THE
WORLD
REPUBLIC
OF LETTERS

Pascale Casanova

T0385771

TRANSLATED BY
M. B. DeBevoise

HARVARD UNIVERSITY PRESS
Cambridge, Massachusetts
London, England

This book was originally published as *La république mondiale des lettres*, by Éditions du Seuil, copyright © 1999 Éditions du Seuil, Paris.

Publication of this book has been aided by grants from the French Ministry of Culture and the JKW Foundation.

First Harvard University Press paperback edition, 2007

Library of Congress Cataloging-in-Publication Data
Casanova, Pascale
[République mondiale des lettres. English]
The world republic of letters / Pascale Casanova:
translated by M.B. DeBevoise
p. cm. — (Convergences)
Index index.
ISBN-13 978-0-674-01345-2 (cloth: alk. paper)
ISBN-10 0-674-01345-X (cloth: alk. paper)
ISBN-13 978-0-674-01021-5 (pbk.)
ISBN-10 0-674-01021-3 (pbk.)
1. European literature—History and criticism.   I. Title.   II. Series.
PN703.C3713 2004
809'.894—dc22   2004054359

Designed by Amber Frid-Jimenez

CONVERGENCES
Inventories of the Present
Edward W. Said, General Editor

e tanto onesta pare / La donna mia quand'ella altrui saluta, / Ch'ogne lingua deven tremando muta, / E li occhi no l'ardiscon di guarda

est un capital dont l'accroissement peut se poursuivre pendant des siècl

melancolia... / Minha mulher, a solidão... /

dabei zum Ungeheuer wird. Und wenn du lange in einem Abgrund blickst, blickt der Abgru

foi que me trocaram... / Cai chuva do céu cinzento... / Eu am

time they are living is th

civiliza

As nu

A ciência... / Tudo quanto penso, tudo quanto sou... Ah quanta melancolia... / Minha mulher, a s

n is the thing seen by everyone living in the living they are doing,

Por quem foi que me trocaram... / Cai chuva do cé

Une civilisation est un capital dont l'accroissem

To my father

CONTENTS

Preface to the English-Language Edition

IS IT LEGITIMATE to speak of world literature? If so, how are we to take in so huge a body of work and to make sense of it? Must one speak of literature, or of literatures? What theoretical instruments are available for analyzing literary phenomena on this scale? Does the comparative study of literature help us think about such things in new terms?

In grappling with these questions it is not enough to geographically enlarge the corpus of works needing to be studied, or to import economic theories of globalization into the literary universe—still less to try to provide an impossibly exhaustive enumeration of the whole of world literary production. It is necessary instead to change our ordinary way of looking at literary phenomena.

As a result of the appropriation of literatures and literary histories by political nations during the nineteenth century, although we do not always realize it, our literary unconscious is largely national. Our instruments of analysis and evaluation are national. Indeed the study of literature almost everywhere in the world is organized along national lines. This is why we are blind to a certain number of transnational phenomena that have permitted a specifically literary world to gradually emerge over the past four centuries or so. The purpose of this book is to restore a point of view that has been obscured for the most part by the "nationalization" of literatures and literary histories, to rediscover a lost transnational dimension of literature that for two hundred years has been reduced to the political and linguistic boundaries of nations.

This change of "vantage point" (to use Fernand Braudel's term) implies a modification of the instruments used to measure, analyze, appraise, understand, and compare texts. A change of literary lenses, as it were, also involves retracing another history of literature: a non-national history of strictly literary events, of the rivalries and competitions, the subversions and conservative reactions, the revolts and revolutions that have taken place in this invisible world.

In what follows, then, I will speak not of world literature, but of international literary space, or else of the world republic of letters. By these terms I mean that what needs to be described is not a contemporary state of the world of letters, but a long historical process through which international literature—literary creation, freed from its political and national dependencies—has progressively invented itself.

The central hypothesis of this book, which borrows both Braudel's concept of an "economy-world" and Pierre Bourdieu's notion of a "field," is that there exists a "literature-world," a literary universe relatively independent of the everyday world and its political divisions, whose boundaries and operational laws are not reducible to those of ordinary political space. Exerted within this *international literary space* are relations of force and a violence peculiar to them—in short, a *literary domination* whose forms I have tried to describe while taking care not to confuse this domination with the forms of political domination, even though it may in many respects be dependent upon them.

This immense detour through transnational space has been undertaken for the sole purpose of proposing a new tool for the reading and interpretation of literary texts that may be at once, and without any contradiction, internal (textual) and external (historical). At bottom it is a matter of rejecting a difference in orientation that has long profoundly divided literary studies, separating the practitioners of internal history—on which "close reading," in particular, is founded—and the partisans of an external history of literature. The method I propose, which consists chiefly in situating a work on the basis of its position in world literary space, will make it possible to understand, at least in part, not only texts that more or less closely touch on the colonial or imperial question but also works, such as those of Beckett and Kafka, that at first glance would appear to be furthest removed from any historical or political determination. The effects of literary domination are so powerful, in fact, that by examining them it becomes possible to understand, above and beyond historical variations, literary texts from dominated regions of the world, *literarily* dominated regions among them.

The present work, employing theoretical tools seldom used until now in literary criticism, is thus conceived as a sort of pivot between two traditions that until today have remained almost wholly foreign to each other: the postcolonial critique, which has played an important role in reintroducing history, and in particular political history, into literary theory; and the French critical tradition, based exclusively on the internal reading of texts, frozen in a certain aestheticizing attitude, refusing any intrusion of history—and, a fortiori, of politics—in the supposedly "pure" and purely formal universe of literature. This is not, in my view, an insuperable antinomy. I have tried to reconstruct the stages of a historical process that illustrates the *relative* dependence and independence of literary phenomena with regard to politics. I have tried to show, in other words, that the great writers have managed, by gradually detaching themselves from historical and literary forces, to invent their literary freedom, which is to say the conditions of the autonomy of their work.

Translation, despite the inevitable misunderstandings to which it gives rise, is one of the principal means by which texts circulate in the literary world. And so I am pleased that this book, aimed at inaugurating an *international literary criticism,* should itself be internationalized through translation into English. In this way its hypotheses will be able to be scrutinized in a practical fashion, and its propositions debated at a truly transnational level, by the various actors in international literary space.

Critical texts, no less than literary texts, need mediators and intermediaries in order to make their way in the world republic of letters. In the present instance it was Edward Said who played this rare and precious role. I owe him an enormous debt of thanks. I would like also to express my deepest gratitude to Jean Stein for her unfailing support, and to thank Lindsay Waters for his patience.

Nos autem, cui mundus est patria . . .

—DANTE

INTRODUCTION | *The Figure in the Carpet*

HENRY JAMES IS one of the few writers who dared to treat in literary form, in "The Figure in the Carpet" (1896), the thorny and inexhaustible question of the relationship between the writer (and therefore the text) and his critics. But far from asserting the critic's powerlessness in the face of literature, whose essential quality necessarily remains beyond his grasp, James affirmed two principles contrary to the ordinary conception of literary art: on the one hand, there is indeed an object to be discovered in each work, and this is the legitimate task of criticism; on the other, this "secret" is not something unsayable, some sort of superior and transcendent essence that imposes an ecstatic silence. James's metaphor of the figure, or pattern, in a carpet—"as concrete there," he emphasized, "as a bird in a cage, a bait on a hook, a piece of cheese in a mouse trap"—was meant to suggest that there is something to be sought in literature that has not yet been described.[1]

Addressing the writer Verecker, whose "little point" he confesses has always eluded his powers of hermeneutic subtlety, and the meaning of whose work he confesses never to have understood, James's disappointed critic asks: "Just to hasten that difficult birth, can't you give a fellow a clue?" To this Verecker replies that the critic is perplexed only because he has "never had a glimpse" of the "exquisite scheme" that links all his books: "If you had had one the element in question would soon have become practically all you'd see. To me it's exactly as palpable as the marble of this chimney." His professional honor wounded, the critic insists on reviewing one by one, with great diligence, all the available critical hypotheses. "Is it a kind of esoteric message?" he asks, venturing: "I see—it's some idea *about* life, some sort of philosophy"—persuaded that it is necessary to search texts for the expression of a deep meaning that goes beyond their manifest sense. "Is it something in the style or something in the thought? An element of form or an element of feeling?" he queries—now embracing the useless dichotemy between form and content. "Unless it be," the critic grasps in desperation, "some kind of game you're up to with your style, something you're after in the language. Perhaps it's a preference for the letter P! . . . Papa, potatoes, prunes—that sort of thing?"—thus proposing a purely formal hypothesis.[2]

"There's an idea in my work," replies the novelist, "without which I wouldn't have given a straw for the whole job. It's the finest, fullest intention of the lot." This, the critic finally succeeds in working out, is something "in the primal plan; something like a complex figure in a Persian carpet." The "right combination" of patterns "in all their superb intricacy" remain—like the purloined letter—exposed for all to see and yet at the same time invisible. "If my great affair's a secret," Verecker reflected, "that's only because it is a secret in spite of itself . . . I not only never took the smallest precaution to keep it so, but never dreamed of any such an accident."[3]

In criticizing the critic and his usual assumptions, "The Figure in the Carpet" invites a rethinking of the whole question of critical perspective and of the aesthetic foundations on which it rests. In his feverish quest for the secret of the writer's work, it never occurs to James's critic to question the nature of the questions that he puts to texts, to reconsider his chief presupposition, which nonetheless is the very thing that blinds him: the unexamined assumption that every literary work must be described as an absolute exception, a sudden, unpredictable, and isolated expression of artistic creativity. In this sense, the literary critic practices a radical monadology: because each work is seen as being unique and irreducible, a perfect unity that can be measured in relation only to itself, the interpreter is obliged to contemplate the ensemble of texts that form what is called the "history of literature" as a random succession of singularities.

The solution that James proposes to the critic—discerning the "figure in the carpet," which is to say the pattern that appears only once its form and coherence are suddenly seen to emerge from the tangle and apparent disorder of a complex composition—is to be sought not above and beyond the carpet itself, but by looking at it from another point of view. If one is prepared to shift one's perspective, to step away from a particular text in order to examine it in relation to other texts, to try to detect similarities and dissimilarities between them and look for recurring patterns—in short, if one tries to take in the composition of the carpet as a whole, to see it as a coherent design, then it becomes possible to perceive the particularity of the pattern that one wishes to make appear. The persistent tendency of critics to isolate texts from one another prevents them from seeing in its entirety the configuration (to use Michel Foucault's term) to which all texts belong; that is, the totality of texts and literary and aesthetic debates with which a particular work of literature enters into relation and resonance, and which forms the true basis for its singularity, its real originality.

Understanding a work of literature, then, is a matter of changing the vantage point from which one observes it—of looking at the carpet as a whole. This is why, to extend James's metaphor, the "superb intricacy" of the mysterious work finds its expression in the overall pattern—invisible and yet there for all to see—of all the literary texts through and against which it has been constructed. On this view, everything that is written, everything that is translated, published, theorized, commented upon, celebrated—all these things are so many elements of a vast composition. A literary work can be deciphered only on the basis of the whole of the composition, for its rediscovered coherence stands revealed only in relation to the entire literary universe of which it is a part. The singularity of individual literary works therefore becomes manifest only against the background of the overall structure in which they take their place. Each work that is declared to be literary is a minute part of the immense "combination" constituted by the literary world as a whole.

What is apt to seem most foreign to a work of literature, to its construction, its form, and its aesthetic singularity, is in reality what generates the text itself, what permits its individual character to stand out. It is the global configuration, or composition, of the carpet—that is, the domain of letters, the totality of what I call world literary space—that alone is capable of giving meaning and coherence to the very form of individual texts. This space is not an abstract and theoretical construction, but an actual—albeit unseen—world made up by lands of literature; a world in which what is judged worthy of being considered literary is brought into existence; a world in which the ways and means of literary art are argued over and decided.

In this broader perspective, then, literary frontiers come into view that are independent of political boundaries, dividing up a world that is secret and yet perceptible by all (especially its most dispossessed members); territories whose sole value and sole resource is literature, ordered by power relations that nonetheless govern the form of the texts that are written in and that circulate throughout these lands; a world that has its own capital, its own provinces and borders, in which languages become instruments of power. Each member of this republic struggles to achieve recognition as a writer. Specific laws have been passed freeing literature from arbitrary political and national powers, at least in the most independent regions. Rival languages compete for dominance; revolutions are always at once literary and political. The history of these events can be fathomed only by recognizing the existence of a literary measure of time, of a "tempo" peculiar to literature; and by recognizing that this world has its own present—the literary Greenwich meridian.

My purpose in analyzing the world republic of letters is not to describe all of the world's literature, still less to propose an exhaustive and equally impossible critical rereading of it. The aim of this book is to bring about a change of perspective: to describe the literary world "from a certain vantage point," in the historian Fernand Braudel's phrase, which is to say to change the point of view of ordinary criticism, to explore a universe that writers themselves have always ignored;[4] and to show that the laws that govern this strange and immense republic—a world of rivalry, struggle, and inequality—help illuminate in often radically new ways even the most widely discussed works, in particular those of some of the greatest literary revolutionaries of the twentieth century—Joyce, Beckett, and Kafka, to be sure, but also, among others, Michaux, Ibsen, Cioran, Naipaul, Kiš, Faulkner, and Schmidt.

World literary space as a history and a geography—a space constituted by writers, who make and actually embody literary history—has never been properly traced or described. The ambition of the international literary criticism that I propose in the pages that follow is to provide a specifically literary, yet nonetheless historical, interpretation of texts; that is, to overcome the supposedly insuperable antinomy between internal criticism, which looks no further than texts themselves in searching for their meaning, and external criticism, which describes the historical conditions under which texts are produced, without, however, accounting for their literary quality and singularity. It therefore becomes necessary to situate writers and their works in this immense territory, which may be thought of as a sort of spatialized history.

Fernand Braudel, as he was preparing to write the economic history of the world from the fifteenth through the eighteenth centuries, noted with regret that general works on this subject were typically "confined to the European context." "I am convinced," he said, "that history would benefit immeasurably from comparisons made on the only valid scale—that of the world . . . [For] it is easier to make sense of the economic history of the world than of the economic history of Europe alone." At the same time he acknowledged that the analysis of historical phenomena on a world scale might be thought sufficiently daunting an enterprise "to discourage the most intrepid and even the most naive."[5] I shall therefore heed Braudel's advice in what follows, looking to the literary world as a whole in trying to account for the interdependence of local phenomena, while respecting his counsel of caution and modesty. Just the same, trying to make sense of a space of such gigantic complexity means having to abandon all the habits associated with specialized historical, linguistic, and cultural research, all the divisions between disciplines—which, to some extent, justify our divided view of the world—because only by going beyond these boundaries will it be possible to think outside conventional frameworks and to conceive of literary space as a worldwide reality.

It was a writer and translator, Valery Larbaud, who more than fifty years ago was the first to hope for the advent of an "intellectual International"[6] and to have called, with a fine fearlessness, for a global approach to literary criticism. To his mind it was necessary to break with the national habits of thought that create the illusion of uniqueness and insularity, and above all to erase the boundaries assigned by literary nationalism. The few attempts that until then had been made to describe world literature, he observed in *Sous l'invocation de saint Jérôme* (Under the Protection of St. Jerome, 1944), amounted to "a simple juxtaposition of the textbooks of different national literatures."[7] But, he continued, "it is quite plain that the future science of Literature—renouncing at last all criticism other than the descriptive—can lead only to the constitution of an ever-growing body of work that will answer to these two terms: *history* and *international*."[8] And it was Henry James who announced, as the reward of such an enterprise, an approach to the meaning of texts that was both novel and at the same time obvious—so obvious, in fact, that there was not "the smallest reason why it should have been over-looked": "It was great, yet so simple, was simple, yet so great, and the final knowledge of it was an experience quite apart."[9] The present work therefore places itself under the dual patronage of Henry James and Valery Larbaud.

PART I | *The Literary World*

Our historical study should set forth the circumstances relevant to all the extant books of the prophets, giving the life, character and pursuits of the author of every book, detailing who he was, on what occasion and at what time and for whom and in what language he wrote. Again, it should relate what happened to each book, how it was first received, into whose hands it fell, how many variant versions there were, by whose decision it was received into the canon, and, finally, how all the books, now universally regarded as sacred, were united into a single whole. All these details, I repeat, should be available from an historical study of Scripture.

—Spinoza, *Tractatus Theologico-Politicus*

1 | *Principles of a World History of Literature*

A civilization is a form of capital whose increase may continue for centuries.
   —Paul Valéry, "Spiritual Freedom"

I am dismayed not to be able to lay out for you a more ample Catalogue of our good productions: I do not accuse the Nation: it lacks neither spirit nor genius, but it has been delayed by
causes that have prevented it from growing up at the same time as its neighbors . . . We are
ashamed that in certain genres we cannot equal our neighbors, [and so] we desire through
tireless efforts to make up for the time that our calamities have caused us to lose . . . Let us
therefore not imitate the poor who wish to pass for the rich, let us acknowledge our destitution in good faith; that this may encourage us instead to obtain by our own efforts the treasures of Literature, whose possession will raise national glory to its full height.
   —Frederick II of Prussia, *On German Literature*

MANY WRITERS HAVE described, albeit partially and in quite diverse ways,
the difficulties associated with their position in the world of letters and
the problems they had to resolve in creating a place for themselves
within the peculiar economy of literature. But so great is the force of
denial and rejection in this world that all works that in one way or another address questions that are dangerous and prejudicial to the established literary order find themselves immediately opposed. Since Du
Bellay, many authors have tried to expose the violent nature of literary
competition—to show what is really at stake in it. A literal reading of
their texts reveals the existence of an unsuspected world, which is to say

the world of letters as it actually operates. But every use of terms drawn from the world of commerce, every assertion of the existence of "verbal marketplaces" and "invisible wars" (Khlebnikov), every invocation of a "world market of intellectual goods" (Goethe), every reference to "immaterial wealth" or to culture as a form of "capital" (Valéry), is firmly denied and rejected by critics in favor of a metaphorical and "poetic" interpretation.

The fact remains, however, that at different times and in different places many of the most prestigious contestants in the game of letters have sought to realistically describe what Valéry called the "spiritual economy" underlying the structure of the literary world. As grand strategists of the economy peculiar to literature, they have not only succeeded in giving an exact, though inevitably incomplete, picture of the laws of this economy; they have also created novel and unorthodox instruments for the analysis of their own literary practice. Even so, no author—not even the most dominated, which is to say the most lucid, for he alone is able to understand and describe his own position in the world of letters—is aware of the general principle that generates the structure he describes as a particular case. The prisoner of a particular point of view, he glimpses a part of the structure of the literary world without, however, seeing it whole, because literary belief obscures the very mechanism of literary domination. It is therefore necessary to consider carefully what these writers have said, while deepening and systematizing some of their intuitions and most subversive ideas, in order to give an adequate description of the international republic of letters.

What Valery Larbaud called the "politics of literature" has its own ways and its own reasons, of which the politics of nations is unaware. "There is a great difference," Larbaud observed in *Ce vice impuni, la lecture: Domaine anglais* (Reading, This Unpunished Vice: English Domain, 1925), "between the political map and the intellectual map of the world. The one changes its look every fifty years; it is covered with arbitrary and uncertain divisions, and its major centers are constantly shifting. The intellectual map, by contrast, changes slowly, and its boundaries display great stability . . . Whence an intellectual politics that has almost no relation to economic politics."[1] Fernand Braudel also noted a relative independence of artistic space with respect to economic (and therefore political) space. In the sixteenth century, though Venice was the economic capital of Europe, it was Florence and the Tuscan dialect that prevailed in the intellectual sphere; in the seventeenth century, though Amsterdam was now the great center of European commerce, it was Rome and Madrid that triumphed in the arts and in literature; in the eighteenth century London became the center of the world economy, but it was Paris that imposed its cultural hegemony. "Similarly," Braudel remarked, "in the late nineteenth century and early twentieth, France, though lagging behind the rest of Europe economically, was the undisputed centre of Western painting and literature; the times when Italy and Germany dominated the world of music were not times when Italy or Germany dominated Europe economically; and even today, the formidable economic lead [enjoyed] by the United States has not made it the literary and artistic leader of the world."[2] The key to understanding how this literary world operates lies in recognizing that its boundaries, its capitals, its highways, and its forms of communication do not completely coincide with those of the political and economic world.

International literary space was formed in the sixteenth century at the very moment when literature began to figure as a source of contention in Europe, and it has not ceased to enlarge and extend itself since. Literary authority and recognition—and, as a result, national rivalries—came into existence with the formation and development of the first European states. Previously confined to regional areas that were sealed off from each other, literature now emerged as a common battleground. Renaissance Italy, fortified by its Latin heritage, was the first recognized literary power. Next came France, with the rise of the Pléiade in the mid-sixteenth century, which in challenging both the hegemony of Latin and the advance of Italian produced a first tentative sketch of transnational literary space. Then Spain and England, followed by the rest of the countries of Europe, gradually entered into competition on the strength of their own literary "assets" and traditions. The nationalist movements that appeared in central Europe during the nineteenth century—a century that also saw the arrival of North America and Latin America on the international literary scene—generated new claims to literary existence. Finally, with decolonization, countries in Africa, the Indian subcontinent, and Asia demanded access to literary legitimacy and existence as well.

This world republic of letters has its own mode of operation: its own economy, which produces hierarchies and various forms of violence; and, above all, its own history, which, long obscured by the quasi-systematic national (and therefore political) appropriation of literary stature, has never really been chronicled. Its geography is based on the opposition between a capital, on the one hand, and peripheral dependencies whose relationship to this center is defined by their aesthetic distance from it. It is equipped, finally, with its own consecrating authorities,[3] charged with responsibility for legislating on literary matters, which function as the sole legitimate arbiters with regard to questions of recognition. Over time, owing to the work of a number of pioneering figures remarkable for their freedom from nationalist prejudice, an international literary law came to be created, a specific form of recognition that owes nothing to political fiat, interest, or prejudice.

But this immense realm, a hundred times surveyed yet always ignored, has remained invisible because it rests on a fiction accepted by all who take part in the game: the fable of an enchanted world, a kingdom of pure creation, the best of all possible worlds where universality reigns through liberty and equality. It is this fiction, proclaimed throughout the world, that has obscured its real nature until the present day. In thrall to the notion of literature as something pure, free, and universal, the contestants of literary space refuse to acknowledge the actual functioning of its peculiar economy, the "unequal trade" (to quote Braudel once more) that takes place within it.[4] In fact, the books produced by the least literarily endowed countries are also the most improbable; that they yet manage to emerge and make themselves known at all verges on the miraculous. The world of letters is in fact something quite different from the received view of literature as a peaceful domain. Its history is one of incessant struggle and competition over the very nature of literature itself—an endless succession of literary manifestos, movements, assaults, and revolutions. These rivalries are what have created world literature.

THE BOURSE OF LITERARY VALUES

Paul Valéry, seeking to describe the structure of intellectual commerce in terms of what he called a "spiritual economy," felt he had to justify having recourse to the vocabulary of economic life: "You see that I borrow the language of the stock exchange. It may seem strange, adapted to spiritual things; but I feel there is nothing better, *and that there may be no other way to express the relations of this kind,* for both the spiritual economy and the material economy, when you pause to consider the matter, may quite aptly be described as a conflict among valuations."[5] In the same essay, "La liberté de l'esprit" (Spiritual Freedom, 1939), he went on to say:

I say that there is a value called "spirit," as there is a value [assigned to] *oil, wheat,* or *gold.* I have said value, because it involves appreciation and judgments of importance, as well as discussion about the price one is prepared to pay for this value: *spirit.* One can invest in this value; one can *follow* it, as the men at the Bourse say; one can observe its fluctuations, in whatever quotations reflect people's opinion of it. In these quotations, which are printed on every page of the newspapers, one can see how it continually comes into competition with other values. For there are competing values . . . All these values that rise and fall constitute the great market of human affairs.

"A civilization is a form of capital," he went on to say, "whose increase may continue for centuries, like that of certain other forms of capital, and which absorbs into itself its compound interest." All this, to Valéry's mind, was evidence of "a wealth that has to be accumulated like natural wealth, a capital that has to be formed by successive strata in people's minds."[6]

Extending Valéry's line of thought to apply more precisely to the specific economy of the world of letters, one may describe the competition in which writers are engaged as a set of transactions involving a commodity that is peculiar to international literary space, a good that is demanded and accepted by everyone—a form of capital that Valéry called "Culture" or "Civilization," which includes literary capital as well. Valéry believed that it is possible to analyze the course of a specific commodity that is traded only in this "great market of human affairs," appraising its value with reference to norms proper to the cultural world. The recognition of this value, which is incommensurate with the values of ordinary commerce, is the certain sign of the existence of an intellectual space, never identified as such, in which literary transactions take place.

The literary economy is therefore based on a "market," to adopt Valéry's term, which is to say a space in which the sole value recognized by all participants—literary value—circulates and is traded. But Valéry is not the only one to have perceived, behind this apparently antiliterary formulation, the functioning of the literary world. Before him Goethe had sketched the outlines of a literary world governed by new economic laws, and described "a market where all nations offer their goods," a "general intellectual commerce."[7] As Antoine Berman has observed, "The appearance of a *Weltliteratur* was contemporaneous with that of a *Weltmarkt*."[8] The deliberate use of the vocabulary of commerce and economics in these texts was in no way metaphorical, no more for Goethe than for Valéry: Goethe, for his part, upheld the concrete notion of a "commerce of ideas among peoples," referring to a "universal world market of exchange." At the same time he insisted on the necessity of laying the foundations for a realistic view of literary commerce, free from flights of fancy that conceal the reality of competition between nations, without thereby reducing such commerce to purely economic or nationalist interests. This is why Goethe saw the translator as a central actor in the world of letters, not only as an intermediary but also as a creator of literary value: "It is thus necessary," he wrote, "to consider each translator as a mediator seeking to promote this universal spiritual commerce and setting himself the task of assisting its progress. Whatever one may say of the inadequacy of translation, this activity nonetheless remains one of the most essential tasks and one of the worthiest of esteem in the universal market of world trade."[9]

"Of what," Valéry asked, "is this capital called *Culture* or *Civilization* composed? It is constituted first by things, material objects—books, paintings, instruments, etc., which have their own probable lifespan, their own fragility, the precariousness that things have."[10] In the case of literature, these material objects include texts—collected, catalogued, and declared national history and property. Age is one of the chief aspects of literary capital: the older the literature, the more substantial a country's patrimony, the more numerous the canonical texts that constitute its literary pantheon in the form of "national classics."[11] The age of a national literature testifies to its "wealth"—in the sense of number of texts—but also, and above all, to its "nobility," to its presumed or asserted priority in relation to other national traditions and, as a result, to the number of texts regarded as "classics" (works that stand above temporal rivalry) or "universal" (works that transcend all particular attachments or qualities). The names of Shakespeare, Dante, and Cervantes summarize at once the greatness of a national literary past, its historical and literary legitimacy, and the universal (and therefore ennobling) recognition of its greatest authors. The classics are the privilege of the oldest literary nations, which, in elevating their foundational texts to the status of timeless works of art, have defined their literary capital as nonnational and ahistorical—a definition that corresponds exactly to the definition that they have given of literature itself. The classic embodies the very notion of literary legitimacy, which is to say what is recognized as *Literature:* the unit of measurement for everything that is or will be recognized as literary.

Literary "prestige" also depends on the existence of a more or less extensive professional "milieu," a restricted and cultivated public, and an interested aristocracy or enlightened bourgeoisie; on salons, a specialized press, and sought-after publishers with distinguished lists who compete with one another; on respected judges of talent, whose reputation and authority as discoverers of unknown literary texts may be national or international; and, of course, on celebrated writers wholly devoted to the task of writing. In countries highly endowed with literary resources, great writers can become literary "professionals": "Note these two conditions," Valéry says. "In order for the material of a culture to constitute capital, it is also necessary that there be men who have need of it and who are able to make use of it . . . and who know, on the other hand, how to acquire and exercise what is necessary in the way of habits, intellectual discipline, conventions, and practices for using the arsenal of documents and instruments that has been accumulated over the centuries."[12] This capital is therefore embodied by all those who transmit it, gain possession of it, transform it, and update it. It exists in various forms—literary institutions, academies, juries, critics, reviews, schools of literature—whose legitimacy is measured according to the age and authority of the recognition that they decree. Countries of great literary tradition continually renew their literary patrimony, through the efforts of all those who participate in it and who consider themselves accountable for it.

Valéry's analysis can be made more precise by incorporating the "cultural indicators" devised by Priscilla Clark Ferguson for the purpose of comparing literary practices in various countries and measuring their respective stocks of national capital. Ferguson analyzed not only the number of books published each year, the sales of books, time spent reading per inhabitant, financial assistance available for writers; but also the number of publishers and bookstores, the number of writers whose portraits appear on banknotes and stamps, the number of streets named after famous writers, the space allotted to books in the press, and the time given over to books on television programs.[13] To all these things, of course, it is necessary to add the number of translations of a nation's literary output and, above all, to take into account the fact that the "concentration of the production and publication of ideas," as Valéry put it elsewhere, is not exclusively literary, since it depends to a large extent on contacts between writers, musicians, and painters;[14] that is, on the conjunction of several types of artistic capital that works to enrich each one of them.

Conversely, it is also possible to measure the relative lack, or even absence, of national literary capital in certain countries. Thus the Brazilian literary critic Antonio Candido describes what he calls the "cultural weakness" of Latin America, noting the absence of almost all the things just mentioned: first, the high rate of illiteracy, which implies "the nonexistence, dispersion, and weakness of publics disposed to literature, due to the small number of real readers"; in addition to this, "the lack of the means of communication and diffusion (publishers, libraries, magazines, newspapers)"; and, finally, "the impossibility, for writers, of specializing in their literary jobs, generally therefore realized as marginal, or even amateur, tasks."[15]

Besides its relative age and volume, another characteristic of literary capital is that it rests on judgments and reputations. The amount of "credit" that is extended to a space endowed with a great "immaterial wealth" depends on "people's opinion," as Valéry says—that is, on the degree of recognition that is granted it and on its legitimacy. The place reserved for economics by Ezra Pound in his *Cantos* is well known; also in his *ABC of Reading* (1934), in which he affirmed the existence of an economy internal to ideas and to literature: "Any general statement is like a cheque drawn on a bank. Its value depends on what is there to meet it. If Mr. Rockefeller draws a cheque for a million dollars it is good. If I draw one for a million it is a joke, a hoax, it has no value . . . The same applies with cheques against knowledge . . . You do not accept a stranger's cheques without reference. In writing, a man's 'name' is his reference. He has, after a time, credit."[16] The idea of literary credit in Pound's sense makes it possible to see how value in the literary world is directly related to belief.[17] When a writer becomes known, when his name has acquired value in the literary market—which is to say, once it is believed that what he has written has literary value, once he has gained acceptance as a writer—then credit is given to him. Credit—Pound's "reference"—is the power and authority granted to a writer by virtue of the belief that he has earned his "name"; it is therefore what he believes himself to have, what others believe him to have, and consequently the power to which it is agreed he is entitled. "We are," as Valéry says, "what we think we are and what we are believed to be."[18]

The existence, at once concrete and abstract, of this literary capital—this "spiritual gold," in Larbaud's phrase—is therefore possible only by virtue of the very belief that sustains it and of the real and tangible effects of this belief, which supports the functioning of the entire literary world. All participants have in common a belief in the value of this asset—an asset that not everyone possesses, or at least not to the same degree, and for the possession of which everyone is prepared to struggle. Literary capital is both what everyone seeks to acquire and what is universally recognized as the necessary and sufficient condition of taking part in literary competition. This fact makes it possible to measure literary practices against a standard that is universally recognized as legitimate. Literary capital so surely exists, in its very immateriality, only because it has—for all those who take part in the competition, and above all for those who are deprived of capital—objectively measurable effects that serve to perpetuate this belief. The immense profit that writers from literarily impoverished spaces have obtained in the past,[19] and still obtain today, from being published and recognized in the major centers—through translation and the prestige conferred by imprints that symbolize literary excellence, the distinction that accompanies a formal introduction of an unknown writer by an internationally renowned author, even the award of literary prizes—supplies evidence of the real effects of literary belief.

Literariness

Language is another major component of literary capital. The political sociology of language studies the usage and relative "value" of languages only in political and economic terms, ignoring that which, in the world of letters, defines their linguistic and literary capital—what I propose to call *literariness*.[20] Certain languages, by virtue of the prestige of the texts written in them, are reputed to be more literary than others, to embody literature. Indeed, literature is so closely linked to language that there is a tendency to identify the "language of literature"—the "language of Racine" or the "language of Shakespeare"—with literature itself. For a language to acquire a high degree of literariness it has to have a long tradition, one that in each generation refines, modifies, and enlarges the gamut of formal and aesthetic possibilities of the language, establishing, guaranteeing, and calling attention to the literary character of what is written in it. This tradition functions, in effect, as a certificate of literary value.

Literary value therefore attaches to certain languages, along with purely literary effects (notably connected with translation) that cannot be reduced to the strictly linguistic capital possessed by a particular language or to the prestige associated with the use of a particular language in the worlds of scholarship, politics, and economics. This sort of value must be clearly distinguished from what political sociologists who study the "emergent world language system" mean when they refer to indicators of a language's centrality.[21] Depending on the history of a language and the country in which it is spoken, as well as on the literature written in it and the position it occupies in world literary space, the literary heritage of a language is linked also to a set of techniques devised over the course of centuries—poetical and narrative forms and constraints, the results of formal investigations, theoretical debates, and stylistic innovations—that enrich its range of possibilities. As a consequence, literary and linguistic wealth operates through both ideas and things, through beliefs and through texts.

It is for this reason that certain authors writing in "small" languages have been tempted to introduce within their own national tongue not only the techniques, but even the sounds, of a reputedly literary language. Frederick II, king of Prussia, published in Berlin in 1780 a brief essay in French (the text appeared some time later in a German translation by a civil servant of the Prussian state) titled *De la littérature allemande, des défauts qu'on peut lui reprocher, quelles en sont les causes, et par quels moyens on peut les corriger* (On German Literature, the Defects for Which It May Be Reproached, the Causes of These, and by What Means They May Be Corrected). Through an extraordinary accord of language and argument, the German monarch called attention to the specifically literary domination exercised by French over German letters at the end of the eighteenth century.[22] Accepting this predominance as something altogether obvious—and so forgetting the great works in the German language by poets and writers such as Klopstock, Lessing, Wieland, Herder, and Lenz—he regarded the reform of the German language as the necessary condition of giving birth to a classical German literature. To carry out his program for "perfecting" the German language—a "half-barbarous" and "unrefined" tongue that he accused of being "diffuse, difficult to handle, unpleasing to the ear," by contrast with "elegant" and "polished" languages—Frederick II proposed to Italianize (or Latinize) it: "We have a great quantity of auxiliary and active verbs whose final syllables are dull and disagreeable, such as *sagen, geben, nehmen:* put an 'a' after these endings and make them *sagena, gebena, nehmena,* and these sounds will flatter the ear."[23]

In the same way, Rubén Darío, the founder of *modernismo,* undertook at the end of the nineteenth century to import the French language into Castilian; that is, to transfer into Spanish the literary resources of French. The Nicaraguan poet's boundless admiration for the French literature of his time—Hugo, Zola, Barbey d'Aurevilly, Catulle Mendès—led him to invent a technique he called "mental Gallicism." "The admiration that I have felt for France for as long as I can remember," he wrote in an article published in *La Nación* of Buenos Aires in 1895, "is immense and profound. My dream was always to write in French . . . And this is how it came about that, thinking in French and writing in a Castilian whose purity the academicians of Spain approved, I published the slender volume that was to initiate the present American literary movement."[24]

The Russian poet Velimir Khlebnikov, who in the second decade of the twentieth century sought to achieve universal recognition for the Russian language and Russian poetry, introduced the notion of "verbal marketplaces."[25] Describing the inequalities of linguistic and literary commerce with unusual acuteness, by means of an economic analogy surprising for its realism, he wrote:

> Nowadays sounds have abandoned their past functions and serve the purposes of hostility; they have become differentiated auditory instruments for the exchange of rational wares; they have divided multilingual mankind into different camps involved in tariff wars, into a series of verbal marketplaces beyond whose confines any given language loses currency. Every system of auditory currency claims supremacy, and so language as such serves to disunite mankind and wage spectral wars.[26]

What is needed, then, is an index or measure of literary authority that can account for the linguistic struggles in which all contestants in the game of literature take part without even knowing it, by virtue simply of belonging to such a linguistic area, and clarify the mediating role of texts and translations, the making and breaking of reputations, and the process of literary consecration and excommunication. Such an index would incorporate a number of factors: the age, the "nobility," and the number of literary texts written in a given language, the number of universally recognized works, the number of translations, and so on. It therefore becomes necessary to distinguish between languages that are associated with "high culture"—languages having a high degree of literary value—and those that are spoken by a great many people. The former are languages that are read not only by those who speak them, but also by readers who think that authors who write in these languages or who are translated into them are worth reading. They amount to a kind of licence, a permit of circulation certifying an author's membership in a literary circle.

One way to devise such an index, in order to measure the strictly literary power of a language, would be to transpose the criteria used by political sociology to the literary world. Considering the set of world languages as an emergent system that derives its coherence from multilingualism, Abram de Swaan argues that the political centrality of a language—or, as I wish to say, the volume of its strictly linguistic capital—can be determined by the number of multilingual speakers it has: the greater the number of polyglots who speak a language, the more central, or dominant, the language is.[27] In other words, even in the political sphere, the fact that a language has a large number of speakers does not suffice to establish its central character in the system, which exhibits what Swaan calls a "floral figuration"—a pattern in which all the languages of the periphery are linked to the center by polyglots. "Potential communication," or the extent of a linguistic territory, is "the product of the proportion of speakers of a language among all speakers in the (sub)system and the proportion of speakers of that language among the multilingual speakers in the (sub)system, that is, the product of its 'plurality' and its 'centrality,' indicating respectively its size and its position within the (sub)system."[28] By similarly conceiving the literary world in terms of a floral pattern, which is to say as a system in which the literatures of the periphery are linked to the center by polyglots and translators, it becomes possible to measure the literariness (the power, prestige, and volume of linguistic and literary capital) of a language, not in terms of the number of writers and readers it has, but in terms of the number of cosmopolitan intermediaries—publishers, editors, critics, and especially translators—who assure the circulation of texts into the language or out of it.[29]

Cosmopolitans and Polyglots

The great, often polyglot, cosmopolitan figures of the world of letters act in effect as foreign exchange brokers, responsible for exporting from one territory to another texts whose literary value they determine by virtue of this very activity. Valery Larbaud, himself a notable cosmopolitan and a great translator, described these men and women as members of an invisible society—legislators, as it were, of the Republic of Letters:

> There exists an aristocracy open to all, but which has never been very numerous, an invisible, dispersed aristocracy, devoid of external signs, without officially recognized existence, without diplomas and without letters patent, and yet more brilliant than any other; without temporal power and yet possessing considerable authority, such that it has often led the world and determined the future. From it have come the most truly sovereign princes that the world has known, the only ones who for years—in some cases, centuries—after their death direct the actions of many men.[30]

The power of this "aristocracy" can be measured only in literary terms. For its "considerable authority" consists in the supreme power to decide what is literary, and lastingly to recognize, or to consecrate, all those whom it designates as great writers: those who, in a strict sense, make literature; whose work incarnates (in some cases for "centuries after their death") literary greatness itself in the form of universal classics, and sets the limits and standards of what is and will be considered literary—thus literally becoming the model for all future literature. This society of letters, Larbaud continues,

> is one and indivisible in spite of boundaries, and literary, pictorial, and musical beauty is for it something as true as Euclidian geometry is for ordinary minds. One and indivisible because it is, in each country, that which is at the same time the most national and the most international: the most national, since it incarnates the culture that has

brought together and formed the nation; and the most international, since it can find its like, its level, its milieu, only among the elites of other nations . . . Thus it is that the opinion of a German who is suf- ficiently well-read to be acquainted with literary French will probably coincide, with respect to any French book whatever, with the opinion of the French elite and not with the judgment of Frenchmen who are not literarily minded.[31]

The stature of these great intermediaries, whose immense power of consecration, of determining literary quality, is a function of their very independence, therefore derives from the fact that they are citizens of a particular nation, which paradoxically supplies the basis for their literary autonomy. Collectively they form a society that, in conformity with the law of literary autonomy, disregards political, linguistic, and national di- visions—a world that, as Larbaud says, is one and "indivisible in spite of boundaries"—and sanctions texts in accordance with an analogous principle of indivisibility in literature. By rescuing texts from imprison- ment within literary and linguistic boundaries, they lay down auton- omous—that is, nonnational, international—criteria of literary legiti- macy.

Thus it becomes clear why critics are regarded as creators of literary value. Valéry, who assigns them responsibility for evaluating texts, uses the word "judges" in praising

these connoisseurs, these invaluable amateurs who, if they do not cre- ate the works themselves, create their true value; these . . . passionate, but incorruptible, judges, for whom or against whom it is a fine thing to work. They know how to read: a virtue that has been lost. They know how to hear, and even how to listen. They know how to see. This is to say that what they insist on rereading, rehearing, and resee- ing is constituted, by this act of going back, as a *sound value*. Universal capital increases as a result.[32]

By virtue of the fact that the competence of critics is acknowledged by all members of the literary world, including the most prestigious and the most fêted figures (such as Valéry), the judgments and the verdicts that they deliver—consecration or anathema—have objective and measur- able effects. The recognition of James Joyce by the highest authorities of the literary world established him right away as a founder of literary modernity, transforming him into a sort of standard of measurement against which the work of other authors was reckoned. By contrast, the excommunication pronounced against Charles Ferdinand Ramuz (although he was unquestionably one of the first, before Céline, to exploit the resources of spoken French in fictional narration) relegated him to the hell of minor provincial roles in French literature. The huge power of being able to say what is literary and what is not, of setting the limits of literary art, belongs exclusively to those who reserve for themselves, and are granted by others, the right to legislate in literary matters.

Translation, like criticism, is a process of establishing value—what Larbaud calls enrichment: "At the same time as he increases his intellectual wealth, [the translator] enriches his national literature and honors his own name. Bringing over into a language and a literature an important work from another literature is not an obscure enterprise devoid of grandeur."[33] Similarly, as Valéry argues, the "sound value" that arises from the recognition conferred by true criticism makes it possible to increase literary wealth by adding the value of newly recognized works to the existing stock of capital held by those who recognize it. Critics, like translators, thus contribute to the growth of the literary heritage of nations that enjoy the power of consecration: critical recognition and translation are weapons in the struggle by and for literary capital. But the case of Valery Larbaud shows that these great intermediaries are naively committed to a pure, dehistoricized, denationalized, and depoliticized conception of literature; more than anyone in the world of letters, they are firmly convinced of the universality of the aesthetic categories in terms of which they evaluate individual works. More than anyone else, they are responsible for the misunderstandings and misreadings that characterize the literary recognition conferred by the leading centers (and particularly, as we shall see, Paris)—misreadings that are evidence of the ethnocentric blindness of these centers.

Paris: City of Literature

As against the national boundaries that give rise to political belief and nationalist feeling, the world of letters creates its own geography and its own divisions. The territories of literature are defined and delimited according to their aesthetic distance from the place where literary consecration is ordained. The cities where literary resources are concentrated, where they accumulate, become places where belief is incarnated, centers of credit, as it were. Indeed, they may be thought of as central banks of a specific sort: thus Ramuz described Paris as "the universal bank of foreign exchange and commerce" in literature.[34] The emergence and universal recognition of a literary capital, which is to say of a place where literary prestige and belief converge in the highest degree, is a direct result of such belief. The existence of a literary center is therefore twofold: it exists both in the imaginations of those who inhabit it and in the reality of the measurable effects it produces.

And so it was that Paris became the capital of the literary world, the city endowed with the greatest literary prestige on earth. It was, as Valéry put it, a necessary "function" of the structure of the literary world.[35] As the capital of France, Paris combined two sets of apparently antithetical properties, in a curious way bringing together all the historical conceptions of freedom. On the one hand, it symbolized the Revolution, the overthrow of the monarchy, the invention of the rights of man—an image that was to earn France its great reputation for tolerance toward foreigners and as a land of asylum for political refugees. But it was also the capital of letters, the arts, luxurious living, and fashion. Paris was therefore at once the intellectual capital of the world, the arbiter of good taste, and (at least in the mythological account that later circulated throughout the entire world) the source of political democracy: an idealized city where artistic freedom could be proclaimed and lived.

Political liberty, elegance, and intellectuality constituted a unique configuration, both historical and mythical, that made it actually possible to invent and to perpetuate the liberty of art and of artists. Victor Hugo, perhaps the most eminent of the many contributors to the *Paris Guide* of 1867, identified the French Revolution as the city's major form of "symbolic capital"—what set it apart from all other cities. Without 1789, he wrote, the supremacy of Paris is an enigma: "Rome has more majesty, Trier is older, Venice is more beautiful, Naples more graceful, London wealthier. What, then, does Paris have? The Revolution . . . Of all the cities of the earth, Paris is the place where the flapping of the immense invisible sails of progress can best be heard."[36] For a very long time, until at least the 1960s, the image of Paris was bound up with the memory of the French Revolution and the uprisings of 1830, 1848, and 1870–71; with the Declaration of the Rights of Man and respect for the principle of the right to asylum; but also with the great "heroes" of literature. Nearly a century after Hugo composed his tribute to Paris, the

German writer Georg K. Glaser recalled: "In my small homeland, the name 'Paris' had the ring of legend about it. My later readings and experiences did not rob it of this splendor. It was the city of Henri Heine, the city of Jean-Christophe, the city of Hugo, of Balzac, of Zola, the city of Marat, Robespierre, Danton, the city of eternal barricades and of the Commune, the city of love, of light, of lightness, laughter, and pleasure."[37]

Other cities, notably Barcelona, which during the years under Franco acquired a reputation for relative political tolerance and became a great intellectual capital, may seem to have characteristics similar to those of Paris. But the Catalan capital served as a literary center only on a national scale—or, in a broader sense, as a literary center of a linguistic area, if one includes the Spanish-speaking countries of Central and South America. Paris, on the other hand, owing to the extent of its literary resources, unrivaled in Europe, and to the exceptional nature of the French Revolution, played a special role in creating a world literary space. Walter Benjamin, in *Das Passagen-Werk* (The Arcades Project, 1927–1939), showed that the historical particularity of Paris was connected with the demand for political freedom, which in turn was directly associated with the invention of literary modernity: "Paris is a counterpart in the social order to what Vesuvius is in the geographic order: a menacing, hazardous massif, an ever-active hotbed of revolution. But just as the slopes of Vesuvius, thanks to the layers of lava that cover them, have been transformed into paradisal orchards, so the lava of revolutions provides uniquely fertile ground for the blossoming of art, festivity, fashion."[38] In his letters, Benjamin also referred to the "infernal worldview" of the nineteenth-century French socialist and revolutionary theorist Louis Auguste Blanqui, which he saw as bearing an "obscure and profound relationship to Baudelaire"; together, Blanqui and Baudelaire symbolized—indeed personified—the connection between literature and revolution.[39]

This unique configuration was reinforced by literature itself. Innumerable descriptions in novels and poems of Paris in the nineteenth and, especially, the twentieth century made the city's literariness manifest. Roger Caillois noted the "fabulous picture of Paris that the novels of Balzac in particular, as well as those of Eugène Sue and Ponson de Terrail, helped to popularize."[40] Indeed, Paris had become synonymous with literature, transformed through the evocations of novelists and poets into a character in its own right, a novelistic place par excellence—one thinks of Hugo's *Notre-Dame de Paris* (1828–31); Balzac's *Le Père Goriot* (1835), *Illusions perdues* (Lost Illusions, 1837–1843), and *Splendeurs et misères des courtisanes* (Splendors and Miseries of Courtesans, 1838–1847); Sue's *Les mystères de Paris* (1842–43); Baudelaire's *Le spleen de Paris* (1869); Zola's *La Curée* (The Spoils, 1871) and *Le ventre de Paris* (The Belly of Paris, 1873). Paris in some sense objectified—almost proved—its uniqueness in a special and irrefutable way. "The city of a hundred thousand novels," as Balzac called it, literarily embodied literature. Underlying the indissoluble link between literature and politics that supplied the basis for its unique power was the classic tableau of revolutionary Paris. It might in fact be said that the descriptions of popular uprisings in Hugo's *Les Misérables* (1862) and *Quatre-vingt-treize* (Ninety-three, 1874), Flaubert's *L'éducation sentimentale* (Sentimental Education, 1869), and Vallès's *L'Insurgé* (The Insurrectionist, 1886) condense all the images on which the legend of Paris rests. By its ability to convert great political events into literature, Paris further strengthened belief in its preeminent position as the capital of the literary world.

These countless descriptions of Paris—a literary genre inaugurated in the late eighteenth century—were gradually codified, so that over time they amounted (to use Daniel Oster's term) to a "recitation"—an immutable leitmotif, obligatory in form and content, that sang the glories and virtues of Paris by casting the city as a miniature version of the world.[41] The extraordinary repetition of this exaggerated discourse is evidence of the long but steady accumulation of a literary and intellectual heritage peculiar to Paris, since symbolic resources are able to increase only once they are believed to exist, which is to say once the number of believers reaches a certain level; and since the recitation of its glories, by virtue of being repeated as something obvious, gradually comes to acquire a reality of its own.

All authors, French and foreign alike, who have attempted to describe, understand, and define the essence of Paris have faithfully echoed the inexhaustible refrain of the city's uniqueness and universality—an exercise in style that developed over a virtually unbroken period lasting more than one hundred fifty years, from the end of the eighteenth century until at least 1960, and swiftly became a set routine for anyone who aspired to be a writer.[42] Thus Edmond Texier, in describing Paris in his preface to the celebrated *Tableau de Paris* (Picture of Paris, 1852) as "summary of the world," "humanity made city," "cosmopolitan forum," "grand Pandemonium," "encyclopedic and universal city," was only repeating a series of formulas that were already clichés.[43] Comparison with the great capitals of world history was a favored (and indeed hackneyed) method of calling attention to Paris. Valéry was later to compare it with Athens and Alberto Savinio with Delphi, the navel of the world;[44] the German essayist and critic Ernst Curtius, in *Die französische Kultur* (French Culture, 1930), preferred Rome: "Ancient Rome and modern Paris are both unique examples of the fact that the political capital of a great state can become the central point of the whole of its national and intellectual life, and that it can also gain worldwide importance as a cosmopolitan center of culture."[45] It was not until the theme of the apocalyptic destruction of Paris—an obligatory aspect of chronicles and evocations of Paris throughout the nineteenth century[46]—gained currency that it became possible to raise the city, through the tragic fate that awaited it, to the rank of the great mythical cities, Ninevah, Babylon, and Thebes: "All the great cities have met a violent death," wrote Maxime Du Camp. "World history is the account of the destruction of great capitals; these excessive and hydrocephalic bodies seem fated to disappear in cataclysms."[47] To evoke the disappearance of Paris was therefore only a way of making it appear still greater than it was and, by snatching it from the clutches of history, of elevating it to the rank of universal myth.[48]

Thus Roger Caillois, for example, in his study of Balzac, called Paris a modern myth created by literature.[49] It is for this reason that historical chronology is of little importance: the commonplaces of descriptions of Paris are transnational and transhistorical. They are a measure of the form and the dissemination of literary belief. Descriptions of Paris are hardly the privilege of French writers—belief in the special supremacy of Paris quickly spread throughout the world. The accounts of Paris composed by foreigners and brought back to their own countries became remote vehicles for belief in its literary power. The Yugoslav writer Danilo Kiš remarked that the legend of Paris on which he had been brought up was less the invention of French literature and poetry, with which he was thoroughly acquainted, than of Yugoslav and Hungarian poets:

It suddenly became clear to me that I had not constructed the Paris of my dreams from [reading] the French, but that—curiously and para-doxically—it was a foreigner who had inoculated me with the poison of nostalgia . . . I thought of all those survivors of shipwrecked hopes and dreams who had cast anchor in a Parisian haven: Matoš, Tin Ujević, Bora Stanković, Crnjanski . . . But Ady[50] was the only one who succeeded in expressing and putting into verse all these nostal-gias, all the dreams of poets who had prostrated themselves before Paris as though before an icon.[51]

Writing on the occasion of his first trip to Paris, in 1959, Kiš captured this wholly "literacized" vision—this conviction of having attained the very seat of literature—better than any of them:

I did not come to Paris as a foreigner, but as someone who goes on a pilgrimage in the innermost landscapes of his own dreams, in a *terra nostalgia* . . . The panoramas and sanctuaries of Balzac, the naturalist "underbelly of Paris" of Zola, the spleen of Baudelaire's Paris in the *Petits poèmes en prose* as well as its old women and its half-breeds, the thieves and the prostitutes in the bitter perfume of the *Fleurs du mal,* the salons and the fiacres of Proust, the Pont Mirabeau of Apollinaire . . . Montmartre, Pigalle, the Place de la Concorde, the Boulevard Saint-Michel, the Champs-Élysées, the Seine . . . all these were only pure impressionist canvases spattered with sunlight whose names en-livened my dreams . . . Hugo's *Les Misérables,* the revolutions, the barri-cades, the murmur of history, poetry, literature, the cinema, music, all these things were mixed together and boiling over, all ablaze in my head before I set foot in Paris.[52]

Octavio Paz, in *Vislumbres de la India* (In Light of India, 1995), recalled his discovery of Paris in the late 1940s as a sort of materialization of what until then had been purely literary acquaintance: "Exploration and recognition: in my walks and rambles I discovered new places and neighborhoods, but there were others that I recognized, not by sight but from novels and poems. Paris for me is a city that, more than invented, is reconstructed by memory and the imagination."[53] The Spanish writer Juan Benet testified in his own way to the same attraction:

I believe it is fair to say that between 1945 and 1960 Paris still focused the attention of almost all the artists and students [of Madrid] . . . Only muffled echoes of the culture of the interwar period could any longer be heard. Paris after the war still occupied the privileged place that Spanish liberals had traditionally reserved for it . . . Paris still retained a bit of the multifaceted charm that it had exercised since 1900, and not only as the sole place where the awkward Spanish naiveté would not do, summed up in the seductive invitation of the nightclubs to young people: Come in here and you will see Paris.

Beyond this attraction, new ones were added after the war: on the one hand, the anti-Francoist hospitality and the possibility of carrying on the ideological war against the dictatorship from there and, on the other, the furious and nocturnal modernity of existentialism, which, having no rivals, for many years was to have a monopoly on academic anticonformism.[54]

This improbable combination of qualities lastingly established Paris, both in France and throughout the world, as the capital of a republic having neither borders nor boundaries, a universal homeland exempt from all professions of patriotism, a kingdom of literature set up in opposition to the ordinary laws of states, a transnational realm whose sole imperatives are those of art and literature: the universal republic of letters. "Here," wrote Henri Michaux with reference to Adrienne Monnier's bookshop, one of the chief places of literary consecration in Paris, "is the homeland of [all] those free spirits who have not found a homeland."[55] Paris therefore became the capital of those who proclaimed themselves to be stateless and above political laws: in a word, artists. "In art," Brancusi said to Tzara during a meeting at the Closerie des Lilas in 1922, "there are no foreigners."[56] The almost systematic appearance of the theme of universality in evocations of Paris is one of the most conclusive proofs of its status as literary capital of the world. It is because this universality was universally acknowledged (or very nearly so) that Paris came to be invested with the power of conferring universal recognition, which in turn affected the course of literary history. Valery Larbaud, in *Paris de France* (1925), drew a portrait of the ideal cosmopolitan (whose independence he was anxious to reaffirm after the closing of national ranks during the war of 1914–1918):

. . . the Parisian whose horizon extends far beyond his city; who knows the world and its diversity, who knows at least his continent, the neighboring islands . . . who is not content to be from Paris . . . And all this for the greater glory of Paris, so that nothing may be foreign to Paris, so that Paris may be in permanent contact with activity everywhere in the world, and conscious of this contact, and that it may become the capital—beyond all "local" politics, whether sentimental or economic—of a sort of intellectual International.[57]

To the belief in its literature and its political liberalism, Paris added faith in its artistic internationalism. The incessantly proclaimed universality that, by a sort of mutual contamination of causes and effects, made Paris the intellectual capital of the world produced two types of consequences: the one imaginary, which helped construct and consolidate a Parisian mythology; the other real, associated with the inflow of foreign artists, political refugees, and isolated artists who came to get their start in Paris—without its being possible to say which ones were the consequences of the others. The two phenomena increased and multiplied, each one helping to establish and support the other. Paris was thus doubly universal, by virtue both of the belief in its universality and of the real effects that this belief produced.

Faith in the power and the uniqueness of Paris produced a massive stream of immigration, and the image of the city as a condensed version of the world (which today appears as the most pompous aspect of this rhetorical tradition) also attests to its genuine cosmopolitanism. The presence of a great many foreign communities—Poles, Italians, Czechs and Slovaks, Siamese, Germans, Armenians, Africans, Latin Americans, Japanese, Russians, and Americans who had settled in the French capital between 1830 and 1945—as well as political refugees of every stripe and artists who had come from all over the world to mix with the powerful French avant-garde—evidence of the improbable synthesis of political asylum and artistic consecration that occurred during this period—made Paris a new "Babel," a "Cosmopolis," a crossroads of the artistic world.[58]

The personal freedom associated with Paris as an artistic capital found expression in "bohemian" lifestyles. Indeed, tolerance of artists' unconventional behavior is one of the most frequently remarked characteristics of Parisian life. Arthur Koestler, who fled Nazi Germany and arrived in Zurich in 1935 via Paris, later compared the two cities in his autobiography:

we found it more difficult to be poor in Zurich than in Paris. Although the largest town in Switzerland, Zurich has an intensely provincial atmosphere, saturated with prosperity and virtue. To be poor on Montparnasse could be regarded as a joke, a bohemian eccentricity; but Zurich had neither a Montparnasse nor cheap bistros, nor that kind of humour. In this clean, smug, orderly town, poverty was simply degrading; and, though no longer starving, we were very poor indeed.[59]

The contrast with life in Zurich illuminates one of the French capital's great attractions for artists the world over: owing to its unique concentration of a specific sort of capital, and an exceptional conjunction of political, sexual, and aesthetic freedoms, Paris offered the possibility of living what is rightly called *la vie d'artiste,* which is to say elegant and elective poverty.

Almost from the beginning foreigners came to Paris to demand and proclaim political independence for their homelands while at the same time inaugurating national literatures and arts. Paris became the political capital of the Poles after the "great immigration" of 1830, and that of Czech nationalists in exile after 1915. Organs of the émigré press calling for national independence in their various homelands proliferated, among them *El Americano* (founded in 1872), which championed nationalist causes in Latin America, *La Estrella del Chile,* and *La República Cubana* (1896), organ of the Cuban republican government established in Paris.[60] The Czech colony launched the national newspaper *Na Zdar* in 1914, followed the next year by *La Nation Tchèque,* a political journal of the nationalist resistance, and then in 1916 by *L'Indépendance Tchèque,* founded in Switzerland and shortly thereafter relocated to Paris, where it became the official organ of Czech exiles.[61] Paradoxically, as the American art critic Harold Rosenberg pointed out in the 1950s, because "Paris was the opposite of the national in art, the art of every nation increased through Paris." Thus Rosenberg summed up, somewhat in the manner of Gertrude Stein, what America owed to Paris: "In Paris, American speech found its measure of poetry and eloquence. Criticism born there achieved an appreciation of American folk art and music; of the motion-picture technique of Griffiths; of the designs of New England interiors and of early Yankee machines; of the sand paintings of the Navajo, the backyard landscapes of Chicago and the East Side."[62] This sort of national reappropriation, which reflected what might be called the neutrality or denationalization of Paris, has also been emphasized by historians of Latin America, many of whose writers and intellectuals discovered their national identity in Paris and, more generally, in Europe. The Brazilian poet Oswald de Andrade (1890–1954), his friend Paulo Prado wrote in 1924, "discovered with wonder his own country in a studio above the Place Clichy—navel of the world,"[63] while the Peruvian poet César Vallejo (1892–1938) exclaimed, "I set out for Europe and I learned to know Peru."[64]

It was in Paris that Adam Mickiewicz (1798–1855) wrote *Pan Tadeusz* (1834), considered today to be the Polish national epic. Jkai (1825–1904), one of the most widely read authors in his native Hungary until the 1960s, wrote in his memoirs: "We were all Frenchmen! We did not read anything but Lamartine, Michelet, Louis Blanc, Sue, Victor Hugo, and Béranger; and if an English or German poet could find favor with us, then [it was] only Shelley or Heine, both denied by their own nations, English or German only in their language but French in their spirit."[65] The American poet William Carlos Williams styled Paris the "artistic Mecca"; the Japanese poet Kafu Nagai (1879–1959) prostrated himself before Maupassant's tomb when he arrived there in 1907. The Italian "Futurist Manifesto," signed by Marinetti, was published in the 20 February 1909 issue of *Le Figaro* before appearing in Italian in the Milanese review *Poesia*. The Spanish composer Manuel de Falla, who spent time in Paris between 1907 and 1914, wrote to a friend: "For everything that has to do with my profession, my homeland is Paris."[66] Paris was also the "Black Babel" for the first intellectuals from Africa and the West Indies who arrived in the French capital in the 1920s.[67]

Faith in the universality of Paris was so great that, in certain parts of the world, writers began to write in French: the Brazilian Joaquim Nabuco (1849–1910), who wrote a play in alexandrines, *L'Option* (The Choice, 1910), about an Alsatian's moral qualms after the Franco-Prussian war; also the Peruvian short-story writer Ventura García Calderón (1886–1959), the Brazilian poet of the abolition of slavery, Antônio de Castro Alves (1847–1871), the Peruvian Surrealist poet César Moro (1903–1956), and the Ecuadoran poet Alfredo Gangotena (1904–1944), a friend of Michaux, who lived in Paris for many years. Another Brazilian, the novelist Joaquim Maria Machado de Assis (1839–1908), described the French as the "most democratic people in the world" and made Lamartine and Alexandre Dumas known in his native land.

The fascination with Paris in Latin America reached its apogee at the end of the nineteenth century: "From my earliest childhood I dreamed so much of Paris," Darío recalled, "that when I prayed, I asked God not to let me die without seeing Paris. For me Paris was a kind of heaven where one could breathe the essence of happiness on earth."[68] The same nostalgia was evoked by the Japanese poet Sakutaro Hagiwaro (1886–1942), a product of this extraordinary international faith in Paris:

> Ah! I would like to go to France
> But France is too far
> With a new jacket at least
> Let us set off and wander as we please
> When the train passes through the mountains
> Pressed against the window, blue sky
> Alone I shall think of happy things
> The dawn of a morning in May
> Obeying the heart's whims, blades of grass sprouting.[69]

It was out of admiration for Frédéric Mistral that the Chilean poet Lucila Godoy Alcayaga (1889–1957) chose to call herself Gabriela Mistral. In 1945 she became the first Latin American writer to receive the Nobel Prize for Literature, in recognition of a body of work whose models were wholly European and in which she sang even of villages on the Rhône, softened by water and cicadas.[70] In 1871 Walt Whitman composed a hymn to France, vanquished the previous year in the war against Prussia, that appeared in *Leaves of Grass* under the title "O Star of France" and that contains all the mythic images of Paris, symbol of liberty:

> Dim smitten star
> Orb not of France alone, pale symbol of my soul, its
>   dearest hopes,
> The struggle and the daring, rage divine for liberty,
> Of aspirations toward the far idea, enthusiast's dreams of
>   brotherhood,
> Of terror to the tyrant and the priest.
> Star crucified—by traitors sold,
> Star panting o'er a land of death, heroic land,
> Strange, passionate, mocking, frivolous land.[71]

My reason for noting so many expressions of admiration for Paris has nothing to do with ethnocentrism, much less some form of nationalist pride; to the contrary, I was obliged to acknowledge their force—much to my surprise, and against my will in fact—in trying to account for the effects of the prestige attaching to Paris. Moreover, it is clear that the dominant position enjoyed by Paris has often entailed a peculiar blindness, particularly with regard to writings from those countries that are most distant from it. The ignorance—or, more accurately perhaps, the rejection—of a historicized view of literature, the insistence on interpreting texts only in terms of "pure" categories, which is to say categories purified of any historical or national reference, has often had catastrophic consequences for the interpretation and diffusion of foreign works consecrated in Paris. The formalist bias of these authorities was the result of huge misunderstandings that sometimes infected critical discourse, as in the cases of Beckett and Kafka, which we shall examine later.

On the other hand, literary capital has regularly been put to political and national uses in France. In their colonial ventures, but also in their relations with other nations, the French have practiced what Pierre Bourdieu has called an "imperialism of the universal."[72] Their use of denationalized capital for national purposes—in styling France, for example, the "mother of the arts"—has lent support to the least reputable forms of nationalism, notably in connection with writers who most stridently proclaimed their loyalty to national tradition.

LITERATURE, NATION, AND POLITICS

The particular case of Paris, denationalized and universal capital of the literary world, must not make us forget that literary capital is inherently national. Through its essential link with language—itself always national, since invariably appropriated by national authorities as a symbol of identity—literary heritage is a matter of foremost national interest.[73] Because language is at once an affair of state and the material out of which literature is made, literary resources are inevitably concentrated, at least initially, within the boundaries of the nation itself. Thus it is that language and literature jointly provide political foundations for a nation and, in the process, ennoble each other.

The National Foundations of Literature

The link between the state and literature depends on the fact that, through language, the one serves to establish and reinforce the other. Historians have demonstrated a direct connection between the emer-

gence of the first European states and the formation of "common languages" (which then later became "national languages").[74] Benedict
Anderson, for example, sees the expansion of vernaculars, which supplied administrative, diplomatic, and intellectual support for the emerging European states of the late fifteenth and early sixteenth centuries, as
the central phenomenon underlying the appearance of these states.[75]
From the existence of an organic bond, or interdependence, between
the appearance of national states, the expansion of vernaculars into
common languages, and the corresponding development of new literatures written in these vernaculars, it follows that the accumulation of literary resources is necessarily rooted in the political history of states.

More precisely, both the formation of states and the emergence of literatures in new languages derive from a single principle of differentiation. For it was in distinguishing themselves from each other, which is to
say in asserting their differences through successive rivalries and struggles, that states in Europe gradually took shape from the sixteenth century onward, thereby giving rise to the international political field in its
earliest form. In this embryonic system, which may be described as a
system of differences (in the same sense in which phoneticists speak of
language as a system of differences), language evidently played a central
role as a "marker" of difference. But it also represented what was at stake
in the contests that took place at the intersection of this nascent political
space and the literary space that was coming into existence at the same
time,[76] with the paradoxical result that the birth of literature grew out of
the early political history of nation-states.

The specifically literary defense of vernaculars by the great figures of
the world of letters during the Renaissance, which very quickly assumed the form of a rivalry among these "new" languages (new in the
literary market), was to be advanced equally by literary and political
means.[77] In this sense the various intellectual rivalries that grew up during the Renaissance in Europe may be said to have been founded and
legitimized through political struggles. Similarly, with the spread of nationalist ideas in the nineteenth century and the creation of new nations,
political authority served as a foundation for emerging literary spaces.
Owing to the structural dependence of these new spaces, the construction of world literary space proceeded once more through national rivalries that were inseparably literary and political.

From the earliest stages of the unification of this space, national literary wealth, far from being the private possession of nations whose natural "genius" it was supposed to express, became the weapon and the prize that both permitted and encouraged new claimants to enter international literary competition. In order to compete more effectively, countries in the center sought to define literature in relation to "national character" in ways that in large measure were themselves the result of structural opposition and differentiation. Their dominant traits can quite often be understood—as in the cases of Germany and England, rising powers seeking to challenge French hegemony—in deliberate contrast with the recognized characteristics of the predominant nation. Literatures are therefore not a pure emanation of national identity; they are constructed through literary rivalries, which are always denied, and struggles, which are always international.

Given, then, that literary capital is national, and that there exists a relation of dependence with regard first to the state, then to the nation, it becomes possible to connect the idea of an economy peculiar to the literary world with the notion of a literary geopolitics. No national entity exists in and of itself. In a sense, nothing is more international than a national state: it is constructed solely in relation to other states, and often in opposition to them. In other words, no state—neither the ones that Charles Tilly calls "segmented" (or embryonic) nor, after 1750, "consolidated" (or national) states, which is to say the state in its modern sense—can be described as a separate and autonomous entity, the source of its own existence and coherence.[78] To the contrary, each state is constituted by its relations with other states, by its rivalry and competition with them. Just as the state is a relational entity, so the nation is inter-national.

The construction (and reconstruction) of national identity and the political definition of the nation that developed later, notably during the course of the nineteenth century, were not the product of isolated experience, of private events unfolding behind the ramparts of an incomparable and incommensurate history. What nationalist mythologies attempt to reconstitute (after the fact, in the case of the oldest nations) as autarkic singularities arise in reality only from contact between neighboring peoples. Thus Michael Jeismann has been able to demonstrate that Franco-German antagonism—a veritable "dialogue des ennemis"—permitted nationalism to flourish in each country in reaction against a perceived "natural" enemy.[79] Similarly, Linda Colley has shown that the English nation was constructed through and through in opposition to France.[80]

The analysis of the emergence of nationalism needs to go beyond the assumption of a binary and belligerent relation between nations to take into account a much more complex space of rivalries that proceed both for and through a variety of forms of capital, which may be literary, political, or economic. The totality of world political space is the product of a vast range of national competition, where the clash between two historical enemies—such as the one described by Danilo Kiš between Serbs and Croats—represents only the simplest and most archaic form.[81]

Depoliticization

Little by little, however, literature succeeded in freeing itself from the hold of the political and national authorities that originally it helped to establish and legitimize. The accumulation of specifically literary resources, which involved the invention and development of a set of aesthetic possibilities, of forms, narrative techniques, and formal solutions (what the Russian formalists were to call "procedures")—in short, the creation of a specific history (more or less distinct from national history, from which it could no longer be deduced)—allowed literary space gradually to achieve independence and determine its own laws of operation. Freed from its former condition of political dependency, literature found itself at last in a position to assert its own autonomy.

Writers, or at least some of them, could thus refuse both collectively and individually to submit to the national and political definition of literature. The paradigm of this refusal is undoubtedly Zola's "J'accuse."[82] At the same time, international literary competition, now also detached from strictly national and political rivalries, acquired a life of its own. The spread of freedom throughout world literary space occurred through the autonomization of its constituent spaces, with the result that literary struggles, freed from political constraints, were now bound to obey no other law than the law of literature.

Thus, to take an example that is apparently most unfavorable to the argument I am making, the German literary renaissance at the end of the eighteenth century was associated in part with national issues, being the literary counterpart to the founding of the German nation as a political entity. The rise of the idea of a national literature in Germany is explained first by political antagonism with France, then the culturally dominant power in Europe. Isaiah Berlin in particular has argued that German nationalism had its roots in a sense of humiliation:

> The French dominated the western world, politically, culturally, militarily. The humiliated and defeated Germans . . . responded, like the bent twig of the poet Schiller's theory, by lashing back and refusing to accept their alleged inferiority. They discovered in themselves qualities far superior to those of their tormentors. They contrasted their own deep, inner life of the spirit, their own profound humility, their selfless pursuit of true values—simple, noble, sublime—with the rich, worldly, successful, superficial, smooth, heartless, morally empty French. This mood rose to fever pitch during the national resistance to Napoleon, and was indeed the original exemplar of the reaction of many a backward, exploited, or at any rate patronized society, which, resentful of the apparent inferiority of its status, reacted by turning to real or imaginary triumphs and glories in its past, or enviable attributes of its own national or cultural character.[83]

The prodigious development of German literary culture, beginning in the second half of the eighteenth century, was therefore initially connected with matters of immediate political import: to insist on cultural grandeur was also a way of affirming the unity of the German people beyond the fact of its political disunion. But the arguments that were employed, the principles that were at issue in the debates of the period and the very form that these debates assumed, the stature of the greatest German poets and intellectuals, their poetical and philosophical works, which were to have revolutionary consequences for all of Europe, and for French literature in particular—all these things gradually gave German romanticism an exceptional degree of independence and a power all its own. In the German case, romanticism was, and at the same time was not, national; or, rather, it was national to start with and then subsequently detached itself from national authority. As a consequence, the challenge to French dominance in literature in the nineteenth century needs to be analyzed on the basis of the literary, rather than the political, history of the two countries.

Similarly, notwithstanding differences of time and place, Latin American writers managed in the twentieth century to achieve an international existence and reputation that conferred on their national literary spaces (and, more generally, the Latin American space as a whole) a standing and an influence in the larger literary world that were incommensurate with those of their native countries in the international world of politics. Here, as in the German case, literature enjoys a relative autonomy when the accumulation of a literary heritage—which is to say the international recognition that attaches to writers who are designated by critics in the center as "great" writers—enabled national literary cultures to escape the hold of national politics. As Valery Larbaud pointed out, the literary and intellectual map cannot be superimposed upon the political map, since neither literary history nor literary geography can be reduced to political history. Nonetheless, literature remains relatively dependent on politics, above all in countries that are relatively unendowed with literary resources.

World literary space has therefore developed and achieved unity in accordance with a parallel movement that, as we shall see, is ordered in relation to two antagonistic poles. On the one hand, there is a progressive enlargement of literary space that accompanies the spread of national independence in the various parts of the world. And, on the other, there is a tendency toward autonomy, which is to say literary emancipation in the face of political (and national) claims to authority.

The original dependence of literature on the nation is at the heart of the inequality that structures the literary world. Rivalry among nations arises from the fact that their political, economic, military, diplomatic, and geographical histories are not only different but also unequal. Literary resources, which are always stamped with the seal of the nation, are therefore unequal as well, and unequally distributed among nations. Because the effects of this structure weigh on all national literatures and on all writers, the practices and traditions, the forms and aesthetics that have currency in a given national literary space can be properly understood only if they are related to the precise position of this space in the world system. It is the hierarchy of the literary world, then, that gives literature its very form. This curious edifice, which joins together writers from different spaces whose mutual rivalry is very often the only thing they have in common—a rivalry whose existence, as I say, is always denied—was constructed over time by a succession of national conflicts and challenges to formal and critical authority. Unification of the literary world therefore depends on the entry of new contestants intent upon adding to their stock of literary capital, which is both the instrument and the prize of their competition: each new player, in bringing to bear the weight of his national heritage—the only weapon considered legitimate in this type of struggle—helps to unify international literary space, which is to say to extend the domain of literary rivalry. In order to take part in the competition in the first place, it is necessary to believe in the value of what is at stake, to know and to recognize it. It is this belief that creates literary space and allows it to operate, despite (and also by virtue of) the hierarchies on which it tacitly rests.

The internationalization that I propose to describe here therefore signifies more or less the opposite of what is ordinarily understood by the neutralizing term "globalization," which suggests that the world political and economic system can be conceived as the generalization of a single and universally applicable model. In the literary world, by contrast, it is the competition among its members that defines and unifies the system while at the same time marking its limits. Not every writer proceeds in the same way, but all writers attempt to enter the same race, and all of them struggle, albeit with unequal advantages, to attain the same goal: literary legitimacy.

It is not surprising, then, that Goethe elaborated the notion of *Weltliteratur* precisely at the moment of Germany's entry into the international literary space. As a member of a nation that was a newcomer to the game, challenging French literary and intellectual hegemony, Goethe had a vital interest in understanding the reality of the situation in which his nation now found itself. Displaying the perceptiveness commonly found among newcomers from dominated communities, not only did he grasp the international character of literature, which is to say its deployment outside national limits; he also understood at once its competitive nature and the paradoxical unity that results from it.

A New Method of Interpretation

These resources—at once concrete and abstract, national and international, collective and subjective, political, linguistic, and literary—make up the specific heritage that is shared by all the writers of the world. Each writer enters into international competition armed (or unarmed) with his entire literary "past": by virtue solely of his membership in a linguistic area and a national grouping, he embodies and reactivates a whole literary history, carrying this "literary time" with him without even being fully concious of it. He is therefore heir to the entire national and international history that has "made" him what he is. The cardinal importance of this heritage, which amounts to a kind of "destiny" or "fate," explains why even the most international authors, such as the Spaniard Juan Benet or the Serb Danilo Kiš, conceive of themselves, if only by way of reaction against it, in terms of the national space from which they have come. And the same thing must be said of Samuel Beckett, despite the fact that few writers seem further removed from the reach of history, for the course of his career, which led him from Dublin to Paris, can be understood only in terms of the history of Irish literary space.

None of this amounts to invoking the "influence" of national culture on the development of a literary work, or to reviving national literary history in its traditional form. Quite the contrary: understanding the way in which writers invent their own freedom—which is to say perpetuate, or alter, or reject, or add to, or deny, or forget, or betray their national literary (and linguistic) heritage—makes it possible to chart the course of their work and discover its very purpose. National literary and linguistic patrimony supplies a sort of a priori definition of the writer, one that he will transform (if need be, by rejecting it or, as in the case of Beckett, by conceiving himself in opposition to it) throughout his career. In other words, the writer stands in a particular relation to world literary space by virtue of the place occupied in it by the national space into which he has been born. But his position also depends on the way in which he deals with this unavoidable inheritance; on the aesthetic, linguistic, and formal choices he is led to make, which determine his position in this larger space. He may reject his national heritage, forsaking his homeland for a country that is more richly endowed in literary resources than his own, as Beckett and Michaux did; he may acknowledge his patrimony while trying at the same time to transform it and, in this way, to give it greater autonomy, like Joyce (who, though he left his native land and rejected its literary practices and aesthetic norms, sought to found an Irish literature freed from nationalist constraints); or he may affirm the difference and importance of a national literature, like Kafka, as we shall see, but also like Yeats and Kateb Yacine. All these examples show that, in trying to characterize a writer's work, one must situate it with respect to two things: the place occupied by his native literary space within world literature and his own position within this space.

Determining the position of a writer in this way has nothing to do with the usual sort of national contextualization favored by literary critics. On the one hand, national (and linguistic) origin is now related to the hierarchical structure of world literature as a whole; and, on the other hand, it is recognized that no two writers inherit their literary past in exactly the same fashion. Most critics, however, are led by a belief in the singularity and originality of individual writers to privilege some aspect of their biography that hides this structural relation. Thus, for example, the feminist critic who studies the case of Gertrude Stein concentrates on one of its aspects—the fact that she was a woman and a lesbian—while forgetting, as though it were something obvious not needing to be examined, that she was American.[84] Yet the United States in the 1920s was literarily a dominated country that looked to Paris in order to try to accumulate resources it lacked. Any analysis that fails to take into account the world literary structure of the period and of the place occupied in this structure by Paris and the United States, respectively, will be incapable of explaining Stein's permanent concern to develop a modern American national literature (through the creation of an avant-garde) and her interest in both American history and the literary representation of the American people (of which her gigantic enterprise *The Making of Americans* is no doubt the most outstanding proof).[85] The fact that she was a woman in the community of American intellectuals in exile in Paris is, of course, of crucial importance for understanding her subversive impulses and the nature of her aesthetic ambitions. But the deeper structural relationship, obscured by critical tradition, remains paramount. Generally speaking, one can point to some feature of every writer's career—important, to be sure, but nonetheless secondary—that conceals the structural pattern of literary domination.

The dual historicization proposed here makes it possible not only to find a way out from the inevitable impasse of literary history, which finds itself relegated to a subordinate role and accused of being powerless to grasp the essence of literature; it also allows us to describe the hierarchical structure of the literary world and the constraints that operate within it. The inequality of the transactions that take place in this world goes unperceived, or is otherwise denied or euphemistically referred to, because the ecumenical picture it presents of itself as a peaceful world, untroubled by rivalry or struggle, strengthens received beliefs and assures the continued existence of a quite different reality that is never admitted. The simple idea that dominates the literary world still today, of literature as something pure and harmonious, works to eliminate all traces of the invisible violence that reigns over it and denies the power relations that are specific to this world and the battles that are fought in it. According to the standard view, the world of letters is one of peaceful internationalism, a world of free and equal access in which literary recognition is available to all writers, an enchanted world that exists outside time and space and so escapes the mundane conflicts of human history. This fiction, of a literature emancipated from all historical and political attachments, was invented in the most autonomous countries of world literary space. It is in these countries, which for the most part have managed to free themselves from political constraints, that the belief in a pure definition of literature is strongest, of literature as something entirely cut off from history, from the world of nations, political and military competition, economic dependence, linguistic domination—the idea of a universal literature that is nonnational, nonpartisan, and unmarked by political or linguistic divisions. It is perhaps not surprising, then, that very few writers at the center of world literature have any idea of its actual structure. Though they are familiar with the constraints and norms of the center, they fail to recognize them as such since they have come to regard them as natural. They are blind almost by definition: their very point of view on the world hides it from them, for they believe that it coincides with the small part of it they know.

The irremediable and violent discontinuity between the metropolitan literary world and its suburban outskirts is perceptible only to writers on the periphery, who, having to struggle in very tangible ways in order simply to find "the gateway to the present" (as Octavio Paz put it), and then to gain admission to its central precincts, are more clearsighted than others about the nature and the form of the literary balance of power.[86] Despite these obstacles, which are never acknowledged—so great is the power of denial that accompanies the extraordinary belief in literature—they nonetheless manage to invent their own freedom as artists. It is by no means a paradox, then, that authors living today on the edges of the literary world, who long ago learned to confront the laws and forces that sustain the unequal structure of this world and who are keenly aware that they must be recognized in their respective centers in order to have any chance of surviving as writers, should be the most sensitive to the newest aesthetic inventions of international literature, from the recent attempts of Anglo-Saxon writers to devise a worldwide cross-fertilization of styles to the latest narrative techniques of Latin American novelists, among others. This lucidity, and the impulse to rebel against the existing literary order, are at the very heart of their identity as writers.

For all these reasons, ever since French hegemony reached its height at the end of the eighteenth century, radical challenges to the existing literary order have appeared in the most impoverished territories of the international republic of letters, shaping and lastingly modifying its structure, which is to say the very forms of literature. Particularly with Herder, the challenge to the French monopoly on literary legitimacy succeeded so well in establishing itself that an alternative pole was able to be created. But it is nonetheless true that dominated men and women of letters have often been incapable of grasping the reasons for their special lucidity. Even if they are clearsighted with regard to their particular position and to the specific forms of dependency in which they are caught up, their perception of the global structure of which they are a part remains incomplete.

2 | *The Invention of Literature*

How the Romans Enriched Their Language . . . Imitating the best Greek authors, transforming themselves into them, devouring them; and after having well digested them, converting them into blood and nourishment, taking for themselves, each according to his nature, and the argument he wished to choose, the best author of whom they observed diligently all the most rare and exquisite virtues, and these like shoots, as I have already said, they grafted and applied to their own tongue.
— Joachim du Bellay, *The Defense and Illustration of the French Language*

We imitate [in Brazil], there is no doubt. But we are not confined to imitation . . . We have something quite different to do . . . We are putting an end to the domination of the French spirit. We are putting an end to the grammatical domination of Portugal.
— Mário de Andrade, letter to Alberto de Oliveira

LITERATURE IS OBVIOUSLY and directly connected, albeit in very complex ways, to language. The writer's relationship to his literary language (which is not always either his mother tongue or his national language) is infinitely singular and personal. But the whole problem of grasping the relationship between language and literature has to do with the very ambiguity of the status of language. It is clearly used for political purposes,[1] yet at the same time it supplies the raw material with which writers work. Literature is invented through a gradual separation from political obligations: forced at first to place their art in the service of the national purposes of the state, writers little by little achieved artistic freedom through the invention of specifically literary languages. The uniqueness and originality of individual writers became apparent, indeed possible, only as the result of a very long process of gathering and concentrating literary resources. This process of continuous and collective creation is nothing other than the history of literature itself.

Literary history rests therefore neither on national chronologies nor on a series of neatly juxtaposed works, but on the succession of revolts and emancipations thanks to which writers, despite their irreducible dependence on language, have managed to create the conditions of a pure and autonomous literature, freed from considerations of political utility. It is the history of the appearance, then of the accumulation, concentration, distribution, and diversion of literary wealth, which first arose in Europe and subsequently became the object of belief and rivalry throughout the world. The critical moment in the early accumulation of literary capital—a formula very far removed from literary enchantment and derealization—was the publication by Joachim du Bellay (1522–1560) of *La deffence et illustration de la langue françoyse* (The Defense and Illustration of the French Language, 1549).

I am quite aware that it may seem paradoxical, or arbitrary, or even deliberately Gallocentric to adopt as a point of departure for a history of world literature a literary event that is (or at least appears to be) so typically French. An earlier moment could easily enough be found: even within the same tradition one might point to an older work such as *La concorde des deux langages* (The Harmony of the Two Languages, 1513), by Jean Lemaire de Belges; or, within another tradition, the Italian for example, Dante's *De vulgari eloquentia* (On Vernacular Eloquence, 1303–04), which James Joyce and Samuel Beckett cited in 1929 with an altogether similar view to appropriating its fame and legitimacy on behalf of Joyce's own pioneering enterprise, *Finnegans Wake.*[2] But du Bellay's work marked the first time that a national literature had been founded in complex relation to another nation and, through it, another language, one that moreover was dominant and apparently indomitable, namely Latin—a paradigmatic initiative having both national and international implications that was to supply the model, reproduced over and over again in the course of a long history that will be traced here in its broad outlines, of a world republic of letters. Similarly, the claim that Paris is the capital of literature is not an effect of Gallocentrism but the result of a careful historical analysis showing that the exceptional concentration of literary resources that occurred in Paris over the course of several centuries gradually led to its recognition as the center of the literary world.

This history has until now remained so invisible that it needs to be completely reconstructed, which means having to go back to works that have been commented upon a hundred times according to the ordinary habits of literary criticism, as those of du Bellay, Malherbe, Rivarol, and Herder have been—which is to say with reference solely to the works themselves, and never on the basis of the hidden, structural relations that obtain among all of them. A few historians, notably Marc Fumaroli, have examined the initial stages in the development of these relations during the sixteenth and seventeenth centuries in Europe; but this process has continued until the present day with the emergence, on a worldwide scale, of still more new literatures, new literary nations, new international writers, all of them the product of a rupture whose paradigm is furnished by du Bellay's *Defense and Illustration*.

Confronted with a phenomenon that is so poorly known and so generally misunderstood, the historian needs to treat it in broad perspective, keeping in mind the difficulties and the risks inherent in description concerned with the long term (in Braudel's sense) while at the same time being alert to events and mechanisms ordinarily masked by the falsely obvious and misleadingly familiar picture due to academic literary criticism. Moreover, it will be possible to reconstruct such a history only if one is prepared to go beyond not only the political and linguistic borders within which literary histories are invariably confined—and which such histories fail even to take into account, especially in the case of the great literary traditions, such as the French—but also the boundaries between disciplines, which are no less difficult to get clear of.

Three major stages may be distinguished in the genesis of world literary space. The first involves its initial formation, which may be dated to the appearance of the French Pléiade and of du Bellay's manifesto in the mid-sixteenth century. This was the age of what Benedict Anderson calls the "revolutionary vernacularizing thrust of capitalism"[3]—a revolution that gained momentum during the fifteenth and sixteenth centuries and that saw the exclusive use of Latin among educated men give way first to a demand for intellectual recognition of vulgar tongues, then to the creation of modern literatures claiming to compete with the

grandeur of ancient literatures. The second major stage in the enlargement of the literary world corresponds to the "philological-lexigraphic
revolution" described by Anderson,[4] which began in the late eighteenth
century and unfolded throughout the nineteenth century. This revolution saw the appearance in Europe of new nationalist movements associated with the invention or reinvention (to use Eric Hobsbawm's terms)
of self-consciously national languages and, subsequently, the creation of
"popular" literatures, summoned to serve the national idea and to give it
the symbolic foundation that it lacked.[5] Finally, the process of decolonization represents the third major stage in the enlargement of the literate
world, marking the entry into international competition of contestants
who until then had been prevented from taking part.

HOW TO "DEVOUR" LATIN

At the moment when *The Defense and Illustration* appeared, the debate
over the status of the French language occupied center stage in the
world of letters. The whole question of vernaculars (which was to be
posed and discussed in all of Europe) is bound up with that of Latin.
During this period, as Fumaroli puts it, there was "a dizzying difference
of symbolic altitude" between the vulgar tongues and the Latin language. Latin—together with Greek, reintroduced by humanist scholars—had accumulated all of the literary and, more generally, cultural
capital then in existence; but it was also a language on which Rome and
the entire religious establishment had a monopoly, the pope being invested with a dual authority that by itself summarized the exhaustive
domination to which the secular intellectual world was subject, extending from *sacerdotium*—things of the faith—to include *studium,* which is
to say everything that touches on learning, study, and intellectual matters. As the language of knowledge and faith, Latin exercised almost
complete control over existing intellectual resources and thus imposed
(to quote Fumaroli once more) a genuine "linguistic servitude."[6]

The humanist enterprise is therefore to be understood at least in part
as an attempt by the laity, in its battle against Latinist clerics and the
scholastic tradition, to achieve intellectual autonomy by reappropriating
a secularized Latin heritage. Thus the humanists made their purpose
plain in opposing to the "barbaric" Latin of the scholastics the refinement of "Ciceronian" Latin. By reintroducing a corpus of original
Latin texts—among them treatises on grammar and rhetoric, notably

those of Cicero and Quintilian—as well as the practice of translation and commentary, they diverted the ancient heritage of the "classics" by secularizing it—that is, by challenging the monopoly of the church. European humanism thus represents an early instance of the emancipation of the literate world from the control and domination of the church.[7]

The dominant power in this emerging intellectual space, as Fernand Braudel managed to establish after lengthy debate, was Italy.[8] Until then only three "modern" poets had succeeded in establishing themselves in a vernacular, and they were all Tuscan: Dante Alighieri (1265–1321), Petrarch (1304–1374), and Boccacio (1313–1375). Still in the sixteenth century they enjoyed immense prestige throughout Europe. It was in their homeland, then, that a cultural patrimony was first able to be accumulated. In the second half of the fifteenth century, Braudel observed, "Europe was ravaged in its center, France. Italy, by contrast, was protected: the succession of generations of humanists, who in the end prevailed, favored progress and the accumulation of knowledge, from Petrarch via Salutati to Bruni." And precisely because "all humanism is twofold, national first, European next," internal rivalries and quarrels developed in the worlds of scholarship and letters.[9] While some humanists who advocated a return to Ciceronian Latin also lent their support to what Dante called the "illustrious vernaculars," others resisted.

The battle over the status of vulgar tongues was in fact the logical outcome of the enterprise of humanist secularization. But in the case of the French humanists, this enterprise held out the doubly attractive prospect of challenging the power and preeminence of Italy, in both scholarship and poetry, by establishing a language capable of rivaling the Tuscan dialect; and also of offering an alternative to submission to Latin, whether Ciceronian or scholastic. The campaign for the legitimacy of the French language was therefore conceived as a way of freeing the worlds of learning and literature from the influence of the church while at the same time contesting the hegemony of the Italian humanists.[10]

In northern Europe, the spread of the Reformation had likewise challenged the monopoly of Latin and the hitherto unquestioned supremacy of the church. In this context the translation of the Bible into German by Luther in 1534 plainly represented a rejection of the church's claim to authority,[11] and furnished the basis for a standard written language that later became modern German. Throughout Protestant Europe the same tendency gave impetus to the development of vernaculars that, through the reading of the Bible, were to be massively disseminated among the lower classes of society.[12] Leaving to one side the special case of Germany, which long remained a disunified collection of states, in all the countries that adopted Lutheranism or other Protestant faiths (Anglicanism, Calvinism, and Methodism) the rise of vernaculars was associated with the growth of state structures. In northern Europe particularly, in Finland, Norway, and Sweden, translations of the Bible made possible the formation of politically unified nations.

Thus on either side of the great divide created by the Reformation in western Europe, the challenge to the total domination of the church and of Latin was the driving force behind the campaign on behalf of vulgar tongues. Following the denominational clashes of the years 1520–1530, however, the humanist movement gradually lost its religious character and began to come apart under the strain produced by the increasingly divergent interests of philologists and church reformers. From the 1530s onward, the schism between the Protestant north and Catholic south amounted in effect to a sort of division of labor. Although the church exercised, as we have seen, a dual authority of *sacerdotium* and *studium*— of faith and learning—the Reformation challenged the former, which is to say ecclesiastical control over strictly religious practices and institutions, while humanism contested the latter, which is to say ecclesiastical control over scholarship, poetry, and rhetoric. The distinctive separation of powers taking shape in France—unlike in England, where, as we shall see, political decentralization prevented a challenge to the church's monopoly upon *studium* from developing—was marked by the abandonment (except in the case of Calvinism, which remained a minority faith) of the demand for the reading and dissemination of the Bible in French and for lay participation in determining theological doctrine: even at the height of the battle between the upholders of Latin and those who defended the vulgar tongue, after 1530 there was no longer any question of French replacing the Latin of the schoolmen or disputing the privileged position of liturgical and theological Latin. Despite the structural dependency of the kingdom with respect to the church, the battle on behalf of the "king's language" therefore set in motion a unique process of secularization.

Within humanism itself, rivalries assumed political form. To offset the influence of Rome and of Italian men of letters, the Pléiade advocated the use of the French language, which was also the language of the king. In opposing the humanist universalism that sustained the domination of Latin, French men of letters embraced the cause of their king and the advance of royal sovereignty and authority in the face of papal power. But in order for the language of the king of France to be able to pretend to the rank of "Latin of the moderns," for its defenders to be able to dare openly to compare their vulgar language to that of the pope and the clerics, it needed to assure its own superiority, both literarily and politically, over the *langue d'oc* in the southern part of the kingdom and the other dialects of the *langue d'oïl* in the north. The language of the Île-de-France was associated with the royal principle from a very early time; indeed, Fumaroli argues that France was constructed around "a King-Word." Until the sixteenth century it was through a royal institution—"the Chancellery of France and its prestigious corps of royal notaries and clerks, all of whom were laymen"—that "an unbroken tradition" was carried on by "high functionaries of the royal language and style."[13] In a sense, these functionaries constituted a corps of royal writers who, by drafting legal documents and writing historical chronicles, worked to promote the political and diplomatic prestige of the royal language and the "increase," as du Bellay remarked, of its stylistic, literary, and poetic wealth.[14] In the sixteenth century, then, the vulgar language began to acquire an incontestable legitimacy as much on the political level—the famous Ordinance of Villers-Cotterêts in 1539, which stipulated that legal rulings be handed down in French rather than Latin, is evidence of this—as on the literary level, for it was at this time that grammars, lexicons, and treatises on orthography appeared.

If the poets of the Pléiade sided with the royal court—their first victory was to be the selection of Dorat, leader of the new school, as preceptor of the children of King Henri II—this is because for them the question was as much political as aesthetic. To take a position, as du Bellay did in *The Defense and Illustration,* against the recognized poetical genres practiced in the powerful feudal courts of the kingdom of France ("leave aside all these French poesies to the floral games of Toulouse, and the contest of Rouen, the rondels, ballades, virelays, chants royal, songs, and other such spices which do corrupt the taste of our tongue, and serve not, save to bear witness to our ignorance"), was to explicitly declare oneself against feudal prerogatives in the political sphere while at the same time, in the literary sphere, opposing the proponents of the "second rhetoric," who were also partisans of the poetic usage of the vulgar tongue, only conceived as a set of codified poetical forms.[15] Up until this time the court of the king was distinguished from other feudal courts solely by its status as *primus inter pares.*[16] But now the French crown achieved decisive victories against its rivals, laying claim to the hegemony that the feudal courts had previously exercised in the cultural domain. Beginning in 1530, François I founded the Collège des Lecteurs Royaux, ordered the construction of libraries and the purchase of paintings, and commanded the translation of ancient works after the example of the Italian humanist courts.

The new royal policy regarding language triggered an initial accumulation of political, linguistic, and literary resources, on the strength of which competition between the language of the king of France, the doubly sacred language of Rome, and the very literary Tuscan dialect was able to be established and proclaimed. It should be added that this program, though at the time it no doubt appeared to be overly ambitious, if not actually unachievable, was also favored by the French doctrine of *translatio imperii et studii,* according to which France and its king were predestined to exercise the supremacy that had lapsed with the fall of Rome and that Charlemagne had reclaimed for himself seven centuries earlier.[17]

Du Bellay's treatise (translated in part from a dialogue by the Italian author Sperone Speroni) was a frank declaration of war against the domination of Latin. To be sure, the debate over the question of vernaculars, over the primacy of one or another among them and their complex and conflictual relations with Latin, was not new. It had begun in Tuscany in the twelfth century with Dante (whose declaration of linguistic independence ultimately failed to create a national literature, as we shall see) and was later carried on in France, notably by Christophe de Longueil and then by Jean Lemaire de Belges in *The Harmony of the Two Languages.* But this treatise, far from inaugurating a competition between French, Latin, and Tuscan, linked the two vulgar sisters—French and Tuscan, daughters and heirs of Latin—in a "felicitous equality."[18] Its author refusing to choose between them, the quarrel between the two languages ended in reconciliation. If therefore *The Defense and Illustration* marked a break with the past, this is because it heralded a new era, not one of linguistic concord and serenity, but of open battle and competition with Latin.

Du Bellay's essay, regarded today by most scholars as a mere pamphlet, is usually thought to be of interest only insofar as it illuminates continuities and discontinuities in the humanist tradition and provides an opportunity for spotting classical citations and detecting Italian influences. Moreover, since poetry is associated much more strongly than other literary genres with national traditions, it has typically been regarded as evidence of a special national purpose, with the result that no attempt has been made to relate the development of poetry to any larger transnational history. But *The Defense and Illustration* was in fact a revolutionary text, an assertion of strength, a program for the enrichment of the French language; above all it was a manifesto for a new literature and a manual giving French poets the literary tools they needed to enter into competition with Latin and its modern successor, Tuscan. It was not a call for a return to the past, still less a plea for simple imitation of the ancients; it was a deliberate declaration of war. Du Bellay no longer sought, as his predecessors had done, merely to inherit the splendor of the classics, but actually to prevail over Greek and Latin, as well as Tuscan, in open combat—a combat that was not only linguistic, rhetorical, and poetic, but also political.

The Latin language, logically enough in view of its dominance, served as the unique measure of literary excellence. In order to undermine the dual hegemony of the ecclesiastical and Ciceronian Latin defended by the Italians, du Bellay proposed a brilliant and unsuspected solution: a *diversion of capital* that conserved the gains of Latinist humanism—a vast collection of knowledge derived from translations and commentaries on ancient texts—while diverting them to the profit of French, a language that was, as he put it, less "rich." This could be done very simply. First, du Bellay strenuously rejected translation, which in his view only encouraged "slavish" imitation, endlessly reproducing Greek and Latin texts without taking anything from them—that is, without contributing to the enrichment of the language: "What think they then to do, these replasterers of walls, who day and night break their heads with striving to imitate? Do I say to imitate? nay, to transcribe a Virgil and a Cicero, building their poems with hemistiches of the one, and swearing fealty in their proses to the words and thoughts of the other . . . Think not then, imitators, servile flock, to attain to the top point of their excellence." To "enrich his language," du Bellay proposed "to borrow from a foreign tongue thoughts and words and appropriate them to our own . . . Therefore I do admonish thee (O thou who desirest the increasing of thy language, and wouldst excell therein) not to imitate lightly (*à pié levé* as someone lately said) the most famous authors therein, as ordinarily do for the most part our French poets, a thing indeed as vicious as it is *profitless* to our common speech."[19]

To emphasize the importance he attached to appropriation, du Bellay employed the metaphor of devouring,[20] comparing this process to what the Romans did: "Imitating the best Greek authors, transforming themselves into them, *devouring* them; and after having well digested them, *converting* them into blood and nourishment."[21] Plainly this process of conversion must be understood in its implicit, though long denied, economic sense as well: French poets were being counseled to seize, devour, and digest an ancient heritage in order to convert it into national literary "assets." The peculiar sort of imitation du Bellay had in mind consisted in carrying over the immense achievement of Latin rhetoric into French. Confident that the French language would one day succeed to the dominant position of Latin and Greek, he offered his fellow "Poëtes Françoys" a way of achieving superiority over their rivals in Italy and elsewhere. In rejecting the "vieilles poësies Françoyses," he condemned as outmoded not only poetical norms that were current only within the borders of the kingdom of France but also all those forms that, by their failure to embrace humanist modernity (which is to say, paradoxically, Latin poetry), had forfeited any claim to take part in the new European competition.

With *The Defense and Illustration of the French Language,* du Bellay therefore laid the foundations of a unified international literary space. In retrospect he can be seen to have signaled the advent of what Fumaroli calls "a grand European competition, with the Ancients as coaches and referees; the French were expected to win every match . . . The enthusiasm of the French would ensure their victory over their Italian and Spanish rivals. The participation of the English was not yet envisaged."[22] Du Bellay—and with him the whole Pléiade school—sought to "enrich" the French language by means of a diversion of assets. Within a century and a half France had succeeded in reversing the balance of power in its favor, so that by the time of Louis XIV it reigned as the dominant literary power in Europe.

To this initial Tuscan-French core were gradually added Spain, and then England, which together formed the first group of major literary powers, each endowed with a "great language" as well as a sizable literary patrimony. The highpoint of the Golden Age had passed by the mid-seventeenth century, however, by which point Spain entered upon a period of slow decline that was inseparably literary and political. This "vast collapse, this very slow sinking" created a growing gap between Spanish literary space and that of the French and the English, now poised to assume their place as the leading literary powers in Europe.[23]

Italy: An Argument from Contraries

The case of Italy furnishes an argument from contraries in favor of the proposition that there is a necessary link between the founding of a state and the formation, first of a common language, and then of a literature. Historically, where a centralized state fails to emerge, neither the attempt to legitimize a vulgar tongue nor the hope of creating a national literature is able to succeed. In the fourteenth century, in Tuscany, Dante had sought to free the regional vernacular from the domination of Latin. Indeed, he was the first to have used his native dialect, in *Il Convivio* (The Banquet, 1304–1307), in order to reach a larger public. And in the treatise *On Vernacular Eloquence,* composed in Latin and begun at the same time, he had propounded the idea of an "illustrious vulgar tongue," a poetic, literary, and scientific language that would be founded on the basis of several Tuscan dialects. The influence of this treatise was to be decisive in France (for the poets of the Pléiade) and in Spain in marshaling support for the vernacular language as the vehicle of literary, and consequently national, expression.

The novelty and importance of Dante's agument led it to be adopted much later by writers who found themselves in a structurally similar position. Thus James Joyce and Samuel Beckett in the late 1920s pointed to it as model and precursor at a moment when the influence of English—the result of colonial domination in Ireland—bore comparison with that of Latin in Dante's time. Beckett, anxious to defend Joyce's literary and linguistic purposes in *Finnegans Wake,* explicitly claimed the Tuscan poet as a noble predecessor in setting out to oppose the monopoly enjoyed by English in their homeland.

In Italy, and more particularly in Tuscany, literary production in the vernacular was both earlier and more prestigious than elsewhere: consecrated as classics during their own lifetimes, the three great Tuscan poets—Dante, Petrarch, and Boccaccio—presided over the accumulation of the greatest literary wealth of the time, not only in Italy but also in the whole of Europe. Accordingly, their work was invested with the dual prestige of priority and perfection. But in the absence of forces tending to produce a unified Italian kingdom, and also because of the influence of the church, which was greater in Italy than elsewhere, this enormous initial stock of literary capital failed to produce a unified literary domain. The Italian courts remained divided, with the result that none was powerful enough to adopt and fully authorize the use of the "illustrious vulgar tongue" advocated by Dante, or indeed of any other: Latin remained the common and dominant language. As Fumaroli observes, Petrarch, "like his disciple Boccaccio and his sixteenth-century heir Bembo . . . was torn between Latin literature, which enjoyed supremacy in Italy and throughout Christian Europe thanks to Roman sacerdotal authority, and Italian literature, which lacked the support of an uncontested central political authority."[24]

The central debate in Italy during the sixteenth century opposed the supporters of the vernacular tongue to the Latinists. In the end it was the arguments of Pietro Bembo (1470–1547), whose *Prose della volgar lingua* (Essays on the Vernacular Language, 1525) advocated a return to the Tuscan literary and linguistic tradition of the fourteenth century, that carried the day. Bembo's "archaic" sensibility, marked by a thoroughgoing purism, halted the creation of a fund of literary capital, arresting poetical creativity and the renewal of an ancient tradition by restoring the sterilizing rule of imitation (on the model of the Latin humanists). The example of Petrarch, now established both as a stylistic model and a grammatical norm, helped slow the pace of innovation in Italian letters. For a very long time the poets were confined to imitation of Dante, Petrarque, and Bocaccio: in the absence of any centralized state structure that might have helped to stabilize and "grammatize" common languages,[25] it fell to poetry, whose fundamental role as the incarnation of perfection had now assumed mythical proportions, to act as guardian of the order of the language and as the measure of all things literary. Broadly speaking, it is true to say that poetical, rhetorical, and aesthetic problems were subordinated in Italy to the debate over linguistic norms until the achievement of political unity in the nineteenth century. Owing to the inability to exploit the political power of an organized state, and so accumulate a specifically literary wealth through the creation of a stable common language having a standard grammar and lexicon, an autonomous literary space was very late in being formed in Italy. Its literary heritage was able to be reappropriated as a national asset—symbolized by the elevation of Dante to the status of national poet—only after the establishment of a unified kingdom in 1861.

The same analysis, allowing for differences in historical context and development, may be applied to Germany. Here again, despite the early and significant accumulation of resources, the political division of the country prevented it from gathering sufficient literary wealth to be able to compete with other nations in Europe before the end of the eighteenth century, when the first stirrings of national unity made it possible to reclaim the German-language literary tradition as part of a national heritage. As for Russia, it did not begin the process of accumulating literary assets until the beginning of the nineteenth century.[26]

THE BATTLE OVER FRENCH

The Pléiade represented the first great revolution in French poetry. It was to shape poetical theory and practice in France for at least three hundred years, as much from the point of view of privileged genres (the rondeau, ballad, and other forms promoted by the second rhetoric gradually disappeared, not truly to be encountered again until Mallarmé and Apollinaire) as of the new metrics and prosody (verses of eight and of six feet, and above all the "mètre-roi," the Alexandrine, which was to become the standard meter for the whole classical period) and stanza patterns that came to be generalized and adopted throughout French literary space—not omitting, of course, the obligatory references to antiquity.[27]

Nonetheless, this opening salvo in the war with Latin in no way signaled the readiness of French to rival, either in fact or in belief, the immense power—symbolic, religious, political, intellectual, literary, rhetorical—of the older language. The history not only of French literature, but also of French grammar and rhetoric during the second half of the sixteenth century and the whole of the seventeenth, can be described as the continuation of the same struggle for the same prize—a struggle that was unacknowledged yet unmistakably real, carried on with the object of obtaining for the French language equality and, ultimately, superiority in relation to Latin. What is traditionally called "classicism," the highpoint of this cumulative process, is a shorthand for the set and succession of strategies that enabled France in only a little more than a century to realize its ambition of competing with the most powerful language and culture in the world (thus du Bellay's inaugural gesture in *The Defense*), achieving an indubitable victory over Latin during the "century of Louis XIV." The triumph of French—now considered the "Latin of the moderns"—was unhesitatingly and universally recognized throughout Europe.

What historical linguists call the process of codifying or standardizing a language,[28] marked by the appearance of grammars and treatises on rhetoric, rules of proper usage, and so on, seems in this case almost to amount to an immense collective undertaking aimed at increasing French literary and linguistic wealth—so much so that the extreme attention shown to the question of *bon usage* throughout the kingdom of France during the seventeenth century appears to be evidence of an attempt to rob Latin of its continental preeminence and thereby acquire title to the famous *imperium* that it had exercised for so long. Neither of these things is true, of course: there was neither a generalized will to power nor an explicit policy of state transmitted from generation to generation and devoted to obtaining political and cultural supremacy for the kingdom of France. In France, as elsewhere, struggles between the learned and the worldly (*doctes* and *mondains*), and between grammarians and writers, played themselves out in ways that were at once tacitly understood and publically denied. These formative rivalries gave French literary space its distinctive character by determining what was at stake and defining the specific form that its literary resources were to assume after the Pléiade—hence the importance, which was as much political as literary, attached to the language debate. Looked at from the narrow perspective of domestic literary and political experience, however, the historical course of French letters resists all explanation. We need to take a wider view and examine the international dimension of these rivalries, not only with other European languages but also with a dead yet still enormously influential tongue, which for a very long time were to remain the driving force of literary and linguistic innovation and debate in France.

Latin in the Schools

Despite the growing legitimacy of French as a language of administration and the arts, Latin continued to occupy a central place in national life, notably through the educational system and the church. Thomas Pavel has described the life of the *collèges* during the classical age of the seventeenth and eighteenth centuries, where students not only received instruction in Latin but were obliged to speak it (even among themselves) and permitted to read only the most reputable Latin authors. Divided into centuries and decuries, they were rewarded for success in their studies by the titles of senator and consul. A scholar's apprenticeship amounted to little more than the assimilation of a repertoire of histories—lives of illustrious men and women of antiquity, famous sayings, examples of strength and virtue. "In these closed *collèges*," Pavel notes, "carefully isolated from the rest of the world . . . the imaginary nature of [ancient] rhetorical culture . . . was celebrated each year by productions of neo-Latin plays written for the benefit of the students."[29]

Émile Durkheim, in his lectures on education in France, described this world in the same vein: "The Greco-Roman milieu in which students were made to live was emptied of all Greek and Roman reality, so that it became a sort of unreal, ideal place, populated no doubt by figures who had lived in the past but who, presented in this way, no longer had anything of the past about them. They were emblematic figures, nothing more, illustrating virtues, vices, all the great passions of humanity . . . Types so general, so indeterminate, [that they] could easily serve to exemplify the precepts of Christian morality." The sole pedagogical innovation introduced before the second half of the eighteenth century originated in the Petites Écoles des Messieurs de Port-Royal (opened in 1643 in Port-Royal and three years later in Paris), the first secondary schools to allow a place for French in the curriculum. "Port-Royal," noted Durkheim, "did not limit itself to protesting against the absolute prohibition that had been placed upon [the teaching of] French . . . but challenged the supremacy that, by unanimous opinion, had been attributed until then, throughout the Renaissance, to Latin and Greek."[30] And Pellisson himself, the historian of the Académie Française and historiographer to the king, testified to the influence of Latin in the training of "the learned men" of his time: "On leaving school I was given I know not how many new novels and plays, which, young and childish though I was, I did not cease to mock, always returning to my Cicero and my Terence, which I found much more reasonable."[31]

The battle of the "moderns" against the teaching of Latin began quite early. In 1657 Monsieur Le Grand, Sieur des Herminières, led the attack on "pédants,"[32] whose heads he claimed were so full of ancient languages that they were incapable of using French correctly:

> No doubt minds that are encumbered with Greek and Latin, that know so many things of no use in their own language, that burden their discourse with learned nonsense and elaborate pedantry, can never acquire the natural purity and naïve expression that are essential and necessary to compose a truly French prayer. So many different grammars and locutions are at war in their heads that there is a chaos of idioms and dialects: the construction of one sentence contradicts the syntax of another. Greek contaminates Latin, and Latin contaminates Greek, while Greek and Latin combined corrupt French . . . They are familiar with the dead languages and cannot use the living.[33]

Ten years later, Louis Le Laboureur, in his treatise *Des avantages de la langue françoise sur la langue latine* (Advantages of the French Language over the Latin Language, 1667), addressed the question whether the early education of the dauphin, the eldest son of Louis XIV, ought to be devoted to the "Latin Muses" or the "French Muses." But the learning of Latin enforced by the schools had made bilingualism a reality, and classical culture, despite the growing acceptance of the modern tongue, continued to furnish a repertoire of models and themes that were long to nourish literary composition in French.

The Use of French as a Spoken Language

The first great codifier of the language and of poetry was, of course, François de Malherbe (1555–1628). He was also for this reason the second great revolutionary of the French language; and although he was opposed to the aesthetics of the Pléiade and to the poetry of Philippe Desportes—a disciple of Ronsard—he may be considered a direct successor to du Bellay insofar as he pursued by other means the same enterprise of "enriching" French. But Malherbe was an innovator who found a way to escape the problem of imitation: once what was needed had been imported from Latin, the true differences between the two languages could be affirmed.

Malherbe, as is well known, attached priority to the need to encourage a refined use of the spoken language. He sought to invent an "oral prose"[34] that would make it possible to recreate the "charm," the "sweetness," and the "naturalness" that were peculiar to the French language while helping to devise norms of "proper speech," which stood in contrast to the abstraction of a language that was only written, and for that very reason dead: Latin. Malherbe also carried out a literary revolution by rejecting, like du Bellay, two traditions: on the one hand, the worldly and precious poetry of the courtiers and the verse of the learned men and the neo-Latin poets ("in order to mock those who wrote verse in Latin," his disciple Racan recalled, "he said that if Vergil and Horace were to come back to life, they would take the whip to Bourbon and Sirmond");[35] and, on the other hand, the practice of the Pléiade's descendants, who freely used many dialect words, employed a convoluted syntax, and practiced esotericism. Malherbe sought instead to affirm and codify the unarguable "beauties" of French, and thereby establish a standard of proper and euphonious usage on the basis of the particular characteristics of the living language. This did not mean having to forgo imitation of Latin masters. To the contrary, Malherbe wished to reconcile the revolution introduced by the Pléiade, namely the importation of Latin techniques to the French language (to which he added the "clarity" and "precision" inherited from Ciceronian prose and the elegance of Virgilian verse), with a desire to liberate French— through the vital and malleable use of the spoken tongue—from the sluggishness induced by unimaginative imitation. This doctrine, which rapidly gained acceptance among the ruling classes (not only the small elite of magistrates and men of letters from which Malherbe himself came, but also the court nobility), enabled French poetry to continue the process of accumulating literary resources begun by the Pléiade while avoiding the danger of becoming fossilized (as was the case in Italy) through too "faithful" imitation of ancient models.

Malherbe's call for elegant usage and "naturalness" (by contrast with precious "archaism"), combined with his insistence on the need to cultivate the spoken, living language, which otherwise risked being frozen in written models, therefore gave additional impetus to the creation of a specifically French stock of literary and linguistic capital. The famous reference to the "hay-pitchers at the Port-au-Foin"—with its implication than an "ignorant" layman's mastery of the royal tongue was surer than that of the learned humanists—is clear evidence of Malherbe's desire to break with the inertia of scholarly models.[36] The attempt to create a new oral prose, unencumbered by the rigidities of ancient and Renaissance canons, was to revolutionize the whole of French letters and, notwithstanding the lexical and grammatical codifications to which it gave rise, give poets the freedom the innovate.

Surprisingly, the same strategy was later to be employed in a variety of dominated literary spaces located in very different times and contexts. In Brazil during the 1920s, for example, modernists called for the standardization and literary use of a "Brazilian language" on the basis of a similar oral prose, relegating to the past the static norms of Portuguese—"the language of Camões"—which was likened in much the same way to a dead language. In the United States at the end of the nineteenth century, Mark Twain founded the modern American novel through the introduction of an oral, popular language by which he declared his opposition to the norms of literary English. In both cases, association of literature with the development of a changing and unfinished language, abandoning older, sclerotic models, made it possible to accumulate fresh literary resources.

Claude Favre de Vaugelas (1585–1660) took up the task begun by Malherbe with his *Remarques sur la langue françoise* (Remarks on the French Language, 1647). This was a sort of "linguistic courtesy book,"[37] consisting of recommendations for defining the *bon usage* of spoken language that relied on the rules of conversation of "society" and the literary practice of the best authors: "Here then is how good Usage is defined . . . it is the manner of speaking of the soundest part of the Court, in conformity with the manner of writing of the soundest Authors of the time. When I say the Court, I understand by it women as well as men, and various persons from the city where the Prince resides, who, through their communication with the people of the Court, share in its good taste [*politesse*]."[38] The importance attached to the conversation of "society," now regarded as the standard of proper speech and the model of good writing, is a patent sign of the distinctive character of French linguistic capital during its phase of accumulation, which underwrote innovation within the literary language and within newly codified genres. Because the written was subordinate to the oral, literary forms that were usually the most fixed and unchanging, especially ones associated with the models of antiquity, were able to develop more rapidly than in other countries, such as Italy, where archaic written models continued to serve as the basis for the spoken usage of the common language.

THE CULT OF LANGUAGE

With the quasi-permanent establishment of the king and his entourage in Paris at the end of the sixteenth century, and then throughout the seventeenth century the centralization and strengthening of monarchical power, which reached its height during the reign of Louis XIV, there was a corresponding shift of virtually all intellectual activity to Paris. The capital's preeminence was accompanied by the growing influence of the court and the increasing power of salons, where the various elements of the world of letters met—scholars and gentlemen, well-bred ladies (whose essential role in the dissemination of a new art of living and conversing has been much emphasized), scientists and poets. And it was through these salons that the issue of language came to be discussed by the ruling class as a whole. In no other part of the world during this period were the proper use of language and literary art taken out of the hands of teachers and scholars and placed in the service of and art of living and conversation to the degree they were in France. "The king's French, Parisian French, was being transformed," Fumaroli notes, "by literate conversation into the living language at once most concerned with its own distinctive character, originality, and naturalness and most eager to borrow the stylistic traits that humanist philologists had praised in Ciceronian prose."[39]

The intense effort at codification undertaken during the seventeenth century has long been attributed to the "aesthetic sensibilities" of the grammarians: since the "exuberance of the sixteenth century [had] left a great deal of 'linguistic untidiness' to be cleared up," it was necessary to restore the order, symmetry, and harmony of the language.[40] Walther von Wartburg, for example, interpreted the grammarians' concern as the expression of a political imperative, namely that France dispose of a single and uniform language in order to improve social communication after the anarchy and disorder of earlier times. On this view, the ruling class joined together to defend the long-term interests of the country.[41] One might have thought, to the contrary, that the codification of French was the result of a system of shifting alliances and rivalries between grammarians and gentlemen, officers of the Chancellery, jurists, and members of the worlds of letters and polite society—a system that worked to produce definitions of good usage and to formulate the principles on which these were based, including rules governing poetic composition, while appealing to the example of the most prestigious authors in order to establish criteria of linguistic correctness. The rivalries among *doctes* and *mondains,* writers, grammarians, and courtiers[42] gave rise to an extraordinary and altogether novel debate of immense social import, the like of which was found nowhere else in Europe.[43] Ferdinand Brunot's observation that the "reign of grammar . . . was more tyrannical and long-lasting in France than in any other country" perfectly captures its special linguistic and literary character.[44] In no other country were prescriptive works concerning vocabulary, grammar, spelling, and pronunciation more numerous.[45]

A turning point occurred around 1630, when Descartes chose to renounce Latin—until then the language of philosophy—and composed several important works in French, most notably the *Discours de la méthode* (Discourse on Method, 1637), at the end of which he explained his decision by saying, "I expect that those who use only their natural reason in all its purity will be better judges of my opinions than those who give credence only to the writings of the ancients."[46] A generation later, the *Grammaire générale et raisonnée* (General and Analytical Grammar, 1660), by Antoine Arnauld and Claude Lancelot, better known as the "Port-Royal grammar," was to rely on the Cartesian method in advancing the idea of an "analytical" grammatical doctrine.

The "standardization" of the French language during the seventeenth century cannot be reduced, then, to a simple need for improved communication in order to promote political centralization.[47] Instead it was a matter of gathering the various resources—theoretical, logical, aesthetic, rhetorical—necessary for creating literary value and for transforming the "langue françoyse" into a literary language. This process amounted to a sort of aestheticization, or progressive *littérarisation,* which in a relatively short time endowed French with the autonomy it needed to become the language of literature. "Throughout the seventeenth century," Anthony Lodge notes, "the symbolic value of language and the most minute refinements of the linguistic norm were central preoccupations of the upper echelons of a society where [as Brunot put it] 'beauty of language is one of the chief ways of distinguishing oneself.'"[48] Language therefore became the object and purpose of a unique form of belief.

In 1637 the Hôtel de Rambouillet found itself party to a "grammatical dispute" over the word *car* (meaning "because" or "for"). This unfortunate conjunction had aroused Malherbe's the displeasure—Gomberville congratulated himself on having avoided it in the five volumes of his *Exil de Polexandre et d'Ériclée* (Exile of Polexander and Ericlea, 1629)—with the result that the matter was brought to the attention of the Academy, which studied it with an attentiveness later mocked by Saint-Évremont in his comedy *Les Académistes* (The Equestrian Masters, 1650). The Academy's preference for *pour ce que* led to a war of pamphlets. Mlle. de Rambouillet called upon Vincent Voiture, a leader of the society faction, to come to the rescue. Voiture responded with a plea for the defense that parodied the "noble" style:

> At a time when fortune stages tragic dramas in all parts of Europe, I see nothing so worthy of pity as when I see that one is prepared to hunt down and bring to trial a word that has so usefully served this monarchy and that, in all the troubles of the kingdom, has always shown itself to be good French . . . I do not know for what reason they try to take away from *car* what belongs to it in order to give this to *pour ce que,* nor why they wish to say with three words what they can say with three letters. What is most to be feared, Mademoiselle, is that in the wake of this injustice others will be undertaken. There will be no difficulty attacking *mais,* and I do not know if *si* will long be safe. So that after all the words that link the others have been removed, the great minds will wish to reduce us to the language of the angels, or, if this cannot be done, they will oblige us at least to speak only through signs . . . Yet it happens that after having lived for eleven hundred years, full of strength and credit, after having been employed in the most important treaties and having always honorably assisted in the deliberations of our kings, it falls suddenly into disgrace and finds itself threatened with a violent end. The moment is not far off, I fear, when mournful voices will be heard to fill the air, which will say: *le grand car est mort,* and the demise neither of the great *Cam* nor of the great *Pan* would seem to me so important or so strange.[49]

By the beginning of the reign of Louis XIV in 1661, the accumulated capital of French was so great, and the belief in the power of this language so strong, that its victory over Latin and its triumph throughout Europe began to be celebrated. In 1667 Louis Le Laboureur published *Des avantages de la langue françoise sur la langue latine,* as though it were still necessary to affirm the preeminence of French; four years later, however, in 1671, Father Bouhours' *Entretiens d'Ariste et d'Eugène* (Conversations between Ariste and Eugene) appeared, a work that praised the superiority of French "not only to the other modern languages but also to Latin, even to the perfected Latin of the early imperial age."[50] And in 1676 François Charpentier, in his *Defense de la langue françoise pour l'inscription de l'Arc de triomphe* (Defense of the French Language for the Inscription on the Triumphal Arch), asserted that the French language was more "universal" than Latin at the time when the Roman Empire was at the height of its power and, a fortiori, than the neo-Latin of the *doctes*. Charpentier styled his monarch "a second Augustus," claiming that "like Augustus, he is the Love of Peoples; the Restorer of the State; the Founder of laws and of Public Happiness . . . All the Fine Arts have felt the effects of this Marvelous Progress. Poetry, Eloquence, Music—all these have attained a degree of excellence never before equalled."[51]

The following decade saw the quarrel between the ancients and the moderns pit the director of the Academy, Charles Perrault, whose poem *Le siècle de Louis le Grand* (The Century of Louis the Great, 1687) asserted the superiority of his monarch's century over that of Augustus Caesar, against Boileau (supported by La Bruyère, La Fontaine, and others).[52] The triumph of the moderns was to mark the end of the age opened by du Bellay in 1549. By the end of the seventeenth century the moderns could claim to have put an end to the supremacy of the ancients, vindicating du Bellay's strategy of imitating classical texts for the purpose of appropriating their resources. In the meantime, however, the moderns had taken a new tack: imitation was now held to be useless, and the process of importation and emancipation was finished. In the four volumes of his *Parallèles des anciens et des modernes* (Parallels between the Ancients and the Moderns, 1688–1697), Perrault claimed preeminence for the moderns in all genres, holding that in the seventeenth century the arts had been brought to a higher degree of perfection than they enjoyed among the ancients. Those who were rightly called "classics," and who borrowed their references and literary models from antiquity, made Perrault's manifesto possible: they were reckoned to mark the apogee of the century of Louis XIV, the triumph of French language and literature, because they had achieved the greatest possible "increase" of literary resources. In their works, and in the language they used, they incarnated the victory of French over Latin. Perrault could announce his opposition to the policy of imitating the ancients and proclaim the end of the reign of Latin precisely because these writers had put an end to the process of imitation by bringing it to its most extreme point. The achievement of the moderns was to have reached the limits of literary freedom first glimpsed by Greek and Latin authors: if Perrault granted not only Corneille, Molière, Pascal, La Fontaine, and La Bruyère but also Voltaire, Sarasin, and Saint-Amant superiority over the ancients, it was because he considered them as having arrived at the summit of perfection.

This is why one cannot reduce the quarrel, as traditional literary historiography does, to simple political partisanship.[53] The received view openly endorses an anachronistic conception of history in making the ancients supporters of the absolute monarchy and the moderns upholders of a more liberal form of government. But in that case how are we to explain the unqualified apology for the reign of Louis XIV in Perrault's *Le siècle de Louis le Grand?* Only an analysis of the historical accumulation of literary capital within French literary space allows us to account both for what was really at issue—the unspoken and specifically literary basis of the quarrel, namely the balance of power with Latin—and for the political stakes of the conflict, which is to say the place and the power of the language in the face of the declining and contested hegemony of Latin.

THE EMPIRE OF FRENCH

The triumph of French was now so complete, both in France and in the rest of Europe, and its prestige so unchallengable, that its claim to superiority came to be true as a matter of fact no less than of opinion; or rather, it began to exist in fact because its truth was universally thought to be obvious. The French had come so fully to believe in the definitive victory of their language over Latin, and moreover had so completely succeeded in causing it to be believed by others (with the result that the authority of the language was acknowledged by all other elites in Europe), that the use of French very quickly spread throughout the continent. With the wars of Louis XIV and the treaties that concluded them, French became the language of diplomacy and international agreements. This transnational usage established itself only by virtue of the "empire," as Rivarol put it, over which French now "naturally" presided because it had at last managed, after a century and a half of struggle, to accumulate literary resources, to overturn the power relations that formerly had subjected France, and with it the whole of Europe, to the domination of Latin.

French became almost a second mother tongue in aristocratic circles in Germany and Russia; elsewhere it was adopted as a sort of second language of conversation and "civility." Belief in the supremacy of French was strongest in the small German states. Throughout the eighteenth century, and particularly during the years 1740–1770, the German principalities were unsurpassed in their attachment to its worldly use. Elsewhere, in central and eastern Europe, even in Italy, one finds the same enthusiastic embrace of the French model. Patent evidence of the literary value that was attributed to it is supplied by the writers who elected to compose their literary works in French: the Germans Grimm and Holbach, the Italians Galiani and Casanova, Catherine II of Russia and Frederick II of Prussia, the Irishman Anthony Hamilton, and a growing number of Russian authors who had abandoned German in its favor, among others.

The striking thing about the pretension of the French language to universality, founded and modeled on that of Latin, is that it did not impose itself as a form of French domination; that is, as a system deliberately organized in such a way as to redound to the advantage of France as a nation. French came to be generally established, without the assistance or cooperation of any political authority, as a common language—the language of cultivated and refined conversation, exercising a sort of jurisdiction that extended to all of Europe. Its cosmopolitan character is evidence of the curious "denationalization" of French,[54] whose dominance, never recognized as national, was accepted instead as international. It was neither a form of political power nor an example of cultural influence in the service of a nation-state, but the vehicle of a symbolic supremacy whose ramifications were long to be felt, never more plainly than at the moment when Paris emerged as the universal capital of literature and began to administer its "government" (in Victor Hugo's phrase) over the entire world. Thus, under Louis XV, Abbé Desfontaines asked: "What is the source of this attraction to the language coupled with aversion to the nation? It is the good taste of those who speak and write it naturally; it is the excellence of their compositions, their turns of phrase, their subject matter. French superiority in matters of delicate and refined luxury and sensuality has also helped our language to travel. People adopt our terms with our fashions and finery, about which they are extremely curious."[55]

This reversal of the terms of cultural domination in favor of French, now regarded as the language of "civilization" (as the Germans were to say some years later), therefore marked the founding of a new "secular international order."[56] Indeed, the secularization of European political and literary space stands out as one of the fundamental traits of the French *imperium*. To the extent that it was the ultimate consequence of the enterprise inaugurated by du Bellay and the humanists against the supremacy of Latin, it can be understood as a first step in the direction of autonomy for European literary space as a whole. Having succeeded in escaping the influence and domination of the church, it remained for writers—this would be the work of the eighteenth and, especially, the nineteenth century—to free themselves first from dependency on the king, and then from subjection to the national cause.

Clearly, this extraordinary belief in the perfection of the language of the king was able to be accepted, not only by the entire French literary world but by all the European elites as well, only because the enormity of accumulated literary capital, and the singular character of the struggle engaged in by French men and women of letters made it irresistible. But this belief, as well as the belief in the grandeur of what Voltaire was to call "the century of Louis XIV," also generated a system of literary, stylistic, and linguistic representations whose effects can still be felt today.

Voltaire himself was perhaps the chief architect of the unequalled and unmatchable grandeur of the French classical age.[57] In *Le siècle de Louis XIV* (The Century of Louis XIV, 1751), he constructed out of whole cloth the myth of a golden age that was at once political and literary. He invented the notion of an eternal classicism, created a nostalgia for the glorious days of the Sun King, and above all elevated those writers henceforth called classic to an unattainable summit of literary art. By giving a historical appearance to the mythical conception of history that this belief assumed, he established the reign of Louis XIV as a "perfect" age, which could only be reproduced or imitated:

> It seems to me that when, in a century, one has had a sufficient number of good writers who have become classics, it is hardly permissible to use expressions other than theirs, and that it is necessary to give [such expressions] the same meaning, or else very shortly the present century will no longer understand the previous century . . . It was a time worthy of the attention of times to come, when the heroes of Corneille and Racine, the characters of Molière, the symphonies of Lully, and (because here one is speaking only of the arts) the voices of Bossuet and Bourdaloue made themselves heard by Louis XIV, by Madame, so famous for her taste, by Condé, Turenne, Colbert, and that

throng of superior men who appeared in every genre. This time will never be met with again, when the Duc de La Rochefoucauld, the author of the *Maximes,* on emerging from conversation with Pascal or Arnauld, went to see a play by Corneille.[58]

The belief in the model of French "classicism," and the avowed determination of writers and intellectuals to go beyond it, can be understood only in terms of this notion of a "perfection" incarnated at a certain historical moment by a country with which there was no alternative but to try to compete. In the same way, nearer to our time, one cannot comprehend the fascination with the language of French classicism exhibited by a writer such as E. M. Cioran, or his desire to reproduce it, without taking into account the belief—inherited mainly from Germany—in the unequaled state of perfection of the language and literature of France.

One finds the doctrine of French classical perfection given full expression in the treatise *De la littérature allemande,* published in French by the king of Prussia in 1780.[59] I have already observed that this text is an extraordinary indication of the complete dominance enjoyed at the time by the French language. But it must also be said that the conception of history (and of the history of art) that underlies the book, and that was to be upheld by future generations of German intellectuals and artists, ascribed to classicism a sort of discontinuous permanence, first manifested by the Greece of Plato and Demosthenes and continuing with the Rome of Cicero and Augustus, the Italy of the Renaissance, and the France of Louis XIV. Germany could not hope for a more brilliant destiny than to assume its place in a universal history of culture, conceived as a succession of "centuries" in which each nation in its turn incarnated the classical ideal before stepping aside, overcome by decadence, as another slowly reached maturity.

In order to make up for German "backwardness" and bring forth new German "classics," Frederick II therefore needed to take the French language as a model:

> under the reign of Louis XIV, French spread throughout Europe, and this partly out of love for the admirable authors who then flourished, also for the excellent translations of the ancients that were made then. And now this language has become a master key that lets you into every house and every city. Travel from Lisbon to Petersburg, and from

Stockholm to Naples speaking French, you will make yourself understood everywhere. By this idiom alone, you spare yourself the need to know a great many languages, which would overburden your memory for words . . . We shall have our classic authors; each person, in order to profit from them, will wish to read them; our neighbors will learn German, courts will speak it with delight; and it will come to pass that our polished and perfected language extends on behalf of our admirable Writers from one end of Europe to the other.[60]

It was with this Voltairean model, ratified by Frederick the Great, that Herder was later to break.

Antoine de Rivarol's famous *Discours de l'universalité de la langue française* (Discourse on the Universality of the French Language, 1784) was a response to a series of questions set by the Academy of Berlin in its competition of the previous year: "What has made the French language universal? Why does it merit this primacy? Is it to be presumed that it will keep [this primacy]?" The very fact that the contest was announced in these terms is the ultimate proof of undisputed French dominance—but proof also that it had already entered into decline. Some twelve years earlier, Johann Gottfried Herder had advanced the first arguments against French universalism before the same academy in Berlin. His essay, *Abhandlung über den Ursprung der Sprache* (Treatise on the Origin of Languages, 1772), served as the banner for the new national ideas that were to be used as weapons in the struggle against French hegemony and that were subsequently to spread throughout Europe. In effect, then, Rivarol delivered a sort of funeral oration rather than a panegyric.

But Rivarol's *Discourse* nevertheless marked a crucial moment in the formation of the French literary heritage: on the one hand, because it brought together and reviewed all the commonplaces underlying the belief in the universality of French and, by stating them in a clear and organized way, made it possible to explain and understand the origin of a form of cultural domination that was recognized and accepted in all of Europe; and, on the other, because it signaled the appearance of a new and rising power across the Channel that called French sovereignty into question. The campaign against the "empire" of French was henceforth to be conducted on two fronts, England and Germany, with decisive consequences for the structure of European literary space throughout the nineteenth century.

In the opening sentence of the *Discourse,* Rivarol drew a parallel with the Roman Empire: "The time seems to have come to say [that] the French world, as formerly the Roman world, and philosophy, having grown weary of seeing men forever divided by the various interests of politics, now rejoices at seeing them, from one end of the earth to the other, form themselves into a republic under the domination of a single language."[61] It is necessary to recall the definition of universality as it was understood in France (and as it was to be challenged by Herder), namely, as the reestablishment of a unity in a world sundered by political rivalries. In other words, French domination was accepted by one and all because it placed itself above all partisan advantage, personal or national: "It is no longer merely the French language," Rivarol explained; "it is the human language." This sentence, often cited as proof of French arrogance, was actually another way of making the point that, owing to its incontestable dominion, the French language was not seen as an expression of national character, and therefore an instrument of the particular interests of France and the French people, but rather as a universal language, which is to say one that belonged to all people and so rose above national interests. With the Age of Louis XIV, France had come to exercise a symbolic power that no military victory could have imposed: "Since this explosion," Rivarol went on to observe, "France has continued to provide surrounding states with theater, clothing, taste, manners, a language, a new art of living, and novel pleasures—a kind of empire that no other people has ever exercised. Compare it, I beg you, with that of the Romans, who everywhere disseminated their language and slavery, battened on blood, and destroyed until they themselves were destroyed."[62] In other words, the power of French, by its very civility and refinement, surpassed that of Latin.

This universality was in a sense founded on what Rivarol called the "conflict of nations," which is to say the competition and rivalry among them. The victory of France and French, notwithstanding the merits of all other languages—acknowledged in a very refined and cultivated way—was due to its unmatched "clarity." In offering the customary explanation for the intrinsic "superiority" of French over other languages, Rivarol formulated what was already a commonplace with the extraordinary arrogance characteristic of dominant powers: "What is not clear is not French; what is not clear is only English, Italian, Greek, or Latin."[63]

The *Discourse* was also an engine of war, manufactured for the purpose of fighting France's most dangerous rival in this eternal conflict of nations, the one that then challenged most directly the universal domination of French universality: England. The English and the French, Rivarol wrote, were "neighboring and rival [peoples] who, having contended for three hundred years, not over who would have empire, but over who would exist, still fight over the glory of letters and for a century have commanded the attention of the world." At bottom, the rivalry with England grew out of the threat represented by its commercial power. London had become in economic terms the richest and most important place in Europe. Rivarol was very careful not to confuse what he called "the immense credit" enjoyed by the English in respect of commerce with their supposed power in literature; to the contrary, he tried to dissociate the two things so that France might be in a position to perpetuate its literary empire, arguing that symbolic power could not be inferred from economic power: "Accustomed to the immense credit that he has in business, the Englishman seems to bear this fictive power in letters, and his literature has contracted from it an exaggerated character contrary to good taste."[64] There is a hint in this of a distinction between an economic order and a literary order; but because Rivarol was not yet really able to formulate the concept of literary autonomy, he could not imagine—as Valery Larbaud was to do two centuries later—a literary map distinct from the political map.

The English Challenge

At the end of the eighteenth century, then, the great challenge to the prevailing French order came from England. "The English," observed Louis Réau, "boastful of their victories over Louis XIV, proud of the new popularity of their literature as illustrated by Dryden, Addison, Pope, and Swift, impatiently endured the pretensions of the French language to universality."[65] In England, the economic and political ascendancy of the crown was accompanied by a codification of the language and a specific claim to literary capital. Through the efforts of men of letters, grammarians, and lexicographers, the main outlines of English in its modern form were fixed.

The establishment of French as the official language following the Norman Conquest in 1066 was to have lasting consequences, and it was only in the fifteenth century that standard English emerged. The peculiarity of the history of the English nation is that the emancipation from Roman ecclesiastical authority led, in the sixteenth century, to the transfer of all powers to the king: in proclaiming himself, by the Act of Supremacy (1534), the supreme head of the Church of England, Henry VIII seized a power that was absolute as much in the political as in the religious sphere. The standardization of the language was thus linked to an attempt to establish uniform religious texts in English: the *Great Bible* (1539), the *Book of Common Prayer* (1548), and the *King James Bible* ("Authorized Version," 1611) were read at Sunday services throughout the land. But the legitimation of the vernacular language occurred rather belatedly. As in the German case, the challenge to Roman preeminence in theological matters prevented the dominance of Latin from being contested in the realm of learning and poetry—as though, as I suggested earlier, the adoption of Protestant faiths somehow prevented literary and linguistic challenges to the established order from assuming a secular form. Surely this is why, despite the schism, Latin conserved all its properly literary prestige for a very long time in England, and the work of grammarians was able to emancipate the common language from the Greco-Latin model only much later.[66]

It was not until the eighteenth century that the results of this activity were affirmed, but without the creation of any central legislative institution on the model of the Académie Française. "The setting of standards," Daniel Baggioni remarks, "was the business of grammarians, men of letters, and pedagogues, ratified by a social consensus that was respectful of established hierarchies."[67] This apparent autonomy obscures a national appropriation of literature that, without being limited to England, was no doubt particularly marked there. The habit of seeing literature as the outstanding expression of national character, which is to say the chief incarnation of national identity, is peculiarly English.[68] In England more than anywhere else, literature became one of the principal devices for the affirmation and definition of national identity, which in turn had a great deal to do with the declared rivalry with France. Even if English nationalism did not assume the same forms as in the rest of Europe— and this is essential for understanding English "exceptionalism"—it is fair to say that the definition of national identity in England was first elaborated at the end of the eighteenth century in reaction against French hegemony. This challenge took the form of a pronounced Gallophobia that was unquestionably commensurate with French arrogance and assertions of supremacy. The task of national construction, expressly undertaken in opposition to a France supposed to be hostile, tyrannical, and Catholic, was based on the "difference" constituted by Protestantism.[69] In the same way, literature was gradually nationalized—which is to say designated as "English," as national property—and affirmed against French pretensions to preeminence.

Stereotypes of the English national character—likewise conceived as a defense against the threat of French domination—were expressed and developed through literature.[70] The idea of an innate "genius" for individualism and sincerity, for example, is closely bound up with a sense of political identity directly opposed to that of France: thus the French fondness for dialectical juxtapositions (between despotism and revolution, for example) was associated with artificial formality—the famous "French polish"—and the doubtful morality of their literature.[71] Similarly, the notion of an English "gift" for liberty and representative government grew up in reaction to French political mythology and in combination with a supposed and self-proclaimed inability to construct a system of thought based on general ideas—the talent of "English literature" consisting in a faithfulness to the richness and complexity of life and a refusal to reduce them to abstract categories.[72] These elements of structural opposition to the hegemony of France made England its foremost rival in the world of letters.

THE HERDERIAN REVOLUTION

Between 1820 and 1920 in Europe, alongside the nationalist movements of the period, there occurred what Benedict Anderson has called a "philological-lexigraphic revolution." The theories of Johann Gottfried Herder (1744–1803), formulated in the late eighteenth century and thereafter rapidly and widely disseminated, brought about the first enlargement of literary space to include the European continent as a whole. Herder not only proposed a new manner of contesting French hegemony that was to be of value to Germany; he also provided the theoretical basis for the attempt made in politically dominated territories, both in Europe and elsewhere, to invent their own solutions to the problem of cultural dependence. By establishing a necessary link between nation and language, he encouraged all peoples who sought recognition on equal terms with the established nations of the world to stake their claim to literary and political existence.

The ascendancy of the French literary and historical model and the prestige of the philosophy of history that French culture implicitly, but nonetheless powerfully, transmitted were such that Herder was obliged to forge an utterly new set of theoretical and conceptual tools. One of his first efforts in this direction, *Auch eine Philosophie die Geschichte zur Bildung der Menschheit* (Another Philosophy of History for the Education of Mankind, 1774), amounted to a declaration of war against Voltaire's philosophy and his belief in the superiority of the "enlightened" age of French classicism over all other periods of history. Herder, by contrast, laid stress on the equal value of past ages, particularly the medieval period, arguing that each epoch (and nation) possesses its own special character and so must be judged according to its own criteria;[73] and that each culture therefore has its own place and its own value, independent of the place and value of others. He joined with Goethe and Möser in arguing against "French taste" in *Von deutscher Art und Kunst* (On German Style and Art, 1773), a work notable for its admiration of what for Herder were three incomparable examples of naturalness and strength in literature: popular song, Ossian, and Shakespeare. They also represented so many weapons to be directed against the aristocratic and cosmopolitan power of French universalism: the people; the literary tradition issuing from sources other than Greco-Latin antiquity (as against the "artifice" and "embellishment" of French culture, Herder advocated a poetry that would be at once "authentic" and "immediately popular"); and, finally, England. The unequal distribution of power in the emerging international literary world helps explain why the Germans were to rely on England and Shakespeare, its major and incontestable source of capital: given two poles of opposition to French power, each would be able to lend support to the other. In the same way, the critical reassessment of Shakespeare by the German Romantics was used by the English to claim him as the chief repository of their national literary wealth.

Herder sought to explain why Germany had not yet produced a universally recognized literature. Nations, he argued, likening them to living organisms, needed time to develop their own peculiar "genius." As for Germany, it had not yet reached maturity. In calling for a return to "popular" languages, he devised a wholly novel and genuinely revolutionary strategy for accumulating literary capital that was to enable Germany to overcome its "backwardness" and join at last in international literary competition. By granting each country and each people the right to an existence and a dignity equal in principle to those of others, in the name of "popular traditions" from which sprang a country's entire cultural and historical development, and by locating the source of artistic fertility in the "soul" of peoples, Herder shattered all the hierarchies, all the assumptions that until then had unchallengably constituted literary "nobility"—and this for a very long time.

The new definitions that he proposed both of language (the "mirror of the people") and of literature ("language is the reservoir and content of literature")—as he had described them earlier in *Über die neure deutsche Literatur: Fragmente* (Fragments concerning Recent German Literature, 1767)—contradicted the dominant aristocratic French conception and, by exploding the notion of literary legitimacy, changed the rules of the international literary game. Since a nation's people were now regarded as the source and conservatory of literary inspiration, it thereby became possible to gauge the "greatness" of a literature by the importance and the "authenticity" of their traditions. This alternative notion of literary legitimacy, at once national and popular, permitted the accumulation of another type of resource, unknown until then in the literary world, that was to link literature still more closely with politics. Henceforth, all the "little" nations in Europe and elsewhere were able, on account of their ennoblement by the people, to claim an independent existence that was inseparably political and literary.

The Herder Effect
Herder's thought was to play a central role in modern German intellectual life. His ideas exercised a profound influence upon the Romantic writers, who adopted his philosophy of history as well as his interest in the medieval period, the East, and language; the same is true of his study of comparative literature, and of his conception of poetry as the primary vehicle of national "education." Hölderlin, Jean Paul, Novalis, Wilhelm von Schlegel and his brother Friedrich, Schelling, Hegel, Schleiermacher, and Humboldt were all great readers of Herder. The very concept of "romantic," in the sense of "modern"—by contrast with that of "classic" and "ancient"—has its origin in Herder's thought, which supplied the basis for the Germans' claim to modernity in their struggle against French cultural hegemony. It was with Möser and Herder that the Germans began to reproach France for "superficiality, frivolity, and immorality while claiming for Germany solidity, integrity, and fidelity."[74]

With respect to the rest of Europe, it would be more accurate to speak of a sort of "Herder effect," at least to the extent that outside Germany it was more a question of the practical consequences flowing from a few key ideas due to Herder than of the strictly theoretical and political elaboration of his thinking. The *Ideen zur Philosophie der Geschichte der Menschheit* (Reflections on the Philosophy of the History of Mankind, 1784–1791)—unquestionably Herder's most famous work—enjoyed an immense and immediate success in Hungary, where it was read in German; and the brief chapter devoted to the Slavs in the *Ideen* had an electrifying effect in the Balkans, where Herder was hailed as the "master of the Croat race" and "the first to defend and praise the Slavs."[75] His major theme, endlessly repeated by Hungarians, Romanians, Poles, Czechs, Serbs, and Croats, was the right and the necessity of writing in one's native tongue. In Russia the work was known through the French translation by Edgar Quinet. In Argentina its political influence was great at the end of the nineteenth century. In the United States the constellation of themes summarized by the formula "literature, nation, mankind" and popularized through the work of George Bancroft (one of fifteen Americans who studied with Herder's disciples at Göttingen) constituted the chief doctrine of American Herderianism: "The literature of a nation is national," Bancroft wrote.[76] "Each [nation] bears in itself the standard of perfection, totally independent of all comparison with that of others."[77]

The equivalence between language and nation posited by Herder explains why the national demands that appeared throughout Europe during the nineteenth century were indissociable from linguistic demands. The new national languages that were championed had either come close to disappearing from use during a period of political domination—as in the cases, for example, of Hungarian, Czech, Gaelic, Bulgarian, and Greek—or existed only in the oral form of a patois or peasant language—as in the cases of Slovene, Romanian, Norwegian, Slovak, Ukrainian, Latvian, Lithuanian, Finnish, and so on.[78] With the affirmation of a national culture, the language of the people—seen as the instrument of emancipation and the means for defining a distinctive national character—very rapidly found (not always for the first time) grammarians, lexicographers, and linguists ready to take responsibility for its codification, writing, and teaching. The paramount role of writers and, more broadly, intellectuals in the construction of national identity explains to some extent the submission of literary and scholarly work to national norms.[79]

The collections of popular poetry and traditional songs edited by Herder himself (and published before the famous folktales of the Brothers Grimm) served as a model for the anthologies of folktales and legends that were subsequently to appear throughout Europe. Between 1822 and 1827 the Czech writer František Čelakovsky published three volumes of Slavic folk songs, followed by a collection of fifteen thousand Slavic proverbs and sayings; in Slovenia, Stanko Vraz published an edition of Illyrian poems; and Vuk Karadžič, encouraged by correspondance with Jacob Grimm, brought together Serbian folk songs. The young Henrik Ibsen, an enthusiastic adherent of the movement to promote a national identity in Norway, set out a bit later to study the manifestations of the Norwegian "soul" among peasants.

In short, the "invention" of popular languages and literatures throughout Europe in the nineteenth century (and later, as we shall see, in other parts of the world as well) corresponds exactly to the grammatization undertaken in the sixteenth and seventeenth centuries, which had allowed emerging European nations to devise new weapons to combat the still formidable domination of Latin. The upheaval brought about in the republic of letters by what I have called the Herder effect can therefore be understood only by examining the genesis of international space, sketched here in its broad outlines. Because entering literary space meant entering into a type of competition, and because this space was formed and unified on the basis of the rivalries that emerged within it, the new theoretical concepts that underlay the assault against the established philosophical and literary order must be described and recognized as so many instruments in the struggle for literary legitimacy. Before the twentieth century in Europe, this struggle took the form of an attempt to nationalize language and literature.

The period of decolonization, which began roughly after the Second World War (and which is not yet finished), marks the third great stage in the formation of international literary space. In one sense, it is only the continuation and extension of the revolution inaugurated by Herder: the newly independent nations of Africa, Asia, and Latin America, obeying the same political and cultural mechanisms, moved to assert linguistic and literary claims of their own. The consequences of decolonialization in the literary world were of a piece with the national and literary upheavals of nineteenth-century Europe, carrying on the Herderian revolution by other means. Popular legitimacy, in the form of various political avatars of the notion of the "people," provided these newcomers with a way to achieve linguistic and cultural autonomy.

As in Europe during the nineteenth century, recollection of popular tales and legends made it possible to translate an oral tradition into written literature. The first attempts by European folklorists to collect popular tales—an enterprise linked, as we have seen, to the romantic belief in the "soul" and the "genius" of the people—subsequently found support in the colonial science of ethnology, which worked to promote a reappropriated cultural identity. By perpetuating the belief in a popular peasant "origin," it became possible to push further back in time the inventory of an oral heritage that henceforth could be claimed by a nation as its own. Acting on the same belief in the singular and popular identity of the nation, and in accordance with the same logic underlying the accumulation of literary and intellectual wealth, writers from countries emerging from colonization set out to do what writers in European countries had done before them, this time relying on the model provided by ethnology.

The linguistic question was raised in very similar terms as well. Like many European countries during the nineteenth century, the newly decolonized countries had often inherited languages having no real literary existence, associated instead with extensive oral traditions. The choice facing these countries—whether to adopt the language of their colonizers or to create their own linguistic and literary patrimony—obviously depended on the wealth and literariness of these nonnative languages, but also on the level of economic development. Daniel Baggioni has noted that the same problems that arose at the end of the nineteenth century "for young nation-states such as Poland, Romania, Bulgaria, Yugoslavia, Albania, and even Greece, which combined the disadvantages of a largely agricultural and underdeveloped economy with massive illiteracy, recent and fragile national unity, a weak technological base, and a small elite whose intellectual interests lay abroad," were later experienced by emerging countries in Africa and Asia.[80]

But the postcolonial situation is distinguished from what came before by the fact that the use of European languages had been systematically imposed in colonized territories, leading to greater complexity in the forms of dependency that developed and therefore in the strategies adopted to escape them as well. For a national literary space to come into being, a nation must attain true political independence; but because the newest nations are also the ones that are the most vulnerable to political and economic domination, and because literary space is dependent to one degree or another on political structures, international forms of literary dependency are to some extent correlated with the structures of international political domination.

Writers in postcolonial nations on the periphery of international literary space therefore have to struggle not only against the predominance of national politics, as writers in the richest spaces do, but also against international political forces. The external forces exerted upon the least endowed literary spaces today assume the forms of linguistic domination and economic domination (notably in the form of foreign control over publishing), which is why proclamations of national independence do not suffice to eliminate outside pressures. To one degree or another, then, literary relations of power are forms of political relations of power.

3 | *World Literary Space*

There is *one* thing of which one can say neither that it is one metre long, nor that it is not one metre long, and that is the standard metre in Paris.—But this is, of course, not to ascribe any extraordinary property to it, but only to mark its peculiar role in the language-game of measuring with a metre-rule.

    —Ludwig Wittgenstein, *Philosophical Investigations*

As people of the fringes, inhabitants of the suburbs of history, we Latin Americans are uninvited guests who have sneaked in through the West's back door, intruders who have arrived at the feast of modernity as the lights are about to be put out. We arrive late everywhere, we were born when it was already late in history, we have no past or, if we have one, we spit on its remains.

    —Octavio Paz, *The Labyrinth of Solitude*

THE HIERARCHICAL STRUCTURE that orders the literary world is the direct product of the history of literature in the sense I have described, but it is also what makes this history. Indeed, one is tempted to say that literary history is incarnated in the structure of the world of letters, which supplies its motive force; that the events of the literary world take on meaning through the structure that produces them and gives them form and, in so doing, makes literature at once stake, resource, and belief.

In the world republic of letters, the richest spaces are also the oldest, which is to say the ones that were the first to enter into literary competition and whose national classics came also to be regarded as universal classics. The literary map that has taken shape in Europe since the six-teenth century cannot be regarded, then, simply as the result of a gradual extension of literary belief or the idea of literature (in keeping with the familiar image of the "dissemination," "fortune," or even "influence" of a literary form or work). It is a consequence of the unequal structure (to recall Fernand Braudel's phrase once again) of literary space, the uneven distribution of resources among national literary spaces. In measuring themselves against one other, these spaces slowly establish hierarchies and relations of dependency that over time create a complex and dura-ble design. "So the past always counts," as Braudel rightly insisted. "The inequality of the world is the result of structural realities [that are] at once slow to take shape and slow to fade away . . . An economy, society, civilization or political complex finds it very hard to live down a depen-dent past."[1] So, too, the structure of the literary world lastingly perpetu-ates itself despite the various transformations it appears to undergo, par-ticularly in its political aspect.

The world of letters is a relatively unified space characterized by the opposition between the great national literary spaces, which are also the oldest—and, accordingly, the best endowed—and those literary spaces that have more recently appeared and that are poor by comparison. Henry James, who chose English nationality as though it were a matter almost of literary salvation, who made the gap between the American and European worlds the subject of a great part of his work, and who in his own practice of literature had direct experience of the literary desti-tution of America at the end of the nineteenth century, lucidly de-scribed art as a flower that can flourish only in a thick soil. It takes a great deal of history, as James once remarked, to produce a little bit of lit-erature.

But it is not sufficient to imagine a simple binary opposition between dominant and dominated literary spaces. One would do better to speak of a *continuum,* for the many forms of antagonism to which domination gives rise prevent a linear hierarchy from establishing itself. Obviously, not all those who are literarily dominated find themselves in the same situation. Their common condition of dependency does not imply that they can be described in terms of the same categories: each one is de-pendent in a specific way. Even within the most richly endowed region of literary space—which is to say in Europe, which was the first to en-ter into transnational competition—one finds newer literatures that are dominated by older ones. This is notably the case in nations that long remained subject to external political control, as in central and eastern Europe, or to colonial domination, as in the case of Ireland. It is necessary also to include in this group—which may be thought of as a subset of outlying areas within a larger central space—all those countries that were dominated not politically but literarily, through language and culture, such as Belgium, French-speaking and German-speaking Switzerland, Austria, and so on.

These dominated areas within Europe were the cradle of the great literary revolutions. As heirs by language and shared culture to the richest traditions in the world of letters, already by the time the first nationalist claims began to be asserted in the nineteenth century they had accumulated sufficient assets of their own to cause upheavals that were registered in the centers, upsetting the old hierarchies of the established literary order. Thus between 1890 and 1930, in a literarily destitute country under colonial rule, there occurred one of the greatest literary revolutions—the "Irish miracle"—marked by the appearance of three or four of the most important writers of the twentieth century. The case of Franz Kafka illustrates the same point: although he belonged to an emerging Czech literary space and took an enthusiastic interest in the Jewish nationalist movement, he managed to create one of the most enigmatic and innovative bodies of work of the century by virtue of the fact that he was heir to the whole of German language and culture—an heir who nonetheless sought to subvert his inheritance.

The same logic applies to the formation and development of American literatures. The new states that emerged in the Americas at the end of the eighteenth and the beginning of the nineteenth centuries do not lend themselves to interpretation in terms of the Herderian model, in part because decolonization in these regions was achieved by Creoles—persons of European descent born in the Americas: "Language was not an element that differentiated them from their respective imperial metropoles," as Benedict Anderson observes. "[It] was never even an issue in these early struggles for national liberation."[2] Nor were what Marc Ferro calls "colonist-independence movements," which unfolded between 1760 and 1830 in the United States, the Spanish colonies, and Brazil, consequences of the revolution Herder inaugurated;[3] they were the product instead of the spread of the French Enlightenment, and relied on a critique of imperial "anciens régimes" that ignored the whole notion of popular belief, founded on nation, people, and language.[4] Examining the distinctive characteristics of Latin American history, the Venezuelan writer and intellectual Arturo Uslar Pietri (1906–2001) described the originality of America in relation to other colonized countries: "Our case is different, original," he wrote, "above all because the American continent has known from the beginning, and, through language and religion, the most sensitive cultural fibers there are, an integration with Western culture that the other areas of European expansion never knew. Latin America [is] a living and creative part of this whole region, the West, which is steeped in particularities; and why not call it the Extreme West, since it possesses distinctive signs that no modern empire has engendered?"[5]

Both North American and Latin American literature are therefore the direct descendants, through the colonists who demanded independence from their home countries, of European literatures. The freedom to build upon the literary heritage of England, Spain, and Portugal enabled them in the twentieth century to trigger unprecedented literary upheavals (of which the works of Faulkner, García Márquez, and Guimarães Rosa are the three outstanding examples). By appropriating the literary and linguistic assets of the European countries whose heritage they claimed, the writers of the Americas succeeded in establishing a sort of transatlantic patrimony. "My classics are those of my language," Octavio Paz stated unequivocally. "I consider myself to be a descendant of Lope and Quevedo, as any Spanish writer would . . . Yet I am not a Spaniard. I think that most writers of Spanish America would say the same, as would writers from the United States, Brazil, and Francophone Canada with regard to the English, Portuguese, and French traditions."[6]

ROADS TO FREEDOM

The construction of national literary space is closely related, as we have seen, to the political space of the nation that it helps build in turn. But in the most endowed literary spaces the age and volume of their capital—together with the prestige and international recognition these things imply—combine to bring about the independence of literary space as a whole. The oldest literary fields are therefore the most autonomous as well, which is to say the most exclusively devoted to literature as an activity having no need of justification beyond itself. The scale of their resources gives them the means to develop, in opposition to the nation and its strictly political interests, a history and logic of their own that are irreducible to politics.

Literary space translates political and national issues into its own terms—aesthetic, formal, narrative, poetic—and at once affirms and denies them. Though it is not altogether free from political domination, literature has its own ways and means of asserting a measure of independence; of constituting itself as a distinct world in opposition to the nation and nationalism, a world in which external concerns appear only in refracted form, transformed and reinterpreted in literary terms and with literary instruments. In the most autonomous countries, then, literature cannot be reduced to political interests or used to suit national purposes. It is in these countries that the independent laws of literature are invented, and that the extraordinary and improbable construction of what may properly be referred to as the autonomous international space of literature is carried out.

This very long process, through which autonomy is achieved and literary capital hoarded,[7] tends also to obscure the political origins of literature; and, by causing the link between literature and nation to be forgotten, encourages a belief in the existence of a literature that is completely pure, beyond the reach of time and history. Paradoxically, it is time itself that enables literature to free itself from history. But if still today (and even in those countries that are the freest) literature remains the most conservative of the arts, which is to say the one that is the most subject to traditional conventions and norms of representation—norms from which painters and sculptors, through the revolution of abstraction, were long ago liberated—this is because the denied link with the political nation, camouflaged by well-worn euphemisms, remains very powerful.[8]

Autonomy is nonetheless a fundamental aspect of world literary space. The most independent territories of the literary world are able to state their own law, to lay down the specific standards and principles applied by their internal hierarchies, and to evaluate works and pronounce judgments without regard for political and national divisions. Indeed, autonomy amounts to its own categorical imperative, enjoining writers everywhere to stand united against literary nationalism, against the intrusion of politics into literary life. In other words, the structural internationalism of the most literary countries strengthens and guarantees their independence. Autonomy in the world of letters is always relative.

In France, the volume of accumulated capital was so great, and the literary domination exerted over the whole of Europe from the eighteenth century onward so uncontested (and indeed incontestable), that it became the most autonomous literary space of all, which is to say the freest in relation to political and national institutions.

The emancipation of literary activity in France from many, if not all, of the constraints of political life had one striking consequence. French literary space, having imposed itself as universal, was adopted as a model: not insofar as it was French, but insofar as it was autonomous—which is to say purely literary. In other words, French literary capital belonged not to France alone, but to all nations. Indeed, it is this very capacity for being universalized, or denationalized, that allows varying degrees of autonomy among literary spaces to be recognized. Valery Larbaud, by virtue of his position as one of the most eminent figures in French letters responsible for introducing a great deal of world literature to Paris, was able to state what was to become the fundamental article of faith in the great literary centers: "Every French writer is international, he is a poet, a writer for all of Europe and for a part of America as well . . . All that which is 'national' is silly, archaic, disreputably patriotic . . . It served a purpose under certain circumstances, but that time has passed. There is now a country of Europe."[9]

It was through this very process of emancipation from national politics that Paris became the world capital of literature in the nineteenth century. Because France was the least national of literary nations, it was able to manufacture a universal literature while consecrating works produced in outlying territories—impressing the stamp of *littérarité* upon texts that came from farflung lands, thereby denationalizing and departicularizing them, declaring them to be acceptable as legal tender in all the countries under its literary jurisdiction. Thanks to its promotion of the law of universality in the world of letters against the ordinary political laws of nations, France became an alternative model for writers from every part of the literary world who aspired to autonomy.

THE GREENWICH MERIDIAN OF LITERATURE

The unification of literary space through competition presumes the existence of a common standard for measuring time, an absolute point of reference unconditionally recognized by all contestants. It is at once a point in space, the center of all centers (which even literary rivals, by the very fact of their competition, are agreed in acknowledging), and a basis for measuring the time that is peculiar to literature. Events that "leave a mark" on the literary world have a "tempo" (to use Pierre Bourdieu's terms) that is unique to this world and that is not—or is not necessarily—"synchronous" with the measure of historical (which is to say political) time that is established as official and legitimate.[10] Literary space creates a present on the basis of which all positions can be measured, a point in relation to which all other points can be located. Just as the *fictive* line known as the prime meridian, arbitrarily chosen for the determination of longitude, contributes to the *real* organization of the world and makes possible the measure of distances and the location of positions on the surface of the earth, so what might be called the Greenwich meridian of literature makes it possible to estimate the relative aesthetic distance from the center of the world of letters of all those who belong to it. This aesthetic distance is also measured in temporal terms, since the prime meridian determines the present of literary creation, which is to say modernity. The aesthetic distance of a work or corpus of works from the center may thus be measured by their temporal remove from the canons that, at the precise moment of estimation, define the literary present. In this sense one may say that a work is contemporary; that it is more or less current (as opposed to being out of date—temporal metaphors abound in the language of criticism), depending on its proximity to the criteria of modernity; that it is modern or avant-garde (as opposed to being academic, which is to say based on outmoded models that belong to the literary past or otherwise fail to conform to the criteria that at any given moment determine the present).

Gertrude Stein neatly summed up the question of the localization of modernity in a single phrase: "Paris," she wrote in *Paris, France* (1940), "was where the 20th century was."[11] As site of the literary present and capital of modernity, Paris to some extent owed its position to the fact that it was where fashion—the outstanding expression of modernity— was made. In the famous *Paris Guide* of 1867, Victor Hugo insisted on the authority of the City of Light, not only in political and intellectual matters but also in the domain of taste and elegance, which is to say of fashion and everything modern: "I defy you," he declared, "to wear another hat than the hat of Paris. The ribbon worn by the woman in the street [in Paris] rules. In every country, the way in which this ribbon is tied has the force of law." This law was part and parcel of what Hugo identified as the city's special authority:

> Paris, it needs to be emphasized, is a government. This government has neither judges, nor police, nor soldiers, nor ambassadors; it operates through infiltration, which is to say omnipotence. It falls drop by drop upon humanity and everywhere leaves its impression. Apart from whoever officially exercises authority, above or below, lower or higher, Paris exists, and its way of existing rules. Its books, its newspapers, its theater, its industry, its art, its science, its philosophy, the procedures associated with its science, the fashions that are part of its philosophy, its good and its bad, its good and its evil—all these things arouse the spirit of nations and lead them.[12]

The ability to decree without fear of challenge what is or is not "fashionable," in the domain of haute couture and elsewhere, permitted Paris to control one of the main routes of access to modernity. Stein described the link between fashion and modernity in her own ironic faux-naive way:

> And so in the beginning of the twentieth century when a new way had to be found naturally they needed France . . . It was important too that Paris was where fashions were made . . . and so quite naturally Paris which has always made fashions was where everyone went in 1900 . . . It is funny about art and literature, fashions being part of it. Two years ago everybody was saying that France was down and out, was sinking to be a second-rate power, etcetera, etcetera. And I said but I do not think so because not for years not since the war have hats been as various and lovely and as french as they are now . . . I do not believe that when the characteristic art and literature of a country is active and fresh I do not think that country is in its decline . . . So Paris was the place that suited those of us that were to create the twentieth century art and literature, naturally enough.[13]

By combining all these structural elements, Paris managed to sustain its position—at least until the 1960s—as the center of the system of literary time.

The temporal law of the world of letters may be stated thus: *it is necessary to be old in order to have any chance of being modern or of decreeing what is modern.* In other words, having a long national past is the condition of being able to claim a literary existence that is fully recognized in the present. This is what du Bellay had in mind when he conceded, in *The Defense and Illustration of the French Language,* that the handicap of French in the battle against Latin was what he called its "lateness." At stake in the competition between literary centers, all of which by definition enjoy the privilege of antiquity, is mastery of just this measure of time (and space), which is to say the power to claim for oneself the legitimate present of literature and to canonize its great writers. Among all the central spaces that contend with each other by virtue of the antiquity and nobility of their literature, it is the Greenwich meridian, the source of literary time, that stands as the capital of literature—the capital of capitals.

The continually redefined present of literary life constitutes a universal artistic clock by which writers must regulate their work if they wish to attain legitimacy. If modernity is the sole present moment of literature, which is to say what makes it possible to institute a measure of time, the literary Greenwich meridian makes it possible to evaluate and recognize the quality of a work or, to the contrary, to dismiss a work as an anachronism or to label it "provincial." It needs to be emphasized that the relative notions of aesthetic "backwardness" and "advance," which all writers have in the back of their minds (though the structure of the literary world is never explicitly described in such terms, since one of the unwritten laws of the world republic of letters requires that literary talent and recognition be universal), are not introduced here in order to lay down some fixed and immutable definition of literature. Nonetheless the existence and influence of these notions needs to be acknowledged, without any judgment being made as to their value or normative character, for they are part of the logic of temporal competition.

Frederick II of Prussia, who, as we have seen, wished to bring his people into the European literary world at the end of the eighteenth century, proposed his own version of German backwardness together with a chronology of the formation of literary space: "I am dismayed not to be able to lay out for you a more ample Catalogue of our good productions: I do not accuse the Nation: it lacks neither spirit nor genius, but it has been delayed by causes that have prevented it from growing up at the same time as its neighbors." It was therefore a question, considering the logic of literary competition, of making up for lost time in order to overcome its backwardness: "We are ashamed," he wrote, "that in certain genres we cannot equal our neighbors, [and so] we desire through tireless efforts to make up for the time that our calamities have caused us to lose . . . there can be little doubt that, [taking note of] such feelings, the Muses will lead us in our turn into the Temple of Glory." This curious delay was the source of what the Prussian king readily acknowledged to be a special form of poverty, which implied the existence of a literary marketplace characterized by great inequalities: "Let us therefore not imitate the poor who wish to pass for the rich, let us acknowledge our destitution in good faith; that this may encourage us instead to obtain by our own efforts the treasures of Literature, whose possession will raise national glory to its full height."[14]

What Is Modernity?

Modernity's connection with fashion is a sign of its inherent instability. It is also inevitably an occasion of rivalry and competition: because the modern by definition is always new, and therefore open to challenge, the only way in literary space to be truly modern is to contest the present as outmoded—to appeal to a still more present present, as yet unknown, which thus becomes the newest certified present. The success of new-comers to literary space and time in breaking into the ranks of the estab-lished moderns, and earning for themselves the right to take part in de-bates over the definition of the latest modernity, therefore depends to some extent on their familiarity with the most recent innovations in form and technique.

The necessity of being up-to-date in order to obtain recognition ex-plains why the concept of modernity is so frequently and so emphati-cally invoked by writers claiming to embody literary innovation, from its first formulation by Baudelaire in the mid-nineteenth century to the very name of the review founded by Sartre a hundred years later—*Les Temps Modernes*. One thinks of Rimbaud's famous injunction ("One must be absolutely modern"); also of the *modernismo* founded by Rubén Darío at the end of the nineteenth century, the Brazilian modernist movement of the 1920s, and "futurist" movements in Italy and in Rus-sia.[15] The rushing after lost time, the frantic quest for the present, the rage to be "contemporaries of all mankind" (as Octavio Paz put it)—all these things are typical of the search for a way to enter literary time and thereby to attain artistic salvation.[16] Danilo Kiš perfectly expressed the importance of this extraordinary belief in literary modernity: "I still want to be modern. But I don't mean that because things are constantly changing we need to keep up with them; I mean that there is something in the way a work is written and the times in which it is written that makes it part of its age."[17]

The modern work is condemned to become dated unless, by achieving the status of a classic, it manages to free itself from the fluctuations of taste and critical opinion. ("We pass our time arguing over tastes and colors," Valéry observed. "It is the same at the stock exchange, on countless juries, in the Academies, and it cannot be otherwise").[18] Literarily speaking, a classic is a work that rises above competition and so escapes the bidding of time. Only in this way can a modern work be rescued from aging, by being declared timeless and immortal. The classic incarnates literary legitimacy itself, which is to say what is recognized as constituting *Literature;* what, in serving as a unit of measure, supplies the basis for determining the limits of that which is considered to be literary.

All writers from countries that are remote from literary capitals refer, consciously or unconsciously, to a measure of time that takes for granted the existence of a literary present. Determined by the highest critical authorities, this moment confers legitimacy on certain books by including them among those works judged to be contemporary. Thus Octavio Paz (1914–1998), in the passage from *The Labyrinth of Solitude* that serves as an epigraph to this chapter, spoke of Latin Americans as "inhabitants of the suburbs of history . . . intruders who have arrived at the feast of modernity as the lights are about to be put out"—people who "were born when it was already late in history."[19] In his 1990 Nobel Prize acceptance speech—significantly titled "La búsqueda del presente" (In Search of the Present)—Paz described his discovery at a very young age of a curious dislocation of time, and his subsequent quest—poetic, historical, and aesthetic—for a present that his country's separation from Europe ("a constant feature of our spiritual history") had deprived him of contact with:

> I must have been about six. One of my cousins, who was a little older, showed me a North American magazine with a photograph of soldiers marching down a wide avenue, probably in New York. "They've returned from the war," she said . . . But for me, the war had taken place in another time, not here and now . . . I felt dislodged from the present. After that, time began to fracture more and more. And space,

to multiply . . . I felt that my world was disintegrating, that the real present was somewhere else. My time . . . was a fictitious time . . . that was how my expulsion from the present began . . . For us Spanish Americans this present was not in our own countries: it was the time lived by others—by the English, the French, the Germans. It was the time of New York, Paris, London.[20]

What Paz recounts here is nothing other than his personal discovery of central time, which is to say his own decentering, his own sense of disadvantaged remoteness. The process of unification, in art no less than in politics, assumes a common measure of absolute time that supersedes other temporalities, whether of nations, families, or personal experience. Paz's realization that he lived in a place outside real time and history (this present that was "somewhere else") was succeeded by a sudden awareness of a schism in the world, which led him to set out in search of the present: "The search for the present is not the pursuit of an earthly paradise or of a timeless eternity; it is the search for reality . . . we had to go and look for it and bring it back home."[21] This quest was an attempt to find a way out from the "fictitious time" reserved for the national space into which he had been born and to gain entry to the real time of international life.

But it was the discovery of another present that forced him to acknowledge his backwardness as a writer. He found that there also existed a time specific to literature, a measure of literary modernity: "These years were also the years of my discovery of literature. I began writing poems . . . Only now have I understood that there was a secret relationship between what I have called my expulsion from the present and the writing of poetry . . . *I was searching for the gateway to the present.* I wanted to belong to my time and to my century. Later, this desire became an obsession: I wanted to be a modern poet. My search for modernity had begun."[22] In searching for the poetical present, he joined in the hunt with poets from other nations and thus, by accepting the rules and stakes of this competition, acquired an international identity. It was this discovery of a whole new world of literary and aesthetic possibilities—possibilities unknown to Mexico—that caused Paz to aspire to be a universal poet. On the other hand, he discovered also that he was inevitably starting behind the other competitors. The recognition of central time as the only legitimate measure of political and artistic achievement is an effect of the domination exercised by the powerful; but it is a domination that is recognized and accepted by outsiders while remaining wholly unknown to the inhabitants of the centers, who are also (and especially) unaware of their role in producing literary time and its associated unit of historical measure. Resolved to bring back to his own country the true present, Paz succeeded spectacularly, winning the Nobel Prize—the highest honor the world republic of letters has to give—while at the same time developing an analysis of "Mexicanness."

This specifically literary form of time is perceptible only by those writers on the peripheries of the world of letters who, in their openness to international experience, seek to end what they see as their exile from literature. "National" writers, by contrast, whether they live in central or outlying countries, are united in ignoring world competition (and therefore literary time) and in considering only the local norms and limits assigned to literary practice by their homelands. Indeed, it would not be going too far to say that the only true moderns, the only ones fully to recognize and know the literature of the present, are those who are aware of the existence of this system of literary timekeeping and who, as a result, acknowledge the force of the aesthetic revolutions that have shaped world literary space and the international laws that structure it.

The link between spatial and temporal views of literary distance is condensed in the image, very common among writers on the literary peripheries, of the "province."[23] Thus, for example, the Peruvian author Mario Vargas Llosa (b. 1936) recalled his discovery of Sartre in the 1950s:

> What could [his] works offer to a Latin American adolescent? They could save him from provincialism, immunize him against rustic views, make him feel dissatisfied with that local colour, [with that] superficial literature with its Manichaean structures and simplistic techniques—Rómulo Gallegos, Eustasio Rivera, Jorge Icaza, Ciro Alegría . . .—which was still our model and which repeated, unwittingly, the themes and fashions of European naturalism imported half a century previously.[24]

Danilo Kiš, in a 1973 interview with a Belgrade journalist, described the literature of his country in very similar terms: "In our country we continue to write a poor prose, anachronistic in expression and themes, entirely dependent on the tradition of the nineteenth century, a timid prose, fearful of experimentation, regional, local—a prose in which local color serves mainly as a means of trying to preserve national identity, as the essence of prose."[25] These reflections were echoed in an essay of the same period: "I see my own work, my own defeat, in the provincial setting where it developed, where it was allowed to develop, as a small, distinct defeat in the parade of our defeats, as a permanent and consistent attempt to escape this spiritual province, through myths, themes, and technical devices."[26]

The recurrence of this theme of the literary province—strictly speaking, a sort of disinherited country—is further evidence of the representation of the literary world by writers themselves as one of inequality; and, more generally, of a literary geography that can never be completely superimposed upon the political geography of the world's nations. The gap between "capital" and "province" (which is to say between past and present, between ancient and modern) is an aspect of the world of letters that is perceived only by those who are not quite of their time. This gap is not merely temporal and spatial; it is also aesthetic (indeed, aesthetics is simply another name for literary time). And the only boundary—at once abstract, real, and necessary—that provincial writers are agreed in recognizing is what I have called the Greenwich meridian of literature.

The only way for an Irishman around 1900 (such as James Joyce) or for an American around 1930 (such as William Faulkner) to reject the literary norms of London, to challenge its condemnation or its indifference; the only way for a Nicaraguan around 1890 (such as Rubén Darío) to turn away from Spanish academic literary practice; for a Yugoslav around 1970 (such as Danilo Kiš) to refuse submission to the aesthetic conditions imposed by Moscow; for a Portuguese around 1995 (such as António Lobo Antunes) to escape the restrictive conventions of his native country was to turn toward Paris. Because its verdicts were the most autonomous (that is, the least national) in the literary world, it constituted a court of final appeal. This is why Joyce, for example, ultimately chose exile in Paris and a strategy of dual refusal: by rejecting not only the submission to colonial power that exile in London would have represented, but equally any display of conformity to the national literary norms of Ireland, he was free to carry out an enterprise of unprecedented daring and novelty.

Paris also attracted writers who came to the center to equip themselves with the knowledge and technical expertise of literary modernity in order then to revolutionize the literature of their homelands through the innovations that they brought back with them. Having made their reputation in the center, some of these innovators were able to accelerate literary time, as it were, in their native countries. This was notably to be the case, as we shall see, with Faulkner, who in order to evoke an archaic world created a new novelistic form, recognized and consecrated in Paris. For this he was subsequently held up as a model by writers in many outlying regions of the literary world who found themselves in an equivalent structural position.

The same argument can be used to analyze two exemplary cases: the Nicaraguan poet Rubén Darío (1867–1916), a central figure in the literary history of Latin America and Spain who, though he was not consecrated by Paris, rearranged the literary landscape of the Hispanic world by importing the latest edition of modernity from Paris; and the great Danish literary critic Georg Brandes (1842–1927), who in the late nineteenth century overturned the traditional literary and aesthetic assumptions of the Scandinavian countries by applying the principles of French naturalism. Their appropriation of the innovations and techniques of modernity won both of them fame in their respective cultural areas while also permitting them to create an autonomous pole in spaces that until then had been reserved for political literature.

Darío's first volumes of verse, *Azul,* published in Valparaiso in 1888, and *Prosas profanas,* which came out in Buenos Aires in 1896, broke with the whole poetic tradition of the Spanish language.[27] The revolution that Darío engineered under the name of modernism grew out of his determination to introduce into the Spanish language and Spanish prosody the forms and sounds peculiar to French: "Accustomed as I was to the eternal Spanish cliché of the 'Golden Age,' and to its indecisive modern poetry, I found among the French . . . *a literary mine to exploit.*"[28] What he called "mental Gallicism"—the introduction of French sounds and turns of phrase into Castilian—was an extreme (and yet, owing to the prestige of Paris, literarily acceptable) form of a larger revolt against the literary order of the Spanish-speaking world. In availing himself of the literary power of France, Darío succeeded in changing the terms of Hispanic aesthetic debate and in imposing French modernism, first upon Latin America and then, reversing the terms of colonial subjugation, upon Spain as well. As he put it in an article published in *La Nación* of Buenos Aires in 1895: "My dream was to write in French . . . Was not the course of events that would lead Spanish to this renaissance destined to play itself out in America, from the moment that, in Spain, the language came to be walled in by tradition, surrounded and spiked [like a parapet] with Spanishisms?" Darío's scarcely veiled attacks signaled his intention to launch a literary revolution that would sweep away all the clichés imposed by Spain on its American colonies. He stressed the backwardness of Spanish poetry ("walled in by tradition"), the better to contrast it with modernist novelty: "My success—it would be ridiculous not to acknowledge it—has been due to novelty. Now what was this novelty? It was mental Gallicism."²⁹ It was this stunning innovation— more precisely, renovation—that Jorge Luis Borges referred to in an interview in Argentina published in 1986:

> I was fully convinced that, with the Golden Age . . . Spanish poetry had entered into decadence . . . Everything became rigid . . . And then we have the eighteenth century, the nineteenth century, both of them very poor . . . And then Rubén Darío came along and made everything new again. The renewal began in America and then came to Spain and inspired great poets such as the Machados and Juan Ramón Jimenez, to cite only [three]; but undoubtedly there were others . . . [Darío] was certainly the first of these renovators . . . [u]nder the influence, of course, of Edgar Allen Poe. What a curious thing—Poe was an American: he was born in Boston and died in Baltimore; but he came to our poetry because Baudelaire translated him . . . So [the] influence [exerted by all these poets] was French in a way.³⁰

In the Scandinavian countries, those who recognized the supremacy of Paris were determined to combat the German cultural ascendancy of the period, which had so thoroughly dominated their nations throughout the nineteenth century that they were now little more than aesthetic provinces of Germany. Georg Brandes had lived in Paris for several years and brought back to Denmark the naturalism he discovered there, together with the work of Taine, thus helping found the movement known as *Det moderne Gennembrud,* or the "modern breakthrough." Brandes summed up his approach in a single exhortation: "Submit problems to discussion."³¹ In this way he hoped it would be possible to create a literature on the model of French naturalism, opposed to the idealism advocated by German tradition, that could express social, political, and aesthetic problems and criticize established values. His six volumes of critical essays, written between 1871 and 1890 and collected under the title *Hovedstrømninger i det nittende Aarhundredes Litteratur* (Main Currents in Nineteenth-Century Literature), profoundly altered the literary landscape of the Scandinavian world, exerting a decisive influence not only in Denmark, where writers such as Holger Drachmann and J. P. Jacobsen embraced his ideas, but also in Norway (with Bjørnson and Ibsen) and Sweden (with Strindberg).[32]

Moreover, Brandes' book *Det moderne Gejennembruds Maend* (Eminent Authors of the Nineteenth Century, 1883) launched a literary and cultural movement that had important political ramifications as well: "political radicalism, literary realism and naturalism, the emancipation of women,[33] atheism and religious liberalism . . . [and] the emergence of popular education" were all considered, particularly in Sweden, to be historically linked to the "modern breakthrough."[34] The paradox is that it was necessary to accept the domination of Paris in order to be freed from German control. But the "modern breakthrough" was not a simple reproduction of the revolutionary theoretical and literary discoveries made in Paris; it was an example of the liberation made possible by innovations imported from Paris—innovations that Paris neither imposed nor dictated, any more than it gave them their form. Instead, it supplied the model for them.

The Danish novelist Henrik Stangerup recalls the experience of both his father, Hakon Stangerup, and his grandfather, Hjalmar Söderberg (a very famous writer in his native Sweden, whose anti-German bias was thought scandalous at a time when the great majority of Swedish intellectuals were pro-German),[35] in describing his own relationship with French modernism today:

> From the beginning [my grandfather] was close to Georg Brandes, who was a Dreyfusard. Brandes' review was the first outside France to publish Zola's "J'accuse." Söderberg began his career writing articles on antisemitism in Europe. He died in 1941. He committed suicide in a state of mind very similar to that of Stefan Zweig: he had left Sweden in 1906 to settle in Copenhagen, where he lived the rest of his life, and he was persuaded that Hitler was going to win the war . . . My father was a literary critic, a Francophile as well; he translated many French writers, though his France was rather that of Mauriac and

Maurois. I came to Paris in 1956, and this was *my* France, that of Sartre and Camus. Since I had studied theology and since I came from the land of Kierkegaard, existentialism was my first intellectual adventure. And so there are three Frances in my head: that of my grandfather at the turn of the century, Dreyfusard France; my father's France, more conservative; and mine.[36]

Stangerup's own novels are marked by this intellectual and national dichotemy:

In *Vejen til Lagoa Santa* [The Road to Lagoa Santa, 1981], German culture played a great role. Historically we had always been inspired by Germany—the "big brother." Kierkegaard was inspired by Germany and at the same time he revolted against Hegel and German philosophy. The Danish naturalist Lund in my novel challenges the positivism inherited from German culture. He becomes a Brazilian. But in the nineteenth century, Danish culture was above all a theological culture. It was the pastors who formed the intelligentsia in Denmark. And then, like the Germans, the Danish are Lutherans. With Møller, the great literary critic in Denmark during the 1840s—who figures in my novel *Det er svaert at do i Dieppe* [The Seducer, 1985]—France entered Danish literature for the first time . . . All the writers who made Danish literature—with the exception of those who chose internal exile, such as Kierkegaard, who made only two trips to Berlin—were great travelers. Unquestionably the greatest of them was Hans Christian Andersen, whose travel writing has been completely ignored in France. It was Andersen's dream, and Brandes' dream as well, to be translated into French.[37]

The changes introduced by Darío and Brandes in their respective national, linguistic, and culural spaces had less to do with literary innovation than with speeding up literary time. They were not so much revolutions as an attempt to bring literature up to date. They imported to regions that until then had been far removed from the Greenwich meridian upheavals that had already occurred in the center and that made it possible to measure literary time. Moreover, they gave these regions the assets they needed to enter world competition at once by offering them access to the latest aesthetic innovations—in each case through a gigantic diversion of literary capital. Though the authors and critics behind these modernizing movements could not themselves be hailed by Paris as innovators, they contributed powerfully to the unification of literary space by introducing a measure of autonomy in their regions through the model of Parisian modernity.

Like the cosmopolitans of the center, whose structural counterparts in a sense they are, "eccentric" cosmopolitans on the outer edges of the literary world also contribute to the production of literary value as agents of what Ramuz called "the universal bank of foreign exchange and commerce." Their translations are essential elements in the unification of literary space, assisting the diffusion of the great revolutions carried out in the center and so sharing in the universal credit of the innovations they help transmit.

Anachronisms

Anachronism is characteristic of areas distant from the literary Greenwich meridian. Thus the Brazilian literary critic Antonio Candido describes the literary "backwardness and underdevelopment" of Latin America as a consequence of its "cultural penury." What is striking about this region, he observes,

> is the way aesthetically anachronistic works were considered valid . . . This is what occurred with naturalism in the novel, which arrived a little late and has prolonged itself until now with no essential break in continuity, though modifying its modalities . . . So, when naturalism was already only a survival of an outdated genre in Europe, among us it could still be an ingredient of legitimate literary formulas, such as the social novel of the 1930s and 1940s.[38]

Naturalism—"adapted to the Spanish style" (in Juan Benet's phrase), "imported a century earlier" (as Mario Vargas Llosa put it),[39] converted into a mere technique of "picturesque" description—was the tool of international exoticism par excellence. Like folklore and regionalism, exoticism seeks to describe the distinctive character (whether local, national, or regional) of a place through the use—without their authors' being aware of it, as Vargas Llosa remarks—of aesthetic instruments that have long been outmoded where they were first devised, in a sort of spontaneous reinvention of Herderianism. Thus Benet spoke of the "local color," the "folk perspective" of the Spanish novel of the 1950s: "The novel was reduced to the picturesque; it portrayed the tavern, the street, the boardinghouse, the small restaurant, the small family facing financial difficulties."[40] Local color and the picturesque are attempts to depict a particular reality using the most commonplace and ordinary aesthetic means.

The relative backwardness and poverty of such regions are not permanent conditions: not all writers on the periphery are inevitably "condemned" to backwardness, any more than writers from the center are necessarily modern. To the contrary, very different literary temporalities (and therefore aesthetics and theories) may be found in a given national space, with the result that not infrequently one finds writers who are nearer to ones quite distant in geographical terms than to writers of their own generation and nationality who share the same culture and the same language. The specific logic of the literary world, which ignores ordinary geography and establishes territories and boundaries along lines quite different from those of nations, makes it possible, for example, to connect James Joyce, an Irishman, with Arno Schmidt, a German, or with the Serb Danilo Kiš and the Argentine Jorge Luis Borges; or Umberto Eco, an Italian, with the Spaniard Arturo Pérez-Reverte and the Serbian Milorad Pavić. Conversely, within spaces having the greatest endowment of literary resources, one encounters writers (often academics if not also academicians) whose work lags years behind that of their compatriots; as believers in the eternal nature of conventional aesthetic forms, they go on endlessly reproducing obsolete models. The moderns, on the other hand, relentlessly pursue the invention, or reinvention, of literature.

These discrepancies explain the difficulties that specialists in comparative literature face in trying to establish transnational periodizations. The model of world literary space proposed here, because it is not constructed according to evolutionary principles, makes it possible to compare writers who are not contemporary in the usual sense with reference to a measure of literary time that is relatively independent of the political chronologies that for the most part still organize histories of literature. Thus the global dissemination of a particular stylistic innovation originating in the center (which, for any given moment of literary history, marks the present) allows us to sketch the structure of the literary field in space and time, or, better perhaps, in a time that has become space. Consider, for example, the international success and diffusion of the naturalistic novel, a genuine literary revolution whose chief monument is Émile Zola's series of novels *Les Rougon-Macquart* (1871–1893).

Zola's moment of triumph in Germany may be placed between 1883 and 1888, by which point his success in France was beginning to decline. Joseph Jurt has insisted on the delay in translation and on the "time-lag that separated French literary space from German literary space," noting that in France "the great period of naturalist success fell between 1877 (*L'Assommoir*) and 1880 *(Le roman expérimental)*."[41] The 1880s in Paris saw the emergence of rival tendencies: the psychological novel, with the appearance of Bourget's *Essais de psychologie contemporaine* (Essays in Contemporary Psychology, 1883); the publication of Huysmans' *À rebours* (Against the Grain, 1884); and the rise of a new group of naturalist writers. These challenges to naturalism in its original form occurred in Germany only at the beginning of the following decade, with the publication of Hermann Bahr's *Die Überwindung des Naturalismus* (The Overcoming of Naturalism, 1891), which proclaimed the advent of a new literature based on the integration of the possibilities opened up by Bourget's psychology and Zola's naturalism. The time-lag between events that leave a mark on the literary Greenwich meridian and the moment when their repercussions begin to be felt abroad remains constant.

In Spain in the 1880s, French naturalism—considered as a literary revolution having both formal and political aspects—was the object of long and fierce debate. On the one hand, it was an instrument for criticizing the moralism and conformity of forms associated with the post-romantic Spanish novel. But it was also a tool of social criticism: the widely denounced "crudeness" of Zola's descriptions was a way of literarily subverting all the conventions and conservative tendencies of the day, in art as well as in society. Zola's introducer and translator in Spain, Leopoldo Alas (1852–1901), who wrote under the name of Clarín, was one of the most passionate defenders of naturalism, both as a theorist and as a novelist in his own right; the author of more than 2,000 articles, he regarded literary journalism as a "hygienic" struggle waged in the name of progress. During the same period, Emilia Pardo Bazán (1852–1921) published *La cuestión palpitante* (The Burning Question, 1883), a collection of essays on the realistic novel and French naturalism.

By allying themselves with the literary present, modernists in Spain and elsewhere were able to relegate national literary conventions to the past, using an imported tool to bring about a decisive rupture in national literary chronology. Naturalism permitted writers in all parts of the world who wished to free themselves from the yoke of academicism and conservatism (which is to say, of the literary past) to obtain access to modernity. In much the same way, the dates marking the publication and critical acclaim of James Joyce's work in the various linguistic and national domains of world literary space furnish another measure of its different temporalities: *Ulysses* and *Finnegans Wake,* foundational texts of literary modernity since their translation into French by Valery Larbaud, consititute one of the great indices—along with naturalism, surrealism, and the work of Faulkner—of distance from the Greenwich meridian.

If literature is defined, then, as a unified international field (or a field in the process of being unified), the international transmission of major revolutions such as naturalism and romanticism can no longer be described using the language either of "influence" or of "reception." To explain the introduction of new aesthetic norms with reference only to print-runs, critical notices in newspapers and literary reviews, and translations assumes, in effect, the existence of two synchronic and equal literary worlds. Plainly, this will not do. Only by analyzing revolutions in terms of the specific geography of literature and its unique measure of aesthetic time, which is to say in terms of the balance of power and competition that organizes the literary field—the temporal geography that I have just attempted to describe—will it be possible to understand how a foreign work is actually received and integrated.

LITERARY NATIONALISM

At the beginning of the nineteenth century, when several autonomous literary fields had already appeared, Herder's theories reaffirmed the connection between politics and literature and established a second pole in the world of letters. Henceforth the connection between literature and the nation, no longer an automatic stage in the constitution of a literary space, was seen as something needing to be achieved. The revolution brought about by Herder did not transform the nature of the structural bond linking literature (and language) with nation; to the contrary, Herder strengthened this bond by making it explicit. Instead of neglecting historical dependency, he made it a cornerstone of nationalist claims to independence.

Structural dependency in relation to political authorities and national interests was a characteristic feature, as we have already seen, of the first literary spaces that appeared in Europe between the sixteenth and eighteenth centuries. The differentiation of European political space that began in the late fifteenth and early sixteenth centuries rested in large part on the crucial role claimed for vernaculars, which served as "difference markers." In other words, the various rivalries that emerged in the intellectual world of the Renaissance were able during this period to gain support and claim legitimacy for themselves through political contest. The attempt to establish a standard language and to bring a written literature into existence very quickly came to be identified with the attempt to impose the legitimacy of a new sovereign state. By the same token, the Herder effect did not alter in any profound way the rules of the great game of literature inaugurated by du Bellay; it simply modified the mode of access to it. For all those who discovered that they were late in coming to literary competition, the popular definition of literary legitimacy advanced by Herder offered a new point of entry.

In addition to the general schema laid out in *The Defense and Illustration,* then, the strategies of the most literarily deprived need to be taken into account as well. During the nineteenth century, and throughout the whole period of decolonization in the twentieth century, they were to make the popular criterion in literature an essential tool for the invention of new literatures and for the entry of new contestants into the world of letters. In the case of "small" countries, the emergence of a new literature is indissociable from the appearance of a new nation. Indeed, if literature was directly associated with the state in pre-Herderian Europe, it was only with the dissemination of national ideas in Europe during the nineteenth century that literary claims to existence came in their turn to assume national form. Not only in Ireland at the end of the nineteenth century, but also in Catalonia, Martinique, and Quebec today, as well as in other regions where nationalist movements in politics and literature have emerged, literary spaces have been able to appear in the absence of a formally constituted state.

The new logic that now asserted itself against the definition of literature as an autonomous enterprise worked to enlarge the literary world and to promote the entry of new players into literary competition while at the same time introducing new criteria of legitimacy that were easily politicized. Herder's identification of language with nation, and of poetry with the "genius of the people," supplied new weapons in the struggle for independence, with the further result that literary spaces shaped by his thinking were also the most heteronomous, which is to say the most dependent on political authority at the national level. The idea of the inevitable "nationalization" of literatures, which thereby became "national literatures"—an explicit form of submission by literary authorities to political divisions—gained currency with the emergence of this political pole. Its influence over the whole of international literary space was to have innumerable consequences, since the new form of literary legitimacy that flowed from it stood in contrast to that of the French universalist model. With the advent of this new politico-literary pole, constituted in opposition to the autonomous pole, the whole of world literary space came to be structured around two antagonistic sources of attraction.

The emphasis on the "soulfulness" of a people that German theorists of the nation placed at the heart of their analysis subsequently served to legitimize a curious sophism: intellectual production depends on both language and nation, but literary texts express "the founding principle of the nation."[42] Literary institutions, academies, school syllabuses, the canon—all these things now having become instruments of national identity, the idea of dividing up national literatures on the exact model of political units began to acquire a sort of natural appeal and, indeed, inevitability. With the constitution of national literary pantheons and the associated hagiography of great writers—now considered national assets and symbols of intellectual influence and power—the national organization of literatures became an essential feature of literary competition among nations.

Following the Herderian revolution, then, all literatures had been declared national, which is to say sealed off from each other behind national boundaries like so many monads that contain the principle of their own causality. The national character of a literature was fixed in terms of a series of traits declared to be peculiar to it. Moreover, now that the nation was seen as the natural and unsurpassable horizon of literature, national literary histories were composed and taught in such a way that they became closed in upon themselves, having nothing in common (or so it was supposed) with their neighbors. From this came the belief that national traditions are fundamentally different.[43] Indeed, their very periodizations rendered them incomparable and incommensurable: thus French literary history was imagined to unfold as a succession of centuries, while English historians made reference to the reigns of sovereigns (Elizabethan literature, Victorian literature, and so on), and Spanish critics divided divided literary time into "generations" (the generation of 1898, for example, or the generation of 1927). The nationalization of literary traditions therefore gave rise to the view that their separation from one another is a fact of nature.

By the same token, nationalization had tangible consequences for literary practice. Acquaintance with the texts of a particular national pantheon and knowledge of the major dates of a country's nationalized literary history had the effect of transforming an artificial construction into an object of shared learning and belief. Within the closed environment of the nation, the process of differentiation and essentialization created familiar and analyzable cultural distinctions: national peculiarities were insisted upon and cultivated, chiefly through the schools, with the result that references, citations, and allusions to the national literary past became the private property of native speakers. National peculiarities thus acquired a reality of their own, and helped in turn to produce a literature that was consistent with accepted national categories.

Thus it was that in the course of the nineteenth century, even in the most powerful literary worlds, which is to say the ones that were most independent of national and political interests, literature came to be redefined in national terms. In England, for example, literature was made the primary vehicle of "national self-definition."[44] Stefan Collini has analyzed the nationalization of culture in nineteenth-century England through the lens of popular anthologies (in series such as the one edited by John Morley for Macmillan in London, beginning in 1877, under the title "English Men of Letters") as well as of scholarly enterprises such as the famous *Oxford English Dictionary,* whose declared purpose was to explain the "genius of the English language." Bringing out the tautology implicit in these attempts to define a national literature, Collini remarks: "Only those authors who display the putative characteristics are recognised as authentically English, a category whose definition relies upon the examples provided in the literature written by just those authors."[45]

The literary nations that are most closed in upon themselves, most concerned to equip themselves with an identity, endlessly reproduce their own norms in a sort of closed circuit, declaring them national and therefore necessary and sufficient within their own autarkic market. Thus Japan, which was long absent from international literary space, drew upon a very powerful internal tradition, handed down from one generation to another, that was based on a set of models held not merely to be a necessary part of any writer's training, but actually objects of national piety. This cultural context, inaccessible to most foreign readers and extremely difficult to communicate abroad, inevitably favored a national conception of literature.

By contrast with autonomous literary worlds, the most closed literary spaces are characterized by an absence of translation and, as a result, an ignorance of recent innovations in international literature and of the criteria of literary modernity. Juan Benet described the lack of interest in translations of foreign works in postwar Spain in these terms:

> Kafka's *Metamorphosis* had been translated just before the war, a very slender volume that passed virtually unnoticed. But no one knew Kafka's great novels; they could only be found in South American editions. Proust was a bit better known thanks to the translation in 1930–31 of the first two volumes of *À la recherche du temps perdu* by the great poet Pedro Salinas.[46] They enjoyed a great success, but the war, which came very suddenly, prevented Proust from having any influence whatever. No one, or almost no one, had ever heard of Kafka, Thomas Mann, Faulkner . . . No [Spanish] writer had been influenced by the great writers of the century, in poetry any more than in the theater, the novel, or even the essay. It was almost impossible to know these foreign works; they were not prohibited, but there simply was no importation of books. Only Faulkner's *Sanctuary,* which had been translated in 1935, but no one was interested in it.[47]

This process of literary nationalization was so successful that not even French literary space was untouched by it. The emphasis placed upon regional folklore and traditions in France, and the related interest shown in linguistic and philological issues, were evidence of the growing influence of the German model. Michel Espagne has nonetheless been able to show that this national conception of literature was reappropriated in a very specific way. The creation of university chairs of foreign literature after 1830, for example, illustrates both the attraction of the theories imported from Germany and the paradoxical character of this borrowing. The term "national culture" was used in France at this time primarily to describe foreign cultures: thus, in a striking reversal, philology, instead of serving as an instrument for pressing the claims to independence of various rediscovered nationalities, became an instrument of universalization through the introduction of literatures that were little or not at all known in France, by means of academic essays, collections of popular tales, and histories of Greek, Provençal, and Slavic national literatures. Even if the ideas that inspired this work were to a large extent imported from Germany, France managed to place them in the service of its own universalizing conception of literature.[48]

NATIONAL VERSUS INTERNATIONAL WRITERS

As a consequence of the Herderian revolution, then, international literary space has come to be structured, and lastingly so, according to the age and volume of its constituent literary resources and the relative degree of autonomy enjoyed by each national space. World literary space is now organized in terms of the opposition between, on the one hand, an autonomous pole composed of those spaces that are most endowed in literary resources, which serves as a model and a recourse for writers claiming a position of independence in newly formed spaces (with the result that Paris emerged as a "denationalized" universal capital and a specific measure of literary time was established); and, on the other, a heteronomous pole composed of relatively deprived literary spaces at early stages of development that are dependent on political—typically national—authorities.

The internal configuration of each national space precisely mirrors the structure of the international literary world as whole. Just as the global space is organized with reference to a literary and cosmopolitan pole, on the one side, and a political and national pole on the other, each of its constituent spaces is structured by the rivalry between what I shall call "national" writers (who embody a national or popular definition of literature) and "international" writers (who uphold an autonomous conception of literature).[49] Since the position of each national space in the world structure depends on its relative degree of autonomy, which in turn is a function of its volume of literary capital, and so ultimately of its age, the world of letters must be conceived as a composite of the various national literary spaces, which are themselves bipolar and differentially situated in the world structure according to the relative attraction exerted upon them by its national and international poles, respectively.

This simple structural analogy conceals a fundamental aspect of world literary space. For it is with reference to the autonomous pole of the worldwide field that national spaces manage first to emerge, and then to achieve autonomy themselves. The homology between international literary space and its component national spaces is the product not merely of the very form of the worldwide field, but also of its progressive unification: new national spaces appear and subsequently are unified on the model of the central areas of their respective linguistic domains, whose consecrating authorities permit international writers within each space to legitimize their position on the national level. The international field as a whole thus tends toward greater autonomy through the emergence of autonomous sub-poles in each national space.

In other words, the writers who seek greater freedom for their work are those who know the laws of world literary space and who make use of them in trying to subvert the dominant norms of their respective national fields. The autonomous pole of the world space is therefore essential to its very constitution, which is to say to its *littérisation* and its gradual denationalization: not only does the center supply theoretical and aesthetic models to writers on the periphery; its publishing networks and critical functions jointly strengthen the fabric of universal literature. There is nothing "miraculous" about this tendency toward greater autonomy. Every work from a dispossessed national space that aspires to the status of literature exists solely in relation to the consecrating authorities of the most autonomous places. It is only the romantic image of the artist's singularity—the fundamental element of literary mythology—that sustains the mistaken idea of creative solitude. In reality, the great heroes of literature invariably emerge only in association with the specific power of an autonomous and international literary capital. The case of James Joyce—rejected in Dublin, ignored in London, banned in New York, lionized in Paris—is undoubtedly the best example.

The literary world needs to be seen, then, as the product of antagonistic forces rather than as the result of a linear and gradually increasing tendency to autonomy. Opposed to the centripetal forces that strengthen the autonomous and unifying pole of world literary space and provide both a common measure of literary value and a literarily absolute point of reference (the Greenwich meridian) are the centrifugal forces associated with the national poles of each national space—the inertial forces that work to divide and particularize by essentializing differences, reproducing outmoded models, and nationalizing and commercializing literary life.

Consequently it becomes clear why the unification of international space proceeds for the most part through rivalries within national fields between national and international writers. As the space becomes more unified, a system of structural oppositions takes shape: thus, in Spain, Miguel Delibes and Camilio José Cela are to Juan Benet what, in the former Yugoslavia, Dragan Jeremić is to Danilo Kiš; what V. S. Naipaul is to Salman Rushdie in India and England; what the Gruppe 47 is to Arno Schmidt in postwar Germany; what Chinua Achebe is to Wole Soyinka in Nigeria; and so on. By the same token, it becomes clear that the dichotemies that structure the world space are the same ones that oppose academics to formalists, ancients to moderns, regionalists to cosmopolitans, writers on the periphery to writers in the center. Larbaud had sketched a rather similar typology (at a moment when the literary world was virtually limited to Europe) in *Reading, This Unpunished Vice:* "The European writer is one who is read by the elite of his country and by the elites of other countries. Thomas Hardy, Marcel Proust, Pirandello, etc., are European writers. Authors whose works are popular in their native countries but which are not read by the elites of their countries are . . . let us say, national writers—an intermediate category between European writers and local or dialect writers."[50]

For writers from nationalized spaces, exile is almost synonymous with autonomy. The great literary revolutionaries—Kiš, Michaux, Beckett, and Joyce among them—find themselves so at odds with the norms of their native literary space and, by contrast, so at home with the norms current in the centers of international space that they are able to make their way only outside their homeland. It is in this sense that the three weapons that Joyce claimed as his own in *A Portrait of the Artist as a Young Man* (1916) are to be understood. His character Stephen Dedalus declares, in a well-known phrase, that he tries to live and to create as "freely" and "wholly" as possible, "using for my defence the only arms I allow myself to use—silence, exile and cunning."[51] Of the three, exile is surely the major weapon of the writer who seeks to defend his autonomy against attack at any cost.

In order to understand what is at stake in the struggles that take place in dominated spaces between national writers—for whom literary aesthetics (because they are connected with political questions) are necessarily neonaturalistic—and international writers—cosmopolitans and polyglots who, owing to their knowledge of the revolutions that have taken place in the freest territories of the literary world, attempt to introduce new norms—it will be helpful to look at two cases in particular: Spain during the 1950s and 1960s and Yugoslavia during the 1970s.

Juan Benet (1927–1993) owed his rejection of the canons of Spanish literature to his awareness of their temporal and aesthetic anachronism: "There was no contemporary Spanish literature," he explained. "All the writers between 1900 and 1970, every last one of them, wrote in the manner of the generation of 1898, a naturalism adapted to the Spanish style, to the Castilian tongue. This was a literature that was already ruined; it already belonged to the past before being written."[52] At the end of the 1950s, Benet by himself occupied the first and only international position in Spanish literary space, then dominated and controlled by the dictatorship of General Francisco Franco. On the basis of a single model, the American novel—especially Faulkner, whom he discovered in issues of *Les Temps Modernes* that reached him by clandestine means[53]—Benet singlehandedly revolutionized the Spanish novel, and this in a literary territory totally closed off from news of international innovation.

The political and intellectual isolation of Francoist Spain was at once active and passive (that is, decided on the national level and experienced on the international level), reinforcing local habits.[54] The civil war marked a profound and radical break in the history of Spanish letters. The movements begun by the avant-gardes of the 1910s and 1920s, and then carried on by the generation of 1927, were abruptly ended; the intellectual class was destroyed; and the practice of literature in Spain, even before the censorship of the 1940s and 1950s, was considerably weakened and impoverished. Benet, who came to Madrid in the 1950s, later recalled the political dependency of the literary landscape he found there. The obligatory and unchallenged realism, concerned solely with the world inside the country's borders, was perfectly consistent with an earlier tradition of the novel: "It was above all the literary mediocrity of all the Spanish novelists that made me angry . . . What I couldn't stand is that they copied Spanish reality using the methods, the system, the style of the great tradition of the naturalistic novel."[55] This functionalist and realist aesthetic is, as we have seen, one of the most telling measures of the political dependence of a literary space. Spain—a country whose literary and political history had virtually been arrested—stood out as one of the most conservative and least autonomous spaces in all of Europe, oblivious to the literary upheavals taking place around it.

In this frozen landscape, Benet boldly broke with national preoccupations and proclaimed the necessity of a literature that had to cross political borders in order to be genuinely contemporary. His exceptional and clandestine knowledge of what was being published in Paris allowed him to be open to literary innovation throughout the world: "I received all of Monsieur Coindreau's translations with Gallimard, and this is how I came to read Faulkner, in French translation. France was very, very important—everything came from there. I received *Les Temps Modernes* a month after it came out. I still have at home an entire set of issues from 1945 to 1952. This was where I discovered the American crime novel, for example."[56]

The model and, above all, the diffusion of consecrated texts makes possible the appearance of an autonomous (albeit sometimes clandestine) pole. For a man such as Benet, who in the years following the Second World War found himself in an almost experimental situation of cultural isolation (or at least who thought of his situation in this way) and who yet managed to learn of the upheavals in literary aesthetics and novelistic technique that were taking place elsewhere in Europe and in the United States, the model of an international literature furnished the instruments he needed in order to challenge the dominant body of literary and asthetic practices in his homeland. The Spanish case illustrates the link between stylistic conservatism and national traditions, on the one hand, and literary innovation and international culture on the other.

Benet's determination to write according to the norms that were then in force along the literary Greenwich meridian but unknown in Spain, a country subject to severe political censorship, required unprecedented courage and condemned him to complete neglect during the time it took for the national space—whose contours little by little he succeeded in profoundly modifying by his very presence—to overcome its backwardness and grasp the nature and scope of the revolution he had brought about. It was to be another ten or fifteen years before another generation was ready to take over and able to recognize him as one of the great writers of Spanish modernity. This chronological solitude, which isolated him from the other writers of his generation and prevented him from forming any group or school, strengthened his belief in the importance of literary freedom—a freedom that had been achieved in the face of resistance on all sides—and in the necessity of an ethics that was at once political and aesthetic:

I believe that I brought about a "moral" rupture with the literature that formerly was written in this country. Young novelists such as Javier Marías, Felix de Azúa, Soledad Puértolas are much better educated than the previous generation was; like me, they have very little respect for traditional Spanish literature. They learned their craft by reading English, French, American, and Russian writers . . . and, like me, they broke with tradition. It was not a question of haughtiness, but rather of respecting a certain type of conduct, an ethics.[57]

Before this, subversion in Spain—so far as it existed at all under Franco's dictatorship—was exclusively political. What Benet did was to introduce a law of literary independence, championing the primacy of form and access to international models against the suffocating regulation of literary creativity by an authoritarian regime.

In much the same way, Danilo Kiš (1935–1989) proclaimed the right to literary independence in Yugoslavia. In a literary manifesto published in Belgrade under the title Čas anatomije (The Anatomy Lesson, 1978), he dissected the literature of his homeland and announced his intention to bring about a "permanent shift (in both form and content) vis-à-vis our run-of-the-mill literary production," to introduce a "distance that may not guarantee a work absolute or even relative superiority . . . but [will] at least guarantee it modernity, that is, save it from anachronism . . . If I have applied my experience with the modern European and American novel to my own works . . . it is because I want . . . to do away with canons and anachronisms in at least the literature of my own country."[58] In adopting the "European and American novel" as an aesthetic norm, Kiš broke with the "anachronistic" literary practices of his country and appealed to the international present. Thus he described his own narrative technique as a way of avoiding "the original sin of the realist novel—psychological motivation from a divine point of view; a motivation that, through the platitudes and banalities it engenders, still wreaks havoc with the novel and short story among us [in Yugoslavia] and yet, with its trite, anachronistic solutions and its 'déja vu' quality, arouses the admiration of our critics."[59]

Kiš's situation in Yugoslavia during the 1970s was exactly the same as Benet's in Spain ten or twenty years earlier: trapped in a country whose literature was exclusively concerned with national and political questions, and in an intellectual milieu that was (as he put it) "ignorant" because "provincial,"[60] he nonetheless managed to revise the rules of the game and forge a new fictional aesthetic by arming himself with the results of the literary revolutions that had occurred previously on the international level. But the rupture that he brought about can only be understood in terms of the national world *in opposition to which* he constructed his identity as a writer. *The Anatomy Lesson* is a meticulous description of the Yugoslav literary space of the period, written in response to charges of plagiarism leveled against his novel *Grobnica za Borisa Davidoviča* (A Tomb for Boris Davidovich, 1976). At the time Kiš was one of the most famous writers in Yugoslavia, one of the few of his generation to be really recognized outside its borders, envied and at the same time marginal, a resolutely antinationalist and cosmopolitan figure in a country that was divided and withdrawn into itself. His work, translated already into several languages, was beginning to make its way into a wider world. In short, everything conspired to put him at odds with the national intellectuals of his country.

The accusation of plagiarism brought against him was credible only in a closed literary world that had not yet been touched by any of the great literary, aesthetic, and formal revolutions of the twentieth century. Only in a world that was unaware of "Western" literary innovations (an epithet that invariably carried a pejorative sense in Belgrade) could a text composed with the whole of international fictional modernity in mind be seen as simple copy of some other work. The very accusation of plagiarism was proof, in fact, of the aesthetic backwardness of Serbia, a land located far in the literary past in relation to the Greenwich meridian. What Kiš called "folk kitsch," "petit-bourgeois kitsch," and "prettiness" are aspects of the conformist practice of a literary space so completely closed in on itself that it knows only how to reproduce ad infinitum the neorealist conception of the novel.

The harsh critique of nationalism that opens *The Anatomy Lesson* not only is political in the narrow sense of the term; it is also a way of politically defending a position of literary autonomy, a refusal to recognize the aesthetic canons imposed by the nationalist mind. "The nationalist," Kiš writes, "is by definition an ignoramus."[61] He is in any case (to recall Benet's characterization) an academic, a stylistic conservative, since he knows nothing other than his national tradition. Kiš's "permanent shift" away from nationalism, the "*differential coefficient* [of his writing] in relation to the canonized works of [Serbian] literature," explains in part the very form of his work:[62] in the chronically anachronistic literary space of the former Yugoslavia, Kiš sought to create the conditions for an autonomous literature by reference to international practice.

FORMS OF LITERARY DOMINATION

In the literary world, domination is not exerted in an unequivocal way. Because hierarchical structure is not linear, it cannot be described in terms of a simple model of a single centralized dominant power. If literary space is relatively autonomous, it is also by the same token relatively dependent on political space. This fundamental dependency assumes a variety of forms, particularly political ones, and operates in a variety of ways, most notably through language.

Here we encounter once again the ambiguity and paradox that govern the very enterprise of literature itself: since language is not a purely literary tool, but an inescapably political instrument as well, it is through language that the literary world remains subject to political power. One consequence of this is that forms of domination, which are interlocking and often superimposed upon one another, are apt to merge and become hidden. Thus literarily dominated spaces may also be dominated linguistically and politically: especially in countries that have undergone colonization, the fact that political domination is often exerted by linguistic means implies a condition of literary dependency. Indeed, when the sources of dependency are exclusively linguistic (and cultural)—as, for example, in the cases of Belgium, Austria, and Switzerland—literary domination is unavoidable. But it may also be the case that domination is exerted and measured in literary terms alone. These include the effectiveness of consecration by central authorities, the power of critical decrees, the canonizing effect of prefaces and translations by writers who themselves have been consecrated at the center (thus Gide introduced the Egyptian Taha Hussein and translated Rabindranath Tagore, while Marguerite Yourcenar introduced the work of the Japanese novelist Yukio Mishima to France),[63] the prestige of the collections in which foreign works appear, and the leading role played by great translators.

Since all these forms of domination are liable to become mixed together, and so obscure each other, one of the objects of the present work is to isolate and describe them, while also showing that the literary balance of power is often a disguised reflection of patterns of political domination. Conversely, however, it is also necessary to show that patterns of literary domination cannot be reduced to a political balance of power, as is sometimes done by academic critics who treat perceived differences in rank between national literatures as a simple function of economic domination, analyzed in terms of a binary opposition between center and periphery. This sort of spatialization tends to neutralize the violence that actually governs the literary world and to obscure the inequalities that arise from strictly literary competition between dominant and dominated. A purely political analysis does not allow us to understand the individual struggles waged by writers in dominated spaces against the center or against regional centers associated with different linguistic areas, much less the precise nature of literary reality and aesthetics.

A more sophisticated model would take into account a peculiar ambiguity of the relation of literary domination and dependence, namely, that writers in dominated spaces may be able to convert their dependence into an instrument of emancipation and legitimacy. To criticize established literary forms and genres because they have been inherited from colonial culture, for instance, misses the point that literature itself, as a value common to an entire space, is not only part of the legacy of political domination but also an instrument that, once reappropriated, permits writers from literarily deprived territories to gain recognition.[64]

Literary Regions and Linguistic Areas

Linguistic areas are the emanation and embodiment of political domination. By exporting their languages and institutions, colonizing nations (which is to say dominant literary nations) succeeded in strengthening their political pole. The expansion of linguistic (or linguistic-cultural) areas therefore constituted a sort of extension of European national literary spaces. Afterward, as Salman Rushdie put it, the "pink conquerors crept home, the boxwallahs and memsahibs and bwanas, leaving behind them parliaments, schools, Grand Trunk Roads and the rules of cricket."[65] The age of colonialism was characterized in large part by a process of linguistic and cultural unification. One of the chief aspects of this "propensity for self-exportation," as the West Indian poet Édouard Glissant has noted, is that it typically generated "a sort of vocation for the universal," with the result that the great Western languages came to be regarded as "vehicular languages" that "often took the place of an actual metropolis."[66]

Each linguistic territory has a center that controls and attracts the literary productions dependent on it. London today, even if it now finds itself in competition with New York and Toronto, continues to be central for Australians, New Zealanders, Irish, Canadians, Indians, and English-speaking Africans; Barcelona, the intellectual and cultural capital of Spain, remains a great literary center for Latin Americans; Paris is still central for writers from West and North Africa as well as for Francophone authors in Belgium, Switzerland, and Canada, countries where it continues to exercise influence by virtue of its literary eminence rather than any power of political control. Berlin is the leading capital for Austrian and Swiss writers and remains an important literary center today for the countries of northern Europe as well as for the countries of central Europe that emerged from the breakup of the Austro-Hungarian Empire.

Each of these linguistic-cultural areas preserves a large measure of autonomy in relation to the others: each is what might be called a "literature-world" (to transpose Braudel's notion of an "economy-world"): that is, a homogenous and autonomous sphere in which the legitimacy of its centralized power of consecration is unchallenged; a world having its own pantheon and prizes, its own favored genres, its own distinctive traditions and internal rivalries. The structure of each area mirrors that of worldwide literary space, with a subtle hierarchy being established among its various satellites as a function of their symbolic distance (which is aesthetic rather than geographic) from the center. In some regions there may be more than one center—London and New York, for example, within the Anglophone area. These capitals come into conflict with each other, each one seeking to impose its authority over the shared linguistic hinterland with a view to achieving, and then sustaining, a regional monopoly of literary consecration.

In the aftermath of decolonization, then, the major literary centers have been able to go on maintaining a sort of literary protectorate thanks to the dual character of their languages, which allows them to exert a literary form of political power. Even in the "soft" neocolonial form of language and literature, the perpetuation of such domination is a powerful factor favoring consolidation of the heteronomous (or political and economic) pole of the worldwide literary field.

London is, of course, along with Paris, the other great capital of world literature, not only by virtue of its accumulated literary capital but also

owing to the immensity of its former colonial empire. Its power of recognition, which extends from Ireland to India, Africa, and Australia, is
unquestionably one of the greatest in the world: authors as different as
Shaw, Yeats, Tagore, Narayan, and Soyinka (four of them Nobel Prize
winners) have all looked to London as their literary capital. This power,
and the correspondingly large share of literary credit it implies, continue
to confer real literary legitimacy upon writers from Commonwealth nations, successors to the territories of the old empire. Among writers of
Indian descent, for example, no matter whether they have wholly assimilated British values, as in the case of V. S. Naipaul, or whether they pre-
fer to keep a critical distance from them, as in the case of Salman
Rushdie, consecration by London has allowed them to enjoy literary
existence on the international level, even if this form of ennoblement is
not altogether untouched by political motives.

Of one of the heroes in *The Satanic Verses,* Saladin Chamcha, an Indian immigrant to London, Rushdie writes:

> Of the things of the mind, he had most loved the protean, inexhaust-
> ible culture of the English-speaking peoples; had said, when courting
> Pamela, that *Othello,* "just that one play," was worth the total output of
> any other dramatist in any other language, and though he was con-
> scious of hyperbole, he didn't think the exaggeration very great . . . Of
> material things, he had given his love to this city, London, preferring it
> to the city of his birth or to any other; had been creeping up on it,
> stealthily, with mounting excitement, freezing into a statue when it
> looked in his direction, dreaming of being the one to possess it and so,
> in a sense, become it, as when in the game of grandmother's footsteps
> the child who touches the one who's it ("on it", today's young Lon-
> doners would say) takes over the cherished identity . . . [London's]
> long history as a refuge, a role it maintained in spite of the recalcitrant
> ingratitude of the refugees' children; and without any of the self-con-
> gratulatory huddled-masses rhetoric of the "nation of immigrants"
> across the ocean, itself far from perfectly open-armed. Would the
> United States, with its are-you-now-have-you-ever-beens, have per-
> mitted Ho Chi Minh to cook in its hotel kitchens? What would its
> McCarran-Walter Act have to say about a latter-day Karl Marx, stand-
> ing bushy-bearded at its gates, waiting to cross its yellow lines? O
> Proper London! Dull would he truly be of soul who did not prefer its
> faded splendours, its new hesitancies, to the hot certainties of that
> transatlantic New Rome.[67]

London's power of attraction, it will be noted, shares two characteristics already observed in connection with Paris: a sizable share of literary capital and a reputation for political liberalism.

By virtue of its uncontested political power, London has very often been used as a weapon in the permanent struggle that opposes European capitals to each other. When France's cultural domination was at its height, at the end of the eighteenth and the beginning of the nineteenth centuries, its competitors sought to turn London's prestige against Paris. Between 1750 and 1770 in Germany, for example, when a national literature was in the process of being created, the "preclassical" generation—that of Klopstock and especially of Lessing—proposed to put an end to the imitation (and therefore to the domination) of French authors by relying on English models. Lessing himself was responsible for the great shift in critical and popular opinion regarding the work of Shakespeare.

But London has seldom imposed itself outside the linguistic jurisdiction of the British Empire (now Commonwealth). London publishers today publish very few literary translations, and prizes are awarded only to works written in English.[68] It owes its credit to the vast extent of its linguistic area and to the globally dominant position now enjoyed by the English language; but because its power of consecration has always had a linguistic (and therefore often political) basis, its strictly literary credit is not of the same kind as that commanded by Paris.

In recent years the rivalry between London and New York has produced a very clear bipolarization of English-speaking cultural space. But if New York today is the unchallenged publishing capital of the world in financial terms, still it cannot be said to have become a center of consecration whose legitimacy is universally recognized. Here again the very question of legitimacy is one of the things at stake in the game, and the way it is answered depends on the place occupied by those who are prepared to wager on it. Many writers take advantage of this uncertain balance of power in order to play one capital off against the other.

The Postcolonial Novel

In exporting their languages, European nations have also exported their own political struggles; or rather, the work of writers from outlying lands has become a major element in these struggles. Increasingly it is the case that the literary power of a central nation can be measured in terms of the literary innovations produced by universally recognized writers from its suburbs. For a language no less than for the literary tradition associated with it, these outsiders supply a new way of keeping up with modernity and thereby of revaluing the nation's stock of literary capital. The importance of notions such as "Commonwealth literature" or "francophonie" lies in precisely this, for they make it possible to lay claim to, and then annex, peripheral literary innovations under a central linguistic and cultural aegis.

Since 1981, for example, the Booker Prize, the most prestigious literary prize in Great Britain, has on several occasions been awarded to "not quites," as the Indian writer Bharati Mukherjee calls them—authors whose work has been shaped by immigration, exile, or postcolonization. The first of these to be crowned was Salman Rushdie, for *Midnight's Children* (1981). Subsequently the prize has gone to Keri Hulme, a Maori from New Zealand; Ben Okri, a Nigerian; Michael Ondaatje, a Canadian citizen of Sinhalese birth; and Kazuo Ishiguro, a naturalized Englishman born in Japan. Two Australians, a South African, and several finalists of non-English ancestry profited from critical attention as well, among them Timothy Mo, a Hong Kong Chinese by birth. This was all that was needed for the critics, confusing cause and effect, to deduce the existence of a "new" literature, even of a veritable literary movement originating in the former British colonial empire.

In fact, there was a desire on the part of publishers to create the impression of a group by gathering together under a single label authors who had nothing, or very little, in common. This labeling effect (which may be compared, for example, with the promotion of the Latin American "boom" of the 1960s) turned out to be an extremely effective marketing strategy. Ishiguro, whose parents had emigrated from Japan when he was a child, was unaffected by colonization and had an entirely different relationship to England from an Indian such as Rushdie. Ben Okri was Nigerian, like Wole Soyinka; but Soyinka, despite the international recognition that led to the Nobel Prize, had never been regarded as a neocolonial author—no more than V. S. Naipaul, a Trinidadian who practiced a stubborn assimilationism and was knighted by the queen. Michael Ondaatje, for his part, professed to be interested in "international bastards, born in one place and deciding to live in another."[69] And Rushdie himself, who in various articles published after the success of *Midnight's Children* refused to be treated as a postimperial product, was one of the first to repudiate the geopolitical assumptions of the new

British taxonomy. "At best," he wrote in 1983, "what is called 'Commonwealth literature' is positioned below English literature 'proper'—
. . . it places Eng. Lit. at the centre and the rest of the world at the periphery."[70] By ignoring this ambiguity British critics were able to point to the successful assimilation of which these writers were manifest proof, and the extraordinary extent of the territory over which such assimilation occurred, as evidence of the power and the influence of British civilization. To rally so many disparate writers (Nigerians, Sri Lankans, Canadians, Pakistanis, Anglo-Indians, even Japanese) under the British banner was a curious yet clever way of incorporating as part of official British literary history works that to one degree or another were written *against* it.

What is more, national literary awards—such as the Goncourt and Booker Prizes—were now often influenced by commercial success, with the result that the verdicts of juries tended more and more to coincide with the interests of publishers. And by extending the jurisdiction of the judges to include the work of authors from the former colonial empire (whether in the name of Commonwealth literature or *francophonie* or some other conception), their deliberations suffered a further loss of independence, being subject not only to national norms and commercial criteria but now to neoimperial ambitions as well.

The vogue for exoticism was so great that publishers—particularly in the United States—moved quickly to manufacture bestsellers for an international public. The programmed success of the novel by the Indian writer Vikram Seth, *A Suitable Boy* (1993), perfectly illustrates this phenomenon. Critics in both England and France described the book as an indubitable sign of the revitalization of literature in English, even of the "revenge" of the old colonies against the British Empire—and this despite the fact that the literary techniques employed were both typically English and largely outmoded. Indeed, the publisher proudly announced that the book was set in India in the 1950s and written "in the great tradition of Jane Austen and Dickens." In adopting the perennially popular form of the family saga and enlisting the aesthetic norms of the past century in the service of an eminently Western view of the world, the author (a graduate of Oxford and Stanford) showed his eagerness to satisfy all the most obvious criteria of the commercially successful novel. Far from furnishing evidence of some sort of literary liberation, or of the sudden accession of the formerly colonized to literary greatness, *A Suit-*

able Boy offered irrefutable proof of the virtually total domination of the English literary model over its cultural area.

Unlike London, the scope of whose cultural jurisdiction depended mainly on its stock of literary capital and the extent of its linguistic territory, Paris never took an interest in writers from its colonial territories; or, more precisely, it long despised and mistreated them as a species of extreme provincials, too similar to be celebrated as exotic foreigners but too remote to be considered worthy of interest. France has no tradition of cultural consecration on purely linguistic grounds, and what is called *francophonie* is only a timid political substitute for the influence that Paris once exerted (and to some extent still exerts today) in symbolic terms. Indeed, the few national literary prizes that have been awarded to writers from the former French colonies or from the margins of the Francophone area have been motivated by transparently neoimperial considerations.

In polycentric areas, dominated writers can exploit an unequal balance of power between linguistic and political capitals. Where there is competition between two capitals—between London and New York, for example, or between Lisbon and São Paulo—peripheral literary spaces are subject to a dual form of domination, which paradoxically permits writers to make use of one center in order to do battle with the other. Thus in Canada writers can choose between adopting the critical categories of their neighbor to the south—as in the case of Michael Ondaatje, a native of Sri Lanka who lives in Toronto—or, conversely, relying on London in order to escape the homogenizing and dissipating influence of American norms. This is the case, for example, with the novelists Margaret Atwood and Jane Urquhart, who seek to found an Anglo-Canadian literary identity on the basis of the dichotemy between the British and American traditions that characterizes their nation's literature. "The history of Canada," Atwood observes, "is in part the history of a struggle against the United States. Many Canadians were political refugees who refused to give up."[71] In *The Whirlpool* (1986), Urquhart recreated the birth of the Canadian nation and literature by imagining the encounter in 1889 of a historian and a poet at Niagara Falls, astride the American-Canadian border. This place, the site of the battle of Lundy's Lane in 1812, is thus made the symbol of the founding of a nation, which is to say of a national reappropriation of history:[72] the historian attempts to demonstrate, as against both the official British and American versions, that this battle was really a Canadian victory ("Imagine having a victory stolen from you like that. The Americans are robbing us of our victories! It's unconscionable! . . . Total victory! They never lost a battle, a skirmish, a cockfight! Arrogant bastards!"); the young poet, for his part, hesitates between the view of the world that had been transmitted to him by English romanticism ("'You're never going to find Wordsworth's daffodils here'") and the novelty of the North American landscape.[73]

One cannot really grasp Urquhart's purpose if one ignores this desire to found a nation, inherent in every work produced in a dominated literary space. The difficult situation of double-edged dependence in which Canadian writers find themselves therefore leads them to pit one capital against the other. In the cases of Urquhart and Atwood, the habit of referring to English literary history, to the pantheon of British poetry and fiction, helps strengthen the British pole, which is part of their history as Canadians and furnishes them with a supply of established literary capital with which to oppose the rising power of the Americans. But other deprived members of the English-speaking area of international literary space choose to ally themselves with New York as a way of resisting dependence on London. This is the case with Irish writers today, who in their struggle against neoimperial influence seek to take advantage of the growing literary power (particularly in academic circles) of the United States. The presence of a sizable Irish community that plays a role in both American political and intellectual life further improves the possibility of shifting the balance of literary power away from London.

Similarly, international recognition of the distinctive character of Brazilian letters has now made it possible for writers in other parts of the Portuguese-speaking area, less endowed in cultural and literary resources, to look to the São Paulo pole in attempting to overturn traditional political and literary norms. All those in Portuguese-speaking Africa today who seek to attain literary modernity and autonomy by opposing the influence of Lisbon invoke the example of Brazilian poetry and, more generally, the Brazilian challenge to the linguistic—and therefore cultural—constraints of classical Portuguese. Thus the Angolan writer José Luandino Vieira (who is Portuguese by birth) and, more recently, the Mozambican writer Mia Couto have been able to rely upon Brazilian literary resources in order to counteract the influence of

European models and to create their own literary genealogy and history:[74] "The poets of Mozambique," Couto has said, "are working above all to bring about the transformation of Portuguese. The most important poets for us in Mozambique are the Brazilians, because they were in a sense *authorized* to do violence to the language. People like Drummond de Andrade, Mário de Andrade, Guimarães Rosa, Graciliano Ramos, and many others succeeded in renewing Portuguese."[75] Realizing that they can draw not only upon the literary assets accumulated by the Brazilians since the 1920s but also upon the reserve of solutions to the problem of overcoming intellectual submission to Portugal that have already been devised, Mozambican and Angolan writers have taken up the banner of literary liberation in their turn while making a point of acknowledging their dependence on Brazil, which had been in the same position before them and yet managed to create a distinctive and original national literature.

The position of Francophone writers, on the other hand, is paradoxical if not tragic as well. Since for them Paris is not merely the capital of world literary space, as historically it has been for writers everywhere, but also the very source of the political and/or literary domination under which they labor, they alone have been unable to look to Paris as a second homeland. The possibility is not available to them of escaping Paris—unless by retreating into their national space, as Ramuz did—or of using Paris to invent a form of aesthetic dissidence. Making matters worse, the power of Paris is still more domineering and more keenly felt by Francophone writers for being incessantly denied in the name of the universal belief in the universality of French letters and on behalf of the values of liberty promoted and monopolized by France itself. How can one hope to found a new literary tradition that will be free from the influence of the world's most prestigious literature? No other center, no other capital or authority, can really offer a way out from this impasse.

Still, the problem may not be intractable. Among the solutions that have been proposed by intellectuals on the periphery of the French-speaking world is the acrobatic theory known as the "two Frances." For a long time the belief in a supposed duality—"the colonizing, reactionary, racist France and the noble, generous France, mother of arts and letters, the emancipating creator of the rights of man and the citizen," as Raphaël Confiant put it[76]—permitted Francophone writers to preserve a sense of freedom and cultivate the special identity necessary to their literary existence while at the same time fighting against political subjugation. In recent years, however, a number of writers have adopted more sophisticated strategies. Some, such as the West Indian writers Édouard Glissant and Patrick Chamoiseau (along with Confiant) and the Algerian Rachid Boudjedra, have embraced the Faulknerian model in the hope of escaping French supremacy; others, such as the Guinean writer Tierno Monénembo, explicitly declare their indebtedness to the Latin Americans—notably Octavio Paz—in their quest for creative liberty.[77] But in doing this they have only made a detour: Faulkner, like the great writers of Latin America, was consecrated in Paris. To acknowledge their example amounts still to recognizing the singular power of Paris that continues to make itself felt throughout the world republic of letters.

4 | *The Fabric of the Universal*

It is therefore wholly necessary that this man, if he values being illustrious, bring to the capital his bundle of talent, that there he lay it out before the Parisian experts, that he pay for expertise, and that a reputation is then made for him that from the capital is dispatched to the provinces, where it is eagerly accepted.
—Rodolphe Töpffer, unpublished notes, 1834–1836

Yet up to the day of the occupation, Paris had been the Holy Place of our time. The only one. Not because of its affirmative genius alone, but perhaps, on the contrary, through its passivity, which allowed it to be possessed by the searchers of every nation. By Picasso and Juan Gris, Spaniards; by Modigliani, Boccioni and Severini, Italians; by Brancusi, Roumanian; by Joyce, Irishman; by Mondrian, Dutchman; by Lipchitz, Polish Lithuanian; by Archipenko, Kandinsky, Diaghilev, Larionov, Russians; by Calder, Pound, Gertrude Stein, Man Ray, Americans; by Kupka, Czechoslovak; by Lehmbruck and Max Ernst, Germans; by Wyndham Lewis and T. E. Hulme, Englishmen . . . by all artists, students, refugees . . . Paris represented the International of Culture . . . [r]eleased in this aged and bottomless metropolis from national folklore, national politics, national careers; detached from the family and the corporate taste.
—Harold Rosenberg, *The Tradition of the New*

CONSECRATION, IN THE form of recognition by autonomous critics, signifies the crossing of a literary border. To cross this invisible line is to undergo a sort of transformation—one might almost say a transmutation in the alchemical sense. The consecration of a text is the almost magical metamorphosis of an ordinary material into "gold," into absolute literary value. In this sense the sanctioning authorities of world literary space are the guardians, guarantors, and creators of value, which is nonetheless always changing, ceaselessly contested and debated, by virtue of the very fact of its connection with the literary present and modernity. Valéry justified the reference to value, it will be recalled, on the ground that "it involves appreciation and judgments of importance, as well as discussion of the price one is prepared to pay for this value," noting that "one can see how it continually comes into competition with other values."[1] For texts that come from literarily disinherited countries, the magical transmutation that consecration brings about amounts to a change in their very nature: a passage from literary inexistence to existence, from invisibility to the condition of literature—a transformation that I have called *littérisation*.

THE CAPITAL AND ITS DOUBLE

Paris is not only the capital of the literary world. It is also, as a result, the gateway to the "world market of intellectual goods," as Goethe put it; the chief place of consecration in the world of literature. Consecration in Paris is indispensable for authors from all dominated literary spaces: translations, critical studies, tributes, and commentaries represent so many judgments and verdicts that confer value upon a text that until now has remained outside world literary space or otherwise gone unnoticed within. Because this judgment is pronounced by autonomous literary authorities, it has real consequences for the reception of a text. The belief in the *power* of the capital of the arts is so strong that not only do artists throughout the world unreservedly accept the preeminence of Paris; owing to the extraordinary concentration of intellectual talent there that follows from this belief, Paris has become the place where books—submitted to critical judgment and transmuted—can be denationalized and their authors made universal. By virtue of its status as the central bank of literature, to revert to the terms employed earlier, Paris is able to create literary value and extend terms of credit everywhere in the world.

Samuel Beckett, in an essay titled "La peinture des Van Velde; ou Le Monde et le pantalon" (The Painting of the Van Velde Brothers; or The World and the Trousers, 1945), expressed the obviousness of this power of consecration in a single sentence: "The painting . . . of Abraham and Gerardus van Velde is little known in Paris, which is to say little known."[2] Paris—which Beckett had decided some years earlier, when he was himself perfectly unknown, to make his home—inspired, produced, and crowned works that were totally impossible and ignored elsewhere. Having fled Dublin to escape the establishment of a national art under the political and religious supervision and censorship of the new Irish state, Beckett spoke from personal experience: Paris was, from his point of view, the capital of Art in the purest sense. He chose exile there in order to affirm, as against the claims of an art subjugated to national purposes, the total autonomy of literature.

Larbaud had argued in similar terms, in an article written in the 1920s, that Walt Whitman was unknown in America: "Yes, he was an American . . . But he was not an American because he proclaimed himself the poet of America. Again the immediate rejection: he was as neglected in the United States as Stendhal in Grenoble, or Cézanne in Aix . . . most of 'the happy few' lived in Europe. It was therefore in Europe alone that he could be recognized and that he was recognized."[3] And, as Paul de Man has pointed out, it was in France that the Argentine Jorge Luis Borges was discovered by critics and regularly translated, although he had been a great translator of American poetry and fiction into Spanish.[4]

James Joyce, rejected and even banned in Dublin, was welcomed and consecrated by Paris, which made him an artist who revolutionized universal literature rather than merely an Irish national writer. To escape the linguistic, political, and moral (or religious) constraints of Irish literary space, Joyce devised a paradoxical and apparently contradictory solution by composing an Irish work—*Ulysses*—as an avowed exile from his native land. Thus Larbaud, whose translation established Joyce as one of the greatest writers of the century, managed to rescue him from an invisible provincialism and to universalize him, which is to say to give him an existence in the autonomous literary sphere (like Yeats before him, only more broadly, since Joyce was consecrated outside the cultural area of the English language) but also to make him visible, accepted, and acceptable in his own national literary space. It was in this sense that Larbaud wrote in 1921:

> It must be remarked that in writing *Dubliners, Portrait of the Artist,* and *Ulysses,* [Joyce] has done as much as all the heroes of Irish nationalism to win Ireland the respect of intellectuals everywhere. His work gives

back to Ireland, or rather gives to the young Ireland, an artistic physiognomy, an intellectual identity; it does for Ireland what Ibsen's work did in its time for Norway, what Strindberg's did for Sweden, what Nietzsche's did for Germany at the end of the nineteenth century, and what the books of Gabriel Miró and Ramón Gómez de la Serna have just done for contemporary Spain . . . In short, it may be said that with the work of James Joyce, and in particular with *Ulysses,* which is soon to appear in Paris, Ireland makes a sensational entry into the first rank of European literature.[5]

Sixty years later another exile crowned by Paris, Danilo Kiš, described in quite simple and intuitive terms the mechanisms (of which he had firsthand experience) that continued to make it a unique center for the consecration of literature:

> It seems to me that Paris has always been, only more and more so, a true fair—you know, an auction, where one sells to the highest bidder everything that the world of culture has produced elsewhere, in other parts of the globe . . . In order to exist it is necessary to pass through Paris. Latin American literature existed before the French [noticed it], like existentialism, Russian formalism, etc, etc, but in order to achieve the status of universal patrimony it had to pass through Paris. This is what Parisian cuisine amounts to. Emigrations, universities, theses and prose compositions, translations, commentaries: in a word, cuisine. That's what French culture is.[6]

For Kiš, Paris was therefore at the center of a market, an auction involving the sale and exchange of intellectual goods from all over the world, which must be displayed there if they are to achieve the status of "universal patrimony," that is, to acquire the value recognized in this market.

Owing to its dual literary and political function, Paris also represents the last bulwark against national censorship: its historical reputation as the capital of every form of liberty—political, aesthetic, and moral— makes it a beacon of freedom for writers. It was in Paris that Kiš chose exile in order to escape censorship and official harrassment in Belgrade during the 1970s; and that Nabokov's *Lolita* had been published in the face of American censorship two decades earlier, in 1955, along with William Burroughs' *Naked Lunch* in 1959.

In the 1960s, Jean-Paul Sartre personally embodied the accumulated wealth of four centuries of French literary and intellectual activity, almost single-handedly concentrating the totality of historical belief and

Parisian credit.[7] As an intellectual committed to the cause of the politically repressed, he also became one of the most powerful sources of recognition in the world of literature, notably on behalf of Faulkner and Dos Passos. Mario Vargas Llosa evoked Sartre's stature in the eyes of young intellectuals throughout the world who came to Paris in search of literary modernity:

> It will be as difficult for readers in the future to have an exact idea of the importance of Sartre to this era as it is for us to understand exactly what Voltaire, Victor Hugo or Gide meant to their age. He was, like them, that curious French institution: the intellectual mandarin. That is, someone who is seen as a teacher, beyond what he knows, what he writes or even what he says, a man on whom a huge public confers the power to legislate on matters ranging from the largest moral, cultural and political questions to the most trivial [ones] . . . It will be difficult for those who know Sartre only through his books to understand to what extent the things that he said or did not say, or what it was thought he might have said, had an impact on thousands of people and became transformed into forms of behaviour, "vital choices."[8]

Sartre's immense power of consecration made him a sort of embodiment of literary modernity, someone who fixed the limits of literary art by designating a present of literature: "Apart from stimulating us to move away from a regionalist literary framework," Vargas Llosa remarks, "we realized, albeit secondhand, through reading Sartre that narrative had undergone a revolution, that the range of its themes had diversified in all directions and that the modes of narration were both freer and more complicated . . . the first volumes of *Roads to Freedom* and Sartre's essays enabled many of us to discover literature at the beginning of the fifties."[9]

The road to worldwide recognition for William Faulkner likewise went through Paris. Faulkner's early literary career in the United States was a very difficult one. Coming after *Soldier's Pay* (1926), *Mosquitoes* (1927), and the failure of *Sartoris* (1929), *The Sound and the Fury* (1929) brought him a certain measure of critical notice (though the book sold only 1,789 copies). *As I Lay Dying* (1930) was followed by his first real success, *Sanctuary* (published in a first version in 1931, then in final form the next year)—a *succès de scandale*, in fact, selling more than 6,500 copies in less than two months. Yet for another fifteen years Faulkner was to remain practically unknown in his own country. It was only in 1946—only three years before receiving the Nobel Prize and well after his consecration in France—that Malcolm Cowley's anthology *The Portable Faulkner* won him the recognition of critics in the United States as one of the masters of American literature, reviving sales of his books.

In France, by contrast, he was recognized very early on as one of the great innovators of the century. Already in 1931, two years after the publication of *The Sound and the Fury,* Maurice-Edgar Coindreau published in the *Nouvelle Revue Française* a critical study of the six novels published by Faulkner up until that time.[10] Apart from two brief essays published in the United States and a dozen reviews in the American press, half of which betrayed a total incomprehension, only two other studies of Faulkner had previously appeared.[11] *As I Lay Dying* was translated by Coindreau in 1932, with a preface by Larbaud, but came out in France only after *Sanctuary,* which was issued in 1933 with a preface by André Malraux. Gallimard published *The Sound and the Fury* in August 1938. Sartre's review the following year established Faulkner as one of the greatest novelists of the century.[12] Jean-Louis Barrault had already adapted *As I Lay Dying* for the stage during the 1934–35 season, as Albert Camus was later to do with *Requiem for a Nun* (1951) in 1956. It was on account of his consecration by the most eminent French writers and critics of the day that Faulkner was able to enjoy worldwide recognition during his lifetime, from the late 1940s until his death in 1962. The Nobel Prize, which confirmed his international reputation, was a direct consequence of this Parisian benediction.

Brussels, a capital in open rivalry with Paris, also enjoyed the power of consecrating works of literature. The simplistic picture of Brussels as a minor center under the influence of its more glamorous neighbor needs to be set against the more complex reality of a city that functioned as a crossroads, a rallying point for members of the avant-garde cast out of the great European capitals, a place that offered a second chance for all the moderns rejected and ignored by Paris.[13] Brussels' freedom from nationalist resentment and defensiveness made it attentive to all forms of cultural novelty and modernity. As a country belatedly and artificially created in 1830, the very youth of Belgium shielded it from the ancient antagonisms that divided older European nations. Apart from the invention of a national tradition that borrowed more from painting (from the

Flemish primitives to Rubens) than from popular culture, Belgium's distinctiveness and relative advantage derived from its openness to Europe as a whole. Particularly after 1870, when even French literary elites found themselves held hostage to nationalist sentiment, Brussels provided writers with an alternative to Paris.

In the aftermath of the Franco-Prussian War, anti-German bias blinded the French to aesthetic innovation coming from across the Rhine. But Brussels celebrated Wagner, putting on *Lohengrin* in 1870 and becoming the capital of Wagnerism outside Germany. The aesthetic conformism of the Opéra Français led French composers who had been rejected in Paris to turn to Belgium—among them Jules Massenet, whose *Hérodiade* was an immense success in 1881. Vincent d'Indy settled in Brussels, where he received an enthusiastic welcome. The Cercle des XX, founded in 1883 by a group of young independent painters for the purpose of advancing new artistic ideas, helped artists from all over the world show their work. The *Vingtistes,* as they were known, offered a welcome in Brussels to avant-garde movements in search of critical recognition, proposing a theoretical basis for their work and giving it legitimacy through reviews and exhibitions. It was in Brussels that the Impressionists, Neoimpressionists, and unknown artists such as Toulouse-Lautrec, Gauguin, and Van Gogh (who sold the only canvas that was to find a buyer during his lifetime there) made friends and won admirers. Neoimpressionism, very popular among Belgian painters, was especially commented on and praised (Félix Fénéon, the Paris correspondent of *L'Art Moderne,* was the first to promote the movement as a radical advance over Impressionism).

Similarly, in the hope of dispelling the influence of French realism on fictional aesthetics, Belgian writers lent their support to the Symbolist challenge that first emerged in France, reappropriating its techniques through the filter of Flemish mysticism (Maurice Maeterlinck, for example, translated Jan van Ruusbroec [1293–1381]) and German philosophy and poetry. Their cosmopolitanism—which is to say their bilingualism and cultural openness—allowed them to devise new approaches and even to anticipate the aesthetic innovations of French writers. Brussels very quickly became the capital of Symbolism: Mallarmé found exceptionally favorable conditions for publication there, as he later recounted in the poem "La remémoration d'amis belges" (Remembrance of Belgian Friends, 1899);[14] and Maeterlinck (acclaimed by Octave Mirbeau in a famous 1890 article in *Le Figaro* as the "new Shakespeare") invented Symbolist theater, subsequently popularized by Aurélien Lugné-Poë, a marginal stage director in Paris whose productions of Maeterlinck and Ibsen captured the attention of Belgian critics and theatergoers in 1893.

By supporting German artists in the face of French prejudice, as well as unrecognized French artists against the established avant-gardes in France (such as the Impressionists), and by championing English art and the pre-Raphaelites (admired by the Belgian practitioners of *art décoratif* in the 1890s), Belgian artists managed to avoid, bypass, or otherwise reduce the constant interference of Parisian authorities. The cosmopolitan openness of Brussels to artistic invention in Europe made it a workshop where some of the most important artistic revolutions of the late nineteenth century were able to be carried out, sheltered against the pressure of politics and the weight of tradition that made themselves felt in neighboring countries. In a sense Brussels had become a second Paris: as a claimant to artistic modernity in its own right, it was able to consecrate avant-gardes at a moment when the French capital was beginning to lose some of its special and autonomous character with the revival of ancient antagonisms and the growth of nationalist feeling.

TRANSLATION AS LITTÉRISATION

Translation is the foremost example of a particular type of consecration in the literary world.[15] Its true nature as a form of literary recognition (rather than a mere exchange of one language for another or a purely horizontal transfer that provides a useful measure of the volume of publishing transactions in the world) goes unrecognized on account of its apparent neutrality. Nonetheless it constitutes the principal means of access to the literary world for all writers outside the center. Translation is the major prize and weapon in international literary competition, an instrument whose use and purpose differ depending on the position of the translator with respect to the text translated—that is, on the relation between what are commonly called "source" and "target" languages.[16] We have already examined the literary inequality of languages, which gives rise, at least in part, to the inequality faced by participants in the world literary game. The analysis of translation therefore depends on the point of view adopted—that of the translator or of the author whose work is being translated—and on the relationship between the languages involved. The combination of these two factors determines the selection of cases that are examined in the present work.

For an impoverished target language, which is to say a language on the periphery that looks to import major works of literature,[17] translation is a way of gathering literary resources, of acquiring universal texts and thereby enriching an underfunded literature—in short, a way of diverting literary assets. The program of the German Romantics for translating the classics, carried out during the course of the nineteenth century, was an enterprise of this type, as I shall go on to show in greater detail. Works of great literary subversiveness, ones that leave a mark in the center, are often translated by writers who themselves are international and polyglot and who, determined to break with the norms of their native literary space, seek to introduce into their language the modernity of the center (whose domination they perpetuate by doing just this). Thus Danilo Kiš translated Hungarian poets (Ady, Petőfi, Radnoti), Russian poets (Mandelstam, Yesenin, Tsvetayeva), and French poets (Corneille, Baudelaire, Lautréamont, Verlaine, Prévert, Queneau) into Serbo-Croatian; Vergilio Ferreira introduced Sartre to Portuguese readers; Arno Schmidt translated Poe, Faulkner, and Joyce into German;[18] Borges translated Hart Crane, E. E. Cummings, Robert Penn Warren, and Faulkner into Spanish;[19] Nabokov translated Lewis Carroll into Russian; Daigaku Horiguchi imported works by Verlaine, Apollinaire, Jammes, Cocteau, and Morand into Japanese, thus helping to profoundly alter the aesthetic norms of a developing literary space; Dezsö Kosztolányi translated Shakespeare, Byron, Wilde, Baudelaire, and Verlaine into his native Hungarian. These intermediaries may be seen as having performed an opposite and complementary function to that of the international figures of the great capitals: instead of introducing the periphery to the center in order to consecrate it, they made the center (and what had already been consecrated there) known in the periphery by translating its major productions. By importing to their own countries the modernity decreed at the Greenwich meridian, they played an essential role in the process of unifying literary space.

Considering the same operation from the point of view of a major source language, translation permits the international diffusion of central literary capital.[20] By extending the power and prestige of the great literary countries, with the assistance of polyglot writers in small countries, it broadens the influence of languages and literatures that pretend to universality and thus adds to their supply of credit. Additionally, it disseminates the aesthetic norms prevailing in the center, albeit with a delay, since translation itself takes time.

From the point of view of a major target language, on the other hand, the importation of literary texts written in "small" languages or ones belonging to neglected literatures serves as a means of annexation, of diverting peripheral works and adding them to the stock of central resources: universal capital increases, as Valéry observed, thanks to the activity of the great consecrating translators. The domination that they exert requires them, almost as a matter of noblesse oblige one might say, to "discover" nonnative writers who suit their literary categories. But from the point of view of a minor source language, this operation involves much more than a simple exchange of texts: it amounts, in fact, to acceding to the status of literature, to obtaining a certificate of literary standing. It is this form of translation—as consecration—that interests us here.

The notion of literariness, which is to say the literary credit that attaches to a language independently of its strictly linguistic capital, makes it possible to consider the translation of dominated authors as an act of consecration that gives them access to literary visibility and existence. Writers from languages that are not recognized (or are recognized only to a small degree) as literary are not immediately eligible for consecration. The condition of their works' being received into the literary world is translation into a major literary language. For translation is not simply a form of naturalization (in the sense of exchanging one nationality for another), or the passage from one language to another; it is, much more specifically, a *littérisation*. The writers of the Latin American "boom," for example, began to exist in international literary space only with their translation into French and their recognition by French critics. For the same reason Jorge Luis Borges claimed to be an invention of France. The international recognition of Danilo Kiš coincided with his consecration via translation into French, which lifted him out of the shadow of his native Serbo-Croatian. The universal recognition of Rabindranath Tagore—symbolized by his Nobel Prize—dated from the Bengali poet's translation of his own work into English. The Zairean writer and intellectual Pius Ngandu Nkashama has emphasized, while at the same time denying, the central role of translation in assuring consecration for African writers: "The failing of African authors has often been to believe that a literary text has value only if it has been accredited as such by a magnanimous West . . . It is as though an author in an African language objectively attains literary status only from the moment that he produces a text in other languages, in this case those of the colonizer . . . A moral credit can be granted him on the basis of translations duly authorized in the world."[21]

To define the translation of dominated authors as *littérisation,* which is to say as an actual metamorphosis, a change of literary being, makes it possible to resolve a whole series of problems generated by the belief in the equality—or, better, the symmetry—of different types of translation, uniformly conceived as simple transfers of meaning from one language to another. Literary transmutation is achieved by crossing a magic frontier that allows a text composed in an unprestigious language—or even a nonliterary language, which is to say one that either does not exist or is unrecognized in the verbal marketplace—to pass into a literary language. Accordingly, I define *littérisation* as any operation—translation, self-translation, transcription, direct composition in the dominant language—by means of which a text from a literarily deprived country comes to be regarded as literary by the legitimate authorities. No matter the language in which they are written, these texts must in one fashion or another be translated if they are to obtain a certificate of literariness. Salman Rushdie, who as an English-speaking Indian writer would appear not to have to concern himself with the problem of translation, nonetheless insists upon a sort of constitutive element of self-translation in the act of writing: "The word 'translation' comes, etymologically, from the Latin for 'bearing across.' Having been borne across the world, we are translated men. It is normally supposed that something always gets lost in translation; I cling, obstinately, to the notion that something can also be gained."[22]

The transmutation and translation of literary texts represents a gamut of strategies—a continuum of solutions to the problem of escaping literary destitution and invisibility. In the careers of many writers, looking at the successive stages of their consecration, it is possible to detect all the ways in which the conditions for achieving visibility laid down by the consecrating authorities cause texts to be transformed. For Strindberg it was not a question of writing in French for its own sake, or of being translated into French, any more than it was for Joyce. What mattered to each of them was advancing to the status of a writer—a practitioner of literature—through the adoption, directly or via translation, of a language that was considered to be the incarnation of literature par excellence.

LANGUAGE GAMES

August Strindberg's various attempts to achieve fame in France can be seen as a sort of paradigm of *littérisation*. Resolved from the beginning of his exile in 1883 (at the age of thirty-four) to "conquer" Paris, Strindberg explored the whole range of possibilities for obtaining literary recognition.[23] Although his earliest plays and collections of stories had been rapidly translated into French, they met with no response in Paris. In his first years there, having few friends and fewer contacts, he saw no alternative but to act as his own translator. With the opening of the Théâtre-Libre in 1887, Strindberg hoped that Émile Zola could be persuaded to read his new play *Fadren* (The Father).[24] A little later Strindberg met a translator, Georges Loiseau, with whom he began to collaborate. Thus self-translation was followed by assisted translation, a second stage in which the writer continues to take an active part in rewriting his text in the hope of bringing his work to the attention of a broad public. Strindberg managed at last to attract interest in theatrical circles: on the heels of Antoine's production of *Fröken Julie* (Miss Julie, 1887) at the Théâtre-Libre in 1893, *Fordringsägare* (Creditors, 1888) was successfully staged by Lugné-Poë the following year in a translation credited to Loiseau but based on Strindberg's own version. Finally, somewhat embarrassed no doubt by the need to rely on a translator, Strindberg decided to write directly in French. He composed a few short stories and tales and then, in 1887, *Le plaidoyer d'un fou* (The Confession of a Fool), in which he sought to compete with French novelists by emulating the "light" style of Maupassant.[25]

To Edvard Brandes, brother of the critic Georg Brandes and himself an influential journalist, he explained his situation: "Do I intend to become a French writer? No! I only make use of French for want of a universal language and I will continue to do so when I write."[26] French served solely as an access ramp to literature for Strindberg.[27] Indeed, his present-day editor and translator in France, Carl Bjurström, notes that Strindberg had no particular fondness for the French language. In the event his strategy proved effective: *The Confession of a Fool* found a publisher in Paris in 1895, having already been translated and successfully published in Germany. Then, in 1896–97, Strindberg wrote *Inferno* in French and published it to great acclaim with *Mercure de France* in 1898. It was only once he became famous that he abandoned writing in French. In other words, once literary existence and visibility have been achieved, translation again becomes a simple matter of carrying a text over from one language to another; at this point the writer from an outlying country can begin writing in his native tongue again, free from the need to work directly in the dominant language.

By the end of the 1890s, then, Strindberg had solved the problem of translation by adopting the most radical solution possible: writing in French. At about the same time, as we have seen, Rubén Darío devised a not dissimilar solution, namely to give Spanish a French cast, in effect fusing the two languages through the technique of "mental Gallicism." In this case, the invention of a sort of hybrid language made it possible to get around the translation problem. Self-translation represents an intermediate position between the two. One of the greatest self-translators, of course, was Vladimir Nabokov. Like Strindberg, he came gradually to reject the idea of having to rely on intermediaries, preferring to publish his own translations of himself.

Nabokov was a Russian writer until the eve of the Second World War. Between 1919 and 1921 around a million people had fled Russia, a great many intellectuals among them. Nabokov's family left St. Petersburg in 1920 and settled in Berlin, which became the intellectual center of the Russian disapora in its first decade. Weimar Germany counted some forty Russian publishing houses during the 1920s as well as a great many newspapers and magazines.[28] The young Nabokov, who was fluent in both English and French as well, published his first stories and poems in Berlin, in Russian, notably in the daily paper *Roul* and in various reviews. His first two novels, *Mashen'ka* (Mary, 1926) and *Korol, dama, valet* (King, Queen, Knave, 1928), were also published in Germany.

By the beginning of the 1930s, Paris had taken over from Berlin as the capital of the Russian émigré community.[29] Its most prestigious review, *Sovremennyia Zapiski* (Contemporary Annals), which in the meantime had moved there from Germany as well, agreed to publish Nabokov's new novel, *Zashchita Luzhina* (The Defense, 1930), in three installments. Russian critics greeted it with hostility. But then, with the publication of an enthusiastic review in the 15 February 1930 issue of *Les Nouvelles*

Littéraires by the French critic André Levinson, the situation suddenly changed. In the space of a week, and even before the original Russian version of the novel had appeared in its entirety, Nabokov signed a contract with Fayard for the French translation.[30] Recognition in France allowed him to cross the Rhine without leaving Berlin and at the same time to escape the anathema of Russian critical opinion.

Nonetheless he found it hard to make a living and continued to publish his work in *Sovremennyia Zapiski* as well as *Poslednie Novosti,* the leading Russian daily newspaper in Paris and the largest title of the émigré press—his only sources of money from writing.[31] His novel *Kamera Obskura* appeared first in serial form in 1932,[32] and then in a French edition two years later with Grasset as *Chambre obscure.* This translation brought him further recognition and led to others: shortly afterward he signed contracts for Swedish, Czech, and English versions of his novels. But in 1935, reviewing the English version of *Kamera Obskura,*[33] he discovered its mediocrity: "It was loose, shapeless, sloppy, full of blunders and gaps, lacking vigor and spring, and plumped down in such dull, flat English that I could not read it to the end; all of which is rather hard on an author who aims in his work at absolute precision, takes the utmost trouble to obtain it, and then finds the translator calmly undoing every blessed phrase."[34] Nabokov nonetheless approved the translation, in order not to forgo his first opportunity of being published in English, while resolving to translate his next book, *Otchaianie* (Despair, 1936), himself. Already he seems to have understood, as an author writing in a dominated language and lacking national support, that if he wished to exist literarily in Europe he had no choice but to act as his own translator.

Like E. M. Cioran, Panait Istrati, Strindberg, and many others, Nabokov found rewriting his work in another language a terrible ordeal: "To translate oneself is a frightful business, looking over one's insides and trying them on like a glove, and discovering the best dictionary to be not a friend but the enemy camp."[35] *Despair,* which appeared in England with a publisher of popular novels, went as unnoticed as *Camera Obscura.* But in 1937 he signed a contract with Gallimard for a French edition on the basis of the English translation[36]—as if, paradoxically, he hoped to be able to assure a greater degree of fidelity by insisting upon a translation that he had personally supervised into a language more widely read than Russian. It was also in Paris that Nabokov began his first novel to be written in English, *The Real Life of Sebastian Knight*. After almost twenty years of various attempts to affirm his identity as a Russian author, he found himself confronted with the same dilemmas as all exiled writers. By the late 1930s all hope of returning to Russia had vanished, and he could not hope to make a living by his pen if this meant writing for a public as narrow and as dispersed as the Russian émigré community. In order to attain genuine literary existence and recognition, he had to "carry over" his work into one of the two great literary languages he knew. For a time he hoped to settle in France, but financial and administrative problems combined to make life difficult for him there. In any case his English was better than his French, and with the approach of war in Europe he chose to seek refuge in America. Aside from "Mademoiselle O" and an essay on Pushkin ("Pouchkine ou le vrai et le vraisemblable"), he wrote nothing directly in French.

Nabokov set out for the United States in 1940 and almost at once became an English-language writer: *The Real Life of Sebastian Knight* was published in New York in 1941, with the support of Delmore Schwartz, by the avant-garde publishing house New Directions. But literary recognition and success were still to come from Paris. *Lolita,* which seemed an unbearable provocation in the puritanical atmosphere of postwar America, appeared in Paris in 1955 between the green covers of Maurice Girodias' Olympia Press following rejection by four American publishers—much as Joyce's scandalous *Ulysses* had been published in Paris in the 1920s in defiance of the diktats of moral censorship, first in English and then in a French translation. Hounded by French censors, delayed by trials and English customs, and crowned by a *succès de scandale,* the book was finally published in the United States three years later, in 1958. Nabokov, who until then had been an American author of no great notoriety, suddenly enjoyed an immense international reputation. All this goes to show that he did not, as is often said, have two lives as a writer, one in each of his two literary languages. He knew the difficult fate of all exiled and dominated writers who, in order to be able to exist literarily and to attain true creative autonomy—which is to say, to avoid dependence on unsupervised translations—choose to become, in Rushdie's phrase, translated men.

Samuel Beckett, in the late 1940s, pioneered a novel solution: self-translation in both directions. It needs to be kept in mind that earlier, as a young Anglophone writer from Dublin, he had himself traversed all the stages just described. After having published a collection of stories, *More Pricks than Kicks* (1934), with Chatto and Windus in London—a book that was banned in Ireland and sold only five hundred copies— and a year later, at his own expense, a collection of poems, *Echo's Bones;* and after having submitted the manuscript of *Murphy* to forty-two English publishers in 1936 and 1937—the novel was finally published in 1938 by Routledge in London and translated into French by Beckett and Alfred Péron in 1947 for Éditions Bordas—Beckett looked for other ways to make himself known. Following the publication in *Les Temps Modernes* of a number of poems written in French, and the composition of *Watt* in English during the war,[37] he wrote several short stories directly in French. Then came his great creative period in Paris, during which he composed his first great works in French: in 1946 he wrote *Mercier et Camier* (Mercier and Camier), *Premier amour* (First Love, unpublished until 1970), *L'Expulsé* (The Expelled), and *Suite* (which became *La fin de partie, Endgame* in English); in 1947 he began *Molloy;* in 1948 he finished *Molloy,* wrote *Malone meurt* (Malone Dies), and sketched *En attendant Godot* (Waiting for Godot), which he reworked and completed in 1949, before beginning *L'Innommable* (The Unnameable).

Beckett knew that if he wished to have a chance of being published and seeing his plays performed in the theater he had no choice but to write in French: *En attendant Godot* (1952) and *Fin de partie,* dedicated to Roger Blin and first staged in London (in French) in 1957, finally permitted him to stake his claim to literary existence. But in following this almost canonical course Beckett adopted a strategy so radical that it stands without parallel in the history of literature: rather than choose one language over another, he resolved to remain the rest of his life a translated writer—only a self-translated writer, no longer dependent upon translators but working instead between two languages. Beckett's commitment to bilingualism reflected his determination to create a dual oeuvre: beginning in 1950 with his translation of *Textes pour rien* (Texts for Nothing, 1955) and then the following year of *Molloy* (1951),[38] he translated and rewrote almost everything from one language into the other, both from French into English and from English into French.

The infinitely diverse practice of self-translation is at least to some extent a way for authors to try to achieve literary freedom by retaining control over the form of their writings, and thus to claim an absolute autonomy. We know that Beckett was never, or only very seldom, willing to entrust his translations to others. Joyce, in *Finnegans Wake,* had already taken matters a step further, having got around the painful and apparently intractable problem of translation by composing a text that is effectively *untranslatable,* which is to say almost completely independent of linguistic, commercial, or national constraints.

Literary history as it is ordinarily conceived prevents us from understanding the crucial role played by translators in the international republic of letters. Since historians of literature restrict themselves—to simplify somewhat—to examining the particular (and typically dehistoricized) history of an individual author, or giving a general account of the development of a national literature, or else reviewing the history of the different interpretations ("readings") of a given text over time, the process of consecration and *littérisation*—authorized by critics and carried out by translators—is always passed over in silence, forgotten or simply ignored. It can be perceived only by looking at the general design of the structure of the world of letters, and at the balance of power inherent in this structure: thus the "pattern in the carpet" of which Henry James spoke. The work of a translator such as Valery Larbaud, who discovered a great many authors, who introduced Faulkner, Joyce, Butler, and Ramón Gómez de la Serna among others to readers in France—the work of this one man, as immense as it was invisible, profoundly changed and renewed world literature. It was the great translations of Faulkner's novels by Maurice-Edgar Coindreau that made his consecration and universal recognition possible; yet they go unmentioned in the official history of literature.[39] The translator, having become the indispensable intermediary for crossing the borders of the literary world, is an essential figure in the history of writing. The great translators of the central literary countries are the true architects of the universal, which is to say of the attempt to unify literary space.

Larbaud described himself as an "introducer and intermediary," a member of a "cosmopolitan clergy" that takes its motto from Saint Jerome: "A single religion, all languages."[40] The unitary religion in this case is literature—the handiwork of translators who create unity out of linguistic diversity. Indeed, the autonomy of translators from central literary spaces derives from their obedience to the literary law that prohibits submission to linguistic and political division. Larbaud, conscious of occupying an ignored yet essential place in the world of literature, sought to restore the dignity of the translator's labor. In establishing an impressive genealogy of French Anglicists, he recalled the most eminent names among the many bilingual poets and writers in France who facilitated the passage of texts from English to their native language and, by helping to strengthen the autonomy of these two great literary spaces, founded on mutual knowledge and reciprocal consecration, contributed to their gradual unification:

> It was Voltaire who started everything, who founded the venerable Order of Interpreters of English Thought. A truly venerable order since (to restrict ourselves to France) it counted, apart from its great representatives and its generations of specialists . . . illustrious writers and great poets such as Chateaubriand, Vigny, Hugo, Sainte-Beuve, Taine, Baudelaire, Laforgue, Mallarmé, and Marcel Schwob . . . But Voltaire . . . was the man on account of whom the great posthumous destiny of Shakespeare came to be realized, and the builder of the invisible bridge that linked the intellectual life of England with that of the continent. His achievement is unsurpassable.[41]

When self-translation is impossible, the translator assumes a key role, becoming almost a double, an alter ego, a substitute author responsible for carrying over a text from an unknown and unliterary language into the world of literature. Among the notable instances of authors and translators who have collaborated as inseparable partners in order to achieve literary status, the case of the Polish writer Witold Gombrowicz (1904–1969) stands out. Marooned on the eve of the Second World War in Argentina, where he was to remain for twenty-four years (from 1939 to 1964), he began—just as Strindberg had done before him, and as Beckett was to do afterward—by translating his own writings. In this way he was able to publish Spanish versions of his first novel, *Ferdydurke* (originally published in Warsaw in 1937), and a play, *Slub* (The Marriage), in 1947 in Buenos Aires. Then, at a new stage (or second degree) in the search for literary recognition, he translated *The Marriage* into French with the help of two Frenchwomen and sent the typescript to Albert Camus and Jean-Louis Barrault, as well as the Polish text to Martin Buber. In 1951 he became a contributor to *Kultura,* a Polish émigré review in Paris. The serialization in its pages of his second novel, *Trans-Atlantyk,* led to its publication in book form (though still in Polish, together with *Ślub*) in 1953 as part of the "Bibliothèque de Kultura," a series sponsored by the Institut Littéraire de Paris.

Gombrowicz knew that access to literature necessarily passed through Paris: "It seems that in Poland I am read on the sly," he wrote to his publisher Maurice Nadeau in 1957. "Good news at least. But it is from Paris that everything must start."[42] A few years earlier Gombrowicz had made the acquaintance of Constantin Jelenski, who rapidly became his intermediary, translator, and introducer in the French capital. A member of the secretariat of the Congrès pour la Liberté de la Culture and of the editorial board of the review *Preuves,* Jelenski was (to quote his countryman Francisek Karpiński) "effectively Gombrowicz's double."[43] He not only translated Gombrowicz's work but wrote prefaces and worked to promote it to a wider audience.[44] "Having smashed my Argentinian cage," Gombrowicz wrote in his diary, Jelenski "built me a bridge to Paris."[45] Elsewhere he added, "Each foreign-language edition of my books ought to bear the seal 'thanks to Jelenski.'"[46] From the time of Jelenski's first attempts to make him known in the early 1950s, Gombrowicz, although (or perhaps because) he lived in Argentina, understood that his chance to attain literary recognition lay with his agent across the Atlantic:

> Jelenski—who is he? He appeared on my horizon, over there, very far away, in Paris, and there he is, struggling for me. It has been a long time—never perhaps—since I have experienced so resolute, so disinterested a confirmation of what I am, of what I write . . . Jelenski defends me every step of the way before the Polish emigration authorities. He works to give me all the advantages offered by the situation he has created for himself in Paris and by his growing prestige in high intellectual circles. He takes my manuscripts around to publishers. He has already managed to win me a handful of supporters, and not the least ones.[47]

Considering the case of Gombrowicz and his passage from self-translation to remote collaboration with a translator and personal representative who became a sort of alter ego, acting abroad as his proxy and spokesman, it becomes clear that the problem of translation must be analyzed as a process of gradual emergence in which the writer himself may intervene, directly or indirectly, in a variety of different ways.[48]

If a writer finds himself obliged to engage the services of a translator, but nonetheless is fluent enough in the target language to be able to revise a translator's draft, it very often happens—as we saw in the case of Strindberg—that he assumes an active role in the translation of his own work. This was particularly true of Joyce, who found in Valery Larbaud at once an introducer, a translator, and a unique source of literary legitimacy. Larbaud had read the first episodes of *Ulysses* published in the *Little Review* with enthusiasm. It was the prestige of his name in Parisian literary circles, his willingness to translate the book himself (in the end, to supervise the translation), and his December 1921 public lecture at the Maison des Amis des Livres (many times reprinted and even translated into English for *The Criterion*—further proof that consecration in Paris was the condition of existing literarily elsewhere) that persuaded Sylvia Beach to transform Shakespeare and Company into a publishing house for the sole purpose of bringing out *Ulysses* in its original version, and then Adrienne Monnier to commission a French translation. Although Joyce's reputation was already great in Anglo-American literary circles—especially among American exiles in Paris—he found it impossible at the beginning of the 1920s to find a publisher for *Ulysses:* his writings were considered scandalous and until then had been brought out by small houses that subsequently found themselves the target of British and American censors. Four issues of the *Little Review* (in which the novel appeared in installments between 1918 and 1920) were seized and burned for obscenity by the U.S. Post Office until finally the New York Society for the Suppression of Vice succeeded in having publication prohibited altogether.[49] It was therefore thanks to the literary authorities of Paris that *Ulysses* enjoyed a dual publication; but the book found an English-language publisher only as a consequence of the critical verdict of a great translator.

Despite Larbaud's central and active role in this process of consecration and ennoblement, Joyce refused to leave matters wholly to his judgment. The translators of *Ulysses*—Auguste Morel and Stuart Gilbert, supervised by Larbaud—all found their work subject to review by the author. The title page of the definitive version published in Paris by Adrienne Monnier in 1929 instituted a subtle hierarchy among the participants while confiding the major role to the author: "Unabridged French translation by M. Auguste Morel, assisted by M. Stuart Gilbert, entirely revised by Valery Larbaud and the author." Similar control was exerted over Beckett during his first stay in Paris the same year. At Joyce's request he worked on the French translation of "Anna Livia Plurabelle," one of the most celebrated sections of the *Work in Progress,* in collaboration with Alfred Péron, whom he had met at Trinity College, Dublin, some years earlier. Their text met with the approval of the author, who was about to send it to the printer for the next issue of the *Nouvelle Revue Française* when he happened to show it to three of his friends, Philippe Soupault, Paul Léon, and Ivan Goll. Gradually the translation came to be challenged, reworked, then entirely revised. It appeared in May 1931 in volume 19 of the *NRF* under the names of Samuel Beckett, Alfred Péron, Ivan Goll, Eugène Jolas, Paul Léon, Adrienne Monnier, and Philippe Soupault, "in collaboration with the author."[50]

It is plain that translation into French, owing to Paris' unique power of consecration, occupies a special place in the literary world. Paradoxically, however, it does not require a corresponding belief in the importance of French literature or the French language as such; indeed, neither Joyce nor Strindberg nor Beckett took any interest whatever in French literary life. But the prestige of translation into French had been unquestioned since the eighteenth century. While no one would dream of denying that English literature has been one of the most important in Europe for at least as long, or that it has strongly influenced the whole of European (and especially French) literature, the fact remains that the greatest English authors enjoyed truly universal recognition during the eighteenth and nineteenth centuries only through the translation of their writings into French. Shakespeare was read throughout Europe in Le Tourneur's translations; Byron and Moore in Pichot's versions, Sterne in that of Fresnais, Richardson in that of Prévost. From 1814 (the year *Waverley* was published) until Walter Scott's death in 1832, his novels were translated into French by Defauconpret as they appeared: it was to these versions that they owed their immense worldwide fame. Scott's novels were read either in French or in translations based on the French version. Thus, for example, the entire series of *Waverley* novels was translated after 1830 from French into Spanish.

THE IMPORTANCE OF BEING UNIVERSAL
Literary prizes, the least literary form of literary consecration, are responsible mainly for making the verdicts of the sanctioning organs of the republic of letters known beyond its borders. As the most apparent

of the mechanisms of consecration, they represent a sort of confirmation for the benefit of the general public. Nonetheless, in keeping with the laws of world literature, the more international the prize, the more specific it is. Thus the greatest proof of literary consecration, bordering on the definition of literary art itself, is the Nobel Prize—a European award established at the beginning of the twentieth century that gradually came to enjoy worldwide authority. Today writers everywhere are agreed in recognizing it as the highest honor of the world of letters. There is no better measure of the unification of the international literary field than the effectively universal respect commanded by this prize.

It is also indisputably the most prestigious prize beyond the borders of the literary world. For more than one hundred years now, the Nobel has been the virtually unchallenged arbiter of literary excellence. No one (or almost no one) professes any longer to be surprised at the esteem in which this institution is everywhere held,[51] nor does anyone doubt the validity of the worldwide reputation that it confers upon a single writer each year. By agreeing to act as executor of the provisions of Alfred Nobel's will, the Swedish Academy assumed responsibility for an enterprise that might well have failed or else been dismissed on all sides as a relic of Scandinavian provincialism; since the announcement of the first prize in 1901, however, the Academy's judgments have met instead with remarkable and uninterrupted approval. Over time, its juries managed not only to establish themselves as arbiters of literary legitimacy but also to preserve their monopoly on worldwide literary consecration.[52]

The importance of the prize in helping to accumulate a national stock of literary capital is now so great that South Korea has mounted a campaign on behalf of its writers. The country's press speaks of "the obsession with the Nobel," and in the largest bookstore in Seoul one sees authors advertised as "the future Korean Nobel Prize winner."[53] There is even talk of creating a review exclusively devoted to pursuit of the prize.[54] The official candidate, Pak Kyong-ni (b. 1927), author of the immensely popular roman-fleuve *T'oji* (Land, 16 vols., 1969–1994), is a monumental figure.

Chinese writers, who have long found themselves shut off from the literary world in a state of quasi-autarky, met a few years ago to decide upon a national strategy aimed at presenting candidates and winning at least one prize by the end of the century. One of them was quoted in the Swedish press as protesting: "Among the thousands of writers in a

Chinese population of almost a billion people, not one has won the Nobel Prize!"[55] The prize awarded in 2000 to a Chinese dissident living in
France, Gao Xingjian, only very partially satisfied these demands: the
first Nobel honoring a Chinese-language writer went to an exile and a
French citizen. It hardly comes as a surprise, then, that China does not
regard it as evidence of national recognition.

The sense of entitlement to the Nobel Prize in Literature has taken a
similar form in the Portuguese-speaking world. Jorge Amado addressed
the matter in an interview not long ago:

> I think that a Nobel is owed to the Portuguese language, which has
> never had a single Nobel Prize. Not that I think that the Nobel makes
> literature: it is writers who make the Nobel and not the Nobel that
> makes writers. But I find it sad that a man such as Guimarães Rosa
> should have died without having won the Nobel Prize, that Carlos
> Drummond de Andrade [and other] great Portuguese writers should
> have died without winning the Nobel. There is in Portugal a man
> eighty and some years of age who is a great Portuguese poet, named
> Miguel Torga, who is a thousand times deserving of the Nobel and
> who has not received it. This is to be deplored. But my opinion counts
> for nothing in all of this. Personally, it doesn't matter to me at all, I can
> assure you.[56]

The Nobel awarded to the Portuguese novelist José Saramago in 1998
served to remedy this injustice.[57]

Having put itself in the difficult position of acting as an impartial tribunal whose judgments will be universally accepted as legitimate, the
Academy finds itself forced to rigorously establish standards of criteria of
literary excellence and to openly acknowledge the consequences for the
unification of world literary space of supporting international writers in
their struggles with national writers. Indeed, the history of the prize
since its inception can be seen as an ongoing attempt to develop explicit
standards of universality. Within the Nobel committee itself, the only really decisive disagreements have been over the endorsement or rejection
of this or that criterion for awarding the prize.[58] The effect of the committee's work over the past century has been to broaden the prevailing
conceptions of literary universality, which have been enriched at each
stage by the prior deliberations of the members of the Academy.

In the early years the governing criteria were political, reflecting the most heteronomous notions of literary value. Thus the first definition of legitimate literary art, a quite minimal one, identified it with political neutrality, a sort of *juste milieu* devised before the war of 1914–1918 as a counterweight to the nationalist "excesses" of the literature of the day and, above all, out of respect for the perceived necessity of exercising diplomatic caution. A perfect illustration of this conception is the interest shown by the jury in 1914 in the candidacy of the Swiss—and therefore supposedly neutral—writer Carl Spitteler (in the event the prize was awarded to him only after the war, in 1919). Two decades later, in 1939, the academy's circumspect deference to the "ideal of peace" upheld by Alfred Nobel in his will establishing the prize produced the same situation. Only three candidates were considered that year, all of them from neutral countries: Hermann Hesse, a nationalized Swiss; F. E. Sillanpää, a Finn; and Johan Huizinga, a Dutchman. This ideal—whose political character is proof of the jury's relative lack of autonomy in the early years—was set up as a supreme artistic value, the embodiment of reason and moderation. It found its literary equivalent logically enough in what Nobel in his will called "idealism," initially interpreted by the prize committee as a sort of aesthetic academicism privileging "balance," "harmony," and "pure and noble ideas" in narrative art.[59]

Beginning in the 1920s, however, in order to free itself from a conception that was felt to be too closely associated with political events, the Academy sought to promote another sort of neutrality. Henceforth works deserving of the Nobel Prize—of being universalized—were stipulated to be ones whose national character was neither too pronounced nor too much insisted upon. Quite early on, then, literary excellence was seen as being incompatible with what might be called cultural nationalism. Already in 1915 the committee had proposed the candidacy of the Spanish writer Benito Pérez Galdós (1843–1920) on the grounds that he "presents himself as the supporter not of a party but of general patriotism" and that there is "something typical" about his characters that "makes them more comprehensible to those readers not familiar with Spanish characteristics." In 1929, by contrast, the candidacy of the German poet Arno Holz (1863–1929) was challenged on the ground that his work was "too German": "here we have a purely German affair . . . the committee has not found his poetry of sufficient universal interest." The prize awarded to Anatole France in 1921 may be understood in the same sense, only now no longer in the name of political neutrality but of active engagement against nationalism and anti-semitism: "In the Dreyfus affair he stood in the front rank of those who defended justice against misguided chauvinism."[60]

A third criterion, advanced a little bit later, built in another dimension: the public reception of a work. The first sign of the success of the prize, and its echo throughout the world, was that universality was now interpreted as unanimity. From now on a work worthy of the Nobel had to be accessible to the broadest possible audience. Thus Paul Valéry was eliminated from consideration in 1930 because the committee felt unable "to recommend for the universally intended Nobel prize a poetry so exclusive and inaccessible."[61] This submission of literary judgment to the taste of the greatest number heralded the formation of a third pole essential for understanding the structure of the world field, namely economic forces, which were strengthened by the emergence of powerful national markets.

In addition to these competing criteria, there was pressure at each stage of the progressive enlargement of the literary universe, from the beginning of the century onward, to recognize the international dimension of universality. Opening the field to new contestants, which is to say to new types of literary capital, was done only with great reluctance. Precisely because it touched the very foundations of the literary ideology on which the Nobel Prize had been built, the need to devise new criteria in order to break free of the academy's European-centered definition of literature was long resisted.

The first attempt to move beyond Europe, a considerable one, came early, with the awarding of the prize in 1913 to Rabindranath Tagore, the great Bengali-speaking Indian poet. The presence among the laureates on the eve of the First World War of an author from a colonized country would appear to be a clear sign of great daring and extraordinary independence of mind on the part of the Swedish Academy, were it not for the fact that this unexpected honor was actually the result of ingrained prejudice reinforced by colonial narcissism. Tagore had not been recommended to the committee by a fellow Indian; instead he was proposed by a member of the Royal Society of Literature in London, solely on the basis of an English version of the *Gitanjali* (partially translated by Tagore himself).[62]

The United States did not make its entry until almost two decades later, with the award of the prize to Sinclair Lewis in 1930 (followed by Eugene O'Neill in 1936 and Pearl Buck in 1938); but it was considered, not unreasonably, as a European offshoot. Similarly, it was not until 1945 that the Latin branch of American literature was recognized. The award of the prize that year to the Chilean poet Gabriela Mistral amounted to little more than lip service to the idea of a genuinely worldwide literature, however, crowning as it did a very traditional body of work closely associated with European models. Only with the honoring in 1967 of the Guatemalan writer Miguel Ángel Asturias was there any real awareness of the novelty of the Latin American novel and of the break with older forms that it represented. With these two exceptions, the prize remained the exclusive province of Europeans and Americans during this entire period. Then in 1968 the Nobel committee suddenly turned to the Far East, awarding the prize to Yasunari Kawabata, who, the judges noted in their citation, "with great sensibility expresses the essence of the Japanese mind."[63] Yet it was to be another two decades before the first African and Arab writers were recognized: Wole Soyinka, in 1986; and Naguib Mahfouz, in 1988.

The dominant position of the Nobel Prize in the pyramid of literary recognition and publication is the outstanding feature of a system that permanently accords the work of European authors a central position while relegating to the periphery everything that comes from other parts of the world.[64] Although the problem of internationalizing the prize presented itself fairly early on, in the 1920s (Tagore having only been an apparent exception in 1913), for many years nothing really changed. When the Nobel committee has dared to venture into the non-Western literary world—until quite recently a rare event—its explorations have exactly coincided with the stages by which the world of letters has come to be enlarged.

For this reason the choice of Gao Xingjian in 2000 is an interesting development. It signals, to be sure, the openness of the committee to a new linguistic and cultural area—an immense and, until then, completely neglected area—but it is also fully in agreement with the definition of literary autonomy current at the Greenwich meridian. Gao is not, as the international press would have it, a political dissident. He is a literary dissident who long ago broke with the prevailing norms of his literary universe. A playwright, literary critic, and painter as well as a novelist, he has also translated into Chinese some of the greatest figures

in modern French literature—Michaux, Ponge, Perec, the Surrealist poets. He is, finally, the author of a critical essay on the techniques of the
modern novel, published in Beijing in 1981, which provoked great con-
troversy in Chinese literary circles.[65] By making use of Western literary
innovations and techniques and referring to the aesthetic norms of the
literary present (which, owing to his knowledge of French, he was able
surreptitiously to discover),[66] Gao encouraged the formation of an unprecedented position of autonomy in his native land—a country where
literature is almost entirely instrumentalized and subject to censorship.

Gao is, in other words, the incarnation of what earlier I called an international writer. Having sought refuge in France in 1988 and become
a naturalized French citizen ten years later, he is much more than simply
a Chinese-language novelist exiled in the West; he is also one of the first
to have managed to recreate his own tradition using nontraditional
forms. His magnificent novel *Ling Shan* (Soul Mountain), begun in
China in 1982 and finished in France in 1989, is thus at once a manifesto
of formal liberty and a precise evocation of traditional China.[67] Far from
crowning a "national" oeuvre that reflects a contemporary Chinese history and milieu, the Nobel Committee honored a genuinely autonomous body of work that, by integrating the norms of literary modernity
(inevitably Western, given the configuration of literary power relations
today), has been able to reconceive, in the Chinese language, the forms
of an older Chinese literature. In no way, then, can the Nobel committee
be said to have made a political or diplomatic choice. Its decision in this
case was truly free, literary, and literarily courageous.

The various criteria governing the academy's selections did not in
fact emerge in strict succession, one after the other. Instead they co-
existed and jointly evolved over time—occasionally even reasserting
themselves, just when they were thought to have been rejected, in the
defense of a particular work. The fourth and final definition of universality was laid down after 1945, when the Academy announced its intention to include "pioneers of literary art" among the list of honorees. The
criterion of the greatest number was set aside and in its place a sort of
pantheon of the avant-garde and "future classics" was established, her-
alding a period of remarkable critical activity on the part of the Nobel
selection committees. It was rather as though, due consideration having
at last been given to innovation in literary art, the universality decreed

and upheld by the Swedish judges was now constructed in opposition to the conservative influence of national academies, on the one hand, and to the most leveling conceptions of literary appeal on the other. Thus T. S. Eliot was elected in 1948 "for his outstanding, pioneer contribution to present-day poetry"; Faulkner won the prize the following year, recognized by the jury as "the great experimentalist among twentieth century novelists," though he was still very little known to the general public (and almost unknown in his own country).[68] Samuel Beckett received it in 1969 for an exceptionally original body of work that was then far from finished. Other innovators were to follow, among them Pablo Neruda in 1971, Eugenio Montale in 1975, Jaroslav Seifert in 1984, Claude Simon in 1985, and Dario Fo in 1997.

This new degree of autonomy came about as a result of the structural complementarity obtaining between the Nobel Prize and the power of consecration enjoyed by Paris. In effect, the Academy affirmed (or reaffirmed) the verdicts of the capital of literature and, as it were, grounded them in law: by making these decisions official, the Swedish Academy—with few exceptions at least through the 1960s—endorsed, ratified, and made public the judgments of Paris, consecrating those writers who had been discovered and promoted by its publishers and critics. Testifying to this state of affairs is not only the large number of French authors on the list of winners (France remains the most regularly honored nation, with twelve prizes—fourteen if one includes Beckett, officially counted as an Irish national, and Gao Xingjian) but also, and above all, the prizes awarded to Faulkner, Hemingway, Asturias, and García Márquez, all of whom were first discovered and celebrated in France. Approval by the literary authorities of Paris (rivaled, of course, by their counterparts in London, who managed to achieve recognition for many of their own authors—Kipling, Tagore, Yeats, Shaw, and so on) has long been an essential first step in presenting oneself as a candidate for the highest and the most international award in the world of literature. Sartre's refusal to accept the Nobel in 1964 supplies additional evidence of the redundancy of Swedish recognition in the aftermath of consecration by Paris. He was one of the few persons in world literary space who, as a central figure in the capital, and one who himself had already been honored to an extraordinary degree, could do without the prize, a circumstance that only reaffirmed his eminent position.

ETHNOCENTRISMS

The authority of the great literary capitals is not unambiguous, however. The power to evaluate and transmute a text into literature is also, and almost inevitably, exerted according to the norms of those who judge. It involves two things that are inseparably linked: celebration and annexation. Together they form a perfect example of what might be called Parisianization, or universalization through denial of difference. The great consecrating nations reduce foreign works of literature to their own categories of perception, which they mistake for universal norms, while neglecting all the elements of historical, cultural, political, and especially literary context that make it possible to properly and fully appreciate such works. In so doing they exact a sort of *octroi* tax on the right to universal circulation. As a result, the history of literary celebration amounts to a long series of misunderstandings and misinterpretations that have their roots in the ethnocentrism of the dominant authorities (notably those in Paris) and in the mechanism of annexation (by which works from outlying areas are subordinated to the aesthetic, historical, political, and formal categories of the center) that operates through the very act of literary recognition.[69] Translation therefore stands revealed as an ambiguous enterprise as well: on the one hand, it is a means of obtaining official entry to the republic of letters; and, on the other, it is a way of systematically imposing the categories of the center upon works from the periphery, even of unilaterally deciding the meaning of such works. In this sense the notion of universality is one of the most diabolical inventions of the center, for in denying the antagonistic and hierarchical structure of the world, and proclaiming the equality of all the citizens of the republic of letters, the monopolists of universality command others to submit to their law. Universality is what they—and they alone—declare to be acceptable and accessible to all.

The full extent of the ambiguity associated with the process of consecration is magnificently condensed in the story of how James Joyce's talent came to be recognized by Valery Larbaud. The special attention paid to Joyce by the high literary authorities of Paris aroused the ire of an Irish critic named Ernest Boyd, who violently attacked Larbaud for his "colossal ignorance of Irish literature" and his "complete ignorance of the great Anglo-Irish writers," among whom he mentioned Synge, George Moore, and Yeats.[70] Citing Larbaud's 1921 lecture, in which he asserted that "to write in Irish would be as though a contemporary

French author were to write in modern Breton,"[71] Boyd took the French critic to task—rightly so in this case—for misunderstanding the national literary revival in Ireland and interpreted his remarks as an attack on the identity of Irish literature and its distinctive place among the literatures of the English-speaking world.[72] To this declaration of national interest, Larbaud memorably replied: "It is not at all by chance or on account of a whim or some ill-considered enthusiasm that, having gained entrance to this room filled with treasures, *Ulysses,* I set about making it known to the elite of French letters . . . My sole merit is to have been the first outside the English domain to say without hesitation that James Joyce is a great writer and *Ulysses* a very great book, and this at a moment when nobody *in Ireland* had said it."[73] Here, in one of their very rare direct encounters, one sees the battle between the national view of literature and the dehistoricizing impulse—and through this the annexation effected by French consecration, which, although it unarguably served to ennoble, internationalize, and universalize, at the same time ignored everything that made the emergence of such a work possible. Paris, the denationalized capital of literature, denationalized texts so that they would conform to its own conceptions of literary art.

In the same way, by variously interpreting the work of Franz Kafka in metaphysical, psychoanalytical, aesthetic, religious, social, or political terms, critics in the center (many of them in Paris) give evidence of a specific form of blindness: through an almost deliberate ignorance of history, they make themselves vulnerable to anachronistic readings that reveal the structural ethnocentrism of the literary world. Marthe Robert, who was one of the first to propose a historical analysis of Kafka's work, has magnificently summarized the thoroughgoing dehistoricization practiced by Parisian critics:

> Since Kafka appeared to be exempt from all geographical and historical influence, there was no hesitation in adopting him—one might almost say "naturalizing" him, for indeed there was a sort of process of naturalization at work that gave birth to a French Kafka, nearer to us, to be sure, but no longer having anything more than a distant relation to the true [Kafka] . . . Since Kafka no longer retained any trace of his actual origins, beyond the fact that he was a human being like anyone else, he came quite naturally to be accorded a sort of right of extraterritoriality, thanks to which his person and his work (in exchange, it is true, for their real existence) ended up being granted a degree of per-

fection and purity enjoyed only by abstract things. This right of extra-territoriality was at bottom a heavenly privilege: coming from no-where and belonging to everyone, Kafka quite naturally gave the impression of having fallen from the sky, even to French writers and critics, who were the least inclined to look upward in search of a higher standard.[74]

More recently, the critical benediction bestowed upon Patrick Chamoiseau and Raphaël Confiant—the Martinican novelists of "Cre-oleness"—has demonstrated the power of consecration by the center to depoliticize politically dominated writers, preventing them from formu-lating political or national demands. Such recognition is at once a neces-sary form of autonomy and a form of ethnocentric annexation that de-nies the historical existence of those who are consecrated. Thus the Nigerian novelist Chinua Achebe took issue with the American critic Charles R. Larson,[75] who claimed to be able to discern the universal character of a Gambian novel solely on the ground that, certain substitu-tions having been made, it could easily pass for a work by an American author:

> Does it ever occur to these [academics] to try out their game of changing names of characters and places in an American novel, say, a Philip Roth or an Updike, and slotting in African names just to see how it works? But of course it would not occur to them. It would never occur to them to doubt the universality of their own literature. In the nature of things the work of a Western writer is automatically informed by universality. It is only others who must strain to achieve it . . . I should like to see the word "universal" banned altogether from discussions of African literature until such time as people cease to use it as a synonym for the narrow, self-serving parochialism of Europe, until their horizon extends to include all the world.[76]

In order to achieve literary recognition, dominated writers must therefore yield to the norms decreed to be universal by the very persons who have a monopoly on universality. More than this, they need to situ-ate themselves at just the right distance from their judges: if they wish to be noticed, they have to show that they are different from other writ-ers—but not so different that they are thereby rendered invisible. They must be neither too near nor too far. All writers from countries under the linguistic domination of France have had this experience. Charles

Ferdinand Ramuz, for example, remained imperceptible so long as he tried to appear as though he belonged to the world of French letters; it was only after he proclaimed his separateness as a Swiss writer from the canton of Vaud that he was recognized. In a letter to his publisher, Bernard Grasset, he summed up the problem perfectly: "It is the fate of my country, everything considered, to be at once too similar and too different, too close and yet not close enough—to be too French or not enough; for either one ignores it, or, when one knows it, one no longer knows quite what to make of it."[77] It is precisely this inherent ethnocentrism that produces all literary exoticisms. In an article devoted to the Spanish writer Ramón Gómez de la Serna, published in the *Nouvelle Revue Française* in 1924, Jean Cassou lucidly analyzed the principal mistakes made by the French critical authorities: "We ask foreigners to surprise us, but in a manner we are almost prepared to indicate to them, as if their role were to serve, on behalf of their race, our pleasure."[78]

French Canadians had already understood this difficulty by the late nineteenth century. As the poet Octave Crémazie pointedly observed:

> If we spoke Huron or Iroquoian, the works of our writers would attract the attention of the Old World. This virile and muscular language, born in the forests of America, has that raw poetry of the wilderness about it that delights the foreigner. One would swoon over a novel or a poem translated from Iroquoian while not troubling oneself to read a book written in French by a colonist of Quebec or Montreal. For two decades now, translations have been published every year in France of Russian, Scandinavian, and Romanian novels. Supposing these same books were written in French, they would not find fifty readers."[79]

IBSEN IN ENGLAND AND IN FRANCE

The translation, interpretation, and consecration of Ibsen's work in England and France furnish a superb example of the different ways in which an author's work may be annexed by two literary capitals having discrepant interests in embracing it. The contrary significance attached to Ibsen's plays in London and Paris—seen as models of realism on one side of the Channel, of Symbolism on the other—shows that the consecration of a work is always an appropriation, a diversion of literary capital.

Henrik Ibsen (1828–1906) stands out as a central figure in European literary history between 1890 and 1920. Having almost in spite of himself become the symbol of modernity in European drama, Ibsen was read and performed in theaters throughout the world on the basis of diametrically opposed interpretations corresponding to the literary and aesthetic categories of those who consecrated him. Every director or critic pretending to have special understanding of Ibsen's plays, whose form and subject matter represented a considerable departure from the conventions of European theater at the time, used them for his own purposes and in ways that depended on the position he occupied in his own national literary space. Far from serving the author by presenting his work to audiences on its own terms, as all "discoverers" profess to do, directors and critics took advantage of Ibsen's relative weakness as a foreigner uninitiated in local literary politics in order to modify his work in ways that strengthened their own reputation.

This is why Ibsen was able to be interpreted in England, particularly by George Bernard Shaw, as a realist addressing concrete social problems in a novel fashion, and in France during the same years as a Symbolist conveying universal poetic insights. The characteristic ethnocentrism of these two great literary nations—particularly in the case of France and its intermediaries, who were especially blind to the historical conditions surrounding the appearance of literary works—acted upon a distinctive set of national preoccupations in each case to produce quite different patterns of consecration and annexation.

Ibsen was one of the leading figures of a national literary movement that sought independence not only from Danish domination, which Norway had endured for four centuries, but also from German tutelage, which more recently had provincialized its intellectual life. Literary debate in Norway in the mid-nineteenth century centered on the creation of a new language, based on the dialects of the western rural parts of the country, which was supposed to be more truly national to the extent that it was further removed from Dano-Norwegian, the consequence of Danish colonization. The *Landsmål*, or "country language" (known today as *Nynorsk,* or "new Norwegian"), which was brought into existence through the efforts of intellectuals and writers, soon won approval as a second official language alongside *Riksmål,* the "state language" (currently called *Bokmål,* or "book language"). It embodied a style of national romanticism that was largely inherited from Germany and that, in putting rural traditions at the heart of aesthetic concerns, was to guide the new literature during the 1840s and 1850s. Following the example of the brothers Grimm, Norwegian folklorists traveled the country in search of popular songs, tales, legends, and ballads. In 1862 Ibsen himself set out into the northern provinces to gather folk material, and his first plays testified to a desire to free Norwegian letters from the domination of foreign models.

Before Ibsen there had been no Norwegian theater. He was determined to combat German intellectual influence, which up until then had made Norway a docile province of Germany, by turning its own weapons against it. In this connection *Peer Gynt* (1867)—written in verse using two different meters, one of which copied the style of medieval ballads, and aimed at settling accounts with an outmoded patriotism while drawing upon the resources of popular narrative and the Romantic mood of the time—represented at once the highpoint and the end of this early period of his work. Ibsen boldly declared his intention to oppose Norwegian conformism and narrow-mindedness—to "awaken the people and lead them to take a large view of the world."[80]

Although he had left his native land several years earlier, embarking upon a period of exile that was to last twenty-seven years, *Peer Gynt* was a national success. Immediately afterward Ibsen began work on a play that marked a turning point in his career: *De unges Forbund* (The League of Youth, 1869), a contemporary work in prose written in imitation of the French style associated with Eugène Scribe and Alexandre Dumas fils, then considered the great masters of drama. During the following decade, the modernism *(Gennembrud)* that had been championed first in Denmark by Georg Brandes in his *Æsthetiske Studier* (Aesthetic Studies, 1868) brought about an aesthetic and political revolution in all of the Scandinavian countries. In the same year that Brandes' book appeared, Ibsen was composing *The League of Youth*—a play that affirmed his determination to introduce realism into the theater and henceforth to use French literary tools for the purpose of devising a distinctively Norwegian style freed from German constraints and control.

Ibsen in England

Ibsen's plays were translated in England well before they were in France. A volume of selected writings was published in 1879, and the following year the drama critic William Archer published his first translations. The earliest productions went unnoticed. But in 1889 *Et Dukkehjem* (A

Doll's House, 1879) was well received; and two years later, in 1891, *Gengangere* (Ghosts, 1881) and *Hedda Gabler* (1890) caused a scandal. The following year *Bygmester Solness* (The Master Builder) was panned by the critics. A group of marginal figures opposed to the dominant theater of the day—among them George Bernard Shaw, then a young critic—nonetheless sought to promote the Norwegian's work. The two main pillars of English avant-garde theater at this time were the Independent Theatre Society, which had been founded in 1891 by Jacob Thomas Grein on the model of Antoine's Théâtre-Libre in Paris as a showcase for new European playwrights and whose first production (of *Ghosts*) aroused storms of protest; and the Court (now Royal Court) Theatre, directed between 1904 and 1907 by Harley Granville-Barker, a playwright and friend of Shaw who staged Ibsen's plays and sought to achieve canonical status for the works of Shakespeare, then considered a subversive author, through the creation of a national theater. Shaw gave his first plays to the Court Theatre, where he enjoyed his first great popular success in 1904 with *John Bull's Other Island*. Opposed both politically and aesthetically to the reigning forms of theater in London, which were still marked by Victorian propriety, Shaw saw Ibsen as the standardbearer of a new style of drama—an argument he had developed several years earlier in *The Quintessence of Ibsenism* (1901).

Just as Wagner was Shaw's musical hero, Ibsen was his teacher in the theater.[81] An obscure music critic who had set out penniless from his native Dublin in 1876, at the age of twenty, Shaw relied on Ibsen's ethical and aesthetic example in attempting to overcome the inertia of the London stage at the time. The absence of social criticism and the stale repetition of academic forms and genres led him to write, for example, in 1889: "This year there was a rivival of hope because Mr Pinero . . . walked cautiously up to a social problem, touched it, and ran away.[82] Shortly afterwards a much greater sensation was created by a Norwegian play, Ibsen's *Doll's House,* in which the dramatist handled this same problem, and shewed, not how it ought to be solved, but how it is about to be solved."[83]

The analogy that Shaw continually pressed between Wagner and Ibsen is explained not only by the similarity of their positions as heretical foreigners, which enabled them to undermine the timid conformism of the artistic world in Britain, but also by the similar sorts of contempt that they aroused in English critics. Ibsen, Shaw wrote, "was treated worse than Wagner, though that seemed impossible. It was, however, easy. We had at least not accused Wagner of obscenity, nor called for the prosecution of Her Majesty's Theatre as a disorderly house after the first performance of *Lohengrin* . . . we assured the English nation that [Ibsen] was an illiterate, diseased, half-crazy pornographer, and wanted to persecute the people who performed his plays in spite of the prohibition of the Censor."[84]

Shaw's situation as an Irishman living in England made him highly sensitive to the problems faced by an author from a country on the periphery of the European literary world whose provincialism prevented its artists from being noticed. Thus on the occasion of the London premiere of *Peer Gynt* (set to music by Grieg) in London in 1889, Shaw called attention to both the first signs of international recognition of Norwegian culture and the hegemonic instincts of the English, who were able to appreciate foreign works only in terms of their own cultural assumptions:

> Even the general public is beginning to understand that the Norwegian people are not simply a poor and wretched lot whose land is prized as a refuge for wealthy foreign hunters and fishermen. They are also commencing to be thought of as a people with a vast modern literature and a remarkably interesting political history. Shakespear's supremacy in our own literature has long led us to believe that there is one great dramatist who dominates each national literature. We are used to the idea of one central figure, around whom all the others group themselves. Therefore we are intensely interested in each new word about that "modern Shakespear" looming in Scandinavia— Henrik Ibsen.[85]

Shaw's subversive political views, which led him to adopt realism and naturalism as methods of social criticism in challenging the aesthetic and moral closed-mindedness of the English theater, together with the Independent Theatre's acknowledged debt to Antoine's Théâtre-Libre, which was famously associated with Zola, therefore encouraged a "social" interpretation of Ibsen's work by members of the English avantgarde—the only interpretation, they felt, that was capable of doing justice to both its novelty and its modernity while also remaining fairly close to the modernist aims of the Norwegian dramatist.

Ibsen in France

Ibsen was very quickly co-opted by the avant-garde theater in France as well, but there the configuration of aesthetic positions was so different that his work was to be interpreted in almost opposite terms. Ibsen became a central issue in the quarrels of the theatrical world in Paris, disputes that grew out of the conflict between the Théâtre-Libre, which aligned itself with the naturalist movement, then in decline, and the Théâtre de l'Oeuvre, created by Lugné-Poë in opposition to Antoine in 1893, which sought to promote the rising Symbolist movement.

It was Antoine who first staged Ibsen, beginning with *Ghosts* in 1890 and *Vildanden* (The Wild Duck, 1884) the following year. Zola's name was frequently mentioned by critics looking to characterize the aesthetic temperament of the Norwegian dramatist.[86] But Lugné-Poë, in order to establish his position as an innovator and to assert a different set of aesthetic preferences, turned Ibsen into a Symbolist. His production in December 1892 of *Fruen fra Havet* (The Lady from the Sea, 1884) inaugurated a new style of acting, solemn and monotone, whose emphasis on speaking lines slowly—which had the effect of making the text seem unreal—represented a striking departure from conventional practice. The heroine, played by an actress known for her roles in Maeterlinck's dramas, was transformed into a "strange creature with long veils, a white ghost."[87] The play was a critical success. Ibsen, impatient to become known at last in Paris—the "real heart of the world," as he called it[88]—reluctantly accepted the Symbolist interpretation as the price of fame while continuing to insist on the right to review translations of his work and the details of their performance.

During the summer of 1894, Lugné-Poë took his company on tour in Sweden, Denmark, and Norway to introduce Maeterlinck and Symbolist drama to the Scandinavian public and to show Ibsen's countrymen how he was performed in France. Though the troupe's arrival was hailed as "an event in the national theater movement," its interpretation of Ibsen's work was widely resisted.[89] Yet if the "missionary of Symbolism" failed to convert Scandinavian audiences, the critics, knowing that the Théâtre de l'Oeuvre was a first step to recognition in Paris, approved the French "naturalization" of Ibsen—all except Georg Brandes, who, in an article published in 1897, openly expressed exasperation with Lugné-Poë's approach: "It is not only in France," he wrote, "that there has developed too great a fondness for finding symbols in the most human characters of Norwegian dramas . . . But France does take the prize for these fantastic interpretations."[90] Ibsen himself seemed to qualify his support.

The next year, in 1895, Lugné-Poë organized a tour of England, putting on plays by Maeterlinck and Ibsen in a small theater in London at Grein's invitation. The passionate interest in the work of the Belgian playwright shown by the decadent young poets of the capital, admirers of Oscar Wilde, excited the disapproval of Victorian opinion and, with the start a few days later of Wilde's first trial, encouraged bitter attacks from opponents of innovation in the theater. Nor had Mirabeau's reference to Maeterlinck five years before as the "Belgian Shakespeare" gone unnoticed—another instance of the syndrome experienced by Ibsen and described earlier by Shaw himself, in which foreign authors were interpreted with reference to the categories of English literary history. But Shaw, Ibsen's introducer in England along with William Archer, defended the approach adopted by the Théâtre de l'Oeuvre, acknowledging the reservations of other critics (who criticized "the shabbiness of the scenery" and "the petty parochial squabblings which stand for public life in Ibsen's prose comedies") while yet praising "the true atmosphere of this most enthralling of all Ibsen's works rising like an enchanted mist for the first time on an English stage."[91]

These differences in interpretation make it clear that authors from the periphery are able to obtain recognition in the leading capitals only at the cost of seeing their work appropriated by the literary establishment for its own purposes. In the case of Ibsen, the arbitrary character of the French reading—French critics go on even today imperturbably talking about his Symbolism, simply repeating the familiar readings of the previous century—can be understood only by looking at the dominant categories of artistic and critical understanding from an international perspective, thereby restoring their full complexity.

English words expressing several, although by no means all aspects of *poshlust* are for in-stance: "cheap, sham, common, smutty, pink-and-blue, high falutin', in bad taste" . . . Litera-ture is one of the best breeding places . . . *Poshlust,* it should be repeated, is especially vigor-ous and vicious when the sham is not obvious and when the values that it mimics are considered, rightly or wrongly, to belong to the very highest level of art, thought or emotion. It is those books which are so poshlustily reviewed in the literary supplement of daily pa-pers—the best sellers, the "stirring, profound and beautiful" novels; . . . *Poshlust* is not only the obviously trashy but also the falsely important, the falsely beautiful, the falsely clever, the falsely attractive . . . For in the kingdom of *poshlust* it is not the book that "makes a tri-umph" but the "reading public" which laps it up, blurb and all.

   —Vladimir Nabokov, *Nikolai Gogol*

THE CONFIGURATION OF contemporary literary space is not easy to charac-terize. It may be that we find ourselves today in a transitional phase, pass-ing from a world dominated by Paris to a polycentric and plural world in which London and New York, chiefly, but also to a lesser degree Rome, Barcelona, and Frankfurt, among other centers, contend with Paris for hegemony.

   By the end of the nineteenth century, fierce struggles between emerging powers, each with its own stock of literary capital, had already made the "decline" of Paris an obligatory theme.[1] Since the authority of a center exists, in its objective effects, only in and through the belief that individuals have in it, Paris' loss of preeminence could be announced in the guise of an objective observation. Rejections of the established order are in fact violent attempts to seize literary power. The place of Paris in the world of letters remains a subject of passionate dispute, on which everyone has a settled opinion. For my part, I can only try to suggest ways in which recent developments may be understood, without thereby pretending to be indifferent about so controversial a question, especially as the author of a book devoted to examining the efforts and exploits of all those who have sought to manufacture universality, as it were, and who today find their authority increasingly threatened.

Thus in the rivalry that now opposes Paris to other European capitals and above all to London and New York, it is difficult to make observations that are not seen as expressions of partisan sentiment and therefore used as weapons in the competition among them. The most the analyst can do is to refuse such observations the status of truth that they claim for themselves, and instead show how they are used and catalogue their effectiveness. Today, for example, attempts made in many parts of the literary world to instill doubt in the minds of the authorities in Paris as to the supremacy of French literature have succeeded so well that the theme of decline, unimaginable only a few years ago in France itself, has become an almost inevitable feature of local debate, to the point that it now appears even in French novels. In the second part of this book I shall describe these attempts and, by restoring them to the context of the worldwide space that produced them, try as far as possible to avoid the myopia inherent in the Parisian view of the world of letters, which mistakenly regards the results of international competition as a series of separate national realities.

In the meantime, however, a few facts will show that the situation is still more complex than it may at first seem. From the point of view of the tacit recognition produced by the simple mechanism of literary credit, French literary power remains important in the United States in the form of philosophy or, more precisely, of a philosophy whose style and content are derived from literature and whose dissemination has been assisted by the literary authority and prestige of France. Recent French philosophy and, more generally, outstanding figures of French intellectual life such as Lacan, Foucault, Deleuze, Derrida, and Lyotard were first introduced to the United States through the literature and foreign-language departments of American universities such as Yale and

Johns Hopkins. And if the method of "deconstruction" developed by Derrida, the theme of "power knowledge" elaborated by Foucault, the "minor literatures" described by Deleuze, and the "postmodernity" analyzed by Lyotard have powerfully influenced American campuses and, in particular, the field of cultural studies, this once again has been due to literary studies and criticism. Nor can the *littérisation* of philosophy be seen as illegitimate in the cases of these and other authors, for their work is deeply concerned with literature and readily enlists it in the service of philosophical inquiry. The weight of France in American intellectual life is yet another effect—indirect, to be sure, disguised, even paradoxical—of its literary credit, which no doubt at least partly accounts for the violence of the attacks against these same figures in America.

The recent recognition of major writers such as Danilo Kiš (a Serb), Milan Kundera (a Czech), Thomas Bernhard and Elfriede Jelinek (Austrians), Arno Schmidt (a German), Carlos Fuentes (a Mexican), Mario Vargas Llosa (a Peruvian), Gabriel García Márquez (a Colombian), Julio Cortázar (an Argentinian), Antonio Tabucchi (an Italian), Paul Auster (an American), and António Lobo Antunes (a Portuguese) testifies to the continuing power of consecration enjoyed by the Paris authorities. Kiš, more conscious of the general mechanisms and more clear-sighted perhaps with regard to the structural implications of world literary space than earlier generations of writers recognized by Paris, asserted in 1982: "For here in Paris, you see, at least for me, everything is literature. And Paris, despite everything, still is and will always be the capital of literature."[2] The evolution of world literary space since then lends support to Kiš's contention that Paris' function of discovery and consecration will survive the decline (real or imagined) of French letters. Certainly Paris remains the capital of "deprived" as well as "marginal" literatures—written by Catalans, Portuguese, Scandinavians, Japanese, and others—and it may be expected to continue to give literary existence to writers from countries that are the furthest removed from literary centers.

Cinema illustrates the same mechanism and, particularly in the French case, is a direct consequence of national literary capital. Paris today consecrates, supports, and in some cases finances filmmakers from India, Korea, Portugal, Mexico, Poland, Iran, Finland, Russia, Hong Kong, and even the United States. But it is not the current prestige of French films that accounts for this situation. Thanks to a volume of cinematographic (and literary) capital that is universally recognized, Paris remains not merely the capital of French cinema, but the capital of independent cinema the world over. One thinks of the international reputations established there in recent decades by Satyajit Ray, Manuel de Oliveira, Krzysztof Kieslowski, Aki Kaurismäki, Hou Hsiao-Hsien, Woody Allen, and others.

Translation is therefore an essential measure of the scale and effectiveness of consecration, for it is terms of the number of candidates for legitimacy and of the actual extent of autonomous consecration (via translation, commentary, critical notice, prizes) that the properly literary credit of a capital is reckoned. A recent study of European trends shows that Great Britain, which exports much of its literary production to other countries in Europe, is also the least open to foreign works originating outside its linguistic area: the share of translations into English as a fraction of total British literary production for the year 1990 was only 3.3 percent. To be sure, the existence of a very large American market—which allows British authors to acquire an international audience without changing language—is responsible in large part for this situation. The authors of this study nonetheless insist upon the virtual "autarky of the Anglo-Saxon markets," and indeed the evidence suggests that British resistance to foreign works of literature is far greater today than it was in the 1950s and 1960s.[3]

German writing in recent years has suffered from almost systematic neglect in Great Britain.[4] For many readers the very adjective "German" is associated with heaviness and an absence of humor and style, by contrast with the reputedly easy and popular manner of the English tradition. The great works by German writers published in the 1950s that have since become classics—Thomas Mann, Rilke, Kafka, and Brecht—retain a certain distant authority, as do those by Böll, Grass, Uwe Johnson, Peter Weiss, and other members of the Gruppe 47. But the scholars, poets, translators, and critics who served after the war as indispensable links to German culture, many of them Jewish immigrants to Great Britain, have now died off, and the image of German literature remains the one they left behind. England today is almost forty years behind the times, notwithstanding its familiarity with the work of Gert Hofmann (whose son, Michael Hofmann, a poet and translator of German work into English, lives in London), the Austrians Peter Handke and Thomas Bernhard, and Christa Wolf, an East German writer who has become well known in feminist circles in the United States as well. One translator recently remarked that even a monumental work by one of the most important German authors of his generation, Uwe Johnson's four-volume *Jahrestage* (Anniversaries, 1970–1983), "went practically unnoticed on its appearance in England a few years ago."[5]

By contrast, Spain, Italy, Portugal, the Low Countries, Denmark, and Sweden import a great many books: translations into the languages of these countries represent more than a quarter of total literary production, considerably higher than the European average of 15 percent. Translations account for 33 percent of published works in Portugal, rising to 60 percent in Sweden—an exceptionally high figure attributable in part to the weak volume of local production, but also to the fact that Sweden is the home of the coveted Nobel Prize, which has made it a crossroads for world literature seeking to make itself known to the Swedish Academy. This massive inflow of translated works, unbalanced by a correspondingly high share of homegrown exports (the most sought-after and translated literatures in Europe remain English and French), sets these countries apart from their European neighbors.[6] In France and Germany, foreign works in translation account for between 14 and 18 percent of overall publishing activity—a significant figure that, in combination with a high level of exports, constitutes an important measure of literary power.

The same analysis applies to the United States, where the commitment of commercial publishers to translation continues steadily to decline. It is for this reason that New York and London cannot be said to have replaced Paris in the structure of literary power: one can only note that, as a result of the generalization of the Anglo-American model and the growing influence of financial considerations, these two capitals tend to acquire more and more power in the literary world. But one must not oversimplify the situation by applying a political analysis that opposes Paris to New York and London, or France to the United States. The fiction component of literary production in America, as in France, is divided between two distinct poles. The first consists of novels that belong to what Pierre Bourdieu calls the "subfield of restricted production," which is to say autonomous, avant-garde works that exist on the fringes of mainstream publishing.[7] In France, by contrast, such novels enjoy a large measure of editorial and critical attention. The great French *améri-*

caniste tradition led by Larbaud, Coindreau, and Sartre, who played a key role in the consecration of Faulkner and Dos Passos and the publication of Nabokov's *Lolita,* is carried on today thanks to the efforts of leading critics, translators, historians, and series editors such as Maurice Nadeau, Marc Chenetier, Denis Roche, Pierre-Yves Pétillon, and Bernard Hoepffer. Their many critical anthologies, prefaces, and translations have made them the privileged interlocutors of the most autonomous American authors, including John Hawkes, Philip Roth, John Edgar Wideman, Don DeLillo, Robert Coover, William H. Gass, Paul Auster, Coleman Dowell, and William Gaddis.

The second pole consists of commercial literary production, associated by definition with the least autonomous sectors of publishing, which today exercises all the more attraction as it manages to imitate the achievements of a certain narrative modernity. American (or Americanized) large-scale literary production, having effortlessly succeeded in making articles of domestic consumption pass for "international" literature, poses a grave threat to the independence of the world of letters as a whole. What is being played out today in every part of world literary space is not a rivalry between France and the United States or Great Britain but rather a struggle between the commercial pole, which in each country seeks to impose itself as a new source of literary legitimacy through the diffusion of writing that mimics the style of the modern novel, and the autonomous pole, which finds itself under siege not only in the United States and France but throughout Europe, owing to the power of international publishing giants. The American avant-garde is no less threatened today than the European avant-garde.

The present-day structure of world literary space is therefore considerably more complex than the one I have already described with regard to the nineteenth and early twentieth centuries. Zones of dependency can no longer be identified solely with literarily deprived national spaces. They can also now be observed in the oldest national fields, where the appearance and consolidation of an increasingly powerful commercial pole has profoundly altered publishing strategies, affecting not only patterns of distribution but also the selection of books and even their content.

Now, it may be argued that the commercial pole in each country is simply a transformation of the national pole or merely one of its avatars. The national bestseller, by virtue of its traditional form and themes (drawn from the nation's history), conforms to the expectations and requirements of commercial success. As Larbaud observed, national writers are distinguished not only by the robust sales that their works enjoy in their own country but also by the fact that they are unknown to readers in other countries.[8] The national novelist is one who produces for the literary market of his own country, respecting its commercial customs. In the case of the United States, this market has now come to assume global proportions, giving rise to a new breed of novel whose international success is the combined result of the triumph of the commercial model in the publishing industry and of the universal adoption of popular American tastes in fiction. America's economic dominance, notably in the fields of cinema and literature, has created a global market for its popular national novels (of which *Gone with the Wind* is perhaps the classic example) on the basis of worldwide familiarity with Hollywood culture.

Everywhere today publishing is being transformed: not only is there a growing tendency toward concentration that works to standardize production and to deprive innovative smaller houses of their traditional outlets; more important still, the absorption of publishing by communications conglomerates has changed the rules of the game. Describing the shifting landscape in the United States, the noted independent publisher André Schiffrin points to mergers among mass-media companies and to the spectacular increases in profits associated with the growth of corporate concentration.[9] Whereas since the 1920s the average profit of publishing houses (in Europe as well as America) has been around 4 percent,[10] Schiffrin notes that in recent years, in Great Britain and the United States, "the new owners insist that the level of profit for their book publishing divisions be comparable to the level they require of their other subsidiaries—newspapers, cable television, and film. The objective has therefore been set between 12 percent and 15 percent. This is why there has been a radical change in the nature of the books responsible for achieving short-term profitability objectives."[11]

In Europe, even if the situation has not yet changed so dramatically, the importation of the American economic model has meant that publishers are increasingly concerned with profitability in the near term. Accelerated inventory turnover and constant addition to the number of titles have displaced long-term investment among the priorities of the great publishing houses.[12] Publishers now find it necessary to publish more titles in smaller print runs that are sold in stores for a shorter time and at incrementally higher prices—changes brought about in the United States through a threefold process of consolidation merging publishing houses, distribution channels, and retail outlets that has led in turn to greater participation by technical and marketing staff in editorial decisions. In short, the dissociation of intellectual purpose and editorial policy has provoked a profound crisis in the publishing industry.[13]

The new organization of production and distribution, together with the emphasis at all levels upon immediate profitability, favors the transnational circulation of books conceived for the mass market. Bestsellers, of course, have always sold across borders. What is new today is the manufacture and promotion of a certain type of novel aimed at an international market. Under the label "world fiction," products based on tested aesthetic formulas and designed to appeal to the widest possible readership—novels of academic life by internationally known authors such as Umberto Eco and David Lodge, for example, as well as neocolonial sagas (such as Vikram Seth's *A Suitable Boy*) that adopt all the familiar devices of exoticism[14]—are marketed alongside updated versions of mythological fables and ancient classics that place a recycled "wisdom" and morality within the reach of everyone and books that combine travel writing with aspects of the adventure novel. These productions have created a new composite measure of fictional modernity. Restored to current taste are all the techniques of the popular novel and the serial invented in the nineteenth century: between the covers of a single volume one can find a cloak-and-dagger drama, a detective novel, an adventure story, a tale of economic and political suspense, a travel narrative, a love story, a mythological account, even a novel within the novel (the last a pretext for false self-referential erudition that makes the book its own subject—an effect of the perceived necessity of imitating "Borgesian" modernity).[15] To some extent this trend is due to the changed role of editors, whose traditional function of choosing among the manuscripts that come to them has given way to a tendency to initiate and conceive projects: a growing share of the books published today are commissioned by the publisher.[16]

Even the freest countries in world literary space are therefore subject to the power of international commerce, which, in transforming the conditions of production, modifies the form of books themselves. The rise of multinational conglomerates and the very broad diffusion of internationally popular novels that give the appearance of literariness have called into question the very idea of a literature independent of commercial forces. The "intellectual International" imagined by Valery Larbaud, who in the 1920s foresaw the advent of a small, cosmopolitan, enlightened society that would silence national prejudices by recognizing and promoting the free circulation of great works of avant-garde literature from all over the world, now stands in danger of being fatally undermined by the imperatives of commercial expansion. A world literature does indeed exist today, new in its form and its effects, that circulates easily and rapidly through virtually simultaneous translations and whose extraordinary success is due to the fact that its denationalized content can be absorbed without any risk of misunderstanding. But under these circumstances a genuine literary internationalism is no longer possible, having been swept away by the tides of international business.

PART II | *Literary Revolts and Revolutions*

I am an invisible man . . . I am a man of substance, of flesh and bone, fiber and liquids—and I might even be said to possess a mind. I am invisible, understand, simply because people re- fuse to see me . . . That invisibility to which I refer occurs because of a peculiar disposition of the eyes of those with whom I come in contact. A matter of the construction of their inner eyes, those eyes with which they look through their physical eyes upon reality.

—Ralph Ellison, Invisible Man

6 | *The Small Literatures*

A small nation's memory is not smaller than the memory of a large one and so can digest the existing material more thoroughly. There are, to be sure, fewer experts in literary history employed, but literature is less a concern of literary history than of the people, and thus, if not purely, it is at least reliably preserved. For the claim that the national consciousness of a small people makes on the individual is such that everyone must always be prepared to know that part of the literature which has come down to him, to support it, to defend it—to defend it even if he does not know it and support it . . . [All this] result[s] in the dissemination of literature within a country on the basis of political slogans.
    —Franz Kafka, *Diaries* (25 December 1911)

LITERARY SPACE IS not an immutable structure, fixed once and for all in its hierarchies and power relations. But even if the unequal distribution of literary resources assures that such forms of domination will endure, it is also a source of incessant struggle, of challenges to authority and legitimacy, of rebellions, insubordination, and, ultimately, revolutions that alter the balance of literary power and rearrange existing hierarchies. In this sense, the only genuine history of literature is one that describes the revolts, assaults upon authority, manifestos, inventions of new forms and languages—all the subversions of the traditional order that, little by little, work to create literature and the literary world.

Every literary space, including that of France, has been subject to domination at one moment or another of its history. And the international literary universe as a whole has taken shape through the attempts made by figures on the periphery to gain entry to it. From the point of view of the history and the genesis of worldwide space, then, literature is a type of creation that is irreducibly singular and yet at the same time inherently collective, the work of all those who have created, reinvented, or reappropriated the various means at their disposal for changing the order of the literary world and its existing power relations. Thus new genres and forms have come into being, foreign works have been translated, and popular languages have acquired literary existence.

Ever since 1549, when *The Defense and Illustration of the French Language* first appeared, mechanisms that paradoxically can only be described as both historical and transhistorical have operated on the world of letters. One observes consequences of domination that are everywhere the same, that are exerted in every place and in every period in identical fashion, and that furnish universal (or almost universal) insights for understanding literary texts. By abstracting from the secondary historical features of a given case, this model makes it possible to associate—and so to understand—quite different literary phenomena that are separated from one another in both time and space. The consequences of occupying a dominated and peripheral position are so powerful that it becomes possible to bring together writers who appear to have nothing in common. Whether they are separated from each other in time, as in the case of Franz Kafka and Kateb Yacine, or of C. F. Ramuz and writers in the French West Indies today; whether they use different languages, as in the case of G. B. Shaw and Henri Michaux or of Henrik Ibsen and James Joyce; whether they are former colonials or simply provincials, founders of literary movements or simply renovators of traditional forms, internal exiles within their own country, such as Juan Benet, or émigrés, such as Joyce and Danilo Kiš—they all find themselves faced with the same alternatives and, curiously, discover the same ways out from the same dilemmas. In some cases they manage actually to bring about revolutions, to pass through the mirror and achieve recognition by changing the rules of the game in the centers of the literary world.

The sense of revelation is never greater than when one groups together and compares writers who, though they are separated by linguistic and cultural traditions and appear to be opposed to one another in every respect, nevertheless have in common everything that a shared structural relationship to a central literary power implies. This is the case, for example, with Ramuz and another Swiss author, Robert Walser. Born the same year, 1878, the one at Lausanne, the other at Biel, their careers followed similar paths that decisively affected the nature of their writing: the early attempts to establish themselves in their respective literary capitals—Ramuz settled in Paris, where for more than twelve years he tried to achieve a reputation, while Walser began first in Munich, later moving to Berlin—which culminated in failure and the forced return to their native land; their subsequent claims on behalf of a modest, distinctly Swiss literature; and so on. The imbalance in the literary resources of the regions from which they came explains the differences in the formal choices made by the two writers, who stood in the same relationship of fascination and rupture with their respective traditions: whereas Ramuz's approach to the rural novel was conditioned by the relative absence of literary models in the Vaud, Walser, who as a German Swiss writer was able to rely upon an older literary tradition, adopted more sophisticated forms.

In order simply to achieve literary existence, to struggle against the invisibility that threatens them from the very beginning of their careers, writers have to create the conditions under which they can be seen. The creative liberty of writers from peripheral countries is not given to them straight away: they earn it as the result of struggles whose reality is denied in the name of literary universality and the equality of all writers as creative artists, by inventing complex strategies that profoundly alter the universe of literary possibilities. The solutions that little by little are arrived at—rescued, as it were, from the structural inertia of the literary world—are the product of compromise; and the methods that they devise for escaping literary destitution become increasingly subtle, on the levels both of style and of literary politics.

By taking into account the variety of solutions for overcoming literary dependence, and thereby giving meaning and justification to the works and aesthetic preferences of writers from the literarily least endowed countries, one can construct a "generative" model capable of reproducing the infinite series of such solutions on the basis of a limited number of literary, stylistic, and essentially political possibilities. In this way it becomes possible to uncover unsuspected links between writers whose affinity is suggested by neither stylistic analysis nor national literary histories, and so to assemble literary "families"—sets of cases that, however distant from each other they may be in time and space, display a kind of family resemblance. Ordinarily, writers are classified by nation, genre, epoch, language, literary movement, and so on; or one chooses not to classify them at all, preferring to celebrate the "miracle" of absolute singularity rather than to attempt a genuinely comparative literary history. In the best case, as with contemporary British critics who oppose V. S. Naipaul to Salman Rushdie, setting Naipaul's determination to assimilate the values of a literary center against Rushdie's stance of open resistance to literary neoimperialism, certain extreme positions can be identified. The consideration of literary works on an international scale leads to the discovery of further principles of contiguity or differentiation that make it possible to associate works that are not usually thought of as being related and sometimes to separate ones that are customarily grouped together, thus bringing out neglected properties.

A literary model of this sort plainly consists of a series of theoretical propositions that the infinite diversity of reality can serve only to nuance, correct, and refine. It is not necessary to pretend that the model exhausts or predicts all aesthetic possibilities: the point is simply to show that literary dependence favors the creation of a range of solutions that writers from dominated countries have both to reinvent and to defend in order to create modernity, which is to say to change the structure of the world of letters through revolution.

But the behavior of these authors cannot be accounted for without acknowledging at once that none of them acts or works in accordance with consciously and rationally elaborated strategies—even if they are, as I have said, the most perspicacious figures in the literary world. The "choice" of working for the development of a national literature, or of writing in a great literary language, is never a free and deliberate decision. The "laws" of national loyalty (or attachment) are so well internalized that they are seldom experienced as constraints; to the contrary, they constitute a major part of literary self-definition. What needs to be described, then, is a general structure whose effects are felt by writers on the periphery without their always knowing it, and which goes utterly unnoticed by writers in the centers, whose universalized position prevents them from seeing it.

This model also makes it possible to reconstruct the chronology of the formation of each literary space. Allowance being made for certain minor variations and differences associated with a particular political history, linguistic situation, or literary heritage, the main initial stages of literary formation are, as we shall see, essentially the same for all literary spaces that have belatedly come into being as the result of assertions of national identity. An almost universal and transhistorical order of development—again, allowance being made for some measure of historical and linguistic variation—governs what is normally experienced, analyzed, and reported by historians of literature as an inalienable historical and national peculiarity. Over the four centuries during which the world literary field has been formed and unified, the struggles and strategies of writers seeking to create and marshal their own literary resources have exhibited more or less the same logic. Even if cleavages—and therefore conflict between cultural centers and their hinterlands—have assumed new forms since the beginning of the nineteenth century, and despite the extreme diversity of literary and geopolitical circumstances, aesthetic debates, and political rivalries, the demands for literary freedom and the revolts to which they have given rise can be described in virtually transhistorical fashion, beginning with French literature during the second half of the sixteenth century.

Two great families of strategies supply the foundation for all struggles within national literary spaces. On the one hand there is *assimilation,* or integration within a dominant literary space through a dilution or erasing of original differences; on the other, *differentiation,* which is to say the assertion of difference, typically on the basis of a claim to national identity. These two main sorts of solution, clear-cut at the moment a movement aimed at achieving national independence appears, have long been described by "indigenous" writers, who, more than anyone else, are familiar with the dilemma facing them. Thus André de Ridder, in a book on contemporary Flemish literature published in 1923, wrote:

> Imagine the fate of a few true intellectuals lost on a similarly small island [Flanders], separated from the rest of the world, having for spiritual nourishment only the traditional literature, music, and art of a small homeland. Between the peril of absorption by a powerful culture, endowed with a universal power of expansion—which for us is the Latin culture on our southern borders, and the German culture to the east of us—and the peril of isolation in a petty-minded and sterilizing self-importance, tossed from one rock to the other, our pilots have managed to steer their boat.[1]

The West Indian poet Édouard Glissant has formulated this alternative in rather similar terms, adding to it the problem of language: "'Live in seclusion or open up to the other': this was supposedly the only alternative for any population demanding the right to speak its own language . . . Nations could have only one linguistic or cultural future—either this seclusion within a restrictive particularity or, conversely, dilution within a generalizing universal."[2] Glissant's analysis is confirmed by Octavio Paz, who in his Nobel Prize acceptance speech described the great founding tension of American literatures: "The first [of these literatures] to appear was that of the English-speaking part, and then . . . that of Latin America in its two great branches, Spanish America and Brazil. Although they are very different, these three literatures have one common feature: the conflict, which is more ideological than literary, between cosmopolitan and nativist tendencies, between Europeanism and Americanism."[3]

One of the peculiarities of the relationship that deprived writers maintain with the literary world has therefore to do with the terrible and inescapable dilemma they have to confront and then resolve in their various ways, regardless of differences of political, national, literary, or linguistic history. Faced with an antinomy that is unique to their situation (and that appears only to them), they have to make an unavoidably painful choice: either to affirm their difference and so condemn themselves to the difficult and uncertain fate of national writers (whether their appeal is regional, popular, or other) writing in "small" literary languages that are hardly, or not at all, recognized in the international literary world; or to betray their heritage and, denying their difference, assimilate the values of one of the great literary centers. Thus Édouard Glissant evokes the "sufferings of expression" that are peculiar to dominated countries—so much so that other countries are uncomprehending, because unaware of them: "To our astonishment we also discover people comfortably established within the placid body of their language, who cannot even comprehend that somewhere someone might experience an agony of language and who will tell you flat out, as they have in the United States, 'That is not a problem.'"[4]

More than a half-century earlier, Charles Ferdinand Ramuz's extraordinary lucidity had enabled him to perceive and acknowledge a state of affairs that ordinarily remains inaccessible to consciousness. The situation in which he found himself deserves henceforth to be known as *Ramuz's dilemma:*

> This is the dilemma that I was faced with when I was twenty years old, and that presents itself to all those who find themselves in the same situation, whether they are many or few: outliers, those who are born outside, beyond a frontier; those who, while linked to a culture through language, are in a sense exiled from it through religion or political affiliation . . . The problem presents itself sooner or later: one has either to embark upon a career and first of all yield to a set of rules that are not only aesthetic or literary, but social and political as well, even worldly; or deliberately to break with them, not only by exposing, but also by exaggerating, one's own differences: even if it means accepting [these rules] later on, if one can.[5]

Later in this chapter (and in greater detail in Chapter 10) I shall examine the Irish Renaissance, which will serve as a sort of scale model or paradigm for understanding almost all the problems faced by writers from dominated literary worlds.

LITERARY DESTITUTION

The unequal structure that characterizes the literary world opposes large literary spaces to small ones and often places writers from small countries in situations that are both tragic and unbearable. It needs to be emphasized once more that the adjective "small" is used here in a specific sense to mean literarily deprived. Just as the Hungarian theorist István Bibó (1911–1979) analyzed "the political poverty of the small nations of Eastern Europe,"[6] I propose here to analyze literary poverty—but also literary greatness, and the invention of literary freedom, in dominated spaces.

Though universalist literary belief agrees with Brancusi's dictum that in art there are no foreigners, in reality national attachment is one of the most burdensome constraints felt by writers; indeed, the more dominated the country, the more constraining it is. The Lithuanian author Saulius Kondrotas (b. 1953) described this phenomenon, which is inevitably sensed even by nonnationalist artists, in the following terms: "I do not believe that one can escape one's origins. I am obviously not a patriot; I do not care about the fate of the Lithuanians . . . and yet I cannot stand completely outside, I cannot escape the fact of being Lithuanian. I speak Lithuanian; I also believe that I think Lithuanian."[7] Miroslav Krleža (1893–1981), in the estimation of Danilo Kiš one of the greatest Croat writers, who throughout his life and work sought to explore and understand the paradoxes of "being Croat," likewise made a sort of phenomenology of what is rightly called, through a curious oxymoron, national feeling. Nationality, in joining a singular and subjective concern ("feeling") with a collective sense of belonging ("national"), Krleža saw as consisting of memories, of

> a nostalgia born of pure subjectivity, the recollection of a youth that is long past! Memories of military service, of flags, war, the sound of the bugle, uniforms, the days of yesteryear, memories of carnival and of bloody fighting, a whole theater of memory that seems much more interesting than reality. Nationality consists in large measure of the dreams of individuals who imagine a better life here below; for an intellectual, it is a childhood completely filled with books, poems, and works of art, books read and paintings contemplated, wild imaginings, conventional lies, prejudices, very often an incredibly acute perception of stupidity, and an unspeakable quantity of blank pages! Nationality, in bad, patriotic, sentimental, maudlin poetry, consists of women, mothers, childhood, cows, pastures, prairies, a material condition into which we are born, a miserable, backward patriarchal state in which illiteracy is mixed with lyrical moonlight . . . Children learn from their fathers what their fathers learned according to the law of tradition, namely that their own nation is "great," that it is "glorious," or that it is "unhappy and weighed down," imprisoned, duped, exploited, and so on.[8]

Only the ecumenicism that informs the universalist conception of literature prevents critics in the center from perceiving and understanding the difficulties (in some cases the tragedies) of these writers, who are extremely clear about the fragile and marginal position they occupy, and who suffer both from belonging to a literarily unrecognized nation and from the fact that this very circumstance goes unrecognized. The notion of small nations, Milan Kundera remarked, "is not quantitative; it describes a situation; a destiny: small nations do not have the comfortable sense of being there always, past and future . . . always faced with the arrogant ignorance of the large nations, they see their existence perpetually threatened or called into question; for their very existence is a question."⁹ Small nations, the writer and translator from the Serbo-Croat Janine Matillon observes, "have sorrows that the great ones do not even suspect."¹⁰ The smallness, poverty, backwardness, and remoteness of these literary worlds render the writers who live in them invisible—imperceptible in the strict sense—to international literary authorities. This invisibility and remoteness appear clearly to those writers on the periphery who are "internationally recognized," and therefore able to evaluate precisely the position of their homelands in the tacit and implacable hierarchy of world literature. It is this very invisibility that forces them to come to terms with the smallness of the lands where they were born: "What then are we to do, the rest of us, who have neither action nor expression?" moaned Ramuz on coming back to his native Vaud.¹¹ "Here we are a tiny country that needs to be enlarged, a rather flat one that needs to be deepened, a poor one that needs to be enriched. Poor in legends, poor in history, poor in events, poor in occasions."¹² Beckett's later, more violent characterization of Ireland, in an early poem, as a "haemorrhoidal isle"¹³ and, in one of his first prose works, as a "pestiferous country"¹⁴ likewise summarizes the unhappiness he felt toward his native land, which, though it infuriated him, he nonetheless identified with.

Where the irreversible, in some sense ontological condition of belonging to a literarily disinherited country is bound up with tragedy, it not only impresses its mark on the entire life of an author but also gives his whole work its form. E. M. Cioran's writing, for example, his very philosophical and intellectual purpose, can be understood only by considering his relationship to Romanian intellectual and literary space, which he soon he came to see as a malign inevitability. Even toward the end of his life he maintained that the "pride of a man born in a small culture is forever wounded," although by then he had long been a famous writer, celebrated throughout the world.¹⁵ His ambivalent feelings toward his own small country (which is to say toward himself, insofar as his own identity, as is often the case with intellectuals in small countries, was primarily national) led him at first to become a fascist and nationalist intellectual. He joined the Iron Guard in the 1930s before finally choosing exile and a "despairing contempt" for his people, having abandoned all belief in the "future" of Romania ("With the peasants, one enters history only through the 'small door'").¹⁶ Evoking his fascist youth in a recently published text written in 1949, Cioran recalled: "We, the young of my country, were living on Insanity. This was our daily bread. Located in a corner of Europe, scorned and neglected by the world, we wanted to call attention to ourselves . . . We wanted to rise up to the surface of history: we revered scandals, the only means, we thought, of avenging the obscurity of our condition, our sub-history, our nonexistent past, and our humiliation in the present."[17]

In a way it was the curse of an obscure origin, the anger at having to write in an almost untranslated language, the frustration of being unable to claim any grandiose national "destiny," the humiliation of having to submit to the whims of ordinary people that led Cioran from active political involvement to a haughty disengagement. *Schimbarea la faţă a Romaniei* (Changing the Face of Romania, 1936), a fascist and antisemitic work published on his return from Germany in 1936, can be read as a frightening admission of the historical disappointment of being Romanian, experienced as a kind of ontological inferiority: "I dream," he wrote, "of a Romania that would have the destiny of France and the population of China."[18] Having tried unsuccessfully to work for "national salvation"—the pervasive theme of all his early writings—Cioran thus sought his own salvation in Paris. So that his genealogy and his career up until that point might be forgotten, he had not only to start over again from zero (and thus relinquish the intellectual capital he had accumulated in Bucharest) but also to abandon his native language.

What may be experienced as a historical curse is sometimes also expressed as a linguistic injustice. Max Daireaux, in his study of Latin American literature in the early twentieth century, reports the comment of the Guatemalan writer Enrique Gómez Carrillo (1873–1927), who, having published more than twenty volumes of fiction and criticism and several thousand columns of journalism, had achieved (in Daireaux's words) "the maximum celebrity to which a South American author can aspire." "For a writer who is the least bit universal-minded," Gómez Carrillo remarked, "the Spanish language is a prison. We can pile up volumes, even find readers, it's exactly as though we had written nothing: our voice doesn't carry beyond the bars of our cage! One can't even say that the terrible wind of the pamapas carried it away, it's worse than that: it vanishes!"[19] This remark makes it clear, incidentally, that the balance of power and inequality within the world of letters is continually modified and transformed: if Latin America was an altogether marginal and remote literary space in the 1930s, lacking any international recognition, thirty years later virtually the opposite was true, the continent having in the meantime become one of the best recognized of the dominated spaces, better integrated than most with the center. It is in this sense that the fine phrase—disillusioned and realistic—of the Somalian novelist Nuruddin Farah, who described his own identity as a dominated writer among dominated writers as consisting in a series of "contradictory unsuitabilities," is to be understood:[20] not only are the impoverished—whether their poverty is literary, political, or linguistic—never suitable, which is to say they never conform, never find their place, are never truly at ease in the literary world; more than this, their various unsuitabilities are themselves contradictory, forming an inextricable web of malediction, unhappiness, anger, and revolt.

This effort to supply the means for understanding and interpreting the special character of works from the periphery of the literary world through a structural description of literary relations and imbalances of power on a world scale will perhaps appear shocking to anyone who has a blinkered view of creative freedom. But one really must try to see, as against the widely shared illusion of a universal poetic inspiration that indifferently grants its favor to all the world's artists, that constraints are exerted unequally upon writers; and that these constraints weigh all the more heavily on some writers rather than others as their true nature is obscured to satisfy the official definition of literature as indivisible, universal, and free. To point out that dispossessed writers are subject to such constraints is not a way of blacklisting or ostracizing them; to the contrary, it is a way of showing that their works are even more improbable than others, that they manage almost miraculously to emerge and to make themselves recognized by subverting the literary laws laid down by the centers, through the invention of novel literary solutions.

Although national attachment must be regarded, especially in the case of the small nations, as a sort of destiny, it is not always experienced negatively—far from it. In the early stages of a country's history, and during times of great political upheaval (marked, for example, by the coming to power of dictatorial regimes and the outbreak of war), the nation is claimed as the indispensable condition of political independence and literary freedom. But paradoxically it is the most international writers who, while rejecting adherence to national belief, are the best at describing the literary manifestations of national feeling. Critically, and with a certain vindictiveness, they express a complex truth to which they alone, by virtue of their position both inside and outside national literary space, are capable of bearing witness. The mixture of irony, hatred, compassion, empathy, and reflectiveness that defines both their ambiguous relationship to their country and their fellow countrymen, on the one hand, and, on the other, the rejection of all national pity—a rejection whose very violence is commensurate with the futility of their revolt—perfectly captures the literary sensibility of national belief in small countries. The inevitable perception of a cultural hierarchy in the world, and the need to defend and illustrate the claims of small countries, are signs of the tragic impasse in which national writers find themselves caught up as a result of this inexorable attachment to their nation. Thus Witold Gombrowicz denounced Polish intellectuals in exile who

purport to show once again (yes, again!) that we are equal to the greatest world literatures, except that we are unknown and unappreciated . . . For they, in elevating Mickiewicz, were denigrating themselves and with their praise of Chopin showed that they had not yet sufficiently matured to appreciate him and that by basking in their own culture, they were simply baring their primitiveness . . . I felt like saying to those gathered: ". . . Chopin and Mickiewicz serve only to emphasize your own narrow-mindedness, because, with the naiveté of children, you prance out your *polonaises* under the noses of a bored foreign audience just so you can strengthen the impaired sense of your own worth . . . You are the poor relations of the world, who try to impress themselves and others" . . . This is the source of the respect, the eager humility exhibited toward phraseology, the admiration for Art, the conventional and learned language, the lack of integrity and honesty. Here they were reciting. The gathering was also marked by inhibition, artificiality, and falseness, because Poland was taking part in the meeting and a Pole does not know how to act toward Poland, it confuses him and makes him mannered. Poland inhibits the Pole to such a degree that nothing really "works" for him. Poland forces him into a cramped state—he wants to help it too much, he wants to elevate it too much . . . I thought that this auction with other nations for geniuses and heroes, for merits and cultural achievement, was really quite awkward from the point of view of propaganda tactics because with our half-French Chopin and not quite native Copernicus, we cannot compete with the Italians, French, Germans, English, or Russians. Therefore, it is exactly this approach that condemns us to inferiority.[21]

In the 1920s Miroslav Krleža made the same observation, not only in the same terms but with the same tone of exasperated and desperate irony of one who cannot help but be an example of what he condemns:

> One of the typical weaknesses of petit-bourgeois Croat sentiment, lulled by illusions, is that it resents its own national attachment as an infected wound, that it bears a childish love for its debility, that it adores overestimating itself in the domain of art, and more precisely in that of poetry, a subject on which it nonetheless has no grounds for congratulating itself . . . Old-fashioned, backward, petit-bourgeois, the allegedly aristocratic Croat sentiment suffers from a social inferiority complex . . . We descend the last steps of provincial backwardness, our intelligence is a dog that wags its tail in front of strangers, with the baseness of a slave, with the unconsciousness of a child, and we give proof, in demeaning ourselves in this way, that we are exactly what we deny being: the servile incarnation of nonvalue.[22]

Beckett and Michaux: The Antinational Mood

Only the weight of an indelible national origin, which writers who reject their history and their original literary milieu yet fail to escape, can explain the similarities between two youthful texts, one by Samuel Beckett, the other by Henri Michaux. Each came from a dominated space and sought to make a name for himself in the literary capital of his linguistic area—London for Beckett, Paris for Michaux; each sought to give an account of the young national literature of his country.

"Recent Irish Poetry" (1934), one of Beckett's first essays, published shortly after his arrival in London in the *Bookman,* provides an extensive overview of Irish poetry at the time. Signed with a pseudonym, it stated the author's views on various aesthetic and ethical questions, notably his refusal to endorse the Celtic folklore movement, and unambiguously designated his literary adversaries. He deliberately, and provocatively, rejected the whole national tradition ushered in by Yeats and carried on by Catholic intellectuals, still largely dominant in the early 1930s. "Thus contemporary Irish poets," he observed, "may be divided into antiquarians and others, the former in the majority, the latter kindly noticed by Mr W. B. Yeats as 'the fish that lie gasping on the shore.'"[23] The young Beckett took aim, directly or indirectly, at Yeats himself, the greatest Irish poet of the day, then seventy years old, winner of the Nobel Prize more than a decade earlier, a worldwide celebrity, everywhere honored as the greatest living poet of the English language, national hero and grand old man of international letters. Casting scorn on the obligatory and repetitive mythic themes of Celtic folklore, Beckett's derision extended to the other members of the Irish pantheon as well: James Stephens, Padraic Colum, George Russell, Austin Clarke, F. R. Higgins. In the Gaelicizing and nationalist atmosphere of Dublin in the 1920s and 1930s, Beckett's position amounted to heresy.

Ten years earlier, addressing his "Lettre de Belgique" (1924) to American readers in the prestigious *Transatlantic Review,* Henri Michaux had claimed exactly the same high ground.[24] He began by denouncing the standard cliché of Belgian literature (borrowed, as Pierre Bourdieu has shown, from a stereotypical image of Flemish painting),[25] both as a commonplace ("Foreigners usually imagine the Belgian at table, eating and drinking. Painters recognize him in Jordaens, writers in Camille Lemonnier, tourists in the 'Manneken-Pis'")[26] and as a national reality ("The work of the belly, glands, saliva, blood vessels, seems among [the Belgians] to be something conscious, a conscious pleasure. Translated into literature, the joys of the flesh make up the bulk of their works. One thinks of [Camille Lemmonier, Georges Eckhoud, Eugène Demolder]").[27] Here one notes Michaux's impertinence in treating in a few apparently offhand lines some of the great figures of Belgian literature—though in fact, as we know from one of his few autobiographical writings, all the great writers associated with the review *Jeune Belgique* (founded in 1881) were very important for him.[28] But if he granted the existence of these established writers (including Émile Verhaeren, whom he briefly mentions later), he described contemporary literature in his homeland as a sort of desert. He then went on to ridicule the Belgian "character" ("good-natured, simple, unpretentious"), which he explained by reference to a curious sort of inferiority complex:

> The Belgian is afraid of pretension, has a phobia about pretension, especially the pretension of written or spoken words. Whence his accent, that famous way of speaking French. The secret is just this: the Belgian believes that words are pretentious. He chokes and smothers them as much as he can, so that they will become inoffensive, good-natured . . . The rather general return to simplicity that has made itself felt in the arts therefore finds young men of letters here marvelously well prepared, and is already taking effect . . . Poets in Belgium today I would readily call virtuosos of simplicity, and I would have to cite almost all of them.[29]

The work of these poets ("in general of a caliber strongly influenced by France, and by J. Cocteau") was criticized for its "triteness, banality, and a laxness of language."[30] Michaux mentioned some fifteen names, among them his own.

Here one thinks again of the young Beckett, who sent Samuel Putnam, an American who with Edward Titus edited the review *This Quarter* and who had accepted four of his poems for an anthology of new European poetry,[31] a biographical notice that he had composed himself: "Samuel Beckett is the most interesting of the younger Irish writers. He is a graduate of Trinity College, Dublin, and has lectured at the École Normale Supérieure in Paris. He has a great knowledge of Romance literature, is a friend of Rudmose-Brown and of Joyce, and has adapted the Joyce method to his poetry with original results. His impulse is lyric, but has been deepened through this influence and the influence of Proust and the historic method."[32] Michaux's style of talking about himself was more sober: "Henry [sic] Michaux has sometimes wrongly been judged to be a poet . . . Poetry, if such a thing exists, is the minimum that remains in any humanly true account. He is an essayist."[33] Michaux went on instead, in the "Lettre de Belgique," to defend Franz Hellens, the novelist, poet, and critic who edited the review *Le Disque Vert,* in which he published his first pieces.

In their earliest writings, then, these two young poets adopted the same general attitude of rejection toward their national literary space, displayed a similar critical distance, a similar irony with regard to their elders. All of this plainly suggests a comparison between their careers as exiled poets, determined to break with the literary establishments of their countries. But their evident disdain testified as much to an ineradicable attachment to a national literary space as to a desire to distance themselves from it: even the most international writers, at least in the formative stages of their career, are first of all defined, in spite of their wishes to the contrary, by their native national and literary space.

POLITICAL DEPENDENCIES

Politicization in national or nationalist form—and therefore, in a sense, nationalization—is one of the constitutive features of small literatures: proof, as it were, of the necessary link between literature and nation at the moment when a country takes its first steps toward revolt and dissimilation. The Irish Literary Revival, for example, took over in a certain sense from the late nineteenth-century nationalist movement in politics. The fall and suicide in 1891 of Charles Stewart Parnell—the "shrewd obstructionist" who had embodied immense political hopes throughout Ireland[34]—marked the failure of a certain form of political action and indefinitely postponed a politically acceptable solution. The literary renaissance that followed expressed the political disenchantment of an entire generation of intellectuals. In a strongly politicized country that had long been accustomed to nationalist struggle, the passage from political nationalism to cultural (and above all literary) nationalism amounted to pursuing the same ends by different means; or rather, the national and political question was precisely the issue that would split the literary world, with the Anglo-Irish Protestants—more culturally than politically minded—led by Yeats on one side and, on the other, the more politicized Catholic intellectuals who fought for aesthetic (and political) realism and the rehabilitation of Gaelic. But whether they sought to reject or to embrace it, the "connection with politics" (to adopt Kafka's expression regarding small literatures) was permanent in the case of Irish writers.

If for some years, then, literary activity took the place of political combat, it also furnished political combatants with other weapons: the insurgents of Easter 1916 were fervent readers of Yeats, Synge, and Douglas Hyde. Many of the leaders of this bloody and unsuccessful revolt, including Patrick Pearse and Thomas MacDonagh, were intellectuals ("I who knew," as George Russell recalled in 1934, "how deep was Pearse's love for the Cuchulain whom O'Grady discovered or invented").[35] The chronology of the movement itself is political, since the uprising of Easter 1916 also marked a turning point in Irish drama and poetry. Yeats withdrew afterward, adopting a sort of aristocratic and spiritualist distance. Turning against literary realism, directly assimilated to politics, he sought autonomy in a nostalgic retirement.

The politicization of Irish literary space supplies the measure of its dependence: as late as 1930 it was still a very peripheral area, distant from the great European literary centers and remaining largely under the historical and political domination of London. To a large degree the literary choices of writers in Dublin were determined by their relation to the English authorities; even their aloofness, their refusal to recognize the aesthetic and critical standards of the British capital, is an indication of the influence of its canons in Irish literary life. The description of this space therefore cannot be limited (as it typically is by critics who confuse national boundaries and the borders of literary space) to literary events in Dublin.

Within deprived spaces, writers are condemned, in effect, to develop a national and popular theme: they must defend and illustrate national history and controversies, if only by criticizing them. Because they are for the most part concerned to defend a certain idea of their country, they are engaged in elaborating a national literature. The importance of the national and popular theme in a nation's literary production is surely the best measure of the degree of political dependence of a literary space. The central question, then, around which the majority of literary debates are organized in emerging literary spaces (to differing degrees depending on the date of their political independence and the scale of their literary resources) involves the nation, the language, and the people—which is to say the language of the people and the linguistic, literary, and historical definition of the nation. In politically annexed or dominated regions, literature is a weapon of combat and national resistance. "When Korea lost its sovereignty as a result of its annexation by Japan [in 1910]," one critic has remarked, "the formidable task of assuring the return of this sovereignty fell to literature alone. In a sense, this mission was its point of departure."[36] Entrusted with responsibility for creating a national language and so laying the foundation for a unique and inalienable national culture, writers place their writing in the service of the nation and the people. Literature thus becomes national or popular, or both, devoted to promoting the nation as an idea and helping it, once the idea has become a reality, to join the ranks of all those nations that enjoy literary existence and recognition. Thus a pantheon comes to be established, a history, a line of prestigious ancestors and founders. "A small nation," Milan Kundera has observed, "resembles a big family and likes to describe itself that way . . . Thus in the big family that is a small country, the artist is bound in multiple ways, by multiple cords. When Nietzsche noisily savaged the German character, when Stendhal announced that he preferred Italy to his homeland, no German or Frenchman took offense; if a Greek or a Czech dared to say the same thing, his family would curse him as a detestable traitor."[37]

The link with national struggle therefore produces a dependence upon the new national public, and so an almost total absence of autonomy. In Ireland at the beginning of the twentieth century, this dependence was the source of the various "scandals" that punctuated the life of the Abbey Theatre, which, as one of the only national institutions of occupied Ireland, was used as a meeting place by nationalist militants. Anything that threatened to challenge the mythology of national heroism and the accepted narrative of the nation's founding was immediately rejected by a furious public, denying writers the least measure of creative independence. The violence that attended the premiere of Synge's *Playboy of the Western World* in 1907 is proof of this almost total absence of autonomy, this fundamental dependence with regard to public opinion and the nationalist cause. Two decades later, when O'Casey's *The Shadow of the Gunman* was being performed, a note was inserted in the program warning spectators: "Any gunshots heard during the performance are part of the script. Members of the audience must at all times remain seated."[38] It needs to be kept in mind that when the play was produced in April 1923, the civil war was not yet over. The realistic quality of the performance was in any case directly and immediately related to the political situation and not to any specific dramatic technique, the events depicted on stage having taken place scarcely three years earlier. James Joyce, who claimed a position of autonomy with regard to popular norms by challenging the obviousness of the "national duty" of national writers, deplored precisely this submission of creative artists to the tastes of the public in "The Day of the Rabblement," his violent attack on the Irish Literary Theatre:

> Now, your popular devil is more dangerous than your vulgar devil . . . the Irish Literary Theatre must now be considered the property of the rabblement of the most belated race in Europe . . . the rabblement, placid and intensely moral, is enthroned in boxes and galleries amid a hum of approval . . . If an artist courts the favor of the multitude he cannot escape the contagion of its fetishism and *deliberate self-deception,* and if he joins in a popular movement he does so at his own risk.[39]

Unlike what was happening in the old declining countries of Europe, which saw the rebirth of regressive and nostalgic nationalisms, the new nationalisms were for the most part politically subversive to the extent that they grew up in opposition to a foreign imperialism. Just as nationalisms, whether political or cultural, are not equivalent to one another in either form or content, and differ according to their historical extent, so writers who claim a national role in the newest spaces—as Synge,

O'Casey, and Douglas Hyde did in Ireland at the beginning of the twentieth century—for this reason occupy a complex position, neither academic nor conservative, that obliges them to resort to apparently heteronomous means to achieve their independence. For all those who are deprived of a literary heritage, of an established tradition, who are dispossessed with respect to language, culture, and popular traditions, there is no alternative but to take up political arms in order to gain literary authority—on pain of being crushed and absorbed into another literary tradition. In this struggle, the principal weapons are the people and the language (supposed or proclaimed) of the people.

The political stakes change only when the literary field asserts its independence vis-à-vis national and political imperatives; when antinational (or anational) writers appear—such as Joyce, and then Beckett, in Ireland—and, by reversing the polarity of the space, as it were, relegate national writers to political dependence, aesthetic backwardness, and academicism.

In reality, from the middle of the twentieth century onward, writers from the most deprived spaces have had to *achieve two forms of independence simultaneously:* political independence, in order to give existence to the nation as a state and share in its recognition on the international level; and a properly literary independence, by establishing a language that is both national and popular and then contributing, through their work, to the literary enrichment of their country. The desire of writers from the youngest spaces to free themselves from international literary domination therefore leads them to subordinate their literary practices to political interests to some extent, so that the quest for literary autonomy in these countries proceeds initially through the achievement of political independence, which is to say by means of literary practices that are closely linked to the national question. It is only when a minimum of political resources has been accumulated, and a minimum of political independence attained, that the struggle for a specifically literary autonomy can be carried on.

In older spaces it may also happen that the process of achieving autonomy is abruptly interrupted for one reason or another, with the result that intellectuals are forced to resort to the same strategies as their counterparts in emerging nations. The coming to power of military dictatorships in Spain and Portugal, for example, and the establishment of Communist regimes in newly formed countries in central and eastern

Europe produced the same phenomenon of literary nationalization and intense politicization, thus marginalizing writers. Under the long dictatorships of Franco and Salazar, the Spanish and Portuguese spaces saw themselves subjugated and absorbed by the political sector, through the regulation of the content and form of literary works. Despite an ancient literary history in these countries, and therefore a certain degree of autonomy, the freedom of literary maneuver became directly dependent on the will of the government. Writers were now subjected to censorship and turned into instruments of official policy; every manifestation of aesthetic (and political) independence was repressed, and the historical separation of national and literary authorities suspended. Under such circumstances, writers—no less than opponents of the regime—are obliged to conform to a narrowly political and national definition of cultural identity. Deprived of their independence, they find themselves faced with a choice familiar to authors in emerging worlds of letters: either to produce a political literature in the service of national interests or to go into exile.

What happened in France between 1940 and 1944 must be understood in the same terms. With the German occupation, French literary space suddenly lost its autonomy. The imposition of censorship, together with political and military repression, caused the totality of issues and positions to be redefined over the course of a few months. As in the most deprived emerging spaces, the preoccupation with national concerns in France—which had long been subordinate to an autonomous conception of literary practices—once again assumed the highest importance, forcing intellectuals to reconsider their commitments;[40] and, in a repetition of the experience of young literatures, the battle to regain literary autonomy took the form of a struggle for the political independence of the nation. A striking reversal of positions ensued, with the consequence (as Gisèle Sapiro has shown) that those French writers who before the war were the most independent—which is to say the most formalist, the least political—became after 1939 the most national, joining the Resistance and fighting to defend the nation against the German occupier and the Nazi order.[41] They temporarily abandoned the privileges of formalism in order to fight politically for the autonomy of the literary field. Conversely, those writers who before the war were the most national, the least autonomous, chose collaboration with the foreign occupier.

Apart from extraordinary political situations of this sort, one must be careful not to confuse national writers from small literary nations with national (or nationalist) writers in the most endowed spaces. The pronounced academic tendencies that are perpetuated in the oldest literary countries, in France and Great Britain, for example, are proof that autonomy remains very relative even in these supposedly independent worlds, and that the national pole remains powerful. These writers continue to ignore the existence of a literary present from which they are excluded, and which they oppose, sometimes violently. Using the instruments of the past, they produce national texts. There is today an "International" of academics (and academicians) who continue to profess nostalgia for outmoded literary practices in the name of a lost literary grandeur: at once centrally situated and immobile, they are ignorant of current innovations and inventions in literature; and as members of literary juries and presidents of national writers' associations, they manufacture and help reproduce (notably through national prizes such as the Prix Goncourt in France) conventional criteria that are out of date in relation to the latest standards of modernity. In short, they consecrate works that conform to their aesthetic categories. In older literary countries, the nationalist intellectual is, by definition, an academic in stylistic terms, since he knows nothing other than his national tradition.

The national conformism and conservatism peculiar to French, English, and Spanish academics have nothing in common with the political and literary struggle of the Québécois and Catalans, for example, for national independence. Writers in these societies, no matter what place they occupy in literary space, even the most cosmopolitan and subversive among them, remain to some extent attached to a requirement of national loyalty or, at least, continue to conceive of their work in terms of domestic political debates. Called upon to devote themselves primarily to the building of the symbolic nation, writers, grammarians, linguists, and intellectuals are in the front line, fighting to provide the new idea with a justification (in Ramuz's phrase).[42]

In worlds in which political and literary poles are still indistinct, writers are thus commonly made to act as spokesmen, in the strict sense of the term, of the people. "I think that it is time," the Kenyan writer James Ngugi (who later changed his name to Ngugi wa Thiong'o) asserted in the 1960s, "that the African writers also started to talk in the terms of these workers and peasants."[43] In Nigeria, Chinua Achebe (b. 1930) defended a "political literature" and the necessity of devoting oneself to "applied art" in order to avoid what he called the impasses of "pure art."[44] This inseparably political and aesthetic position illuminates his view, repeatedly reaffirmed, of the role reserved for the writer in young nations. Achebe's two famous articles from the mid-1960s, "The Novelist as Teacher" and "The Role of a Writer in a New Nation"—much discussed and approved by African intellectuals—clearly laid out his conception of the writer as pedagogue and nation-builder: "The writer cannot expect to be excused from the task of re-education and regeneration that must be done. In fact he should march right in front. For he is after all . . . the sensitive point of his community."[45] In choosing to be a literary pioneer, the writer unavoidably places himself in the service of national enlightenment. Thus, like Standish O'Grady and Douglas Hyde, historians of the Irish nation and literature in the late nineteenth century, Chinua Achebe was to become the bard and repository of Nigerian national history. In a series of four novels published between 1958 and 1966, he set himself the task of retracing the history of Nigeria from the beginnings of colonization until independence. The first novel of the cycle, *Things Fall Apart* (1958), a rare African bestseller (selling more than two million copies), described the encounter between the inhabitants of an Ibo village and the first missionaries to visit it. Standing exactly between the two parties, it managed simultaneously to present and explain their antagonistic points of view, seeking in this way to make sense of African reality and civilization in English. At once a realist, didactic, demonstrative, and national novel, its dual ambition was to provide Nigeria with a national history and to teach this history to the people.

In the absence of autonomy, the function of the historian—the person who knows and transmits historical truth, whose narrative establishes a national cultural patrimony for the first time—and the function of the poet are merged. The novelistic form furnishes the initial basis, then, for both a historical account of the nation and a national epic. Kafka had already emphasized this point in connection with the new Czechoslovakia, arguing that the work of the national historian is essential to the constitution of a fund of literature as well.[46]

NATIONAL AESTHETICS

Joyce observed that the national and nationalist writer had difficulty escaping the "deliberate self-deception"—another name for realism—that he ascribed to the people. And still today, in fact, one observes a genuine hegemony of realism in all its forms and denominations—neonaturalist, picturesque, proletarian, socialist, and so on—in the most impoverished (which is to say the most politicized) literary spaces. The gradual emergence of a dominant, indeed, virtually unchallenged literary aesthetic has occurred at the crossroads of two revolutions, the one literary and the other political. Because neorealism in its national and popular versions excludes any form of literary autonomy and makes literary production a function of politics, it is not surprising to find that, despite certain variations, the same realist (or "illusionist") assumption is common to emerging literary spaces and to those that are subject to strong political censorship.

Additional evidence of the essential heteronomy of literary realism is that it is also found in those literary or paraliterary productions that are most constrained by the commercial imperatives of national, and especially international, publishing—thus signaling the triumph of what Roland Barthes called the "appearance of reality" and Michael Riffaterre the "mythology of reality."[47] Naturalism is the only literary technique that gives the illusion of a coincidence between narrative and reality. The belief produced by this illusion allows it to be used in turn either as an instrument of political power or as a critical tool: conceived as the ultimate point of coincidence between fiction and reality, realism, more than any other doctrine, lends itself to political interests and purposes. The "proletarian novel" advocated by the Soviets was perhaps its most complete incarnation.[48] More generally, the conjunction of neorealist aesthetics and the use of a national ("popular," "workers'," or "peasant") language represents the preeminent form of the literary heteronomy experienced by writers in literary spaces under political domination.

Juan Benet very clearly described an example of this situation in Spain under Franco, where literature was wholly subject to government control. Its very dependence was a measure of the monopolistic influence of neorealist aesthetics, as much among intellectuals who collaborated with the regime as among those who tried to oppose it:

> In the 1940s, it was a "right-wing" literature, a "beatific" literature that supported the Franco regime, a unanimous point of view with no opposition . . . In the 1950s social realism began, a "left-wing" realism

that mimicked the Soviet novel and French existentialism. Very tim-
idly an opposition literature developed, but without any open criticism of the regime, of course, because of censorship. Writers took up
themes that were a bit taboo at the time: the nouveau riches, the difficulties of the working class.[49]

Danilo Kiš, in an essay on the limits of prose expression originally
published in the Belgrade review *Savremenik* (The Contemporary) in
the 1970s, evoked the literary atmosphere in Yugoslavia under Tito in
almost the same terms:

> There is no dilemma in our subprefecture, everything is clear as day: so
> long as one sits at one's desk and depicts the man in the street, the nor-
> mal, nice guy, describing how he drinks, beats his wife, how he gets by,
> sometimes siding with the authorities, sometimes opposing them, ev-
> erything will be fine. This is what is called vivid and committed litera-
> ture, this primitive neorealist art that reproduces provincial ways and
> customs, weddings, wakes, burials, murders, abortions, all supposedly
> in the name of political involvement, of a civilizing spirit and a per-
> petually new literary renaissance.[50]

In literary spaces that are closely monitored by political authorities,
formalism is considered for the most part a luxury to be indulged by
countries in the center, which no longer have to concern themselves
with either the national question or political commitment: "The triumph of *engagement*," Kiš remarks, "of commitment—to which, we
must admit, we adhere only too often and which stipulates that literature which is not committed is not literature—shows to what extent
politics has penetrated the very pores of our beings, flooded life like a
swamp, made man unidimensional and poor in spirit, to what extent poetry has been defeated, to what extent it has become the privilege of the
rich and 'decadent' who can afford the luxury of literature, while the
rest of us . . ."[51] Thus he describes the dominance of a national literary
aesthetic imposed in the former Yugoslavia through the combined influence of native literary tradition, the political regime and national history, and the political influence of the Soviet Union. Socialist realism
therefore served to reinforce Russian domination of the Serbs: "Just as
St. Petersburg was a 'window on the world' for Russians at the time of
Peter the Great . . . so Russia is Serb culture's 'window on the world,'
one where two myths converge: pan-Slavism (Orthodoxy) and revolu-

tion, Dostoevsky and the Comintern."[52] The structural dependence that subjects literary practices to political authority is marked above all by the repetition and reproduction of the same exclusively national narrative assumptions. In other words, this realism, practiced in the name of political engagement, is in reality a literary nationalism whose actual nature—national realism—remains obscured.

In South Korea, for example, where all literature is national, most poets claim to be realist.[53] Thus Shin Kyong-Nim (b. 1935) publishes collections of poetry in which he identifies himself with all those who can be designated by the term "people" or "masses" ("He is one of them," remarks the French critic and translator Patrick Maurus, "and has developed the conviction that his role, his duty, is to give voice to their songs and their stories, however great the sorrow that they express")[54] as well as studies and collections of popular songs that he has recorded in order not only to make them more widely known but also to draw inspiration from them in his own writing.

Carlos Fuentes has described the Mexican literature of the 1950s in very similar terms, or at least using a similar vocabulary—nationalism, realism, antiformalism. At that time, he noted in *Geografía de la novela* (Geography of the Novel, 1993), the novel had to respond to "three simplistic requirements, three unnecessary dichotomies that nonetheless were erected as a dogmatic obstacle to the very possibility of the novel: first, realism against fantasy, indeed against the imagination; second, nationalism against cosmopolitanism; third, political commitment against formalism, against art for art's sake and other forms of literary irresponsibility."[55] Fuentes' first collection of short stories, *Los días enmascarados* (Masked Days, 1954), was naturally condemned as nonrealist, cosmopolitan, and irresponsible.

It thus becomes possible to understand how the very content of literary texts is linked to the place in the worldwide structure of national space from which they emerge. The political dependence of emerging literary spaces is signaled by the recourse to a functionalist aesthetic and, taking the criteria of literary modernity as a standard of measurement, the most conservative narrative, novelistic, and poetical forms. Conversely, as I have tried to show, the autonomy enjoyed by the most literary countries is marked chiefly by the depoliticization of literature: the almost complete disappearance of popular or national themes, the appearance of "pure" writing—texts that, freed from the obligation to help to develop a particular national identity, have no social or political "function"— and, as an aspect of this, the emergence of formal experimentation, which is to say of forms detached from political purpose and unencumbered by nonliterary conceptions of literature. In these countries, the writer is able to operate beyond the domain of inspired prophecy and apart from the function of collective messenger, of national *vates,* or seer, that is assigned to him in nonautonomous spaces.

Formal preoccupations, which is to say specifically literary concerns, appear in small literatures only in a second phase, when an initial stock of literary resources has been accumulated and the first international artists find themselves in a position to challenge the aesthetic assumptions associated with realism and to exploit the revolutionary advances achieved at the Greenwich meridian.

KAFKA AND THE CONNECTION WITH POLITICS

Thanks to the extraordinary complexity of the linguistic, national, political, cultural, and aesthetic situation that he had to face, but also to the sophistication of the intellectual and political controversies that this situation aroused, Franz Kafka was undoubtedly one of the first to understand that small literatures can (and must) be conceived in terms of a single schema. He said that a unified theory of their relative position and specific difficulties might prove illuminating, by identifying recurrent patterns in one literature that have gone unperceived in another, and that questions resolved in the case of one could point to a solution in the case of another. As a Jewish intellectual born in Prague in the late nineteenth century, Kafka came to maturity in a city that lay at the heart of the national tensions and conflicts being felt within the Austro-Hungarian Empire. Far from being a writer standing outside time and history, as has usually been claimed, he became a spontaneous theoretician, as it were, of what he himself actually called "small" literatures,[56] describing developments in the nascent Czechoslovakia and within Yiddish political and literary movements, which is to say the complex mechanisms that bring forth all new national literatures. The national question was not only the major political preoccupation throughout the Austro-Hungarian Empire between 1850 and 1918; it also greatly influenced discussion of intellectual and aesthetic problems during the period.

On 25 December 1911, on the eve of the First World War, Kafka undertook in his diary to describe small literatures with a view to exposing the general mechanisms underlying the emergence of young national literatures. He began with an explicit parallel between Yiddish and Czech literatures, drawing upon his recent discovery of Yiddish theater—which he found dazzling—through the Polish director Isak Löwy: "What I understand of contemporary Jewish literature [comes] through Löwy, and of contemporary Czech literature partly through my own insight."[57] Indeed, it was his intimate and passionate knowledge of the literature that was emerging during these years in his homeland—Max Brod noted that Kafka "followed up the development of Czech literature in every detail"[58]—that enabled him to detect similar characteristics in Yiddish writings and plays.

He was thus led to insist upon the necessarily political position of writers in emerging nations—what he called, in an analytical table summarizing his thinking on the subject, the "external connection with politics"—and proceeded to give a lengthy enumeration of the "benefits" that accompany the birth of a national literature: the "stirring of minds, the coherence of national consciousness . . . the pride which a nation gains from a literature of its own and the support it is afforded in the face of the hostile surrounding world." He drew attention to the parallel birth and development of a national press and publishing industry, but above all to the political importance attached to literature, noting "the birth of a respect for those active in literature . . . the acknowledgment of literary events as objects of political solicitude." Literary texts in these small countries are inevitably produced, Kafka argued, in proximity with politics: "Even though something is often thought through calmly, one still does not reach the boundary where it connects up with similar things, one reaches this boundary soonest in politics, indeed, one even strives to see it before it is there, and often sees this limiting boundary everywhere." In other words, individual concerns rapidly become collective: every text has a political character, since one seeks to politicize (which is to say, to nationalize), to shrink the frontier that separates the subjective—the domain reserved for literature in large countries—from the collective. But, Kafka hastened to add, the fact that "the inner independence of literature makes the external connection with politics harmless" results in "the dissemination of literature within a country on the basis of political slogans."[59]

In short, for Kafka, who was able directly to observe contemporary developments in Prague, and to whom Löwy recounted in detail everything that was happening in Yiddish literature and the Yiddishist political movement in Warsaw, a nascent literature existed only through its claim to national identity. Its primary characteristic, its very animating spirit, he saw as the product of this constant and constitutive interplay between its two natures, each of which provides a foundation for the other. The "national struggle that determines every work" of Yiddish literature in Warsaw, as he had come to understand some weeks earlier, also defined all the literary enterprises of small countries.[60]

Of course, small literatures could be characterized in this way only on the basis of an implicit comparison with the dominant tradition in Kafka's world: German literature. This tradition derived not only from the fact that it was "rich in great talents"—a very clear way of referring to the German literary heritage—but also from the fact that it treated elevated subjects—a way of describing literary autonomy. Kafka remarked (and emphasized—proof of his rare perceptiveness) that new national literatures are also popular literatures. The absence of an autonomous literary culture with its own traditions and peculiar concerns explains why in new spaces, as Kafka observed, "literature is less a concern of literary history than of the people." In explicitly stating the fundamental difference between literatures that are great by virtue of their heritage, which is to say their accumulated history, and small literatures, which are defined by an ambient popular culture, Kafka affirmed the reality of the struggle between the two types of legitimacy described earlier. This is why "what in great literature goes on down below, constituting a not indispensable cellar of the structure, here takes place in the full light of day." The inversion of "above" and "below" in the hierarchy of genres, levels of language, and works is an essential mark, in Kafka's view, of small literatures (which occasion "universal delight in the literary treatment of petty themes").[61]

Finally, Kafka invoked the complex and obligatory relationship maintained by every writer from a small country with his national literature: "For the claim that the national consciousness of a small people makes on the individual is such that everyone must always be prepared to know that part of the literature which has come down to him, to support it, to defend it—to defend it even if he does not know it and support it."[62]

This obscure and difficult text is not a fully articulated theory, only a series of notes jotted down in Kafka's journal, his first reflections on a subject that, as we shall see, was to become central to the development of his entire work. But the true interest of these remarks has to do with the position Kafka occupied as both witness and actor, a perspective that was both unusual and valuable owing to his passionate interest in the Yiddishist movement of cultural nationalism he discovered through Isak Löwy, which enabled him to see matters from both a theoretical and a practical point of view. As a close and sympathetic observer of events he came to have a sensitive understanding of the way in which literary domination was actually experienced, while hoping at the same time to be able to develop a general explanation for this experience. His intuitions therefore serve as an exemplary case study, one that demonstrates the practical usefulness of theoretical analysis. It is also clear that the famous diary entry of 25 December 1911, which has been the object of a lengthy commentary by Gilles Deleuze and Félix Guattari,[63] cannot be fully appreciated unless it is set in the context of a general model of the hierarchical structure of the literary world. Kafka himself affirmed the need to speak of small literatures, which is to say of literary worlds that exist only in their unequal structural relationship to large ("great") literatures; he saw these worlds as inherently politicized, and insisted on the inevitably political and national character of the texts written in them—not in order to deplore or devalue literary productions from these worlds but, to the contrary, to try to understand their nature and interest (the "universal delight" they produce) as well as the mechanisms that generate them and render them necessary.

Deleuze and Guattari, in rereading Kafka's text, diminish the specifically literary character of literature by applying to it—particularly in connection with the highly ambiguous notion of "minor literature"—a crude and anachronistic interpretation that deforms his meaning. They argue that Kafka was a political author ("Everything is political, beginning with the letters to Felice"),[64] though they limit their attention to the 25 December 1911 entry in the diary. While it is true that Kafka had political interests, as his biographer Klaus Wagenbach has demonstrated,[65] they could not have been the ones ascribed to him by Deleuze and Guattari, whose anachronistic conception of politics leads them into historical errors. They project upon Kafka their view of politics as subversion, or "subversive struggle," whereas for him, in the Prague of the early twentieth century, it was identified solely with the national question. "It is the glory of such a literature to be minor," they write, "which is to say revolutionary for all literature"—noting that "'minor' no longer characterizes certain literatures; instead [it refers to] the revolutionary conditions of all literature called great (or established)."[66] In other words, Kafka was a political author who had no real political interests, who did not care about the burning political questions of his time.

Failing to grasp the content that Kafka actually gave to the notion of politics, Deleuze and Guattari are obliged to fall back upon an archaic conception of the writer in order to justify their position. Thus they hold that Kafka was political, but only in a prophetic way; he spoke of politics, but only for the future, as if he foresaw and described events to come: "He was a political author through and through, seer of the future world"; in his work, the "creative line of flight carries away with it all of politics, economics, bureaucracy, and law: it sucks them, like a vampire, to make them emit yet unknown sounds, which are from the near future—fascism, Stalinism, Americanism, diabolical powers that are knocking at the door. For expression precedes content and entails it." In short: "The literary machine thus takes over from the revolutionary machine to come."[67]

The anachronism operates in both directions: on the one hand, in evoking the figure of the poet as prophet and seer, capable of divining and announcing events to come, Deleuze and Guttari reach far back into the past to retrieve the most archaic of poetical mythologies; on the other, in identifying politics with revolution, they impose a modern opinion upon a writer from the past who did not share it. Unable even to imagine that nationalism was one of Kafka's great political convictions, Deleuze and Guattari create a political and critical catchword—"minor literatures"—out of whole cloth and freely attribute it to him. Their interpretation of Kafka is further proof that anachronism is a form of literary ethnocentrism used by the centers to apply their own aesthetic and political categories to texts.

At a very early age—in all the poverty and bareness of Trinidad, far away, with a population of half a million—I was given the ambition to write books . . . But books are not created just in the mind. Books are physical objects. To write them, you need a certain kind of sensibility; you need a language, and a certain gift of language; and you need to possess a particular literary form. To get your name on the spine of the created physical object, you need a vast apparatus outside yourself. You need publishers, editors, designers, printers, binders; booksellers, critics, newspapers, and magazines . . . and, of course, buyers and readers . . . This kind of society didn't exist in Trinidad. It was necessary, therefore, if I was going to be a writer, and live by my books, to travel out to that kind of society where the writing life was possible. This meant, for me at that time, going to England. I was traveling from the periphery, the margin, to what to me was the center; and it was my hope that, at the center, room would be made for me.
   —V. S. Naipaul, "Our Universal Civilization"

BY DESCRIBING THE dilemmas, choices, and inventions of writers from outlying spaces as a set of mutually related positions—the definition of one being inseparable from that of any other—it becomes possible to recast the familiar question of the nature and limits of dominated national literatures. One of the immediate practical consequences of this method is that exiled or assimilated authors, who in a sense have disappeared from their native lands, can now be reintegrated with them. Histories of Francophone literature in Belgium, for example, devote by far the greater part of their attention to the founders of the national tradition and those among their successors who thought of themselves as Belgian writers. They generally exclude—or resist including—Marguerite Yourcenar and Henri Michaux, in the same way that Irish literary histories hesitate to include George Bernard Shaw and Samuel Beckett in their national panorama, as if membership in a literary space by birth needs subsequently to be reaffirmed. But in fact the formation of a literary space can be understood only in terms of the often antagonistic relation between two possibilities, the hatred that some writers feel toward their homeland and the passionate attachment that it inspires in others.

Just so, national literary space must not be confused with national territory. Taking into account every one of the positions that characterizes a literary space, including those occupied by exiled writers, and regarding them as elements of a coherent whole, helps resolve the false questions that are posed in connection with small literatures. For it is through the interplay between established national positions and the emergence of autonomous literary positions, which are necessarily international, occupied by writers who often are condemned to a sort of internal exile (like Juan Benet and Arno Schmidt) or to actual exile (like James Joyce in Trieste and Paris, Danilo Kiš in Paris, and Salman Rushdie in London), that the full complexity of a national literary space appears.

One speaks today, for example, of Colombian literature and of Colombian writers as if they form a politicoliterary entity that is a recognized reality, something tangible and obvious that can be uncontroversially described. But owing to the interaction of a great many different figures and factors—internationally celebrated writers such as Gabriel García Márquez, the 1982 Nobel Prize winner, and Álvaro Mutis (b. 1923); national writers such as Germán Espinosa (b. 1938), themselves strongly influenced by the stylistic innovations of their more famous countrymen; the many Colombian exiles in Europe and other parts of Latin America; the proud attachment to Latin America as a distinct cultural and linguistic world; the importance of Paris as an arbiter and mediator; the detour (seductive for García Márquez, repugnant for Mutis) via Cuban politics; the lure of New York; the power of Barcelona publishers and literary agents; the stays in Spain; the rivalries and grand political debates among the best-known Latin American authors to have come out of the "boom"—Colombian literary space has become a sort of divided zone that reaches across territorial boundaries, an invisible laboratory in which a national literature has been created that is irreducible to the borders of the nation that its authors helped fashion. The cleavages characteristic of literary spaces that are the furthest removed from the center and the pattern of their multiple dependencies furnish perhaps the surest sign of the incongruence of literary space and the political nation, which is to say of the relative autonomy of world literary space.

It is the complex conjunction of a great many positions, gradually elaborated and put into play, that creates the history of an emergent literature. These positions construct, and then progressively unify, the spaces in which they appear, each one representing a stage in the genesis of a national space. But no newly created position either makes the prior position outmoded or causes it to disappear; each of them makes the rules of the game more complex and causes them to evolve, triggering a contest for literary resources that has the effect of enriching the space. The whole problem in describing the form of these revolts and subversions is that each option or possibility may be simultaneously described as an initial phase of growth, a structural element, a gradual process through which literary history is made, and one among various contemporary positions that coexist (and compete with each other) within a given literary space.

Assimilation, for example, is the lowest level of literary revolt, the obligatory itinerary of every apprentice writer from an impoverished region having no literary resources of its own—for example, a colonized area prior to the formation of a movement for independence or the proclamation of a distinctive national identity. But it is also an option for writers from dominated spaces that are nonetheless relatively well endowed with resources (as, for example, Michaux, a Belgian, and Shaw, an Irishman) who can thus refuse the fate of becoming a national writer—what the Polish novelist Kazimierz Brandys (1916–2000) called the "patriotic duty" of the writer[1]—and begin by almost clandestine means to appropriate the literary heritage of the centers for themselves. In this way Shaw and Michaux managed to obtain direct access to the freedom of form and content that alone authenticates membership in central literary space. Notwithstanding the fact that those who choose assimilationist exile are apt to disappear from the memory of their homelands, being absorbed by the dominant space, with the result that they are for the most part forgotten or marginalized in national literary histories, this

alternative remains one of fundamental mechanisms by which dominated spaces slowly acquire greater autonomy.

Political assimilation has long been described as a process of fusion and
integration by which an immigrant, exile, or dominated population progressively abandons its religious, cultural, and linguistic differences and
particularities and, forced to accept a subordinate position in its new
country, adopts prevailing customs and practices. A striking passage in
one of the long stories of the *Ghetto Comedies* (1907), by the English
Jewish writer Israel Zangwill (1864–1926), summarizes the ambiguity
and difficulty of this longing for assimilation, through which the dominated seek to forget their origins: "There are many ways," the narrator says, "of concealing from the Briton your shame in being related
through a pedigree of three thousand years to Aaron, the High priest of
Israel." Thus Zangwill's character Solomon Cohen had long "distinguished himself by his Anglican mispronunciation of Hebrew and his
insistence on a minister who spoke English and looked like a Christian
clergyman."[2]

The rabbi who has the appearance of a clergyman might well be
taken as the paradigm of literary assimilation, which likewise (as Ramuz
understood) very often depends on whether or not one has the right accent. For writers who are utterly without recognized literary resources,
it often represents the sole means of access to literature and literary existence. One thinks, for example, of the journey of the many Irish playwrights who came to London prior to the emergence of a movement of
cultural nationalism in their homeland. Oscar Wilde and George Bernard Shaw were only the latest heirs to a long line of Irish dramatists—
among them, in the eighteenth century, Congreve and his successors,
Farquhar, Goldsmith, and Sheridan—who distinguished themselves in
the genre of comedy. For Joyce, this tradition was a form of historical
dependence that he was determined to escape. Thus in an essay devoted
to Wilde he wrote: "*Lady Windermere's Fan* took London by storm. In
the tradition of Irish writers of comedy that runs from the days of
Sheridan and Goldsmith to Bernard Shaw, Wilde became, like them,
court jester to the English."[3]

Joyce's famous and brilliant expression at the beginning of *Ulysses*,
where he proposes the "cracked looking glass of a servant" as the symbol
of Irish art,[4] is likewise to be understood as a violent rejection of any

form of assimilation. Indeed, it may be taken as applying to the artistic and cultural productions of all colonized or otherwise dominated regions. Thus the native art of Ireland, before the birth of the Revival Movement, was a simple mirror—an image that recalls the imitation that was first found, it will be recalled, among those whom du Bellay condemned as "replasterers of walls," who produce only pale imitations of the predominant art. But Joyce, in his fury and realism, went still further in condemning mimetic practices, making the mirror cracked. The very dependence of Irish artists made them unable, Joyce argued, to create anything other than a deformed copy of originals. What is more, they were not even simple imitators; they were no more than domestics in the household service of the English, mere maids—an extraordinarily offensive idea in the nationalist atmosphere of Ireland in the 1920s— who were incapable of lifting themselves, even in the aesthetic domain, above the inferior condition that their colonizers had taught them to believe was naturally theirs. They accepted, in other words, as their sole identity, the lowly self-image imposed by the people who had subjugated them. Thus one understands why assimilation arouses such deep ambivalence in emerging literary spaces: it is at once the primary means of access to literature for writers who lack national resources of their own and the characteristic form of betrayal in such spaces. Artists who seek assimilation in the center, and so betray the national literary cause, in a sense cease to belong to their native land.

NAIPAUL: THE NEED TO CONFORM

V. S. Naipaul, born on the outer edges of the British Empire, is an outstanding example of a writer who wholly embraced the dominant literary values of his linguistic region; who, in the absence of any literary tradition in his native country, had no other choice but to try to become English. Despite all the suffering, all the discrimination and rejection to which he found himself exposed on account of his background, his culture, and the color of his skin—an ineradicable reminder of his distance from the center—he inevitably found himself stranded in a sort of no-man's-land: neither completely English (despite being knighted by the queen) nor completely Indian.

Naipaul was born in 1932 in the West Indies, in Trinidad, then a British colony. He was the descendant of Indian immigrants, rural laborers recruited around 1880 to work the plantations in various parts of the British Empire, including the Fiji Islands, Mauritius, South Africa (where Gandhi found an Indian community at the end of the century), Guyana, and Trinidad.[5] Having gone to England on a university scholarship, with the intention of becoming a writer, Naipaul sought to make himself a part of English society[6]—indeed, to embody the most perfect Englishness.

His book *The Enigma of Arrival* (1987), published almost forty years after his arrival in the capital of the empire, is an act of soul-searching, a disillusioned and moving account of a life spent searching for a definite and lasting place. "It is one of the saddest books I have read in a long while, its tone one of unbroken melancholy," Salman Rushdie wrote when the book came out in London.[7] The absence of a literary and cultural tradition peculiar to Trinidad that he could claim for himself and build upon, and the impossibility of ever fully identifying himself with India, from which he was separated by two generations and thousands of miles, made Naipaul the sorrowful personification of dual exile. He evokes in this book, with the pitiless lucidity of one who has suffered terribly on account of his perceived foreignness, and with a kind of self-inflicted cruelty that recalls Ramuz's account of arriving in Paris more than seventy years earlier in *Raison d'être* (1914), his trip from Port of Spain, the capital of Trinidad, to Southampton. Made to feel "like a provincial, from a far corner of the empire," Naipaul came to understand that he was a "half-Indian," unable to lay claim to the cultural tradition of India, but at the same time very far removed as well, by his background, his education, and the color of his skin, from the intellectual and literary world of England: "But that half-Indian world, that world removed in time and space from India, and mysterious to the man, its language not even half understood, its religion and religious rites not grasped, that half-Indian world was the social world the man knew."[8]

Naipaul describes the experience of settling down in the English countryside, upon completing his studies at Oxford, and his difficult beginnings as a writer. There, in Wiltshire, site of a "second birth," he tried actually to make himself English—to understand the landscape, the passing of the seasons, the history and the life of the people of his adopted land. "But knowledge came slowly to me. It was not like the almost instinctive knowledge that had come to me as a child of the plant and flowers of Trinidad; it was like learning a second language." He recalled learning in the late spring "to fix that particular season, to give it certain associations of flower, trees, river." This frenzied desire to belong to a country, to know its daily intimacies, this way of seizing its history in order to make it his own—"My sense of antiquity, my feeling for the age of the earth and the oldness of man's possession of it, was always with me . . . So in tune with the landscape had I become, in that solitude, for the first time in England"—are continually recalled, as though to compensate for an absence, a lack, or what he experienced as one. To put an end to his condition as a foreigner—defined negatively at first as someone without history, without literature, without country (Trinidad having not yet achieved independence), without tradition, without a culture of his own—in short, everything that made up what he called his "insecure past"—he immersed himself in Englishness.[9]

No doubt this is what explains his unmistakably English view of the world, his almost provocative determination to prove himself more English than the English, more nostalgic than his neighbors for the Empire and England's lost power, his pride in proclaiming himself the product of Western civilization. His 1991 essay "Our Universal Civilization"— whose very title announces an appropriation—is a magnificent illustration of his utter identification with the values of the British Empire.[10] In making an apparently objective comparison between two types of colonialism, the European and the Muslim, he condemns the latter and affirms his sense of belonging and his pride in being the product of the former: "And if I have to describe the universal civilization I would say it is the civilization that both gave the prompting and the idea of the literary vocation; and also gave the means to fulfill that prompting; the civilization that enabled me to make that journey from the periphery to the center."[11] Naipaul remains faithful to this position, which is at once conservative, disillusioned, and impossible: the stigma of his own skin ceaselessly reminds him of his betrayal of his own kind, whom England had once colonized.

Even his perspective on contemporary India—complex, painful, difficult, and ambivalent—bears the imprint of this strange, sad lucidity that makes him see, even in the first stirrings of national independence, the mark of English heritage.[12] It is this distant proximity that allows him to state paradoxical and unbearable truths. Thus, he writes, "the history of old India was written by its conquerors"—for the very notions of country, national heritage, culture, and civilization that were to animate the Indian nationalist movement came from English conceptions of the world and history. Naipaul himself, as a child in distant Trinidad, had learned "what Goethe had said about *Shakūntalā,* the Sanskrit play that Sir William Jones had translated in 1789."[13]

Such are the strange paradoxes and impasses in which a refugee from Trinidad was apt to find himself caught up. Naipaul's pessimistic view of England's future, his regret at the disappearance of a pastoral landscape and the decay of country manors, reminders of ancient grandeur and decline, his almost colonial nostalgia for British power—all these things are so many signs of a curious inversion of perspective, of an unqualified endorsement of a view of the world with which nonetheless he can never completely align himself. The "famous Olympian disgust" evoked by Rushdie, which has led Naipaul in his fiction no less than in his journalism to cast a cynical and disenchanted eye upon the countries of the Third World,[14] is also the effect of his position as an assimilated writer, as a traitor to the colonized condition, and of his habit of radical skepticism.

Naipaul's deliberate quest for Englishness—rewarded in the end by a knighthood—naturally disinclined him to innovate with regard to literary form or style. Evidence of his political conservatism, a sort of hypercorrection (in the linguist's sense) within English political and literary space, can be found in all his writings. The traditional character of his stories and novels is the direct consequence of this pathetic search for identity. Ultimately, to write like an Englishman means having to conform to the canons of England.

The award to Naipaul of the Nobel Prize in 2001 in a sense completed the process of assimilation by giving his literary and national transmutation its highest and most perfect form: an English writer who has now become universal. Most of all, this supreme recognition allowed him to "justify" the ambiguities of his position, on the strength of which he claimed to be able to state the truth about the most disenfranchised peoples of the earth with greater authority than others, while at the same time taking advantage of his membership in both worlds to adopt the least favorable view possible of these peoples.[15]

MICHAUX: WHAT IS A FOREIGNER?

The career of Henri Michaux (1899–1984) is in one sense similar to that of Naipaul, apart from the fact that he did not come from a space that was dominated politically: Francophone Belgium was then, as now, a linguistic dependency of France. Born in Namur, Michaux refused the fate of national poets, choosing to forget his Belgian origins (and make them forgotten by others) in order to become a French poet. The fact of a shared language and, excepting his accent, the absence of external signs of foreign nationality naturally favored this furtive integration into the community of central poets.

As a Walloon, Michaux was free to choose between the path of dissimilation, which is to say claiming Belgian regional or national identity, and assimilation to French literary space. He did not settle in Paris until 1924. In combination with his accent, which he mentions in a poem the following year (and then took care to delete in later versions of the text)[16] and which recalls the "'r's of the other end of Europe" that Cioran was later to admit to,[17] his cultural distance and otherness placed him in the curious position of coming across as provincial without the advantage of seeming foreign.

In certain of Michaux's writings—*Un certain plume* (A Certain Plume, 1931), *Un barbare en Asie* (A Barbarian in Asia, 1933), *Voyage en Grand Garabagne* (Travels in Great Garabagne, 1936), and *Ailleurs* (Elsewhere, 1948)—the emphasis on distance and discrepancy, the division of the world into countries and peoples, foreigners and natives, serves not only to state the premises of a purely literary project. Only a very near neighbor to France, whose accent, manners, and way simply of being betrayed his status as an odd sort of stranger—someone who was a foreigner without quite being one and whose very proximity prevented him from blending in, even though nothing set him apart—could imagine dividing up the world into natives and nonnatives. His parody of ethnographic discourse, notably in *Travels in Grand Garabagne,* is very close to what Swift (another Irish "foreigner" assimilated to England) attempted in *Gulliver's Travels.* And just as the subversive power and provocation of Swift's *Travels* have almost been forgotten, in France at least, Michaux's *Travels* have perhaps not been associated with the author's actual situation as a provincial fascinated by the very fact of foreignness.[18]

It was in the company of another faux-Parisian, the Ecuadoran poet Alfredo Gangotena (1904–1944)—who had come to France from distant Uruguay in 1924 and adopted its language, earning the respect of the greatest writers of his time and getting published in all the leading reviews—that Michaux set out on the famous yearlong journey in Gangotena's native land that produced his first book, *Ecuador* (1929).

Michaux's unfashionable determination in this book, which many readers found shocking, to resist all temptations of poetic exoticism is more readily understood if one realizes that his trip was an occasion for verifying the suspicion that Ecuador was only Gangotena's Belgium. It was their similarity as outsiders fascinated with France, and their common interest in refusing to glorify, to grant any reality to the distance—geographic, linguistic, and cultural—that separated their homelands from Paris, that enabled Michaux to universalize his decentered position. Bilingualism also permitted them to identify with each other: Michaux, a Walloon, had been educated in Flemish and as a young man was intrigued by Esperanto, in which he saw a chance to escape the hold of both Flemish and French. He thus established a sort of equivalence between his hated Belgium and Ecuador, a land of literary exile for Gangotena as well as his native country.

Evidence of the weight of Belgian identity—experienced by the young Henri Michaux as a curse, a sign of inferiority—can be found in "Quelques renseignements sur cinquante-neuf années d'existence" (A Few Particulars concerning Fifty-nine Years of Existence), a short essay first published in 1959 in a book of interviews with Robert Bréchon.[19] Although he was now a very famous author, and despite his reluctance to divulge biographical details (another trait he shared with Cioran: exiled poets who achieve assimilation in a foreign literary environment and manage to conceal their origins are naturally reluctant to recall the stages of their metamorphosis), Michaux gave a memorable portrait of himself as a young Belgian poet in a few pithy and precise strokes. He recalled the importance of his literary training and the cosmopolitan Belgian reviews that interested him in his youth; but above all he openly acknowledged his resolve to rid himself of his Belgian identity: "Belgium left once and for all," he remarked, referring to his departure in 1922; from 1929 onward, "he traveled against. To expel his country from him, attachments of all sorts and everything of Greek or Roman or Germanic culture, and of Belgian habits, that fixed itself in him and in spite of him. Voyages of expatriation."[20]

This explicit rejection of his country constituted the very subject matter of Michaux's early writings. His attempt to disavow what had been bequeathed to him, to claim another cultural and literary tradition and, so far as possible, identify himself with it, was motivated by a desire to deny what he saw as his shameful origins. In the epilogue to *Plume* (as the 1931 book was later known) he had vigorously affirmed his rejection of familial and national heritage: "I have lived against my father (and against my mother and against my grandfather, my grandmother, and my great-grandparents); for want of knowing them, I have not been able to struggle against more distant ancestors."[21]

Thus it was, many years later, that he challenged any attempt at national reappropriation, refusing to be included in anthologies of Belgian literature. Michaux's hatred of his name, which combined adversion to his family and rejection of his native land, sprang from a sense that he bore a special curse. "He continued to sign [his work] with his ordinary name, which he detested," Michaux wrote in "Quelques renseignements"—a name "of which he was ashamed, as though it were a label containing the words 'inferior quality.' Perhaps he kept it out of loyalty to his discontent and dissatisfaction. He was therefore never to take pride in his work, always dragging around with him this ball and chain placed at the end of each work, thus protecting himself against even a small sense of triumph and accomplishment."[22]

CIORAN: ON THE INCONVENIENCE OF BEING BORN IN ROMANIA

The careers of writers assimilated to the great literary centers constitute a sort of repertoire of the different types and forms of literary domination. V. S. Naipaul experienced a political form of domination, reinforced by a literary one; Henri Michaux found himself in a condition of linguistic and literary dependence. But in the case of E. M. Cioran (1911–1995) the dependence was exclusively literary. Born into a relatively recent and deeply impoverished literary space, but one that was neither politically nor linguistically dominated by France, Cioran chose exile far from Romania. He betrayed its national cause to the point of abandoning his native language in favor of French, electing to integrate himself in the capital of literature in order to escape the fate of all writers from small countries.

When Cioran arrived in France in 1937, he already enjoyed a reputation in his own country as a promising young writer, having published four books. Two more were to follow, including the emblematic *Îndreptar pătimaş* (Breviary of the Vanquished, 1945). But in France he was a foreigner—unknown, untranslated, living in extreme poverty. This fall into anonymity and the intellectual underclass recalled and reinforced his original experience as a writer on the margins of Europe.

Completing Cioran's personal transfiguration was the decision, ten years after arriving in France, to adopt French as his literary language—a genuine ordeal, as he later testified: "Changing language at the age of twenty can still be done without too much difficulty, but at thirty-five, thirty-six . . . For me it was a terrible experience . . . The switch to another language can be made only at the price of renouncing one's own language."[23] Cioran's belated rebirth as a French writer meant having to strip away all traces of his Romanian past. In order to participate fully in the rich heritage of French intellectual and literary life, to enjoy a reputation untainted by the infamy of his earlier associations, and to hide from view the contamination of his "genius" by membership in an obscure nation, Cioran had to eradicate the memory of his previous existence. One finds reproduced here almost trait for trait—neglecting, of course, the nationalist and fascist obsession—the entire career of Henri Michaux (to whom Cioran was very close),[24] who similarly sought to erase his Belgian accent, his genealogy, who proclaimed his hatred of his family, his scorn for heredity, and his disgust for traditional Flemish life, wishing with all his might to become French and so erase the stigma of his origins.

But Cioran's conversion can be understood only in terms of his choice of a style: he did not choose merely to write in French; he chose to write in the grand style—the language of Racine. This stylistic classicism, or hyperclassicism, harkened back to an age when the preeminence of French culture was unchallenged. Cioran sought to regain the moment when the language and literary style of France enjoyed their highest degree of universal recognition, as though he were trying to restore contact with "genius" in its pure state. In this hierarchical conception of cultures and triumphant classicism may be seen a trace of the Herderian (or, in the broad sense, German) theories that assumed such importance in the various small European countries that longed for independence in the late nineteenth and early twentieth centuries. Cioran's style—indeed, his entire work—can be regarded as an avatar of the belief, inherited from the eighteenth century, in the superiority of the France of Louis XIV; a belated incarnation of the classicism with which the Germans in particular, as we have seen, were determined to compete.

Cioran's concern with transfiguration, with turning himself into a French writer, his obsession with cultural decadence and failure, and his national conception of history led him first to leave Romania for France; and then, haughtily ignoring all his contemporaries and refusing to acquaint himself with current aesthetic debates and innovations, he reached back (like Naipaul after him) to a stylistic archaism better suited to his ideological conservatism. This improbable reversion was soon crowned by success with the publication in 1949 of *Précis de décomposition* (A Short History of Decay), a work that was praised in France partly on account of the reverence it displayed toward the memory of national literary grandeur ("a twentieth-century La Rochefoucauld," as the critics were later to say), of the homage it represented by a foreigner to an intellectual power that felt itself to be in decline. Unsurprisingly perhaps, many critics found the essential ambiguity of Cioran's thought difficult to grasp. For in and through his work, by means of a sort of historical irony that can be explained only if the world of letters is conceived in international terms, the most conventional images of literary greatness, resuscitated by the nationalist imagination of a Romanian writer who had made himself more French than the French, came to be merged with the literary fantasies of a people haunted by their fear of decline and flattered in their notions of national literary history and their most archaic conceptions of style and thought.

RAMUZ: THE IMPOSSIBLE ASSIMILATION

Before becoming the leader of the *Renaissance vaudoise,* the Swiss writer Charles Ferdinand Ramuz (1878–1947) had tried for ten long years before the First World War to create a place for himself in Parisian literary circles—as Henri Michaux was to do after the war—in the hope that, by achieving recognition as a French novelist, he would be able to conceal his origins. Yet it was his very proximity that prevented him from establishing himself in Paris: because he spoke French with an accent, he was too close—too provincial—in the eyes of the consecrating authorities to be accepted, but not far away enough—not sufficiently foreign, exotic, new—to arouse their interest. Ramuz himself gave a moving account of his experience as a young provincial poet excluded and rejected by Paris in a manifesto titled *Raison d'être,* which constituted both a statement of editorial purpose of the *Cahiers vaudois,* the review he founded in 1914 with his friends Edmond Gilliard and Paul Budry on returning to Switzerland, and its first issue.

Raison d'être is a text of capital importance for understanding Ramuz's career. It gave expression to his desire to overturn Parisian law and to invert the prevailing order of values—to transform what until then had been a badge of inferiority into a proudly proclaimed difference. The return to the land of his birth was the consequence of a quasi-conscious decision to convert the stigma of his accent and his provincial manners into an acknowledged identity. Describing life in Paris, he wrote:

> I tried in vain to take part in it—I was aware of my clumsiness, which only made things worse. The embarrassment when one has become ridiculous (at the age of twenty); one no longer knows how to speak, not even how to walk. The least differences of intonation, or of accent, or of attitude are worse than more marked ones and embarrass you much more. The Englishman remains an Englishman, there's nothing surprising about an Englishman, he's taken for what he is: whereas I'm almost the same as those around me, and, wishing to be just the same, fall short only by a tiny bit, but the gap is terribly obvious.[25]

More than twenty years later, in *Paris: Notes d'un Vaudois* (Paris: Notes of a Vaudois, 1938), he was to return to the theme of the hostility of Paris and the impossibly difficult choices faced by writers from outside the center. It was, he observed, as though the capital of literature was incapable of perceiving, much less consecrating and recognizing, anyone who was not situated at the right distance from it:

> The provincial in Paris wears the outward look of Paris in the street, the appearance of Paris . . . [He] is anxious above all not to be taken for a provincial . . . Paris [is] quite hostile, because it seems to exclude in advance those who do not belong to it: those who do not model their appearance on its appearance, their gestures, their intonations, their facial expressions on its gestures, intonations, and facial expressions . . . Either you are from [Paris] or you are not. If you are not, don't try to give the impression that you are; you will be caught out sooner or later, with the result . . . that the adventure will end in your expulsion, more or less cunning, but definitive.[26]

This remote proximity creates a hybrid character, the false foreigner and true provincial, the eternal peasant who struggles in vain to create a place for himself in the capital. Ramuz analyzed this condition with great acuteness and precision, attempting to calibrate the exact distance required in order to have a chance of being noticed by the consecrating authorities of Paris. What earlier I called "Ramuz's dilemma" expresses this very perceptiveness. The strategy that he finally and—what sets Ramuz apart from other writers—almost consciously adopted in order to get himself recognized by Paris was one of decisive rupture, exaggerating his own differences, and in this way placing just the right distance between himself and a recalcitrant capital that could not be ignored.

The poverty of the means granted to him is so impossible to imagine that it appears to defy all credibility. Language, culture, intellectual values, scales of moral values, none of these gifts that one receives in the cradle are of any possible use to him . . . What to do? The thief gets hold at once of other instruments, ones that have been forged neither for him nor for the ends that he means to pursue. What matters is that they are within his reach and that he can bend them to suit his purposes. The language is not his language, the culture is not the heritage of his ancestors, these turns of thought, these intellectual, ethical categories are not current in his natural environment. How ambiguous are the weapons at his disposal!
—Mohammed Dib, "Thief of Fire"

THE SECOND GREAT family of strategies consists of differentiation and dissimilation, which, at least during the time when a new space is being founded, are at once literary and national.[1] It is astounding to note, by the way, that the earliest stages of the international competition inaugurated by the French Pléiade to contest the obligatory use of Latin and the preeminence of Italian poetry were marked by the appearance of almost all the strategies that literary founders were to employ, in essentially unchanged form, over the next four hundred years.

The principal task pioneering writers face is to manufacture difference, for no specifically national resource can be accumulated so long as literary works are entirely assimilable to the dominant space. The halt demanded by du Bellay to the practice of translating the Greek and Latin classics testified to the fact that the simple transfer of Latin resources into French, without any actual innovation, which is to say without any increase in the value of vernacular production or any advertised and proclaimed difference, had the consequence of perpetuating the total domination exercised by the Latin language. Indeed, taking over the predominant tradition virtually word for word only added to the patrimony of Latin and accentuated the obviousness of its supremacy. In order to struggle against dependency it is necessary to create a distinctive identity and in this way, by laying the basis for rivalry and competition, form a literary space.

All first-generation representatives of a literature, like du Bellay, understand both the phenomenon of literary annexation by the dominant spaces to which they are subject and the necessity of creating distance and difference with respect to these spaces. Thus in 1817, almost three-quarters of a century before the Irish Revival was formally launched, Samuel Burdy observed that in Ireland "no encouragement is given to domestic literature, not only by the government, but even by the people themselves. For unhappily a prejudice prevails among them against every production of their own country, and if any Irishman of talents attain celebrity by his publications, he must have acquired it in England, and not at home. In fact the people have no opinion of their own in matters of literature."[2] And in 1826 the Irish periodical *Bolster's Magazine* remarked: "It is the expatriation of national talents that is the cause of the incontestable impoverishment of the rich intellectual resources of our country . . . Sad to remark, in truth, that the talents of which Ireland has an abundance seem to wilt so long as they have not been transplanted and taken on, in the very land that produced them, the appearance of exotic plants."[3] The absence of any distinctive identity therefore prevents native works from being published and achieving recognition. Only works that are conceived and promoted as national productions can help put an end to the dependence of writers in relation to the dominant literary (and political) space.

This is why one finds among many literary founders the same condemnation—vigorously stated in most cases—of imitation. In the chapter of *The Defense and Illustration* titled "Why the French Language Is Not as Rich as Greek and Latin," du Bellay attacked those imitative poets who "have left us our language so poor and bare that it has need of the ornaments and (so to speak) the plumes of other persons."[4] This theme was later to be met with in reworked form in national histories and cultural contexts quite distant from one another. In "The American Scholar" (1837), a document that served as a sort of declaration of intellectual independence for artists of succeeding generations, Ralph Waldo Emerson laid down the guiding principles of American culture and literature. Calling imitation a "fatal disservice," Emerson proclaimed: "Each age, it is found, must write its own books; or rather, each generation for the next succeeding . . . We have listened too long to the courtly muses of Europe."[5]

Latin America furnishes a telling example of the same phenomenon: throughout the nineteenth century, and up until at least the 1940s, its writers produced an imitative literature. Arturo Uslar Pietri, one of the inventors of "magical realism," which was to become in effect the generative formula of all Latin American literature from the 1960s on, insisted in his essays on the weight of European influence in Central and South America, in particular the importance of French romanticism.[6] Thus Chateaubriand's *Atala* (1801)—subtitled "The Love and Constancy of Two Savages in the Desert" and featuring two artificially exotic Indians, placed in a false landscape, who fall in love and suffer according to the most sophisticated conventions of Romantic sentimentalism—became an obligatory model and helped shape the tradition of tropical nativism. The influence of this work was so profound and long-lasting in Latin America that as late as 1879 the Ecuadoran writer Juan León Mera (1832–1894)—who, Uslar Pietri remarks, lived in a region having a large indigenous population—"ceased to see the Ecuadoran Indians with his own eyes, forgot the actual experience of his whole life, and projected onto the void the false vision of Chateaubriand."[7]

It becomes clear, then, why the Cuban writer Alejo Carpentier (1904–1980) was moved to publish a manifesto in Havana in the early 1930s in which he proclaimed the necessity of escaping this state of intellectual subordination and putting an end to a form of literary production that amounted to nothing more than a faithful copy:

> In Latin America the enthusiasm for what comes from Europe gave rise to a certain spirit of imitation, which has had the deplorable consequence of delaying for a very long time [the development of] our own means of expression (an evil Unamuno pointed out quite a while ago). During the nineteenth century we indulged, with a lag of fifteen or twenty years, in all the latest frenzies of the old continent: Roman-

ticism, Parnassism, Symbolism; Rubén Darío began as the spiritual son of Verlaine just as Herrera Reissig was that of Théodore de Banville . . . We dreamed of Versailles and the Trianon, with marquises and *abbés,* while the Indians were relating marvelous legends in our countries . . . Many American artistic domains live today under the sign of Gide, if not of Cocteau or simply Lacretelle. This is one of our evils—we ought to say one of our weaknesses—that we must strenuously resist. But unfortunately it does not suffice to say "Let us break with Europe" to begin to express ourselves in ways that are genuinely representative of the Latin American sensibility.[8]

To produce this sort of original expression is to manufacture difference: each nation creates its own resources. Since the founding of a literature is therefore related to the founding of a nation, first-generation writers use all the means at their disposal—whether literary or politico-national, or both—to gather and concentrate literary wealth. These means differ according to the initial endowment of the literary space in question. In spaces that are relatively well endowed at the outset, the process of enrichment operates by diverting a central patrimony in various ways, through the importation of canonized texts and literary techniques, the designation of new national literary capitals, and so on.

In spaces that were the last to develop and therefore the most destitute, the great innovation that Herder's theories popularized, and that modified the whole set of strategies and solutions to the problem of literary distance, was the idea of the "people." This notion—along with those of nation, language, and literature, which, in the system inaugurated by Herder, were synonymous with it—supplied literary founders with a number of instruments: the collection of popular narratives, transformed into national tales and legends; the creation of a national and popular theater, which made it possible at once to enlarge the scope of the national language, use folk themes as material for this theater, and attract a national audience; the ability to claim antiquity as a heritage (as in the cases of Greece and Mexico) and to challenge the dominant measure of literary time. Ramuz, who understood this mechanism better than anyone else, himself employed the term "capital" in describing difference as a resource of small countries: "Certain countries . . . matter only through their differences . . . [Yet] they do not manage to make use of these differences, which are their true capital, so as to make an impression at the universal bank of foreign exchange and commerce."[9]

LITERARY USES OF THE PEOPLE

Following Herder, then, nation, language, literature, and the people were defined as equivalent and interchangeable terms. This identity added a fourth term to a long-standing equation that had been fixed since du Bellay, substantially modifying the set of strategies and possibilities, particularly linguistic ones, available to deprived writers everywhere. The notion of the people, which Herder had been the first to promote as part of a new conception of literature, and therefore of literary capital, has been a criterion of literary legitimacy ever since, offering new ways of producing and affirming specific differences.

The effects of the Herderian revolution were so powerful and so durable that appeal to the spirit of the people has remained an effective method, despite changes in political context, of achieving access to literary space. In the nineteenth century, the German model introduced a vague and diffuse definition: "popular" meant everything that was "national." But this protean conception, suited to illustrating the most diverse—if not also the most inconsistent—arguments, enjoyed great political success. To the national (or nationalist) definition was added, at the end of the century, the social conception of the people, now defined as a social class. Hence the ambiguity: from now on the "people" was not only another name for a national community taken as a whole, whose classic incarnation was a mythical peasantry, a sort of quintessence of the nation; it also designated—and these notions were in no way contradictory, but rather cumulative—a part of this national whole, consisting of the so-called *classes populaires,* or working classes.

The fluid and polysemous idea of a popular literature (or language) nonetheless was not inconsistent with the criterion that since Herder had established literary legitimacy at the political pole of the international republic of letters. Because it permitted literary resources to be accumulated, and because for two centuries the number of deprived contestants had continued to grow as a result of the progressive enlargement of international literary space, this notion came to be perpetuated even as its political uses were imperceptibly being transformed. Writers both reinvented and reproduced it in a range of different literary, linguistic, and political contexts. The people were not an actual group or entity, on behalf of which writers acted as spokesmen; for writers they were above all a literary (or literary-political) construction, a sort of instrument of literary and political emancipation having its own distinctive use, a way of producing literary difference—and therefore capital—under conditions of great literary destitution. In the early twentieth century, the spread of Communist ideology and belief in literary and intellectual circles—and notably among nationalist militants in areas that were fighting for political independence—favored the appearance of new political, aesthetic, and literary norms in the name of which the popular character of literature was to be affirmed.

It is this very notion that in all periods gives rise to the first inseparably aesthetic and political rivalries in emerging literary spaces, with each competing conception of the popular character of literature generating its own aesthetic and its own literary forms. The first disagreements are over the "proper" definition of the people and what kinds of literary works can be said to be popular. In the name of people as class, some intellectuals reject a nationalist definition of the people, thus raising the stakes of a debate whose very terms are (and remain) political and, by placing themselves in opposition to political authority, achieving a relative and paradoxical autonomy.[10]

The unfolding of these struggles can be seen in the formation of Irish literary space. In Ireland the literary renaissance developed at the juncture of two political-literary moments, with the passage from Romanticism to realism coinciding with the semantic and political shift that led from the idea of the people as nation to that of the people as class. This shift gave rise in turn to two types of realism: the opposition to the idealist aesthetic promoted by Yeats initially took the form of the peasant realism championed by the Cork Realists, with an urban proletarian realism later being introduced by Sean O'Casey (1880–1964), a nationalist playwright and one of the first Irish writers to openly affirm his Communist beliefs. This latter transformation, apparently aesthetic but actually political, remains to this day one of the last metamorphoses of the popular-national identity.

NATIONAL TALES, LEGENDS, POETRY, AND THEATER

With the invention of the notions of people and nation by Herder, and their reinterpretation by the founders of new national literatures, the popular tales collected, edited, reworked, and published by patriotic writers became the first quantifiable resource of a nascent literary space. The initial purpose of the poets of the Irish Revival, for example, may thus be summed up as the recovery, reevaluation, and diffusion of folktales supposed to express the specific genius of the Irish people and to exhibit the country's literary wealth. It was as spokesmen for the Irish popular genius that Yeats, Lady Gregory, Edward Martyn, George Moore, George Russell (Æ), Padraic Colum, John Millington Synge, James Stephens, and others first came to be known and recognized. Ancient legends and traditional narratives, unearthed and ennobled, gradually came to inspire countless poems, novels, stories, and plays, which in turn completed the *littérisation* of these sources in their various forms (comedy, tragedy, symbolic plays, and rural drama).

In countries such as Ireland at the end of the nineteenth century, in which the rate of illiteracy is high and the written literary tradition limited or absent altogether, the transposition of oral practices to written form amounts to an attempt to create literature and thus convert folk tradition into literary wealth by means of a kind of alchemy, transmuting popular cultural and linguistic forms—the ritualized expression of customs and traditions that have not previously been an object of literary evaluation—into cultural and literary gold. It is an attempt, in other words, to give these practices a recognized value that permits access to the literary world. This act of literary transmutation rests mainly on two types of mechanism: first, as in the case of the Irish revivalists, the collection of folktales and popular stories; then, often as part of the same process, the establishment of a national and popular theater.

In much the same spirit as the great populist and national surveys of folklore in Europe conducted in the wake of the "philological revolution" of the nineteenth century, intellectuals and writers in countries created by decolonization in North and sub-Saharan Africa and in Latin America began to construct a literary heritage in the twentieth century, this time on the basis of a new version of the German model, reshaped by ethnological research and devoted to measuring, analyzing, and converting into written form popular practices that until then had been deprived of national and cultural recognition. In Algeria, for example, novelists conducted ethnological research alongside their literary activities. One thinks of Mouloud Mammeri (1917–1989), a novelist, anthropologist, and playwright who first attracted attention as the author of successful novels, such as *La colline oubliée* (The Forgotten Hill, 1952), that reproduced codified literary models, and who later, in the 1970s and 1980s, wrote plays for the theater while also compiling a Berber grammar and publishing collections of Berber folktales and old Kabyle poetry.[11] Other writers, such as Mouloud Feraoun (1913–1962), opted for a quasi-ethnological novelistic style: the descriptive naturalism of novels such as the prizewinning *La terre et le sang* (Land and Blood, 1953) and *Le fils du pauvre* (The Son of the Poor Man, 1954) conferred upon them a quasi-documentary interest that approached the ethnological ideal. By the same token, as we have seen, the quest for political independence brings with it a need to display and increase the nation's literary wealth, through the adaptation for the stage of the tales and legends (as well as novels) that constituted its heritage. But in order for this process of literary accumulation to get started, writers are needed who can deliberately and explicitly transform these popular assets into literary material. The great novel by the Brazilian writer Mário de Andrade, *Macunaíma* (1928), was thus at once (as the author himself affirmed) an "anthology of Brazilian folklore" and, as we shall see later in greater detail, a national novel.[12]

The Yoruba tales of Daniel Olorunfemi Fagunwa (1903–1963), some of which have been translated into English by Wole Soyinka (b. 1934), need to be considered in the same light. Fagunwa was one of the first to have transcribed the oral tradition of his people into the Yoruba language. His first novel, *Ogboju-ode ninu igbó Irunmale* (The Skillful Hunter in the Forest of Spirits, 1939), deployed the themes and above all the narrative techniques of traditional tales and fables. This "naive" work, a popular classic and quasi-ethnological document that by 1950 had gone through sixteen printings, rapidly achieving popularity among the literate public in Nigeria and a secure place on school reading lists,[13] was raised to the rank of literature and national heritage only many years later through the translation and commentary of a future Nobel Prize winner, himself a product of Yoruba tradition, who praised it especially for its "fusion of sound and action."[14] Later, the narratives of Amos Tutuola (1920–1997) in *The Palm-Wine Drinkard* (1952)—which used a naively transcribed pidgin English to tell fantastic stories, full of monsters, cruel ghosts, and phantoms that suddenly appeared in the lives of his characters—were rejected by the first generation of post-independence Nigerian intellectuals,[15] who, in seeking recognition for themselves outside their native country, exhibited a tendency to linguistic hypercorrection and a preference for the norms of Western narrative.

But these tales were to be championed first by Soyinka, for whom Tutuola's use of popular language represented a sort of limiting case for

the categories of Western literary understanding: "This wildly spontaneous kind of English hit the European critics at their weakest point—
boredom with their own language and the usual quest for new titilla-
tions";[16] and then by Ben Okri (b. 1959), a leading representative of the
most recent generation of Nigerian writers, who attracted critical notice
in the West with the publication in London of his novel *The Famished
Road* (1991). Okri's book represented a stunning break with the neorealism of the Nigerian novel, mixing a world of ghosts and spirits—
very much in the manner of Fagunwa and Tutuola—with careful and
detailed description of contemporary Nigeria. Not only, then, did it embody a distinctive and personal view of the world; it also proposed a new
and very original approach to fiction in emerging literary spaces that relied on indigenous cultural and religious tradition. In this respect Okri's
aims were similar to those of his predecessors, except that he refused to
situate himself in a mythical past, instead using its tales to describe and
analyze the present.

Drama occupies an intermediate position between the spoken and written language. It is almost universally performed in areas characterized by
high rates of illiteracy and low levels of literary capital, such as Ireland in
the early twentieth century and certain African countries today. As the
oral art par excellence, drama is at once a popular genre and an instrument for standardizing the language used in an emerging space. Its performance is directly related to the rediscovery and affirmation of traditional popular narratives: in Ireland, for example, drama was used to
convert folktales into a codified and legitimate literary resource. What is
more, it settles the boundaries of an oral language by giving it written
form and then converting this transcription into declaimed speech having literary value. Drama, in other words, works to transform a popular
audience into a national audience by direct appeal to a nascent literature
that exploits the noblest resources of literary art—as Yeats did—while at
the same time casting them in the popular register of the spoken language. It is therefore also the literary art that is most closely associated
with the concerns and demands that give rise to organized political opposition and subversive activity.[17] In many newly formed literary spaces,
the accumulation of a popular heritage, the demand for (and reinvention
of) a national language distinct from the language of colonization, and
the founding of a national theater go hand in hand.

The immediate and essential link between the turn toward drama and the call for a new national language can be apprehended by comparing the situation of a small literature at the beginning of the twentieth century—the Yiddish literature that Kafka knew—with the experience in the 1970s and 1980s of a pair of postcolonial writers, from different linguistic areas, whose careers were utterly changed by the decision (for political and literary reasons) to work in the theater and adopt a new popular language: Kateb Yacine, an Algerian, and Ngugi wa Thiong'o, a Kenyan.[18]

We have seen that Kafka discovered Yiddish language and culture—both inextricably bound up with what he himself called the "national struggle" of eastern European Jews at the beginning of the century—through the theater. A Yiddish theater troupe passing through Prague from Poland in 1911 gave him a glimpse not only of the new Jewish popular literature then being created, but also of a Jewish national and political movement that, until then, he did not even know existed. As with all national literatures placed in the service of political struggle, the one Kafka encountered found both expression and an outlet through the theater, which brought it before a Yiddish-speaking and often illiterate public in Europe and the United States. The new Yiddish drama filled Kafka with enthusiasm for a living popular art endowed with all the attributes (language, tradition, popular legends, and so on) conventionally recognized by national theorists as constituting an "authentic" national culture. His passionate interest is proof of the impact of drama on national movements, and by itself furnishes an extraordinary tool for understanding the form assumed by national ideas that are disseminated through the theater.

On 6 October 1911, having seen a play two days earlier (and no doubt a few performances in 1910 as well), Kafka wrote in his journal: "Would like to see a large Yiddish theater as the production may after all suffer because of the small cast and inadequate rehearsal. Also, would like to know Yiddish literature, which is obviously characterized by an uninterrupted *tradition of national struggle that determines every work.* A tradition, therefore, that pervades no other literature, not even that of the most oppressed people."[19] Isak Löwy, the troupe's director, introduced Kafka during the several weeks it was in Prague to Yiddish language and literature; and even though Kafka did not know Yiddish, the drama written and performed in it opened his eyes to a struggle for emancipation that was indissociably political, linguistic, and literary.

Reliance on drama for political purposes is attested in very different historical and political contexts. Indeed, far from being a historically and culturally specific event, recourse to the theater is an almost universal move for founders of literary traditions in emerging nations. Consider the case of the Algerian writer Kateb Yacine (1929–1989). Yacine had been consecrated in Paris as a leading representative of literary modernity and a pioneer of formal investigation with the appearance of his novel *Nedjma* (1956), written in French. A few years later, in 1962, when Algeria achieved its independence from France, he turned his attention to the political, aesthetic, and linguistic needs of his country's infant literary space. After a period of exile, he broke completely with his prior literary activity and for almost two decades, between 1970 and 1987, led a theater troupe known as Action Culturelle des Travailleurs (Workers' Cultural Action) that traveled throughout Algeria, helping in this way to lay the foundations for a new national literature. But in order to do this he had to renounce a number of prior attachments, abandoning formal experiments in fiction, converting from French to Arabic, and campaigning for a national language freed from traditional constraints. For Yacine it was a question of "making Algerians understand their history" in their main popular languages,[20] dialectical Arabic and Tamashek: "Given my situation in Algeria," he told an interviewer, "it is obvious that political problems are at the root of everything, since the country and society are in the process of being created. Political problems are paramount—and politics means the popular public, the largest public possible. Since there is a message needing to be transmitted, it ought to be addressed to the maximum number of people."[21] In other words, the choice of drama as a form of communication was directly associated with the new circumstances facing Algerian writers and Yacine's own change of language. In the wake of independence he sought to reach a national audience using forms and a language that were familiar to it and that were at once oral and literary:

> How can we make illiteracy disappear? How can we be something other than writers who talk a little over the heads of their people, who are obliged to resort to cunning to make themselves understood by

their people, [who are] often obliged to pass through France [to reach them]? . . . This is a political problem . . . [The people] like to see and hear themselves acting on a theater stage. How could they fail to understand themselves when they speak through their own mouths for the first time in centuries? . . . *Mohamed prend ta valise* is a spoken play, three-quarters in Arabic and one-quarter in French. So spoken, in fact, that I haven't yet even written it. All I have is a tape [recording].[22]

The Kenyan writer Ngugi wa Thiong'o (b. 1938) followed a very similar route. He began his literary career under the name James T. Ngugi and published his first texts in English. His play *The Black Hermit* (1968) had been performed in Uganda in 1962, prior to its actual publication, as part of the country's independence celebrations. With Kenya's independence the following year he took back his African name and published a series of novels in English dealing with the issue of national history and identity: *Weep Not, Child* (1964), *The River Between* (1965), *A Grain of Wheat* (1967). He also directed plays about the major historical events of the tribal society from which he came. In 1967 he began teaching at the University of Nairobi, subsequently moving to Makerere University College in Uganda, where he helped establish an African literature program. But the political violence that gradually came to dominate the region, together with extreme forms of political censorship, blocked the development of autonomous literary activity in his homeland. Ngugi did not hesitate to denounce the authoritarian regime of Jomo Kenyatta, the founder of Kenyan nationalism and president of the republic from 1964 to 1978. His political involvement then assumed a radical and specific form: after publishing *Petals of Blood* (1977), he resolved to go back to his roots and work on behalf of the villagers of his country.[23] At the price of having to switch languages—just as Kateb Yacine had done—he abandoned English for his mother tongue, Kikuyu, and devoted himself to the theater.[24] Following a performance of his play *Ngaahika ndeenda* (I Will Marry When I Want) in 1977, he was arrested and put in jail, where he wrote his first novel in Kikuyu, *Caitaani mutharaba-ini* (Devil on the Cross, 1980), notable for its formal similarities to drama. Released after a year, Ngugi was forced to accept exile in England, where his prison novel was published in London and subsequently translated into Swahili and English.[25]

Similarly, in Quebec, with the emergence of the first separatist movements (whose leaders saw themselves as victims of English Canadian colonization), it was a play, *Les belles-soeurs,* by Michel Tremblay (b. 1942), that utterly and lastingly changed the rules of the literary game in that province. Written in joual,[26] it concerned the lives of a group of working-class women in Montreal, and enjoyed an immediate and resounding success on first being performed in 1968. By the simple fact of giving joual written form, so that it could be spoken on the stage of a theater, Tremblay legitimized it not only as the language of the Québécois (and the emblem of the movement for independence) but as a literary language as well.

LEGACY HUNTING

Alongside the gathering of folktales and legends and the diffusion (which also amounts to recognition) of vernacular languages through the theater, other strategies have been deployed by dominated writers in various historical and political contexts. A stock of national literary resources can be created only through the diversion and appropriation of available assets. Thus du Bellay, rejecting the pure and simple imitation of the ancients, counseled "poètes françoys" to recast Latin turns of phrase in French and, in this way, enrich their language. The metaphor that he used to describe this process—of first "devouring" ancient authors, then "digesting" and "converting" them—was to be adopted (more precisely, reinvented) during the unification of literary space that took place during the next four centuries by all those who, lacking resources of their own, sought to divert to their advantage a share of the existing literary patrimony.[27]

One way of acquiring literary wealth is through the importation of literary expertise and techniques, as Alejo Carpentier emphasized in a seminal text published in June 1931. As a young Cuban exile in Paris (having been aided in his escape from Gerardo Machado's tyrannical regime three years earlier by the French poet Robert Desnos), Carpentier made the acquaintance of the Surrealists and then sought to develop a specifically Caribbean and Latin American style, in particular by adapting Breton's notion of the "merveilleux" to what he was later to call—on the model of Uslar Pietri's "magical realism"—"marvelous reality."[28] In an essay published in *Cartelas,* the Havana review he had edited before his flight from Cuba, Carpentier commented on the first issue of his latest project, a Spanish-language journal published in Paris called *Imán* (Magnet),[29] in terms that exactly recalled those of du Bellay's *Defense and Illustration of the French Language:*

> All art requires a *professional* tradition . . . This is why it is necessary that the young [artists] of America have a thorough knowledge of the representative values of modern European art and literature: not in order to undertake the contemptible labor of imitation and to write, as many do, small novels lacking either warmth or character, copied from some model from beyond the seas, but in order to try to get to the bottom of techniques, through analysis, and to find methods of construction capable of translating with greater force our thoughts and sensibilities as Latin Americans. When Diego Rivera,[30] a man in whom beats the [heart and] soul of an entire continent, tells us: "Picasso is my teacher," this phrase demonstrates that his thinking is not far from the ideas that I have just laid out. To know exemplary techniques in order to try to acquire a similar expertise and to mobilize our energies to translate America with the greatest possible intensity: this ought to be our constant credo for the years to come, even if in America we do not dispose of a *tradition of expertise.*[31]

Carpentier's appeal for an entirely new direction in Latin American letters made him at once the leader of the campaign to build a fund of artistic and literary wealth in Central and South America and its chief promoter—a position strengthened by his own emergence in the years that followed as one of the region's greatest novelists. With the sort of lucidity peculiar to intellectuals who are torn between two cultures, he frankly acknowledged the total subjection of Latin America. His manifesto, in announcing the intention to substitute autonomy for subservience, marked the opening of a new literary area. Sixty years later it was clear that the cultural revolution it heralded had in fact been accomplished—that Carpentier's text was a self-fulfilling prophecy, proclaiming and thereby bringing about the advent of a literature that was to achieve not merely respectability but honor throughout the world, crowned by four Nobel Prizes. Its success in developing a style common to a whole group of writers, and so attaining a genuine aesthetic autonomy, is explained by an initial diversion of resources that permitted writers throughout the region to enter into competition and, by progressively accumulating over several generations the literary capital necessary to underwrite a new literature, to free themselves from submission to European models. The only way to overcome the inherent dependence of Latin America, as Antonio Candido has pointed out, was

> to produce works of the first order, influenced by previous national examples, not by immediate foreign models . . . Brazilian modernism derived in large part from European vanguard movements. But the poets of the succeeding generation, in the 1930s and 1940s, derived immediately from the Modernists—as is the case with what is the fruit of these influences in Carlos Drummond de Andrade or Murilo Mendes . . . This being the case, it is possible to say that Jorge Luis Borges represents the first case of incontestable original influences, exercised fully and recognized in the source countries, through a new mode of conceiving writing.[32]

In other words, it is only on the basis of a first stage of literary accumulation, itself made possible through a diversion of heritage, that a distinctive and autonomous literature is able to appear.

"Magical realism" (a term coined only once the new style had already blossomed) was both a stroke of genius and a strike against international critical authority. The emergence of an aesthetically coherent body of writing in Latin America in the late 1960s forced critics in the center to confront the fact of a genuine literary unity on a continental scale that until then they had failed to notice. The Nobel Prize awarded to Gabriel García Márquez in 1982 only confirmed this unanimous recognition, foreshadowed by the Swedish Academy's consecration of Miguel Ángel Asturias fifteen years earlier and further emphasized by subsequent prizes to Pablo Neruda and Octavio Paz.

In retrospect it is plain that events did in fact unfold according to the pattern that Carpentier had originally imagined in calling for a distinctive literary style common to all of Central and South America, including Cuba and the other Hispanophone islands of the Caribbean. Still today the special interest of the Latin American case resides in the concentration of literary capital not only within a national space but within a continental one as well. The fact that writers faced with political exile were able to find refuge elsewhere in the continent reinforced its linguistic and cultural unity; indeed, the strategy of the writers (and their publishers) responsible for the "boom" in Latin American literature at the beginning of the 1970s consisted in advertising a regional stylistic unity, the product (or so it was supposed) of a common Latin American character. Today one observes the continuing growth of a literary space on an almost hemispheric scale, with intellectuals and writers engaging in dialogue and debate across the borders of their native countries, defending political and literary positions that are invariably both national and continental.

But given the state of linguistic, literary, and cultural destitution in which certain emerging spaces find themselves, particularly ones that have undergone colonization, this inevitable search for a heritage is liable to take on a moving, even tragic aspect. Thus the Algerian novelist Mohammed Dib (b. 1920), in the lines quoted at the beginning of this chapter, described with both poignancy and realism the necessity facing writers from these countries, deprived of any local resources, of carrying out a diversion of symbolic capital by taking up whatever weapons lay to hand, no matter that they may be the products of a foreign culture.[33]

THE IMPORTATION OF TEXTS

"In-translation," conceived as annexation and reappropriation of a foreign patrimony, is another way of adding to a fund of literary resources. This was the path chosen notably by the Romantic movement in Germany. Throughout the nineteenth century, alongside the invention and manufacture of literature as the expression of a national and popular character, the Germans tried to divert from foreign sources the capital that they lacked—thus employing, three centuries later, exactly the same strategy as du Bellay. By exploiting an ancient heritage they were able to accelerate the process of annexing and nationalizing foreign assets—in the case of Greek and Roman literature, a huge vein of potential wealth. The great enterprise of translating the ancient classics was conceived in quasi-explicit terms as an appropriation of a universal literary patrimony through the importation of these texts into the German language.[34] It was also an attempt to dispute the claim of French to be the "Latin of the moderns" and, more generally, to compete with the oldest and most richly endowed literary nations, the only ones until then whose national classics enjoyed widespread international renown.

The very fact that this ambition was described as one of the greatest tasks facing the German nation indicates that the competition also took the form of a continuation of the struggle against Latin inaugurated by du Bellay in the sixteenth century. The Romantics used the same weapons to pursue the same strategy for literary supremacy: by putting into effect a whole program for translating the ancient classics into German, they, too, signaled their intention to fight on the ground of antiquity.[35] "Quite independently of our own productions," Goethe observed, "we have already attained, through the *full appropriation* of what is foreign to us, a very high degree of culture";[36] and elsewhere, in a tone astonishingly similar to that of du Bellay, "The strength of a language is [its power] not to repel what is foreign, but to *devour* it."[37] Herder, citing Thomas Abt, assigned a national responsibility to the translator: "The aim of the true translator is higher than to make foreign works comprehensible to readers; this aim puts him on the level of an author, and makes of a small shopkeeper a merchant who materially enriches the state . . . These translators could become our classic writers."[38] And Walter Benjamin later remarked, as though he was stating something obvious: "Next to the translation of Shakespeare, the permanent poetic achievement of Romanticism was the appropriation of Romance art forms for German poetry. In full consciousness, Romanticism strove toward the conquest, cultivation, and purification of these forms."[39]

The members of the Romantic movement in Germany thus set themselves the task of making the German language a privileged medium in the market of universal world exchange, of making German a literary language. It was necessary, then, first to import into German the great universal European classics that were missing from the German tradition—Shakespeare, Cervantes, Calderón, Petrarch—and then to "civilize" German through the "conquest" of foreign metrics, which is to say the importation of noble traditions into German poetical forms. Novalis hoped to be able to thoroughly Gallicize German, including even its vocabulary;[40] but it would be more accurate to speak of a Grecization of German poetical language through the translation of ancient classics, notably Johann Heinrich Voss's translation of Homer's *Odyssey* (1781) and *Iliad* (1793). This act of bringing into the language, and its literary forms, what was then taken to be a model for all culture was to permit German to compete with the greatest literary languages. Thus Goethe ventured to announce as a fact what was yet only a wish: "The Germans have long been middlemen and sources of mutual recognition. Whoever understands the German language finds himself in a market where every nation displays its merchandise." In one of his conversations with Eckermann, he was still more explicit: "I do not speak here of

French; it is the language of conversation, and it is particularly indispensable when traveling, because everyone understands it, and one can use it in all countries in place of a good interpreter. But with regard to Greek, Latin, Italian, and Spanish, we can read the best works of these nations in German translations so good that we have no reason . . . to waste time in the painful learning of languages."[41] In launching an immense program of translation, then, the German language asserted its claim to the title of new universal (which is to say, literary) language.

From this perspective the reason for the appearance of theories of translation, central in Romantic thought, is readily apparent: they were one of the only means for competing on the ground of literary and intellectual antiquity. In order to carry out a collective project of national enrichment, it was necessary, as a logical matter, to declare translations into French of these very Latin and Greek texts to be outmoded and thereby to state, in opposition to French practices, a theory of "true" translation. Advances in historical philology were therefore also, and without contradiction, instruments in the German struggle for nationhood. Even the most parochial theories could serve as instruments of struggle in international literary space. Thus the German theory of translation, and the practice that flowed from it, were founded on a thoroughgoing opposition to French tradition. Translation in France during this period, particularly of ancient texts, was done without the least concern for fidelity; the dominant position of French culture encouraged ethnocentrism, and led translators to annex texts by blindly adapting them to their own aesthetic. As August Wilhelm von Schlegel remarked, "It is as though they desired that each foreigner among them behave and dress in accordance with their customs, which implies that they do not, strictly speaking, understand anything foreign."[42] In Germany, by contrast, in order to oppose the French intellectual tradition, the principle of fidelity was given a theoretical basis. Thus Herder was to ask: "And translation? In no case can it be embellished . . . The French, overly proud of their national taste, make everything conform to it, instead of adapting themselves to the taste of another period . . . But we poor Germans, by contrast, still deprived of public and country, still free from the tyranny of a national taste, we wish to see this period as it was."[43]

Moreover, pioneering research into the comparative grammar of Indo-European languages by German linguists and philologists allowed the Germanic languages to be raised to the same rank of antiquity and nobility as Latin and Greek. The claim of these languages to a prominent place in the European family, together with the alleged superiority of the Indo-European languages over all others, were of incomparable value in the struggle against French domination. In tacitly accepting the identification of legitimacy with linguistic and literary antiquity, philologists furnished German authors with scientific arguments. This is not to say that Germany consciously undertook to enter into rivalry with France—remarkable though the lucidity of authors from dominated countries is; only that the study of languages and texts, which during this period was making huge strides, was partner to a debate that was taking place within German intellectual and literary space at the moment of its emergence on the international scene. The new science of linguistics enabled the German language to pretend to an antiquity, and therefore a *littérarité,* that raised it—according to the prevailing hierarchical categories of thought and cultural conceptions of the world—to the level of Latin. The combination of two modes of accumulating literary capital—via translation and via philology—permitted Germany rapidly to join the ranks of European literary powers.

Beyond the importation of literary texts, underprivileged spaces whose cultural resources reside for the most part in the vestiges of a prestigious ancient civilization, such as Egypt, Iran, and Greece, which had seen their patrimony confiscated by the great modern intellectual powers, could also hope to reclaim such resources for themselves, particularly national works of which they had been dispossessed. The task of what might be called internal translation, which is to say bringing the national language forward from an ancient to a modern state, as in the case of translations from ancient to modern Greek, is one way of annexing, and thereby nationalizing, texts that all the great countries of Europe had long before declared to be universal, by claiming them as evidence of an underlying linguistic and cultural continuity. But it might also involve texts that were unknown beyond the borders of a country on the literary periphery. Thus Douglas Hyde, for example, through his English versions of Gaelic popular legends, strongly contributed to the enrichment of Irish literary space—so much so, in fact, that these acts of translation within the native Irish tradition increased national capital in both languages.

It is in this context that the critical edition of the *Rubáiyát* of Omar Khayyám (ca. 1050–1123)—mathematician, astronomer, and poet of the fifth and sixth centuries of the Hegira—by the Iranian writer Sadiq Hidayat (1903–1951) needs to be examined.[44] Hidayat's tragic life can almost stand alone for the terrible situation confronting writers in culturally despoiled countries, condemned to an obscure and difficult life in the shadows of their literary center. Hidayat—generally agreed to be the only modern Iranian writer of international reputation—committed suicide in Paris.[45] He had studied at the Sorbonne in the 1920s and then returned to his homeland, via India, in the early 1940s. In the meantime he wrote what today is considered his major work, *Buf-i kur* (The Blind Owl, 1941), translated into French two years after his death.[46] "It is the only work in the modern literature of Iran," argues the critic Youssef Ishagpour, "able to hold its own not only with the classic works of Persia, but also with the great books of world literature of this century."[47] Hidayat's fascination with the ancient literature of his land did not prevent him from developing a deep knowledge of literature in the West (he translated Kafka into modern Persian); nonetheless he found himself caught between an inaccessible literary modernity and a national grandeur that had all but disappeared, and so had "the joint experience of tradition ruined in the present day, and of the present day through the ruins of tradition."[48]

Hidayat's analysis of Khayyám's texts, carried out with Western critical and historical tools, was aimed at restoring the authentic work, freeing it from the confusions, approximations, and errors of the majority of previous commentators, who were interested only in uniting it with the European literary tradition and who as foreigners, lacking a specifically Persian perspective, failed to see either its unity or its coherence. Nonetheless he made use of Western categories for two reasons: on the one hand, in order to take issue with the religious tradition of his own country; and, on the other, to dispute the claims of the German philological tradition, among others, which until then had monopolized scholarly commentary on Khayyám's work,[49] thus dispossessing Iranian literary space of a classic whose prestige would otherwise have been credited to its account in the international literary market.

The work of the South African writer Mazisi Kunene, who has produced English versions of Zulu epics that he himself was the first to transcribe, derives from the same logic. For writers in small nations, internal translations are an effective way of gathering together available literary resources.

All these strategies, aimed at creating a literary patrimony, amount to so many ways of making up for lost time. Indeed, it is with respect to the antiquity of a nation's heritage that the balance of power is the most unfavorable to small countries, since literary nobility very largely depends on how far back their genealogies can be traced. This is why contests over antiquity—or, what comes to the same thing for societies whose history has in one way or another been interrupted or suspended, continuity—are the classic form assumed by the struggle to accumulate literary capital. In proclaiming the antiquity of their literary foundation and stressing the continuity of their national history, nations seek to establish themselves as legitimate contestants in international competition.

To be recognized as belonging to the oldest literary (and, in the broad sense, cultural) nobility is an honor so ardently desired that even those nations that are the most richly endowed in literary resources look for ways of affirming their historical precedence in order to forestall challenges to their position. Thus Stefan Collini has noted the insistence of nineteenth-century historians of English literature on the unbroken continuity of their nation's literary tradition and the permanence and stability of its language: "continuity," he observes, "is a precondition of identity and hence of legitimate pride in earlier achievements."[50] Thus the great editor of Old and Middle English texts, W. W. Skeat, in *Questions for Examination in English Literature* (1873), argued that the eyes of schoolboys "should be opened to the Unity of English, that in English literature there is an unbroken succession of authors, from the reign of Alfred to that of Victoria, and that the language which we speak now is absolutely one in its essence with the language that was spoken in the days when the English first invaded the island and defeated and overwhelmed its British inhabitants."[51]

Countries at a relatively great distance from the center such as Mexico and Greece that otherwise might have invoked a very great cultural heritage, seeking in this way to improve their position in the world literary space, were unable to do so because of the discontinuity of their past. Neither the modern Mexican nor Greek nation was founded until the nineteenth century, in each case only after a long period marked by profound historical dislocations that prevented them from fully exploiting the cultural resources to which they belatedly laid claim.

In 1950, with the publication of *The Labyrinth of Solitude,* Octavio Paz tried to provide a foundation for Mexican national identity by restoring a continuity that had been disrupted—in particular by reconciling its pre-Columbian heritage with the experience of Spanish colonialization and the social structures that it produced. With this book, which was to become a national classic, Paz hoped above all to lead his country to political and cultural modernity by proclaiming both its historical continuity and its critical duty to preserve this heritage. Forty years later, in his speech accepting the Nobel Prize, he continued to affirm what he saw as an essential element of the constitution and future of Mexico and its culture: "The temples and gods of pre-Columbian Mexico may be a pile of ruins, but the spirit that breathed life into that world has not disappeared; it speaks to us in the hermetic language of myth and legend, in forms of social co-existence, in popular art, in customs. Being a Mexican writer means listening to the voice of that present—that presence. Listening to it, speaking with it, deciphering it, expressing it."[52]

The term "continuity" also appears in the work of the other great Mexican writer, Carlos Fuentes. Although there are surely few examples of a historical rupture comparable to the one caused by the European discovery of America, Fuentes insisted in *El espejo enterrado* (The Buried Mirror, 1992) on the cultural permanence of the continent:

> [This cultural heritage] ranges from the stone of Chichén Itzá and Machu Picchu to modern Indian influences in painting and architecture. From the baroque art of the colonial era to the contemporary literature of Jorge Luis Borges and Gabriel García Márquez . . . Few cultures in the world possess a comparable richness and continuity . . . This book is therefore dedicated to a search for the cultural continuity that can inform and transcend the economic and political disunity and fragmentation of the Hispanic world.[53]

This same aspiration to ennoblement through the reappropriation of an ancient heritage led Greece at the moment of its emergence as a nation in the mid-nineteenth century to try to reestablish a lost historical and cultural unity, particularly in reaction to charges by certain German scholars that modern Greeks did not have a drop of Hellenic blood, that they were a Slavic "race," and that they had no privileged claim to a heritage that did not belong to them in the first place.[54] On the political level, what was called the *Megalè Idea* (Great Idea) gave rise to the ambition of reattaching to the nation territories formerly occupied by its illustrious Byzantine ancestors—notably among them, of course, Constantinople—in an attempt to restore territorial and historical continuity. Among scholars it stimulated historical studies of folklore and linguistics, and encouraged writers to revert to an aesthetic archaism that, it was felt, would give proof of their Hellenicity. In support of this program the historian Konstantinos Paparrigopoulos published a vast and famous five-volume *Historia tou hellenikou ethnous* (History of the Greek Nation, 1860–1872) that purported to establish a continuity between the various periods of Greek history, from ancient times through the Byzantine era and so up until the modern period.

But the Greeks were handicapped in their attempt to enter international literary competition by the relative advantages in legacy hunting enjoyed by older countries. The importation of the texts of Greek antiquity into the German language had the effect, as we have seen, of annexing them first to the literary heritage of the German nation, and then to that of Europe as a whole, thereby dispossessing the young Greek nation of an immense store of potential wealth. The leading classicists of the day, the great philologists and historians, were German; and the de-Grecization of the Greeks (as it might be called) that they carried out in the name of science and history was unquestionably a way, at least in part, of pushing aside anyone who might lay claim to this heritage in the name of exactly that unique national character of which the Germans were the chief theoreticians.

The strategic effectiveness of proclaiming a nation's literary antiquity is so great that even the youngest nations hasten to do it. Thus Gertrude Stein, whose concern with the creation of a distinctively American literature I have already mentioned, decreed in *The Autobiography of Alice B. Toklas* (1933):

> Gertrude Stein always speaks of America as being now the oldest country in the world because by the methods of the civil war and the commercial conceptions that followed it America created the twentieth century, and since all the other countries are now either living or commencing to be living a twentieth century life, America having begun the creation of the twentieth century in the sixties of the nineteenth century is now the oldest country in the world.[55]

Here a pseudohistorical syllogism is placed in the service of a simple self-assertion of nobility: faced with the necessity of giving proof of its national antiquity in order to gain acceptance in the literary world, Stein felt that she had no other option than to launch a preemptive strike.

Even Joyce, despite his customary reluctance in this regard, recalled the priority and great antiquity of Irish tradition during one of his lectures in Trieste, casting his remarks rhetorically in the form of a denial whose irony affirmed the existence of a yawning gap between the Irish cultural nobility and the English common people:

> I do not see the purpose of the bitter invectives against the English despoiler, the disdain for the vast Anglo-Saxon civilization, even though it is almost entirely a materialistic civilization, nor the empty boasts that the art of miniature in the ancient Irish books, such as the Book of Kells, the Yellow Book of Lecan, the Book of the Dun Cow, which date back to a time when England was an uncivilized country, is almost as old as the Chinese, and that Ireland made and exported to Europe its own fabrics for several generations before the first Fleming arrived in London to teach the English how to make bread.[56]

But confronted with the actual difficulties of adducing proof of antiquity, some claimants to literary legitimacy sought to enter international competition by challenging the literary measure of time itself. Thus before Gertrude Stein, though in much the same spirit, Walt Whitman had proposed the paradoxical idea of American history as a history of the future. Unable to draw upon any historical patrimony whose resources he could then hope to increase, it occurred to him to oppose the present to the hereafter of modernity; that is, to discount the present in favor of the future. Ever since Whitman, declaring that the present—as the product and exclusive privilege of history—is no longer an adequate measure of literary innovation, and setting oneself up as the future, and therefore as the avant-garde, has been the solution favored by American writers eager to throw off the tutelage of London who have tried to offset Europe's historical advantages by pronouncing it passé and outmoded. To have any chance of being noticed and accepted, American writers needed to contest the temporal law instituted by Europe by claiming to be, not behind, but actually ahead of Europe. In this way it became possible to reject the Old World and relegate it to the past. It was by setting the newness, innocence, and unknown adventure of a new world where anything could happen against the stale and narrow experience of an Old World in which everything had already been written that a national literature, or in any case the "Americanist" part of American literary tradition (as opposed to the "Europeanist" tendency, to recall Octavio Paz's terms), came to be constituted. In a fragment of *Specimen Days* (1882–1883), titled "Mississippi Valley Literature," Whitman inaugurated a long literary genealogy by declaring:

> One's mind needs but a moment's deliberation anywhere in the United States to see clearly enough that all the prevalent book and library poets, either as imported from Great Britain, or follow'd and doppel-gang'd here, are foreign to our States, copiously as they are read by us all. But to fully understand not only how absolutely in opposition to our times and lands, and how little and cramp'd, and what anachronisms and absurdities many of their pages are, for American purposes, one must dwell or travel awhile in Missouri, Kansas and Colorado, and get rapport with their people and country. Will the day ever come—no matter how long deferr'd—when those models and lay-figures from the British islands—and even the previous traditions of the classics—will be reminiscences, studies only? The pure breath, primitiveness, boundless prodigality and amplitude . . . will they ever appear in, and in some sort form a standard for our poetry and art?[57]

And earlier, in the "Inscriptions" that preface *Leaves of Grass* (1855), dedicated to the glories of the "New World," he had written: "The Modern man I sing . . . I project the history of the future."[58]

In effect, then, Whitman's strategy consisted in turning over the hourglass and decreeing himself the creator of the new and the original. He sought to define his status as an American writer, and the distinctiveness of American literature itself, on the basis of the idea of absolute novelty: these "inimitable American areas," he wrote, must be able to be "fused in the alembic of a perfect poem . . . altogether our own, without a trace or taste of Europe's soil, reminiscence, technical letter or spirit."[59] It is quite clear, too, that his rejection of the central measure of time was first and foremost a rejection of dependence on London, an affirmation of political and aesthetic autonomy.

Charles Ferdinand Ramuz, who found himself in a roughly comparable situation on returning to his native Vaud, in 1914, put yet another strategy into effect. In the absence of any historical or cultural patrimony peculiar to this part of Switzerland that would have enabled him to overcome its disadvantage with respect to literary time, he tried to set history against eternity, the present of literary modernity against the immobile time of the countryside and mountains, the eternal present of agrarian rites and practices. More than an attempt to defend a national or regional particularity, the resolute and purposeful return to one's homeland is very often a way of challenging the legitimacy of central criteria of recognition. In order for those who have gone unnoticed to have a chance of being recognized, it becomes necessary to devalue these criteria, so that they are seen as relative and changeable, by opposing them to an absolute and immutable present. Thus the eternal values of a primordial present are held to be more current than the values—by definition ephemeral—of Parisian modernity. Ramuz recalled the train ride that brought him back home to Switzerland from Paris:

> I had the opportunity, then, to be able to compare, during the course of a brief trip, the two essential poles of life . . . *which are separated [from each other] much more in time than in space, much more by centuries than by leagues,* for here [in the Vaud] was not everything as it had been in the time of Rome or even before Rome? Here nothing was ever changing and down there [in Paris] everything was changing, continually changing. Here there is a sort of absolute, down there everything was relative.[60]

In other words, Ramuz reduced spatial distance to a temporal divide and transformed the objective backwardness of the Vaud into an immutability similar to that of the most distinguished eternity of all—Rome. He thus adopted the subtle strategy of classicism: in order to avoid being condemned to the condition of perpetual anachronism to which the "rural novel" is evidently liable, Ramuz sought a way to escape from time, to establish himself as an artist standing outside time, ever and always present, eternal, who submits neither to history nor to the vagaries of modernity—with which in any case he could not pretend to compete.

THE CREATION OF CAPITALS

One of the essential stages in the accumulation of national literary resources consists in the construction of a literary capital—a symbolic central bank, as it were, a place where literary credit is concentrated. Barcelona, historically both the artistic and political center of Catalonia, united, like Paris and London, the two characteristics that are unarguably constitutive of literary capitals: a reputation for political liberalism and a large concentrated volume of literary capital. The gathering of literary, artistic, and intellectual resources in Barcelona dates from the nineteenth century, when the city became a great industrial center. At the beginning of the twentieth century, Rubén Darío, who found in Catalonia the support he needed in order to establish modernism in Spain, observed: "The tendency that has found expression in recent years, constituting exactly what is called 'modern' or new thought, has emerged and triumphed here [in Catalonia] more than in any other corner of the Peninsula . . . [Catalonians] can be called industrialists, Catalanists, egotists; the fact is that they are, and remain, Catalonians, universal."[61] Barcelona's preeminence as a cultural capital was associated with the Els Quatre Gats group, the architecture of Antoni Gaudí, the theater of Adriano Gual, the newly formed Films Barcelona, and the thought of the philosopher and novelist Eugenio d'Ors.

In the political sphere, Barcelona stood out as a great republican bastion during the civil war and subsequently as a source of resistance against Franco's dictatorship, for which Catalonia especially suffered. It was in Barcelona, too, in the 1960s and 1970s, that a relatively autonomous intellectual life came to be restored toward the end of Franco's regime. A large number of publishing houses were established in the city, and the arrival of writers, architects, painters, and poets—from Catalonia and elsewhere—enabled it to combine a national intellectual role with a political one as a sort of democratic enclave tolerated by the government. "In the 1970s," the writer Manuel Vázquez Montalbán (b. 1939) observed, "Barcelona meant—up to a certain point, given the political context of Spain—democratic inventiveness; the atmosphere was freer than in Madrid. And it was then, as now, the most important publishing center in all of Spain and Latin America."[62] Barcelona thus became the literary capital of the Spanish-speaking world, allowing Latin American writers to reaffirm their cultural bonds and gain a European audience for their writings without political interference. The most famous literary agent in Spain, Carmen Balcells, began her career in Barcelona by selling worldwide rights to the work of Gabriel García Márquez; and it was as a result of her efforts and the interest of certain Catalonian publishers, such as Carlos Barral, that other Latin American novelists were published in Spain in the 1960s and 1970s.

In recent years novelists have given Barcelona a literary prestige and artistic existence of its own by presenting it as an element of their fictions. Vázquez Montalbán was the first, followed by Eduardo Mendoza and a cohort of young Castilian and Catalonian writers (including Quim Monzó), to make Barcelona a central character in his novels. Together they accumulated descriptions and evocations of places and neighborhoods and, in this way, almost deliberately constructed a new literary mythology on the basis of the city itself.

Joyce had proceeded in exactly the same fashion with regard to Dublin, first in *Dubliners* and then to a still greater degree in *Ulysses*. Here again it was a matter of conferring artistic distinction upon a city through literary description—we have already considered the role of descriptions of Paris in creating a literary mythology—and thereby giving it a prestige that it lacked. Moreover, for Joyce, to give his nation's capital a literary existence was also a way to take sides in a national struggle: by the very act of writing about Dublin he announced his intention to break with the rural and folk norms that until then had dominated Irish literary space. The same process is at work today among Scottish authors. Motivated by common political and literary concerns, they seek to rehabilitate "Red Glasgow," the working-class capital of Scotland, and to give it a new literary existence as against Edinburgh, the more "sophisticated" and "civilized" historical capital associated with all the clichés of nationalist conservatism.[63]

In certain national literary spaces, the relative autonomy of literary authorities can be perceived in the presence of (and rivalry between) two capitals: one—often the older of the two—the seat of administration, where political and financial authority are concentrated and a conservative literature dependent upon national and political power is perpetuated; the other, often a port city, open to the outside world, or else a university town, open to foreign ideas, in either case laying claim to literary modernity and advocating the abandonment of literary models that are outdated at the literary Greenwich meridian. This general structure provides a way of understanding the relationship between cities such as Warsaw and Cracow, Athens and Salonika, Beijing and Shanghai, Madrid and Barcelona, and São Paulo and Rio de Janeiro.

THE INTERNATIONAL OF SMALL NATIONS

The special perceptiveness of contestants on the periphery enables them to detect affinities among emerging literary (and political) spaces. Their shared literary destitution leads them to take each other as models and historical points of reference, to compare their literary situations, and to apply common strategies based on the logic of prior experience. This logic showed that small nations—or rather the international writers of small literatures—could act in concert to challenge their domination by the centers. Thus at the beginning of the century Belgium came to be seen as a sort of model for small countries in Europe. The Irish, in particular, who were trying to reclaim their own cultural tradition from English control, saw the Belgian example as proof that small countries could succeed in achieving cultural independence. Linguistically, politically, and religiously divided, and under the cultural domination of France, Belgium furnished a model for each of the two contending factions: the Anglo-Irish could identify with the poets Maeterlinck and Verhaeren, who, although they wrote in French, "were never confused with French men of letters";[64] and the Gaelicizing Irish looked to the example of Hendrik Conscience, who had undertaken to revive the use of Flemish. Yeats later met Maeterlinck in Paris and found in him a transposable model: a Francophone Belgian from Flanders who read German, English, and Dutch, the leader and theoretician of Symbolism, an innovator in drama and poetry who had made a name for himself in Paris while refusing to relinquish his ties to his native land—in sum, a nonnationalist national writer.

A relation of the same type had already come into existence between Ireland and Norway, which, like Belgium a little later, was invoked by the various warring factions. The example of a small European nation recently liberated from the colonial yoke imposed several centuries earlier by the Danes that, through the efforts of a small band of writers, had managed to create a new national language was immediately adopted by Irish Catholic nationalists in their campaign to bring about the renaissance of Gaelic and restrict literary production to plays and novels having a national character.[65] Other Irish intellectuals, however, who advocated opening up the country to European culture—Joyce foremost among them, but also Yeats in a different way—were to use Ibsen's work as a model for introducing the idea of literary autonomy in Ireland; for them, the recognition of the Norwegian playwright in Europe was proof that a national literature worthy of the name, in order to have a chance of being recognized on the international level, must cease to bow down before the canons imposed by religious morality and popular prejudice. Joyce developed a passionate interest in the work of Ibsen at a very early age,[66] identifying himself with the self-exiled playwright (his fascination for Dante was to assume the same form and strengthen his attachment to a literary mythology associating the artist with exile) to the point that Ibsen came to occupy the central place in art that Parnell had assumed for him in politics.[67] He even taught himself Dano-Norwegian in order to be able to read Ibsen's plays in the original. His first essay, "Drama and Life" (1900), largely inspired by Shaw's analysis in *The Quintessence of Ibsenism* and written following an argument with a classmate who criticized the decadence of the modern theater and Ibsen's unhealthy influence upon it, tried to demonstrate Ibsen's superiority to Shakespeare—a direct assault upon the British national pantheon—and urged the necessity of promoting realism in dramatic art. Joyce's admiration for Ibsen was thus a form of identification with a playwright from a small country recently liberated from political domination, writing in a language that was almost unknown in Europe, who gave form to a new national literature and at the same time became the spokesman of the European avant-garde by revolutionizing the whole of European theater. It is for this reason that *Ulysses* can be read, among other things, as a Dublin version of *Peer Gynt*.[68]

Another of Joyce's early essays was a sharp attack on Yeats's management of what was to become the Abbey Theatre. "The Day of the Rabblement" (1901) protested against the nativist orientation of the Irish Literary Theatre (as it was then known) and its conception of the people as the repository of legends and traditions needing to be revived and given literary form.[69] In the opening lines of his essay, the young Joyce placed Ireland alongside Norway: the Irish Literary Theatre, he wrote, "is the latest movement of protest against the sterility and falsehood of the modern stage. Half a century ago the note of protest was uttered in Norway . . . Now, your popular devil is more dangerous than your vulgar devil."[70] In affirming Ibsen's genius and modernity Joyce rejected archaizing and conservative attitudes in both politics and literature while at the same time challenging the nationalism of Catholic theater productions, which were subsequently to proclaim the realist aesthetic, only now for patriotic rather than cosmopolitan purposes. His avowed fascination with Ibsen was therefore a way of affirming his own aesthetic and political positions, and he was often to compare his distant attitude toward political nationalism with that of the Norwegian dramatist.

Earlier, in "Ibsen's New Drama" (1900), Joyce had summed up the violence and the importance of the struggle over Ibsen's work that was taking place throughout Europe:

> Twenty years have passed since Henrik Ibsen wrote *A Doll's House*, thereby almost marking an epoch in the history of drama. During those years his name has gone abroad through the length and breadth of two continents, and has provoked more discussion and criticism than that of any other living man. He has been upheld as a religious reformer, a social reformer, a Semitic lover of righteousness, and as a great dramatist. He has been rigorously denounced as a meddlesome intruder, a defective artist, an incomprehensible mystic, and, in the eloquent words of a certain English critic, "a muck-ferreting dog" . . . It may be questioned whether any man has held so firm an empire over the thinking world in modern times.[71]

There is, then, a certain reading of literary works of which only writers on the periphery are capable; certain homologies and similarities that they alone, as a result of their outlying position, are able to discern. What is more, the interpretation by writers in literarily remote lands of works produced by authors elsewhere on the periphery is apt to be more realistic (that is, more historically grounded) than the dehistoricized reading of critics in the center—a circumstance that has always been poorly understood or ignored, since the structure of worldwide literary domination has itself been poorly understood.

The mutual interest of writers from small countries in each other is as much literary as it is directly political; or rather, their readings of one another are so many implicit affirmations of a structural similarity between the literature and politics of small countries. The ability of Norway and Belgium to serve as reference points and models for Ireland was due in the first place to a political perspective that drew upon a methodical comparison of national experiences. Irish political theorists, for example, saw Hungarian autonomy within the Austrian Empire as a possible model for Ireland within the British Empire. Thus Arthur Griffith, one of the founders of the Sinn Fein movement, urged his colleagues to follow the example of Hungarian deputies in boycotting the Austrian parliament, noting that efforts to revive the use of the Magyar tongue had led to an agreement with the Austrian monarchy on the language issue and a real measure of political autonomy for Hungary.[72]

The success of literary artists from small countries who have joined together to contest the unilateral domination of the centers in achieving emancipation and recognition suggests that international movements in painting may to some extent develop according to the same logic. In postwar Paris, for example, which was still the capital not only of literature but also of painting, the Surrealists tried to reassert their dwindling authority by issuing new excommunications, notably against the Belgian painters grouped around Magritte. Weary of the monopoly on art and internationalism exercised by the old Surrealist avant-garde, a small group of Belgian, Danish, and Dutch artists (Christian Dotremont, Joseph Noiret, Asger Jorn, Karel Appel, Constant Nieuwenhuys, and Cornelis van Beverloo) resolved to secede and in 1948 signed a manifesto in Paris titled *La cause était entendue* (The Cause Was Understood), an insolent proclamation of independence—"Paris is no longer the center of art," Dotremont announced—that marked the founding of a new community: "It is in a spirit of efficiency that we add to our national experiences a dialectical experience between our groups."[73] The acronym CoBrA was derived from the initial letters of the three cities—Copenhagen, Brussels, Amsterdam—that thus declared their union as new centers for the invention of an art less steeped in aesthetic seriousness. The group's radical challenge to the centrality of Paris may explain, in part, the insistence of its members on the geographic division of the movement, which (as its name implied) saw itself as an internationalist force acting in opposition to the concentration of critical authority in one city. The decentering represented by the movement was therefore evidence of its modernity and liberty. Thus Noiret spoke of the "geographical practice of freedom."[74]

The alliance of three small countries that acknowledged not only their cultural kinship but also, more importantly, the similarity of their position as marginal contestants in the world arena who were rejected (or, at best, tolerated) by the centers enabled the members of CoBrA to disregard the injunctions of the Parisian avant-garde. They were angry and, above all, against: against Paris, against the Surrealists, against André Breton, against Parisian intellectualism, against aesthetic diktats, against structuralism, against the monopoly on political dissent ceded to the Communist party, and so on. The proclaimed absence of dogmatism, by deliberate contrast with Breton's aesthetic imperiousness, was itself held up as a unifying principle along with the notion that a work of art is an experiment, always open, forever incomplete; the emphasis on technical innovations and the use of apparently ridiculous materials (breadcrumbs, mud, sand, eggshells, wax, and the like); the refusal to choose between abstraction and representation ("an abstract art that does not believe in abstraction," as Jorn characterized the group's orientation);[75] and the preference for collective work as against the cult of singularity. In short, CoBrA was constructed in almost complete opposition to Surrealist doctrine and the other aesthetic programs then recognized in Paris: Kandinsky, socialist realism (prompting Dotremont and Noiret to enter into a debate with the editors of the Communist literary journal *Les lettres françaises* in 1949), and Mondrian's geometric abstraction. "The unity of CoBrA," Dotremont liked to say, "does not depend on slogans."[76] It revealed itself instead in a joyously provocative explosion of primary colors.

The members of CoBrA had always looked to the north for inspiration—no one more than Christian Dotremont, whose fascination with the landscape of Scandinavia and Lapland led him to create his "logoglace" and "logoneige" word-pictures. The group's often reaffirmed Nordic character was partly due to recent theoretical advances made by Danish painters. Reviews founded before and during the war, in resistance to the Nazi occupation, and particularly the work of Bauhaus-influenced theoreticians of abstract art such as Vilhelm Bjerke-Petersen— whose *Symboler i abstrakt Kunst* (Symbols in Abstract Art) had appeared in 1933—had a considerable impact on the development of painting and pictorial thinking in Denmark in the 1930s and 1940s. Jorn, as one of the principal theoreticians of CoBrA, relied on this Dano-Germanic heritage to give form and coherence to its contrarian spirit, at once serious and joyful. The attention given to popular art in the first issues of the group's review, *CoBrA,* was an affirmation of the North's inalienable character as much as it was a celebration of inventiveness, vitality, and universality ("Popular art is the only international art," as Jorn put it).[77] This spirit of popular freedom, asserted against an artistic elitism that consecrated a few exceptional beings, was identical with the one that animated *art brut* (Dubuffet was a contributor to the group's review) and insisted on the artistic interest of drawings by children and the insane.

CoBrA's official life was brief: in 1951, scarcely three years after its creation, it was decided to put an end to the group's activities. Its members pursued their careers independently, and less angrily than when they had first joined forces. Yet it was their common rejection of the mandates of Paris, more than their personal ties to each other, that permitted them during the group's brief existence to construct a coherent aesthetic. Shortly after dissolving CoBrA these painters were welcomed, and their work exhibited, in Paris. Because they had dared to ally themselves across national and cultural borders against the omnipotence of Paris in art, its blessing was eventually bestowed upon them.

9 | *The Tragedy of Translated Men*

They existed among three impossibilities, which I just happen to call linguistic impossibilities. It is simplest to call them that. But they might also be called something entirely different. These are: the impossibility of not writing, the impossibility of writing in German, the impossibility of writing differently. One might also add a fourth impossibility, the impossibility of writing . . . Thus what resulted was a literature impossible in all respects.
—Franz Kafka, letter to Max Brod (June 1921)

Writing is a minefield of betrayals. I betrayed my mother in becoming not an oral poet but a writer, and a writer in English, which is to say in a language incomprehensible to her; and not only that, but a writer of political texts, which prevented me from living in Somalia, near her. So I thought I ought to write books that might be considered a monument to the memory of my mother . . . I regret having written in English, I regret having not lived in Somalia, I regret that you, my mother, died before I could see you again. I hope that my work is good enough to serve as a eulogy to my mother.
—Naruddin Farah, interview with the author (July 1998)

IT IS IN confronting the question of language that writers from outlying spaces have the occasion to deploy the complete range of strategies through which literary differences are affirmed. Language is the major stake of struggles and rivalries, and also, as the only real material available to writers in search of innovation, the specific resource with—and against—which solutions to the problem of literary domination are invented. Literary revolts and revolutions are therefore incarnated in the forms produced by manipulating language. Examining the linguistic so-lutions devised by deprived writers makes it possible not only to analyze their most sophisticated literary creations, their stylistic choices, and their formal inventions—in a word, to rediscover the internal analysis of texts—but also to understand why it is that the greatest revolutionaries of literature are to be found among the linguistically dominated, con-demned to search for ways out from destitution and dependence.

Because language is the major component of literary capital, the reader will find in the pages that follow discussions of a certain number of solutions that have already been mentioned. Unavoidably, this will re-quire some amount of backtracking and repetition; but in each case I shall try to emphasize the specifically linguistic character of the mecha-nisms upon which these solutions depend.

In rejecting the "slavish" imitation of ancient texts, du Bellay hoped to put an end to the quasi-mechanical addition to Latin capital made by the productions of French poets. The first and chief method that he rec-ommended—one that has been practiced ever since by writers who find themselves in the same structural position—consisted in asserting a dif-ference of language through the creation of a vernacular tongue that, by exploiting the literary forms and privileged themes of a dominant tongue, could hope to displace it as the new literary language. In the wake of the French Pléiade, Herder's arguments served only to make this mechanism explicit, establishing the right to existence of small na-tions on the basis of the particular character of their popular languages. This movement was carried on, as we have seen, long after the high tide of European nationalism in the nineteenth century. Still today it is most often by appeal to a linguistic criterion that emerging political spaces are able to proclaim and legitimize their entry into both the political world and the literary world.

The question of linguistic difference is faced by all dominated writers, regardless of their linguistic and literary distance from the center. Assim-ilated authors, who stand in a relation of foreignness and insecurity to the dominant language, seek by a sort of hypercorrection to make the linguistic traces of their origins disappear, as one does in the case of an accent. What might be called dissimilated authors, by contrast, whether or not they have another language at their disposal, seek by every possi-ble means to distance themselves from the dominant language, either by devising a distinctive (and therefore to some extent illegitimate) use of this language, or by creating—in some cases recreating—a new national (and potentially literary) language. In other words, the "choices" made by dominated writers with regard to language—decisions that are neither conscious nor calculated—do not consist, as in the great literary nations, in docile submission to a national norm, even if they largely depend upon national linguistic politics.[1] For these writers the dilemma of language is complex, and the solutions that they devise are varied.[2]

The range of possibilities open to them depends first on their position in literary space and on the literariness of their mother tongue (or national language). In other words, depending on the nature of their dependence, which is to say whether it is political (and so both linguistic and literary), linguistic (and so literary as well), or only literary, they will search for solutions that, however much they may resemble one another, are nonetheless very different in their content and their actual chances of leading to visibility and literary existence. In world literary space, small languages can nonexhaustively be classified in four main categories according to their degree of literariness. First there are languages that are oral or whose script is unsettled and in the process of being established. By definition lacking in literary capital (since they have no written form), they are unknown in international space and unable to benefit from any translation. This is notably the case of certain African languages that do not yet have a settled written form, and of certain creoles that are now beginning, thanks to the efforts of native authors, to acquire a codified written form and, with it, literary status.

Second, there are languages of recent creation (or recreation) that with the achievement of political independence became the country's national language, such as Catalan, Korean, Gaelic, Hebrew, and "new Norwegian." These languages have few speakers and few literary works; are familiar to few polyglots; and, having no tradition of exchange with other countries, must gradually acquire an international existence through translation. Next come languages of ancient culture and tradition, associated in the modern era with small countries, such as Dutch and Danish, Greek and Persian, that have relatively few speakers, native or polyglot; and, though they have a relatively important history and sizable stock of literary credit, are unrecognized outside their national boundaries, which is to say unvalued on the world literary market. Finally, there are languages of broad diffusion such as Arabic, Chinese, and Hindi that have great internal literary traditions but nonetheless are little known and largely unrecognized in the international marketplace.

The constraints of structure and literariness are not the only determinants of linguistic choice among writers. To these must be added their degree of dependence on the nation. As we have seen, the less endowed the native literary space, the more dependent writers are politically: they are subjected to the national "duty" of "defense and illustration," which is also one of the only routes of emancipation open to them. To the extent that their choices involve their entire literary purpose and the very meaning they give to their work, the relation of dominated writers to their language is singularly difficult, passionate, and, in many cases, agonizing.

All literary authors in small languages are therefore faced in one form or another, and in some sense inevitably, with the question of translation. As "translated men," they are caught in a dramatic structural contradiction that forces them to choose between translation into a literary language that cuts them off from their compatriots, but that gives them literary existence, and retreat into a small language that condemns them to invisibility or else to a purely national literary existence.[3] This very real tension, on account of which poets who convert to a great literary language find themselves sometimes accused of treason, forces many of them to seek solutions that are both aesthetic and linguistic. Dual translation, or self-transcription, is thus a way of reconciling literary imperatives and national duties. The Francophone Moroccan poet Abdellâtif Laâbi thus explains:

> In translating my own works into Arabic, or having them translated while always assisting in their translation, I have set myself the task of bringing them before the public for which they were first intended and the cultural area that is their true parent . . . I feel better now. The dissemination of my writings in Morocco and in the rest of the Arab world has made me fully reestablish my "legitimacy" as an Arabic author . . . I fit into the Arab literary scene to the extent that my works are judged, criticized, and appreciated as Arabic texts, independently of their original version.[4]

The attempts by writers on the periphery to deal with distance and decentering—notions that are subsumed here under the generic term "translation," which includes adoption of a dominant language, self-translation, construction of a dual body of work by means of translation back and forth between two languages, creation and promotion of a national and/or popular language, development of a new writing, and symbiotic merger of two languages (such as the famous "Brazilianization" of Portuguese achieved by Mário de Andrade, the invention of a Malagasy French by Jean-Joseph Rabearivelo, the Africanization of English by Chinua Achebe, and Rubén Darío's "mental Gallicism")—should not be thought of as a set of cut-and-dried solutions separate from one another, but rather as a sort of continuum of uncertain and difficult, sometimes tragic, responses to their predicament. In other words, the various ways in which writers seek access to literary recognition are all of a piece. No clear boundary separates them: all these solutions to literary domination need to be jointly conceived in terms of continuity and movement, recognizing that in the course of his career a writer may successively or simultaneously investigate one or more of these possibilities.

The linguistic situation facing writers in colonized (or newly independent) countries, who are subject to a threefold domination—political, linguistic, and literary—and who typically live in bilingual worlds, such as Rachid Boudjedra, Jean-Joseph Ribearivelo, Ngugi wa Thiong'o, and Wole Soyinka, is not comparable, even considering its literary effects, to the sort of domination exercised by the French language. Some European and American writers—Cioran, Kundera, Gangotena, and Beckett, for example—adopted French as their language for writing, and others, such as Strindberg, did so temporarily. For writers from countries that have long been under colonial domination, however, and for them alone, bilingualism (defined as "embodied" translation) is the primary and indelible mark of political domination. Albert Memmi, in his account of the contradictions and impasses to which the colonized in situations of bilingualism are liable, described the difference in symbolic value between the two languages—a difference that gives the linguistic and literary dilemma facing writers in dominated languages its full intensity:

> The mother tongue of the colonized [writer] . . . has no dignity in [his own] country or in the concert of peoples. If he wishes to practice a trade, make a place for himself, exist in public life and in the world, he

must first submit to the language of others, that of the colonizers, his masters. In the linguistic conflict that goes on inside the colonized [writer], his mother tongue ends up being humiliated, crushed. And since this contempt has an objective basis, he ends up sharing it himself.[5]

For Cioran and Strindberg, by contrast, having been born into small European languages (Romanian and Swedish) that were relatively unrecognized literarily but nonetheless endowed with their own traditions and resources, writing in French, in the one case, and self-translation, in the other, were ways of achieving literary existence, of escaping both the invisibility that systematically affected writers on the periphery of Europe and the hold of the national norms that governed their literary spaces.

The strategies of such writers—which are never implemented in a wholly conscious way—can therefore be described as sorts of very complex equations, containing two, three, or four unknowns, that take into account simultaneously the literariness of their national language, their political situation, their degree of involvement in a national struggle, their determination to achieve recognition in the literary centers, the ethnocentrism and blindness of these same centers, and the necessity of making them aware of the difference of authors on the periphery. Only by examining this strange dialectic, which authors on the periphery alone understand, is it possible to comprehend the issue of language in the dominated countries of the literary world in all its dimensions—emotional, subjective, individual, collective, political—and how the experience of each country differs from that of every other.

THIEVES OF FIRE

We have seen that the centrality and literary credit of a language are measured by the number of polyglots who read it without having to rely on translations. When literary texts, beyond a nation's borders, are read by the central authorities only in translation, which is to say when the central authorities themselves cannot evaluate such texts in their original version, then one is in the presence of a "chronically" translated language in the strict sense—one thinks, for example, of Yoruba, Kikuyu, Amharic, Gaelic, and Yiddish. In regions of extreme literary impoverishment such as the Somalia of Nuruddin Farah, the Congo of Emmanuel Dongala, and the Djibouti of Abdourahman Waberi, these and other novelists—writers in languages that are almost nonexistent in the literary world—manage to exist, paradoxically, only by becoming translated men. They are thus forced to adopt the literary language imported through colonization—what the Dahomean (later Togolese) writer Félix Couchoro (1900–1968) called the "educated foreign language."[6] But in this essential and imposed language they produce a body of work entirely devoted to the defense and illustration of their country and their people. For them, literary usage of the colonial language is not a gesture of assimilation. They would surely endorse the words of Kateb Yacine, who in an 1988 interview remarked: "I write in French in order to say to the French that I am not French."[7]

One glimpses the pathos of their situation in a passage such as the following from the novel *Maps* (1986), by the Somalian English-language writer Nuruddin Farah (b. 1945): "And I grieved at the thought that millions of us were conquered, and would remain forever conquered; millions of us who would remain a traditional people and an oral people at that."[8] Farah's linguistic situation is particularly complex. In an autobiographical essay titled "Childhood of My Schizophrenia" (1990), he evoked his multilingualism, the product of his belonging to a people colonized by a colonized people:

> We spoke Somali at home, but we read or wrote in other languages: Arabic (the sacred tongue of the Koran); Amharic, that of the colonial master, the better to know what he thinks; English, a tongue that might one day afford us entry into a wider world. We moved from one language universe to another with the disquiet of a tenant on a temporary lease. We were conscious of the complicated state of affairs, conscious of the fact that we were being brought up not as replicas of our parents but as a strange new species . . . I have remarked on my people's absence from the roll-call of world history as we were taught it . . . It was with this in mind that I began writing, in the hope of enabling the Somali child at least to characterize his otherness and to point at himself as the unnamed, the divided *other,* a schizophrenic child living in the age of colonial contradiction.[9]

Farah, descended from a culture of oral tradition, first became an Arabic writer: the written form of Somali had been settled only very recently, and it was in Arabic that, as an adolescent, he discovered Victor Hugo and Dostoevsky and composed his first autobiographical essays. But in

the 1960s, upon acquiring a typewriter, he opted for English, thus becoming in a sense the first Somalian writer.

Despite great differences in historical and political context, the ambiguous situation of Gaelic in Ireland in the nineteenth century should
be understood in the same terms. The linguistic and cultural movement
led by the Gaelic League represented an essential moment in the constitution of Irish literary space in the 1890s. But Gaelic accumulated so little credit following its exhumation by Catholic intellectuals that it did
not succeed, despite its official status as the second national language after Ireland won independence in 1921, in achieving true international
literary existence. At the end of the 1930s, the situation of Irish writers
who had chosen Gaelic was described by one critic in these terms:

> The contemporary Gaelic writer therefore finds himself, more than
> any other, faced with the following dilemma: either never to be pub-
> lished; or to please . . . not even the public, but the body that inter-
> poses itself between the public and himself . . . It follows that [a writer
> of] original, independent, free talent finds himself faced with obstacles
> so great that very often he gives up literature altogether and throws
> himself, in order to live, into translation; unless he decides to write in
> English.[10]

It thus becomes clear why many Gaelic writers, playwrights, and poets
were forced to "convert" to English—and, conversely, why there remain
so few Gaelic men and women of letters in Ireland today.

Similarly, the South African novelist and literary theorist Njabulo
Ndebele (b. 1948) tried at first to apply Joyce's "stream of consciousness"
narrative technique to the emerging literary language of Zulu in order
to give it currency and to go beyond the simple denunciations of mili-
tant antiapartheid writing, hoping in this way to raise up a language almost devoid of literary credit to what he considered to be the highest
point of literary modernity, which is to say the norms recognized at the
Greenwich meridian. But he quickly understood the difficulty of an enterprise that, paradoxically, could obtain literary existence only from
English translation. In the absence of any native tradition of modernity,
of any public likely to understand what he was trying to do, of any literary milieu capable of consecrating his work, he saw that this ambition
was both anachronistic and futile, and subsequently devoted himself to
developing a specific and unmediated style of black South African nar-

ration in English.[11] Having since become one of the most celebrated English-language black writers in South Africa, he is therefore a translated author without, however, having passed through the stage of translation in the strict sense.[12]

It may also happen that, as a result of colonization and of cultural and linguistic domination, the dominated writer has no choice in the matter; that, lacking fluency in the language of his ancestors, the only language available to him is that of his country's colonizers. In this case one might say that he translates himself—indeed, produces the definitive translation of his work—in order to gain entry to the literary world. Just as many English-language writers in Ireland at the beginning of the century had no Gaelic, many Algerian intellectuals either did not know Arabic, or did not know it well enough to make it a literary language, when their country achieved independence in 1962.

For many authors, owing to their attachment to their country and their determination to make it exist politically no less than literarily, the decision to write in the language of colonization is not without problems. This all-powerful language is a sort of poisoned chalice or, better perhaps, a form of organized robbery. As a consequence of the power of ideas inherited from Herderian theories (today so thoroughly a part of national political and cultural thinking that their origins have been forgotten), the connection between language, nation, and popular identity came to seem necessary, as we have seen, with the result that nonnative languages came to be regarded as illegitimate. The theme of theft, which so well illustrates this sort of illegitimacy, appears in quite varied historical and political contexts. "When you are in the situation of being colonized," observed the Algerian writer Jean Amrouche (1906–1962), "you are required to use this language that has been lent you, but of which you are only the usufructuary, not the legitimate owner, only a user."[13] Elsewhere Amrouche argued that "those among the colonized who have been able to steep themselves in the great works are all not only coddled heirs, but *thieves of fire*."[14] In appropriating for himself "the benefit of the language of a civilization of which he is not the legitimate heir," Amrouche concluded, the intellectual from a colonized country stands revealed as "a sort of bastard."[15]

This notion of the theft of language is encountered among all literarily dominated authors who have been dispossessed of their own tongue, notably among them Kafka, who, as a German-speaking Czech Jew, stood in the same relation of dispossession, illegitimacy, and insecurity to German as, for example, Algerian writers did to French.[16] Even from the pen of Salman Rushdie, no matter that he is an integrated figure in contemporary English literature, consecrated by the London authorities, one finds the same theme of guilt, which is to say of betrayal:

> The Indian writer, looking back at India, does so through guilt-tinted spectacles . . . Those of us who do use English do so in spite of our ambiguity towards it, or perhaps because of that, perhaps because we find in that linguistic struggle a reflection of other struggles taking place in the real world, struggles between the cultures within ourselves and the influences at work upon our societies. To conquer English may be to complete the process of making ourselves free.[17]

Shakespeare's *Tempest* has been much commented upon, particularly in Anglophone countries, as a prophetic play describing in all their refinement and subtlety the mechanisms of colonization and subjugation (a circumstance that in itself furnishes an excellent practical example of the diversion and appropriation of the colonizer's noblest literary capital).[18] The theory of the poisoned chalice has been widely debated in connection with the outburst by Caliban, who, in response to his master Prospero's statement,

> I pitied thee, took pains to make thee speak,
> . . . When thou didst not, savage,
> Know thine own meaning, but wouldst gabble like
> A thing most brutish, I endowed thy purposes
> With words that made them known

replied:

> You taught me language, and my profit on't
> Is, I know how to curse. The red plague rid you
> For learning me your language![19]

The fundamental ambivalence inherent in this structure of domination explains the importance of debates over the linguistic issue, and the violence of the passions they arouse, which divide all the small nations of the literary world.

It is true that the use of a dominant language is paradoxical and contradictory, for it is as much alienating as it is liberating. First-generation authors, such as R. K. Narayan (1906–2001) in India and Mouloud Mammeri in Algeria, in the absence of any specific national capital, often made use of a "hypercorrect" language in conjunction with very traditional literary forms and aesthetics.[20] Because their double illegitimacy (vis-à-vis both national and central norms) committed them to the most orthodox uses of language and literature, which is to say to the least innovative and therefore the least literary practices, they sought to reconcile a position of national combat (to recall Kafka's phrase) with the literary use of the dominant language in which they wrote and in reaction against which they constructed a sense of literary identity. Using the language of domination, they tried to produce a literature that, mirroring the one that was imposed by colonial authorities, could be assimilated as part of the national literary heritage.

But when a literary space has acquired a certain measure of autonomy, the literary use of one of the great central languages becomes for dominated writers a guarantee of immediate membership in the literary world and allows the appropriation of a whole stock of technical knowledge and expertise. Those who "choose" to write in a dominant language are able, in effect, to take a shortcut on the road to literary status. And since their use of a rich language and the aesthetic categories associated with it makes them immediately more visible, more in conformity with prevailing literary norms, they are also the first to obtain international recognition. Thus, in Ireland, Yeats very quickly earned the approval of the critical authorities in London, which allowed him to establish himself as a leading figure by contrast with poets who had chosen to write in Gaelic. Similarly, the Catalonian writers who are today the best known on the international scene are those who write in Castilian—notably Manuel Vázquez Montalbán, Eduardo Mendoza, and Felix de Azúa. Rushdie himself, famous and celebrated even before the *fatwa* that was pronounced against him, is one of the best-known Indian writers in England. He explicitly recognizes that "major work is being done in India in many languages other than English; yet outside India there is just about no interest in any of this work. The Indo-Anglians seize all the limelight . . . 'Commonwealth literature' is not interested in such matters."[21]

Despite its many ambiguous usages, then, the central language can be claimed by dominated writers as their own property on the condition that the curse of an impossible heritage can be turned against itself. Just as Joyce (who lived in a rather similar colonial—later postcolonial—situation) regarded the English language not as the patent sign of domination, but as the rightful property of his people, Rushdie holds that the "English language ceased to be the sole possession of the English some time ago."[22] Moreover, he points out, the "British Indian writer simply does not have the option of rejecting English, anyway . . . in the forging of a British Indian identity the English language is of central importance. It must, in spite of everything, be embraced."[23] Just so, the "children of independent India seem not to think of English as being irredeemably tainted by its colonial provenance. They use it as an Indian language, as one of the tools they have to hand."[24]

TRANSLATED FROM THE NIGHT

When a peripheral language has acquired at least some resources of its own, one sees the emergence—and this is a path very close to the one just discussed—of literary artists who set themselves the task of producing a dual body of work, maintaining a complex and painfully difficult position between two languages in the process. These "digraphic" texts, as Alain Ricard has suggested they be called, are written *at once* in both of the writer's languages, the mother tongue and that of colonization, and follow a complicated trajectory of translations, transcriptions, and self-translations.[25] This permanent double writing constitutes the substrate, the driving force, the dialectic, and often even the subject of such works.

In the case of the Ivory Coast writer Ahmadou Kourouma (b. 1927), who wrote his great novel *Les soleils des indépendances* (Suns of Independence, 1969) on the basis of a sort of French translation from the Malinke language,[26] the novelty and subversive character of his enterprise depended in large part on his refusal to treat French with the customary respect, his disregard of "proper" usage, and his creation of a hybrid literary language through what might be called the Malinkization of French.

Among Francophone writers, one of the first to experiment with this dual mode of expession was the Madagascar poet Jean-Joseph Rabearivelo (1901–1937). An autodidact who revered the great French poets of the late nineteenth century—the Parnassians, then Baudelaire and the Symbolists, all of whom he had discovered by himself—

Rabearivelo constructed his work in a sort of permanent shuttling back and forth, a kind of reciprocal translation between French and Malagasy. Since the nineteenth century there had existed in Madagascar a standardized written language that permitted the emergence of a true Malagasy poetry, for which Rabearivelo came to develop a passionate feeling. He began his career with a number of articles and essays on the necessity of promoting this culture, and subsequently translated into French the works of both ancient and modern Malagasy authors, collected two years after his death under the title *Les vieilles chansons des pays d'Imerina* (The Old Songs of the Lands of Imerina, 1939), a volume that displays a universal strategy for building a fund of national literary capital. Conversely, and for the same reason, he sought to make known in his country not only Baudelaire, Rimbaud, Laforgue, and Verlaine but also Rilke, Whitman, and Tagore, and himself translated Valéry into Malagasy. He next published in French, in both Tananarive (now Antananarivo) and Tunis,[27] what were to become his most celebrated collections of poetry, *Presque-songes* (Almost Dreams, 1934) and *Traduit de la nuit* (Translated from the Night, 1935), the latter subtitled "Poems Transcribed from the Hova by the Author."[28] Critics, mindful of the distinctive talent and originality required for a poet to be consecrated, were much exercised over the question whether these were genuine translations, and inquired after the original version of the texts on which they were based.

The importance of traditional literature, particularly the *hain-teny* described some twenty years earlier by Jean Paulhan, is obvious in Rabearivelo's writing,[29] which, accordingly, sought to go beyond the usual distinction between collective and individual creation. But Rabearivelo also created a new sort of language, a manner of writing Malagasy in French—much like Rubén Darío's "mental Gallicism"— that yielded a genuinely trans-lated text in which each component was brought over through the other. Rabearivelo wrote neither in French nor in Malagasy, but in an intermediate idiom derived from a continual passing back and forth between the two languages. The title of his 1935 collection, "Translated from the Night," is a magnificent metaphor for this almost impossible translation, snatched from the obscurity of an almost unknown tongue, and so attesting at once to its literary existence and to its literary weakness. Rather than take the ennobling path of assimilation, Rabearivelo had the daring to attempt something unprecedented, setting himself in opposition, on the one hand, to his country's nationalists, for whom such an enterprise was a betrayal of the Malagasy language and its poetry, and, on the other, to the norms of proper usage and of French academic poetry—the daring, in short, to invent a Malagasy poetry (and language) in French. Rabearivelo succeeded in this ambition, renouncing neither his original language nor the literary language, which for him was the language of his country's colonizers. His work was recognized in Paris quite rapidly, earning a place in Léopold Sédar Senghor's *Anthologie de la nouvelle poésie nègre et malgache de la langue française* (Anthology of New Black and Malagasy Poetry in French, 1948), which contained a preface by Jean-Paul Sartre. But by then he was dead, having committed suicide more than a decade earlier, in 1937, without ever having been able to obtain permission from the colonial administration to visit France.

COMINGS AND GOINGS

The various options available to writers in "choosing" a literary language are sometimes so hard to dissociate that it makes more sense to analyze them as elements of a single continuous series of strategies. Linguistic imbalance—the sort of imbalance familiar to a tightrope walker—is inherent in these positions, which are at once difficult, marginal, and prodigiously fertile. The choice of one or another option, the passing back and forth from one language to another, gives rise to wavering, hesitations, regrets, and steps backward. They are not clear-cut choices, but rather a series of possibilities that are dependent on political and literary constraints and on the development of a writer's career (which is to say the degree of national and international recognition his work enjoys).

When a dominated language has an autonomous literary existence, the same writer may experiment successively with various routes of access to literature. The Algerian Rachid Boudjedra (b. 1941), for example, is the author of works written first in French that he then translated himself into Arabic; and also of texts written in Arabic that were then translated into French. Boudjedra is therefore a digraphic author, since he operates continually between two languages, subject to the tension of translation, itself an essential element of his work. His first novels composed in French, *La répudiation* (The Repudiation, 1969) and *L'insolation* (Sunstroke, 1972), won him wide recognition. He then translated the second of these two French novels into Arabic, thus transforming his relationship to the Algerian public: having been consecrated in France, he could now be read in the language of his own country. But, as he explained, the social and literary norms were not the same in Algeria:

> In French [the book] didn't cause a stir. In Algeria, people read it, and when I translated it into Arabic there was a terrible outcry against me, precisely because I had challenged the sacred text, I had made puns on the Koranic text and so on . . . the whole subversive thrust comes through better in Arabic . . . I wrote in French when I was in France because otherwise I wouldn't have found a publisher. Frankly, I'll tell you straight out, I'm very fond of French, it's been of enormous service to me—I've written six novels in it and I've got an international reputation and I've been translated in some fifteen countries thanks to this language. Then I changed over to Arabic, and that also coincided with the rise of an Arab-speaking generation that has gone to school and no longer speaks French . . . But I take part in the translation [of my work] into French. There is a translator and I insist on working with him on the translation, because it has to be by Boudjedra, like the days when I wrote in French.[30]

The porousness between two languages made possible by bilingualism therefore encourages a perpetual transit back and forth between them and produces a succession of linguistic and national reappropriations. Fictional purpose is seamlessly inscribed and constituted in this sense of belonging to two languages.

The case of the South African Zulu poet Mazisi Kunene (b. 1930) is very similar to that of Boudjedra. As a writer involved in the struggle against apartheid who served as the representative of the African National Congress to the United Nations in the 1960s, he started out collecting and analyzing traditional Zulu poetry, later creating works of his own in Zulu. Working with poems from the oral tradition, he composed epics that recounted the memory of his people and translated them himself into English, publishing these versions in London, notably *Zulu Poems* (1970) and *The Ancestors and the Sacred Mountains* (1982). Unquestionably his most important work is *Emperor Shaka the Great* (1979), an epic poem in seventeen books. His decision to write in Zulu, together with a faithfulness to the forms of oral culture, permitted him to reconcile participation in national politics and the need for international recognition. His countryman André Brink (b. 1935), heir as a white Afrikaner to another marginal language in the same literary world, likewise chose self-translation. He composed his first novels in Afrikaans and then, after the banning of his book *Kennis van die Aand* (Looking on Darkness, 1973) by the South African regime in 1974, began to translate his own books into English. This exchange of languages, which amounted to a license to travel beyond the borders of his country, enabled him to achieve international recognition.

KAFKA: TRANSLATED FROM YIDDISH

Against all appearances and contrary to the most common critical assumptions regarding his work, Franz Kafka clearly belongs to this same family of cases. One might in fact describe Kafka's whole literary enterprise as a monument raised to the glory of Yiddish, the lost and forgotten language of the Western Jews, and his work as consisting in a despairing practice of German, the language of Jewish assimilation and the language of those who, by encouraging this assimilation, succeeded in making the Jews of Prague (and more generally of western Europe as a whole) forget their own culture. German was a "stolen" language whose use Kafka persisted in regarding as illegitimate. In this sense his work can be considered as entirely translated from a language that he could not write, Yiddish.

As a native of Prague, as a Jew, and as an intellectual, Franz Kafka occupied a very complex place in the political and literary life of his time. As a native of Prague he found himself at the heart of debates over Czech nationalism; as a Jew he was confronted not only with the question of Zionism but also with the appearance of Bundism in eastern Europe;[31] and as an intellectual he was faced, on the one hand, with problems of national and nationalist engagement and, on the other, with the aestheticism practiced by his friends in the Prague Circle.[32] These three positions were often contradictory and yet, at the same time, indissociable. Kafka found himself at the precise point of intersection of three overlapping intellectual, literary, and political spaces: Prague, at once a seat of administration within the Austro-Hungarian Empire and the cultural capital of Czech nationalism, to be sure, but also a city where the Germanized Jewish intellectuals who made up the Prague Circle still affirmed their identity; Berlin, the literary and intellectual capital of central Europe as a whole; and, finally, the political and intellectual space of eastern Europe, a world in which nationalist movements and Jewish workers parties emerged and Bundist and Zionist ideas clashed—not forgetting New York, the new city of Jewish immigration, center of politics, literature, drama, and poetry for the populations that had come to America from Russia and Poland.

The Jews of central and eastern Europe at the end of the nineteenth century were in a position comparable to that of all the other peoples of the region who sought national emancipation, except for this enormous difference: as victims of antisemitism, ostracized, stigmatized, without a land of their own, and dispersed throughout Europe, more than any other dominated people they faced a huge theoretical and political task in trying to formulate a set of national (and nationalist) claims and, by establishing their legitimacy, to win acceptance for them. It was unarguably this unique state of extreme subjection that gave birth to the conflict that—to oversimplify somewhat—opposed Zionists to Bundists: the former, heirs to Herder, advocates for the founding of a true nation identified with a national territory (Palestine); the latter, defenders of Yiddish language and culture, supporters of diaspora and the formation of autonomous Jewish communities within existing states.

Kafka's literary—but no doubt also political, which is to say national—position and aims must be described on the basis of these inseparably literary, linguistic, and political aspects of domination. As we have seen, he became acquainted with the cultural world as well as the political and linguistic demands of the Yiddishists (typically Bundists, though some were Seimists) through the performances of Yiddish theater presented in Prague for several months at the end of 1911 and the beginning of 1912 by a troupe from Poland. A careful analysis of his discovery of *Yiddishkeit* indicates that he subsequently sought to take part in the formation of a Jewish and secular popular culture. One might go further and, in keeping with the model proposed here, suggest that Kafka was placed (or placed himself) in the position of a foundational writer, struggling for the full recognition of his people and his nation, committed to the development of a national Jewish literature. On this view he thus becomes a paradoxical member of Yiddish-Jewish space, tragically distant yet at the same time actively working on behalf of an emerging Jewish nation and, by virtue of this, dedicated to the creation of a popular and national literature and, more generally, to the service of Jewish culture and the Jewish people.

What makes Kafka's situation difficult to comprehend is that it was the exact opposite of that of his contemporaries in Prague. As a first-generation intellectual in his family, seeking to join an intellectual world that on the whole was more bourgeois than he was, Kafka was very different from the other members of the Prague Circle, among them his friend Max Brod: whereas his companions were Zionists, nationalists, Germanophiles, Hebraists, anti-Yiddishists, he was socialist, Yiddishist, and anti-Zionist.[33] And as a member of a Jewish community in central Europe that was largely assimilated and Germanized, he nonetheless found himself in a tragic and contradictory position, for he did not know Yiddish and therefore could not directly devote himself to the collective enterprise whose grandeur and beauty he described in "Beim Bau der chinesischen Mauer" (The Great Wall of China, written in 1917 but not published until 1931). This is why he was to adopt a paradoxical and yet unimprovable solution: to write in German and recount for the assimilated Jewish people the tragedy of their assimilation. It thus becomes necessary to reread "Forschungen eines Hundes" (Investigations of a Dog, written in 1922 and published in 1931) and *Amerika* (America, written in 1911–1914 and published in 1927) as evidence of Kafka's almost ethnological determination to give Germanized Jews an account of their own forgotten history (it needs to be kept in mind that the actual title, due to Kafka himself, of the text that Brod published under the title *Amerika* was in fact *Der Verschollene,* meaning "The Forgotten One")[34] and to denounce the horror of assimilation—of which he himself was a product, and which he saw as a form of self-negation—by contrast with what he considered the necessary affirmation of a popular and secular Jewish national existence.

In other words, Kafka's desire to work on behalf of a Jewish nationalist and socialist movement made him—like all writers who place themselves in the service of a national cause—a political artist. But he was forced to abandon the language of his people—with great sorrow and regret—in favor of the dominant language. His position was thus exactly the same as that of colonized writers who, with the emergence of national independence movements, discover their unique identity and position in coming to understand the state of dependence and cultural destitution into which assimilation has led them. Just as Joyce decided to write in English in order to subvert the language from within, Kafka resigned himself to German—but in order to pose in literary terms a range of literary, political, and social questions that until then had escaped consideration, and tried to express in German the categories peculiar not only to the new Yiddish literature that then was being produced but to all nascent literatures: what might be called collective literary forms and genres, which is to say those that have in common the fact of belonging to a people (tales, legends, myths, chronicles, and so on). It is precisely in this sense that Kafka's work can be read as a sort of translation from the Yiddish.

The situation of the German Jewish writers of Prague, which Kafka described in his famous letter to Max Brod of June 1921, condenses in an extraordinary way the situation of all dominated writers, driven by the very fact of their cultural and linguistic domination to speak and write in the language of those who have subdued them—to the point, in fact, of making them forget their own language and culture. These writers, as Kafka explained in a passage reproduced at the beginning of this chapter, live between three impossibilities: of not writing, of writing in German, and of writing otherwise; indeed, between four, counting the impossibility of writing at all. In just the same way Kateb Yacine could have said that North African writers are torn between as many possibilities (which it is convenient to call linguistic impossibilities but which are also political impossibilities): the impossibility of not writing, the impossibility of writing in French, the impossibility of writing in Arabic, and the impossibility of writing otherwise. Kafka's friends in the Prague Circle were forced to write in German, in his view, but they were so assimilated that they had actually forgotten that they had forgotten their own culture: writing in German was therefore the manifest sign of their subjection. The burden of this is to say that they were in the position of all dominated or colonized intellectuals who look to language for a way out from the fundamental impasse in which they are trapped. This is why Kafka was explicitly to employ in the same letter— and in almost the same terms later used by Jean Amrouche in connection with Algerian writers in the years immediately after their country's independence—the themes of illegitimacy and the theft of language. For Jewish intellectuals, use of the German language amounted to "appropriation of someone else's property, something not earned, but stolen by means of a relatively casual gesture. Yet it remains someone else's property, even though there is no evidence of a single solecism"; their literature was "a literature impossible in all respects, a gypsy literature which had stolen the German child out of its cradle and in great haste put it through some kind of training, for someone has to dance on the tightrope. (But it wasn't even a German child, it was nothing; people merely said something was dancing.)"[35]

The famous passage in Kafka's *Diaries* where he attributes his incomplete love for his mother to a contradiction of language—wonderfully revealing of the central place in his thought of this missing mother tongue, which until now has invariably been analyzed in exclusively psychological terms—is directly associated with his thinking about the Yiddish language. It appears in the midst of notes devoted to Isak Löwy and his memories of the actor:

> Yesterday it occurred to me that I did not always love my mother as she deserved and as I could [have], only because the German language prevented it. The Jewish mother is no "Mutter," to call her "Mutter" makes her a little comic (not to herself, because we are in Germany); we give a Jewish woman the name of a German mother, but forget the contradiction that sinks into the emotions so much the more heavily. "Mutter" is peculiarly German for the Jew, it unconsciously contains . . . Christian splendor [as well as] Christian coldness; the Jewish woman who is called "Mutter" therefore becomes not only comic but strange.[36]

German, as a foreign language and at the same time mother tongue (a dilemma that Rilke, who experienced it as well, was to find other ways of escaping), was a borrowed language, appropriated through assimilation. To Kafka's mind—echoing exactly the terms of the political debate that was then unfolding in Jewish circles throughout Europe—it had been shamefully stolen at the cost of forgetting oneself and betraying Jewish culture.

This reading, which I shall argue for in greater detail in a forthcoming work, and which accommodates rather than excludes a great many prior interpretations (psychological, philosophical, religious, and metaphysical, among others), may seem somewhat shocking and disillusioning, even blasphemous, for readers accustomed to the standard picture of Kafka as a "pure" artist. It imposed itself upon me, little by little and almost in spite of my own wishes, as a consequence of historical research that led me to put Kafka back into the national (and therefore international) world in which he lived.

CREATORS OF LANGUAGES

The appearance of a national language distinct from the dominant language is primarily a consequence of political decisions, and has the consequence in turn that some authors will come to write in it. Even if this option represents an extreme position in the range of linguistic possibilities, which is to say among the main paths of political and literary differentiation, it is also one of the most difficult and most perilous. Emerging literary spaces today, notably in Africa, are repeating the experience of nineteenth-century Europe, where the new languages that achieved official status were based on a regional dialect. In Europe, as Eric Hobsbawm observed, "literary Bulgarian is based on the West Bulgarian idiom, literary Ukrainian on its southeastern dialects, literary Hungarian emerges in the sixteenth century by combining various dialects," and so on.[37] Norwegian brought together, in an almost experimental way, as we have seen, two national languages: the one, *Bokmål* ("book language"), very strongly Danicized after four hundred years of foreign rule, bore the historical marks of colonization; the other, *Landsmål* ("country language"), later called *Nynorsk* ("new Norwegian"), was the work of intellectuals in the mid-nineteenth century who advocated, as part of the movement for national independence, the creation of a "truly" Norwegian language. The absence of literariness in these and other languages that have little value in the literary marketplace (including languages such as Catalan, Czech, and Polish that dispose of an ancient stock of literary capital) leads to the almost automatic marginalization of the writers who defend them, with the result that they have immense difficulty achieving recognition in literary centers. The more peripheral their language and the more devoid it is of resources, the greater the pressure upon them to become national writers. In effect, writers who take this path suffer the consequences of a dual dependence, which itself is the product of the twofold invisibility and nonexistence of their language, both in the international linguistic and political marketplace and in the literary marketplace.

In literary worlds in which the national language is initially endowed with only an oral tradition, or, as in the case of Gaelic, has a long-interrupted written tradition, literary capital—that is, the traditional forms associated with written tradition—is almost nonexistent. This is why all attempts at "standardization"—at establishing orthographic and syntactic norms, which precede the elaboration of a literary tradition in the strict sense—place intellectuals and writers in the exclusive service of the new language, which is to say the new nation.[38] In Ireland at the beginning of the century, poets and intellectuals who chose to write in Gaelic devoted themselves more to the codification of their language than to the creation of a distinctive literature, which in any case was much less valued than the work of their contemporaries who wrote in English. Writers engaged in a struggle on behalf of their nation must therefore build up literary resources of their own from nothing: they must construct a literary tradition out of whole cloth, a tradition with its own themes and genres that will achieve respectability for a language that, being unknown and unvalued in the literary marketplace, will have to be immediately translated in order to find international legitimacy.

The Kenyan writer Ngugi wa Thiong'o, who, as we have noted, abandoned the literary use of English in favor of his mother tongue, Kikuyu, is a limiting case—and a fascinating one for what it reveals about literary enterprises of this type. Before 1970 there existed very few texts in this language, apart from cheap novels sold in the market.[39] In 1980 Ngugi published his first book in Kikuyu, *Caitaani mutharaba-ini,* and since then the literary corpus in this language seems almost to have grown through his own productions alone.[40] His desire to promote the literary status of his native language is clearly consistent with the logic of initial accumulation:

> Language is both a product of that succession of the separate generations, as well as being a bank for the way of life reflecting those modifications of collective experience in the production and reproduction of their life. Literature, thinking in images, utilizes language and draws upon the collective experience embodied in the language . . . We Kenyans can no longer avoid the question: whose language and history will our literature draw upon . . . ? If a Kenyan writer wants to speak to the peasants and workers of any one Kenyan community, then he should write in the language they speak and understand . . . In making their choices, Kenyan writers should remember that the struggle of our languages against domination by those of Europe is part of a wider historical struggle of the Kenyan national culture against imperialist domination.[41]

Salman Rushdie, recalling his participation with Ngugi in a 1983 colloquium in Sweden devoted to the topic "Commonwealth Literature," noted the usual characterizations of the Kenyan author ("committed

Marxist," "an overtly political writer") and remembered that he "expressed his rejection of the English language by reading his own work in Swahili, with a Swedish version read by his translator, leaving the rest of us completely bemused."[42]

The contradictions in which these authors are caught up are reinforced by the literary forms that they adopt. The less literary credit there is available to them, the more writers are dependent on the national and political order, the more they are obliged to borrow literary forms having very little value along the Greenwich meridian. The absence of a literary tradition of their own, combined with their weakness in relation to the political authorities, has the effect of encouraging the reproduction of the most traditional models. Ngugi himself spoke of the practical problems that he encountered in crafting literary fictions in Kikuyu. Having access to no model other than the Bible, he met with great difficulties in the construction of narrative and in the "temporal marking of quoted speech."[43]

These various obstacles explain why many dominated literary spaces, despite the establishment of a national language of their own, remain bilingual for literary purposes. Just as in the sixteenth and seventeenth centuries there was a Latin/French bilingualism[44] among men and women of letters, instituted and reproduced by the educational system as a consequence of the undisputed dominance of Latin, so it is by virtue of their literary bilingualism (or digraphy in Ricard's sense) that the dependence of many literary spaces can be recognized. Alternatively, one might say that it is in the progressive disappearance of bilingualism (or digraphy)—an unmistakable sign of the overcoming of literary subjection—that the degree of linguistic and literary emancipation and progress in appropriating new national literary wealth can be recognized. Thus it was the accumulation of literary credit attaching to the French language during the sixteenth and seventeenth centuries that permitted the triumph of French described in the first part of this book, its symbolic increase in value, and the gradual retreat from Latin (or, at least, its relegation to a secondary place). Objective measures of the current political and literary position of Arabic by comparison with French in Algeria, of Kikuyu by comparison with English in Kenya, of Gaelic by comparison with English in Ireland, of Catalan (or Galician) by comparison with Castilian in Spain—taking into account the official status of the language, the number of people who speak it, its place in the educational system, the number of books published in it, the number of writers who have chosen to write in it, and so on—make it possible to estimate and analyze the extent of linguistic and literary domination in each of these countries.

In what might be called median literary spaces—ones that are neither central nor located on the remote periphery, such as those of small European countries—the situation is structurally very similar, allowing for differences of degree, to that of very impoverished zones. As in the case of the poorest literatures, the effects of linguistic and literary inequality are still so powerful that it can actually prevent (or at least make very difficult) the recognition and consecration of writers working in small languages. Thus Henrik Stangerup speaks of his mother tongue, Danish, as a "miniature language." The great Danish poet Adam Oehlenschläger (1779–1850) stands for him as the symbol of this linguistic marginality, as a "Danish poet-Napoleon, capable of a titanic output, like a Hugo or a Balzac, worthy of being recruited as a member of their conspiracy—if only he had written in a major language—against the crass stupidity that recognizes no [national] frontiers."[45] Notwithstanding the ecumenical ideology that presides over literary celebrations, writers in small languages are apt to find themselves marginalized. Thus the great Brazilian critic Antonio Candido has noted that at the end of the nineteenth century the stylistic and literary originality of Machado de Assis might have allowed him, had circumstances been different, to exercise an international influence:

> Of the Western languages, ours [Portuguese] is the least known, and if the countries where it is spoken matter little today, in 1900 they mattered even less in the political game. For this reason, two novelists who wrote in our language and who are the equals of the best then writing remain marginal: Eça de Queirós, well suited to the spirit of naturalism; and Machado de Assis . . . a writer of international stature [who] remained almost totally unknown outside Brazil . . . His almost hypertrophic national glory was the counterpart of a discouraging international obscurity.[46]

This great critic, committed to bringing about a reevaluation of his country's literature, was himself a victim of the structural ostracism he described: as Howard Becker has observed, Candido "stayed in Brazil, wrote in its language, and devoted much of his effort to its literature, unfamiliar (with a few exceptions) to non-Portuguese-speaking readers. And so his work is almost unknown elsewhere."[47] In exactly the same sense E. M. Cioran reflected upon the predicament of his old friend Petre Tutea (1901–1991), who he felt would surely have enjoyed international fame had he not lived in Bucharest and written in Romanian: "What an extraordinary man! With his matchless eloquence, if he had lived in Paris he would have a worldwide reputation today."[48]

Instances of bilingualism are also encountered in these median spaces. Today in Catalonia, for example, which asserts its distinctive cultural identity as a "nation," Catalan and Castilian coexist and compete with each other. Success in winning recognition for the region's linguistic and cultural autonomy has made it possible to establish independent networks for the production, marketing, and distribution of its literature.[49] In Barcelona there are now Catalan publishers who issue works for a "national" public that has become more and more numerous thanks to what might be called the Catalanization of the educational system. For a quarter-century or more writers such as Sergi Pámies, Pere Gimferrer, Jesus Moncada, and Quim Monzó have been able to write and publish in the Catalan language and, what is more, they can now hope to be translated directly into the great literary languages without having to pass through the intermediate stage of Castilian. The appearance of a corps of specialized translators has opened literary production to an international audience and gradually given the Catalan language existence not only in international literary space but in international political space as well. But even if Catalan has become an increasingly legitimate option, Castilian has remained in some ways a more attractive alternative. As I have already had occasion to emphasize, Catalan novelists working in Castilian, whose works by definition are available to a broader audience, and who spread a euphemistic version of Catalonian cultural nationalism aimed at the general public—in the form of detective novels by authors such as Manuel Vázquez Montalbán, or of realistic novels evoking the history of Barcelona by Eduardo Mendoza, Juan Marsé, and others—have achieved much greater recognition in the great literary centers. In these worlds, in other words, bilingualism has a tendency to disappear in the work of individual authors: though it no longer serves to express wrenching personal dilemmas, it persists in the form of a struggle for linguistic legitimacy within the national literary space itself.

National and international poles tend to be differentiated in median spaces, however, and the position of what I have called national authors changes meaning. Whereas in the newest spaces these authors struggle politically and literarily for autonomy—their very politicization, as I have argued, constituting in itself a paradoxical but real form of independence—in literatures that have already achieved a certain degree of autonomy national writers turn their back on the wider world and devote themselves to literary conservatism, to closing off aesthetic and political borders. At the same time there appear writers who, refusing total submission to national norms and "duties," look beyond their borders and take inspiration from the aesthetic innovations consecrated along the Greenwich meridian. By the same token, oversimplifying slightly, one may describe these median worlds as structured on the basis of an opposition between national writers who have become nationalists and international writers who have become modernists.

Owing to their decentered position in world literary space, and the fact that they work in a language poorly endowed in literary capital, the national-conservatives go untranslated; having no existence, visibility, or recognition outside their national literary space, they do not exist literarily. The national writer has a national career and a national market: he reproduces in the language of his nation models that are not only the most conventional but also the most consistent with commercial— which is to say national, universally outmoded—criteria. Just as his own work is not exported, neither does he import anything: he is unaware of the aesthetic innovations and debates taking place beyond the borders of his country; unaware of the revolutions that are leaving their mark on the world of letters. Being untranslated, his work never reaches this world—the very idea of literature means nothing to him. The portrait that Juan Benet draws of the Spanish writer Pío Baroja (1872–1956) gives a succinct definition of the national writer:

> Over the course of a life of more than eighty years and a literary career of almost sixty, having hardly altered the premises from which he had begun . . . his work ended at the same point from which it had started . . . between his youth and his maturity, he saw modernism, Symbolism, Dadaism, Surrealism pass by without his pen knowing the slightest quiver; he saw Proust, Gide, Joyce, Mann, Kafka, to say nothing of Breton, Céline, Forster, all the Americans of the interwar period, the lost generation, the literature of the revolution, without raising his

head at their passing . . . His mind was already set when the ideas of Marx and Freud began to circulate, ideas for which he had only disdain. Having immunized himself [against events], he was profoundly unaffected by the war of 1914, the Bolshevik revolution, the chaos of the postwar years or the appearance of dictatorships and fascisms. In a sense he had placed himself outside time.[50]

By "untranslated writers" I do not mean that no author of this type has managed ever to have his work published in another language. I mean that, being by definition "behind" in relation to the literary present, they never really manage to achieve international recognition. In a very curious yet convincing way, one can point to similarities in respect both of style (always realistic) and of content (always national) between the great saga of the Korean writer Pak Kyong-Ni, the official national candidate for the Nobel Prize; the work of Dobrica Ćosić, the former president of Serbia and the author of immensely popular national novels conceived on the Tolstoyan model; that of Dragan Jeremić, dissected by Danilo Kiš in *The Anatomy Lesson,* where it is dismissed as "pretty"; and that of Miguel Delibes in Spain—to name only four examples. The national writer manages to prosper in every part of the world only through the reproduction (and the consolidation in many forms, particularly commercial ones) of poles that are not merely national but nationalist, conservative, traditional—in a word, to recall Kiš's term, ignorant. All these untranslated writers stand opposed to the centripetal forces of world literary space and act as a powerful brake upon the process of unification. By partitioning and dividing world literature, their work promotes political and national dependence.

In these same spaces, by contrast, there also appear authors who reject the closing in of the nation upon itself and embrace international criteria of innovation and modernity. They become, as we have seen, importers of central innovations (via "in-translation) whose own work is exported (via "ex-translation"). Their own work, nourished by the great revolutionaries and innovators who have left a mark in the literary capitals, coincides with the categories of those responsible for consecration in the centers. Like Danilo Kiš, Arno Schmidt, Jorge Luis Borges, and others, they are also translated and recognized in Paris, despite their belonging to destitute literary spaces (in which they remain exceptional figures) very far from the Greenwich meridian.

It is in these worlds that one encounters authors who are naturalized, as it were, in another language; who, in order to overcome the marginality and remoteness to which their national (and native) language mechanically condemns them, have converted to one of the great literary idioms. Thus, at one point or another during their careers, Cioran, Kundera, Panait Istrati, Beckett, Nabokov, Conrad, and Strindberg all adopted one of the great world literary languages—whether in a provisional or a definitive way, whether alternating between two languages or in systematic and symmetrical translation—without having been compelled to do so for any political or economic reason. These comings and goings between two languages, two cultures, two worlds are the result of a bilingualism (or digraphy) that is in no way the consequence of colonial or political domination. It can be explained only by the weight of the unequal structure of the literary world, for only the invisible power of the belief that ennobles certain languages and of the discredit that devalues others can force some authors—without any apparent coercion—to exchange their native language for another.

We have seen that Cioran, having published several books in Romanian in Bucharest, wished to rediscover the language of literature par excellence—which is to say, according to the oldest conceptions of balance of power in the literary world, the language of the "century of Louis XIV"—the essence of classicism—and in this way transmute himself into a French writer. Similarly, but according to a quite different political and aesthetic logic, the poetry of Paul Celan (1920–1970)—composed in and at the same time in opposition to German, whose conventions it shattered—has been seen by some interpreters as having actually been written in order to be translated into French, ultimately the symbol of its deliverance from the language of the Holocaust. On this view, one is dealing with a kind of translation internal to the process of writing itself. Celan (born, like Cioran, in Romania) closely collaborated on the French version of his poems with Jean Daive and André du Bouchet, an example of assisted translation that appeared a year after his death under the title *Strette*. This text must be considered as wholly due to Celan, without in any way preventing other translations from being attempted.

Milan Kundera (b. 1929), a Czech writer exiled in France since 1975, began writing in French after his arrival there. Taking matters a step further, however, having personally gone over and corrected the French translations of all his earlier books in Czech, he has insisted since 1985 that the French version of his work is the only authorized one. By an inversion of the ordinary process of translation (which proves yet again that translation involves not merely a change of language but a change in the very "nature" of a work), the French text of his writings therefore became the original version. "Since then," Kundera writes, "I have considered the French text to be mine, and I allow my novels be translated from Czech as well as from French. I even have a slight preference for the latter option."[51]

LITERARY USES OF THE ORAL LANGUAGE

In linguistically dependent regions, including North America and Latin America, which I have earlier described as exceptions within the set of territories under colonial domination,[52] where as a result of cultural and political traditions writers have available to them only one great literary language, the same distinctive strategies are found in other forms.

In the absence of an alternative language, writers are forced to devise a new idiom within their own language; subverting established literary usages and the rules of grammatical and literary correctness, they affirm the specificity of a popular language. Historically, the category and notion of a popular language—that is, a means of expression intrinsically linked to the nation and the people, which it defines and whose existence it justifies—emerged at the juncture of the two main conceptions of the people, as nation and as social class. It therefore became necessary to reinstate a paradoxical sort of bilingualism by making it possible to be different, linguistically and literarily, within a given language. In this way a new idiom was created, through the *littérarisation* of oral practices. Here, in linguistic form, one encounters the mechanisms underlying the literary transmutation of traditional folk narratives.

Though apparently less radical than adopting a new language, this solution is actually, in the absence of anything better, a way of placing the writer at the greatest possible distance from the political pole of a given literary space. While remaining within the central language it becomes possible, by means of minute deviations, to break with it no less explicitly than if one had adopted another tongue. Ramuz, in embracing the tactic of "exaggerating one's own differences," chose precisely this solution on returning to his native Vaud. Many other writers have likewise sought, through the subversion of conventions that are both social and linguistic, to create more or less marked differences in usage and pronunciation, relying on idiomatic expressions and deliberately incorrect usage, with a view to founding a new and inalienable popular identity.

This approach was magnificently inaugurated by the Irish playwright John Millington Synge (1871–1909), who brought the language of his nation's peasants, Anglo-Irish—a language that was at once real and *littérarisé*—to the stage. Synge's solution was faithful to the popular conception of the national language while at the same time representing a break with the canons of English linguistic propriety. The introduction of an oral language in literature alters the terms of literary debate and undermines the tenets of literary realism everywhere: in both Egypt and Brazil during the 1920s and 1930s,[53] in Quebec during the 1960s, in Scotland during the 1980s, and in the West Indies today, the spoken language made it possible, in different forms and for different purposes, to proclaim an emancipation that was literary or political, or sometimes both.

The invention of a new idiom also made it possible to reject an impossible choice. Just as Synge, in making peasants speak in a "mixed" language in Ireland at the beginning of the twentieth century, refused to choose between English and Irish, so Jean Bernabé, Patrick Chamoiseau, and Raphaël Confiant, in their manifesto of "Creoleness" published in Paris in 1989, expressed an unwillingness to choose between the two terms of a crippling alternative—"Europeanness and Africanness"—that had long shackled writers on the periphery.[54]

The championing of joual in Quebec in the 1960s was as much a rejection of the ascendancy of the English language ("whitespeak") as of the norms of proper French. In embracing a despised dialect (the word *joual,* a phonetic transcription of the popular Québécois pronunciation of *cheval,* was until recently a pejorative shorthand for the gap between the local dialect and academic French) as the linguistic symbol of the political and literary independence they demanded, Michel Tremblay and other authors affirmed their autonomy in the face of the two dominant languages, the English of Ottawa and the French of Paris, championing French against English while at the same time calling for the use of a specific language freed from French norms—one that was oral, popular, and full of slang. Thus a working-class Montreal dialect with rural roots that incorporated many Anglicisms and Americanisms came to be promoted as a North American "Creole." Already by the mid-1960s it had achieved the status (albeit provisional) of a literary language, making it possible politically to establish French as the language of the Québécois in their struggle against the hegemony of English while simultaneously resisting the domination of the French of France. The review *Parti Pris,* founded in 1963, described the situation in Quebec as one of colonial oppression and rapidly made itself the mouthpiece for literary and political protest in the province. The following year the review's publishing arm, Éditions Parti Pris, brought out *Le Cabochon* (The Cabochon, 1964), by André Major, and, still more importantly, *Le Cassé* (Broke City, 1964), by Jacques Renaud—works that, in provoking the quarrel over joual, utterly recast the terms of literary debate. By distancing themselves from academic norms, then, Québécois authors created a means of expression (soon to be challenged) that paradoxically permitted them to reappropriate French for themselves.

Depending on a literary space's degree of emancipation, which is to say the degree to which it has been denationalized, a more or less autonomous—that is, literary—use is made of the popular language. It is nonetheless the case that writers who make exclusive (or almost exclusive) use of a great literary language have a distinct advantage in assembling a patrimony. Unlike those who create new languages devoid of literary credit, writers who inherit a dominant language, even in subverting it and in changing its codes and uses, accomplish a sort of diversion of capital and benefit from all its literary resources, for this is a language capable of conveying literary value and credit from the start, of supporting national mythologies and pantheons, and of providing an anchor for literary belief. Though they run a risk in pushing ahead, the aesthetic of writers who adopt a great literary language with the intention of transforming it is from the outset more innovative, on account of the intrinsic literary capital of this language, than that of writers who promote a new language having no capital at all. This is why dominated authors who are speakers (and writers) of central languages belong at once to relatively well-endowed literary spaces.

ANDRADE: THE ANTI-CAMÕES

The career of Mário de Andrade (1893–1945), commonly regarded as the high priest of Brazilian modernism, needs to be placed within the same perspective of the literary creation of a popular and national language. His most famous work, *Macunaíma* (1928), was conceived as the cornerstone of a national literature, demanding and at the same time creating a written Brazilian language distinct from "the language of Camões," the symbol of proper Portuguese usage. With the same determination showed by Joyce in rejecting the literary and grammatical conventions of English, he declared: "We are confronted with the current, national, moral, and human problem of Brazilianizing Brazil."[55] This affirmation of a culture peculiar to Brazil, transmitted and created through a language that is itself Brazilian, therefore proceeded from a resolve not only to put an end to linguistic dependence upon Portugal but also, more broadly, to literary (and cultural) dependence with regard to Europe as a whole: "Patience is a virtue, brothers," cries the Amazonian emperor Macunaíma. "No! I won't go to Europe . . . I'm an American, and my place is here in America. Without a doubt, European civilization would play havoc with our unspoiled nature."[56] Andrade was certainly not the first Brazilian writer,[57] nor was modernism the first Brazilian literary movement: a long literary history had gone before. But, as in the case of Spanish-speaking America, this history had until then to a large degree consisted of works that reproduced models imported from Europe with various small differences that were not always insisted upon. Modernism, of which Andrade was one of the chief theoreticians and spokesmen, was the first movement that explicitly demanded a national literary emancipation. Indeed, one might say that Andrade was in exactly the same position as du Bellay when he called for an end to be put to the dependence of French upon Latin.[58] Andrade was the founding poet of Brazilian literary space by virtue of the fact that, in proclaiming and creating a national "difference," he was the first (along with the other members of the modernist generation) to bring this space into the great international game, into the world of literature on a global scale. His friend Oswald de Andrade, author of two important literary calls-to-arms—*Manifesto antropófago* (Cannibalistic Manifesto, 1928), with its famous line "Tupi or not tupi, that is the question," and *Manifesto da poesia Pau-Brasil* (Manifesto of Brazilwood Poetry, 1924), which took its title from the red hardwood that was colonial Brazil's leading export—was more explicit in this connection. Oswald de Andrade's sylvan metaphor was meant to affirm his determination to create a poetry that could at last be exported: "A single struggle," he wrote, "the struggle for the way forward. Let us distinguish: Imported Poetry. And Brazilwood Poetry, for exportation."[59]

The modernist project was at once political and literary. During the famous Modern Art Week held in São Paulo in 1922—commemorating the centenary of Brazil's independence—a group of poets, musicians, and painters solemnly tore apart a copy of Camões's *Os Lusíadas* (The Lusiads, 1572), thus symbolically declaring war on Portugal. But they wished also to put an end to the undoubted literary domination of Paris, where the majority of Brazilian intellectuals went to get their start. The French model was so imposing that the modernists resolved, as Mário de Andrade put it, to cut "the umbilical cord that ties us to France. Instead of going to Paris and foolishly strutting about, writers ought to pack their bags and start digging around their own country. Ouro Preto and Manaus rather than Montmartre and Florence!"[60] The strength of the urge to reject Paris was commensurate with the extraordinary (and almost fetishistic) passion and fascination felt by Brazilians for the capital of literature.[61] Here we encounter the predicament of founding writers mentioned earlier in connection with their struggle for both political and literary autonomy: the foundation of a national literary space as an affirmation of differences requires a break with all forms of annexation, whether they are strictly political—as in the case of dependence upon Portugal—or specifically literary—as in the case of submission to Paris: "We are in the process of ending the domination of the French spirit," Andrade wrote to the Brazilian poet Alberto de Oliveira (1857–1937). "We are in the process of ending the grammatical domination of Portugal."[62]

Macunaíma, first published in 1928, was to become one of the great national literary classics. In this joyous, impertinent, and provocative work one finds all the characteristic features of foundational literary works. Andrade proposed to Brazilianize the Portuguese language; that is, to appropriate it through the usages of the Portuguese spoken in Brazil, by integrating in the national patrimony of arts and letters the sounds and expressions of the oral language, which diverged from Portuguese norms. "I was fleeing the Portuguese system," he later explained to another countryman, the poet Manuel Bandeira (1885–1968). "I wanted to write in Brazilian without falling into provincialism. I wanted to systematize the everyday mistakes made in conversation, the idiomatic expressions of Brazilian, its Gallicisms, its Italianisms, its slang, its regionalisms, archaisms, pleonasms."[63] He insisted above all that a halt be put to what he ironically called the "bilingualism" of his country—for in fact it had two languages, "spoken Brazilian and written Portuguese."[64] Here one notices another trait that is also found during the initial accumulation of French literary capital in the sixteenth and seventeenth centuries: the desire for emancipation from an overly rigid set of written norms that prevented the enrichment and transformation of literary expression through recourse to new forms of the spoken tongue. Malherbe's famous appeal to the "hay-pitchers at the Port-au-Foin"—a plea for an oral, free, and popular use of the language—was conceived as a weapon for combating the artificiality and especially the immobility (and therefore the repetitive character) of written models, which, because they are always carefully and endlessly reproduced, can neither renew the language nor develop or increase its resources. In *Macunaíma,* Portuguese—a written and therefore sclerotic, dying language—is directly compared to Latin. Referring to the inhabitants of São Paulo, Andrade remarked with wonder that

> the richness of their intellectual self-expression is so prodigious that they speak in one language and write in another . . . In their conversations the Paulistas use a barbarous and multifarious dialect, uncouth and polluted with colloquialisms, but which does not lack gusto and forcefulness in figures of speech and coital idioms . . . But although such vulgar and ignoble language is used in conversation, as soon as the natives of these parts pick up a pen, they divest themselves of such crudities and emerge every whit as *Homo latinus* (Linnaeus), expressing themselves in another language, closer to that of Virgil . . . a mellow tongue which, full as it is of everlasting grace, could be called—the language of that immortal bard—Camões![65]

It is noteworthy that Andrade's strategy is precisely the same as that of Beckett, who in "Dante . . . Bruno. Vico . . . Joyce" argued that English was an old, if not actually dead, language, no less than Latin was in Europe in Dante's time.[66]

Similarly, and in accordance with a logic similar to Joyce's in *Ulysses,* Andrade's proclamation of a written national literature in a national language went hand in hand with a desire to shatter the taboos—cultural, grammatical, sexual, lexical, and literary—of colonial moralism and social propriety; in short, to refuse to show respect for the dominant hierarchy of literary values. Tropical civilization, or "tropicalism," of which Andrade claimed to be a representative, required the affirmation of a "barbarism" that stood the official cultural order on its head. Thus his

1928 travel journal opens with this observation about the Carioca—the inhabitant of Rio de Janiero—as opposed to the Paulista—the more European native of São Paulo: "So all this marvelous exuberance of the Carioca woman reflects a new country of America, a civilization that is called barbarous because it contrasts with European civilization. But what all these people deprived of our country call barbarous is only a re-education. Exhilarating symptom of Brazil."[67] *Macunaíma* is therefore a deliberately provocative text, slangy, comical, antiliterary, assuming all the apparent contradictions of the struggle against European seriousness in its various forms.

But for Andrade it was not only a question of nationalizing the language. He wanted also, like all founders of national literatures, to gather existing resources in order to transmute them into cultural and literary capital. The only discipline to which he could look for guidance in locating, recording, assembling, and imparting literary value to the tales, legends, rites, and popular myths of his country was ethnology. In other words, although he sought to emancipate his country politically and linguistically from Portugal, and culturally and literarily from Europe, Andrade found himself compelled to turn to the work of European scholars, who had been the first to describe the raw materials out of which a distinctive culture could be created. We know that the idea for his novel came to him after reading the second volume of the German ethnologist Theodor Koch-Grünberg's *Vom Roroima zum Orinoco* (From Roroima to the Orinoco, 5 vols., 1917–1928), a collection of Indian legends and mythical narratives in which the character of Macunaíma appears.[68] On the basis of ethnological, linguistic, and geographical data, of scholarly analysis and interpretation, and through his own collection of materials scattered throughout the country that were destined to furnish the basis for a properly Brazilian culture, Andrade attempted to summarize all the knowledge and learning that existed about his native land. This project was animated by an explicit desire to culturally unify the Brazilian nation: Andrade sought to bring together within a single text ("one Brazil and one hero," as he described the subject matter of his book in 1935) all the regions of the country, its cultural and geographical diversity, and its distinguishing features.[69] "One of my purposes," he remarked, "was—in the manner of legends—not to respect geography and [the] geographical [distribution of] flora and fauna. I thus deregionalized creation as far as possible and at the same time succeeded in imagining Brazil literarily as a homogeneous entity—as a national and geographic ethnic concept."[70] To avoid realism (and therefore regionalist divisions) he situated the legends of the south in the north, mixed expressions of gauchos with turns of phrase found in the northeast, and relocated animals and plants. But Andrade also developed a very sophisticated and double-edged position: while gathering and explicitly ennobling the elements of a cultural patrimony that until then had been monopolized by ethnology, at the same time he adopted an ironic and parodistic tone that, in a literary mode, denied and undermined the foundations of his enterprise as a whole.

Apart from the exposition of myths and legends, Andrade's narrative (subtitled a "rhapsody") was also the occasion for an inventory of his country's indigenous vocabulary.[71] By compiling lists—frequently characterized as Rabelaisian and often comic in their effect—Andrade assembled a repertoire of terms that acquired a specifically Brazilian character in the process. Owing to the fact that they were employed in a literary context for the first time, in Andrade's hands they came to have a dual existence: national (since now they had entered into the authorized, or at least recognized, lexicon) and literary (indeed poetic): "They inquired of all the creatures there: tortoises, marmosets, little armadillos, river turtles, lizards, poisonous wasps, swallows, small owls of ill omen, woodpeckers, motmots . . . from the lizard that plays hide and seek with the rat; from fish with scales and fish without; and from the sandpipers that skitter along the sandy beaches—all these living things they asked; not one had seen anything or knew anything."[72] Here again one finds evidence of a virtually universal strategy at work. Long ago du Bellay had exhorted "poëtes françoys" to enrich the vocabulary of French poetry by employing the technical terms used in various professional trades—modern words that could not exist or even have an equivalent in Latin, thus constituting a source of truly French originality: "Again I would urge thee to haunt at times, not only the learned but also all kinds of workmen and mechanics, as mariners, founders, painters, engravers, and others, to know their inventions, the names of their materials, their tools and the terms used in their arts and crafts, to draw there from those fine comparisons and lively descriptions of all things."[73]

The best proof that *Macunaíma* is indeed a national text, and one of national ambition, is that whereas it was to enjoy immense success throughout Brazil, translation proposals aroused little interest abroad.

Today it is a Brazilian classic that figures in examination syllabuses and has been the object of dozens of critical studies, commentaries, interpretations, and annotated editions as well as cinematic and theatrical adaptations; it has even become the marching theme of a samba school.[74] But it had great difficulty going beyond the boundaries of Brazil, and only very belatedly achieved international recognition. The same year that the book was published in São Paulo, Valery Larbaud asked Jean Duriaud, one of the principal translators of Brazilian literature in France, to inquire into the possibility of translating it. "No, I know nothing about Mário de Andrade," Duriaud replied to Larbaud in October 1928. "On your advice I wrote to him, but—an illustration of what I was saying earlier—he hasn't bothered to reply."[75] Andrade, refusing to submit himself to the judgment of the center, and fully absorbed in his national task, was quite uninterested—like all literary founders concerned to resist systematic central annexations of national work—in possible translations of his text.[76] But this characteristic lack of concern with translation is not the only point of interest: the ignorance of *Macunaíma* in European centers was, conversely, the proof of their critical ethnocentrism. An Italian translation of the book appeared only in 1970, followed by a Spanish translation in 1977. The first French translation (by Jacques Thiériot) did not come out until 1979—more than fifty years after its publication in Brazil, having been rejected by several publishing houses (despite the favorable opinions of Roger Caillois and Raymond Queneau). And instead of conferring belated but well-deserved recognition, the French translation rested finally on a gigantic misunderstanding: published in a series devoted to Hispanophone writers of the "boom," Andrade's book was said to display affinities with their "baroque" aesthetic that plainly it did not.

The subsequent course of Andrade's career, which in a sense only served to amplify his initial purpose, unambiguously showed the true nature of what was at bottom a national literary and cultural enterprise. After the book's original publication in 1928, Andrade devoted himself to collecting examples of music and folklore that might be used to found and enrich a national Brazilian culture. A trained musicologist, he undertook research into popular songs and dances for a dictionary of Brazilian music, regularly published essays on ethnomusicology, organized the first conference on the language of Brazilian song, and took part in the creation of a governmental department for national historical and artistic heritage. Additionally, in 1938, along with Claude Lévi-Straus, he was a founder of the Society of Ethnography and Folklore in Rio de Janeiro.

Andrade's commitment to nation-building was so strong, in fact, that he never left Brazil to travel to Europe. But for all this he was not an arrogant and naive nationalist; to the contrary: the peculiar thing about his "heroi sem nenhum caráter"—the hero without a character referred to in the subtitle of the book—is that he is a "bad" savage, conceived in opposition to the standard view of a national hero as the incarnation of the nation's values. He is devoid of good feelings, lazy, cunning, a liar, a boaster, a brawler. His first words are: "I can't be bothered." According to Koch-Grünberg, his name in Taulipang legend is formed from the word *maku* (malicious) and the augmentative suffix *–ima:* Macunaíma therefore means "Big Nasty." Andrade chose him as the main character of his story, and as a national emblem, precisely because he was struck by the fact that Koch-Grünberg described Macunaíma as a hero without a character—a word that Andrade interpreted in the sense of *national* character. In the unpublished preface of 1926 he explained his purpose in the following terms:

> The Brazilian has no character . . . And with the word "character" I do not refer only to a moral reality; I understand rather a permanent mental entity, manifesting itself in everything, in customs in outward action in feeling in language in History in process, as much in good as in evil. The Brazilian has no character because he possesses neither a civilization of his own nor a traditional conscience. The French have a character, and so do the Yoruba and the Mexicans. Whether a distinctive civilization contributed to it, an imminent danger, or a secular conscience, the fact remains that they have a character. Not the Brazilian. He is like a young man of twenty: one can readily perceive general tendencies, but it is too early yet to make any positive statement . . . And while I was reflecting upon these things I came across Macunaíma in Koch-Grünberg's German [text]. And Macunaíma is a stunningly characterless hero.[77]

The strength of Andrade's enterprise lies in its clear-sightedness and what might be called its critical and self-reflective nationalism. As a native of a young and impoverished country, Andrade knew that he could not do battle with the great cultural nations on equal terms; he knew that inequality was not only suffered but internalized, and that Brazil's history of dependency, its distinctive poverty, and the absence of literary resources prevented the formation of a national character, which is to say a stock of capital, as well as the emergence of a common language and a common literature as sources of national pride and reverence. He thus described inequality—the absence of history, of culture, of literature, of language—in terms of a sort of physiological deformity: "The hero sneezed and fell to the ground. As he was wiping himself he felt himself growing bigger and getting stronger until he reached the size of a strapping young man. However, his head, which had not been doused, stayed the same as before—the nasty, oafish mug of the child he had been."[78] Andrade's proclamation of literary independence was not conceived as a gesture of naive national celebration, nor did it spring from a simple desire to ennoble a culture at any cost; it was the expression of a deliberate attitude of self-derision and of a scathing inquiry into national weakness and cowardice.

Andrade invented instead a paradoxical form of nationalism, a way of belonging that through its awareness of the many paradoxes—indeed, impasses—on which Brazilian identity was based, and through its unusually keen sense of irony, managed to overcome the curse that hangs over an impoverished people. Despite his disillusionment (and his realism), Andrade made a genuine attempt to provide the Brazilian nation with foundations: hence the metaphor of Macunaíma and his two brothers representing the three constituent ethnic groups of Brazil—white, black, and red—and affirming, as Pierre Rivas has put it, the "vitality of a young people rich in its diversity" as against "the earlier eugenicist and racist myths deploring the decadence of a mongrel Brazil."[79]

Someone capable of writing "I am a Tupi Indian playing the lute"—a striking epitome of Andrade's cultural sense of being torn between two cultures, of his sense of personal and collective tragedy—could not help but present himself as a living paradox.[80] It is for this reason that *Macunaíma* can today be considered as standing for all founding national narratives, a multiple and complex work—at once national, ethnological, modernist, ironic, disillusioned, political and literary, lucid and willful, anticolonial and antiprovincial, self-critical and fully Brazilian, literary and antiliterary—that raises the constitutive nationalism of destitute and emergent literatures to its highest degree of expression.

This kind of dissimilating approach therefore consists in the complex reappropriation of a central language that permits native writers to draw attention to their differences. Their defense of the claim of a spoken popular language to national and/or literary status is capable of accommodating a variety of forms and degrees of dissimilation—simple differences in accent, regional modes of expression, dialects or creoles. The *littérarisation* of the oral language makes it possible not only to manifest a distinctive identity but also to challenge the standards of literary and linguistic correctness—which are inseparably grammatical, semantic, syntactical, and social—imposed by literary, linguistic, and political domination; and also to provoke dramatic ruptures that are at once political (the language of the people as nation), social (the language of the people as class), and literary. One of the techniques most commonly employed by writers involves the use of obscenity and offensive language (what mainstream literary critics call "vulgarity"),[81] which expresses a desire to break with established conventions through an act of specifically literary violence.

Walt Whitman, for example, altered not only the rules of poetic form but the English language itself in *Leaves of Grass,* introducing archaicisms, neologisms, slang and foreign words, and, of course, Americanisms. Indeed, the birth of the American novel may be said to coincide with the pioneering use of the oral language in Mark Twain's *Huckleberry Finn* (1884), whose crudeness, violence, and anticonformism marked a definitive break with British literary norms. The American novel asserted its difference by insisting upon a specific idiom freed from the constraints of the written language and the rules of English literary propriety. As Hemingway famously remarked, "All modern American literature comes from one book by Mark Twain called *Huckleberry Finn* . . . There was nothing before. There has been nothing as good since."[82] With *Huckleberry Finn* the literary world and the American public became aware of the existence of a peculiarly American oral language—and therefore of a distinctive "Americanness," a national difference resting on all the dialectical variants of the American melting pot, a joyous, iconoclastic distortion of the language bequeathed by the English.

In the same fashion, if it has been possible to speak of a Glasgow School in connection with three Scottish novelists who first appeared in the early 1980s—Alasdair Gray (b. 1934), James Kelman (b. 1946), and Tom Leonard (b. 1944)—this is because they all made explicit use of a popular language that carried with it political implications: all of them were associated with the Scottish nationalist movement, and all of them sought to give literary existence to an urban working-class language that was seen as an essential element of the Scottish nation—this as against the bucolic rural images of the nation, familiar since Herder, as the conservatory of ancient legends and of the genius of the people. Kelman's great subversion, for his part, consisted in the radical (indeed, exclusive) use of this popular language in his novels. In so doing he broke with the convention (itself indissociably literary and political) that when ordinary people speak in a novel, the register and level of language must be changed: thus so-called spoken style is reserved for dialogue while the narrator employs an elevated diction in keeping with literary canons of elegance. This convention, Kelman argued, rests on an assumption inherent in the functioning of literature as a social practice: there is "a wee game going on between writer and reader and the wee game is 'Reader and writer are the same' and they speak in the same voice as the narrative, and they're unlike these fucking natives who do the dialogue in phonetics."[83] Thus in his novel *The Busconductor Hines* (1984) Kelman reproduced the rhythms and idioms of Glaswegian speech (without, however, resorting to phonetic transcription in the way that Tom Leonard was to do) and signaled the equivalence of dialogue and narration through the absence of commas and quotation marks. Kelman emphatically rejected characterizations of his language as "crude" and "obscene," despite the high frequency in his writings of terms that violate the customary norms of literary propriety: in challenging national and social hierarchies he also meant to erase the distinction between polite words and dirty words. While remaining within the English language, he managed through the illustration and defense of a popular language—affirmed as a specifically Scottish mode of expression—to create a difference that was both social and national.

The issue of language can therefore be seen to be the primary force at work in the formation of literary space, the occasion and subject of debates and rivalries. Historians of Brazilian literature, for example, have shown that the desire, reaffirmed by several generations of poets and novelists, to create a language that is specifically Brazilian in its usages as well as in its vocabulary has been the catalyst for the emergence of a national literature and a national literary culture. There the very attempt to define the use and form of the language gave the first internal quarrels their own content and, in providing a focus around which the entire space could be organized and unified, revealed what was at stake in these struggles.

The disagreements between Jorge Amado (1912–2001) and Mário de Andrade in Brazil in the 1930s are characteristic of the type of contests that take place everywhere and lead to the unification of literary space. Amado's early works drew their inspiration from working-class life and were marked by a frankly political perspective.[84] He joined the Communist Youth in 1932, and at the end of that year and the beginning of 1933 wrote his second novel, *Cacáu* (Cacao, 1933), under the influence of the Soviet "proletarian novel" that was beginning to appear in translation with several publishing houses in São Paulo. While searching for the techniques he needed to describe the poverty of the peasants and working classes in the northeastern part of the country, he remained faithful to the neonaturalist conventions inherited from the proletarian novel: "The decisive event for us was the Revolution of 1930, which displayed an interest in Brazilian reality that modernism did not have, and a knowledge of the people that we had and that the modernist writers absolutely did not have." He wished to introduce to Brazil a literary revolution that would also, unavoidably, be a political revolution as well: "We did not want to be modernists but modern: we were fighting for a Brazilian literature that, being Brazilian, would have a universal character; for a literature integrated with the historical moment that we were living through and *that took inspiration from our reality* in order to transform it."[85]

Amado therefore rejected Brazilian modernism, which appeared to him as an expression of a "bourgeois" sensibility, and whose formal innovations seemed to him contrived precisely because it could not lay claim to any popular "authenticity": "The language of *Macunaíma* is an invented language, it's not a language of the people . . . modernism was a formal revolution, but, from the social point of view, it didn't have much to offer."[86] Synge had been violently attacked in the same terms in Dublin at the beginning of the century, accused of bringing to the stage a language of the people that was doubly false—incorrect from the point of view of national norms and unacceptable as a means of portraying the people in political terms.

The case of Brazil shows that writers who succeed in bringing about a linguistic rupture within their own language can lead a country to genuine literary (and national) independence. This break with the past makes it possible to give form and expression to the difference that is thereby proclaimed as a national identity. Brazil managed to establish an autonomous literary existence on the basis of the dispute over modernism in the 1920s—a dispute that was sustained and, in a sense, reinforced politically by the ongoing linguistic struggle that it legitimized. The campaign for a distinctively Brazilian language—different from Portuguese in every detail, right down to its spelling—was to a large extent the result of this upheaval, which lastingly altered the rules of writing, both for writers and lexicographers. In this sense, the use of the oral language pioneered (or revived) by Mário de Andrade in *Macunaíma* was one of the most important stages in the recognition of the specificity of Brazilian language and culture.

SWISS CREOLENESS

The embrace of an oral (often popular) language as a specifically literary instrument of emancipation unites writers who otherwise seem to have nothing in common: despite their discrepant literary histories, they occupy very similar positions in world literary space. Thus it becomes possible to make an almost term-by-term comparison of two manifestos calling for the literary conversion and use of popular languages, one a rural dialect (or "patois") and the other a creole. Issued seventy-five years apart, these manifestos were composed by writers from regions dominated by French literary space in two distinct ways. The author of the first, Charles Ferdinand Ramuz, a Francophone Swiss, belonged to an area that was literarily (though not politically) dominated by France, the canton of Vaud, where a literary patrimony had not yet been able to be constituted, since all its literary productions up until then had been annexed to those of France. Ramuz's manifesto was called *Raison d'être*, which, as we have noted, appeared as the first issue of the *Cahiers vaudois* in 1914. The authors of the second manifesto, Jean Bernabé, Patrick Chamoiseau, and Raphaël Confiant, were born on the island of Martinique in the West Indies, a department of France and an emerging literary space that had long endured colonial domination. Their manifesto, *Éloge de la créolité* (In Praise of Creoleness), appeared in 1989, exactly three-quarters of a century after Ramuz's proclamation of literary independence.

Ramuz, having failed to make a name for himself as a writer in Paris, returned to his native land and attempted to create a distinct voice for himself in French. The Martinicans, for their part, asserted a creole identity in order to oppose both French literary norms and the poetical and literary revolution launched in the 1930s by their elder compatriot, Aimé Césaire (b. 1913), under the banner of Negritude. Their first joint gesture was to reject the stigma ordinarily attached to the popular language of their country and to proclaim as a positive difference what had previously been condemned as provincial and incorrect. Like Bernabé, Chamoiseau, and Confiant after him, Ramuz emphasized that patois and creoles had long been despised and exposed to ridicule, above all by the very persons who spoke them, victims of the imposition of the norms of French in their lands; their languages—*vaudoiseries* on the one hand, *petit-nègre* on the other—had always been an object of caricature, the "old shell of self-defamation" in the Martinican case,[87] mockery in the Vaudois case. Ramuz wrote in praise of "our patois which has so much flavor, apart from [its] briskness, cleanness, decisiveness, straightforwardness (precisely the qualities that are most lacking to us when we write 'in French'); we seem to remember this patois only in broad comedy or farce, as if we were ashamed of ourselves."[88]

These authors also wished to give written form, which is to say both a codified grammar and literary existence, to a popular language that until then had had only an oral existence.[89] "O accent," Ramuz wrote, "you are in our words, you are the thing that informs, but you are not yet in our written language. You are in our gestures, you are in our walk."[90] The Caribbean writers, for their part, declared it necessary to learn "the Creole language, its syntax, its grammar, its vocabulary, its most appropriate writing (even if this is foreign to French habits), its intonations, its rhythms, its spirit . . . its poetics."[91]

As almost everywhere in the world at moments of literary formation and foundation, the first move was to reappropriate oral popular culture: "Caribbean literature does not yet exist," the Martinican writers announced at the outset of their manifesto. "We are still in a state of preliterature."[92] This is why use of the spoken language and reference to oral popular culture were to be the basis of this new literature:

> Provider of tales, proverbs, "titim," nursery rhymes, songs, etc., orality is our intelligence; it is our reading of this world . . . To return to it,

yes, first in order to restore this cultural continuity (which we associate with restored historical continuity) without which it is difficult for collective identity to take shape . . . To return to it, so as simply to invest *the primordial expression of our common genius . . . In short, we shall create a literature,* which will obey all the demands of modern writing while taking root in the traditional configurations of our orality.[93]

For Ramuz, it was a question of restoring linguistic authenticity. As the founder of a new style, the product of a country and a countryside, Ramuz pioneered the literary transcription of the language of his native land as it was actually spoken there. The stylistic revolution that he carried out in the 1920s (and that conventional literary history attributes to Céline alone) consisted in letting the "people" speak in novelistic fiction, in making them talking characters, even narrators in the unfolding of the story. Popular speech is not only embodied in dialogue in his books; it is integrated into the narration itself. The formal, linguistic, aesthetic, and social aspects of Ramuz's innovation—everything, in fact, except his political perspective—were to be recreated sixty years later by the Scottish novelist James Kelman. Ramuz explained his deliberate technique in a letter to Paul Claudel in which he summed up the lowly literary status assigned to popular language: "The novel has furnished innumerable authors with an excuse both to despise and to flatter the people (what is left of them) and the language of the people, which is the only one that counts, because everything comes from it, because everything goes into it, and because it cannot be mistaken; but which these fugitives from the Sorbonne use only between quotation marks, which is to say they touch it only with tweezers."[94]

Ramuz and the three Caribbean writers share the same view of the "littleness" of their lands that led Ramuz to form a higher opinion not only of his country but of its countryside: "It is quite small, our country, but so much the better. This way I can get my arms around all of it and at a glance take it all in . . . And in envisaging it thus, in its entirety, at a glance, I manage to understand it more easily, to understand its 'tone,'[95] its character, and then I can forget about all the rest."[96] "Our world," wrote Bernabé, Chamoiseau, and Confiant, "however small it might be, is large in our minds, boundless in our hearts, and for us will always reflect the human being."[97] Their affirmation of the intrinsic value of the country and the people, despised, neglected, and devoid of literary resources though they might be, was another way of battling against the norms instituted by the center, a way of claiming the right to literary existence and equality. Just as Ramuz insisted that the most humble things and people, notably the country people of his region, be made legitimate literary subjects, the creole writers stated that the literature they were determined to invent "takes it as a principle that there is nothing petty, poor, useless, vulgar, or unworthy of a literary project in our world."[98]

The managing editor of the *Cahiers vaudois* and the architects of creoleness also have in common a distaste for theoretical approaches to literature: "Ordinary terrorism," the three Caribbean writers claimed, "supported distinguished theory, both powerless to save the least light-hearted song from oblivion. Thus went our world, steeped in intellectualist piety, completely cut off from the roots of its orality."[99] In Ramuz one finds a similar preference for "sensibility" and "emotion," a return to basic things in opposition to academicism in texts and language: "Ought we not therefore to break at last with our intellectualism, if that is what it is called, as I suppose, and to unleash instinct?"[100]

Finally, all these writers are united in rejecting regionalism and concerned to defend themselves against the charge of retreating into themselves. Ramuz remarked:

> One hears a great deal of talk these days about "regionalism." We have nothing in common with these lovers of "folklore." The word (an Anglo-Saxon word) seems to us as unpleasant as the thing itself. Our practices, our customs, our beliefs, our ways of dressing . . . all these petty things, which until now have alone seemed to interest our literary enthusiasts, not only are of no importance to us, but moreover seem to us singularly suspect . . . The particular can be, for us, only a point of departure. One attends to the particular only out of love for the general and in order to attain it more surely.[101]

But even though Ramuz, using the rhetoric of denial, dissociated himself from any ambition of founding a national literature, plainly the same logic is involved: "Let us leave to one side," he wrote, "any claim to a 'national literature': this is at once too much and not enough to claim. Too much, because a literature can be called national only when there is a national language and *we do not have a language of our own;* not enough, because it seems that the things by which we then claim *to distinguish ourselves* are simply our *external differences.*"[102] But he intended to claim a boundary that had been assigned to it as a literary stigma, in order to find a position that would permit him to "invent" a novel approach and to avoid the alternatives of annexation pure and simple (that is, of becoming French) and nonexistence (of being Swiss and marginalized as a provincial). For their part, Bernabé, Chamoiseau, and Confiant declared: "We object to the parochialism and self-centeredness that some people find in [creoleness]. There can be no real opening to the world without a [prior] and absolute apprehension of what we are." Considering the necessity of attaining universality as another type of submission to the French order, they called for the creation of "diversality"—a universality reconciled with the diversity of the outlying regions of the world: "Creole literature will have nothing to do with the Universal, which is to say the disguised adherence to Western values . . . This exploration of our singularities . . . leads back to what is natural in the world . . . and opposes to Universality the great opportunity of a world diffracted but recomposed, the conscious harmonization of preserved diversities: Diversality."[103]

Reading the two manifestos together brings out an essential point that separate studies would undoubtedly miss: though they come from wholly different historical situations and apparently incomparable literary worlds, Ramuz and the Creole novelists call for a break with prevailing aesthetic norms in very similar terms, using the same arguments. Several points of difference and divergence ought nonetheless to be emphasized in order to make the similarities clearer. One needs first to distinguish the purely literary—but nonetheless real and symbolically constraining—domination suffered by Francophone Switzerland from the political domination exerted over the island of Martinique, where it gave rise in turn to literary domination. In other words, Ramuz sought to legitimize the cause of literary emancipation through the demand for a popular literary language that to some extent he succeeded in creating; his counterparts sought to escape a form of control that was both literary and political while refusing a purely political alternative.

A second major distinction has to do with the importance of literary resources. In the interval since Césaire launched his revolution in the name of Negritude—a movement recognized and consecrated in the center—a genuinely Caribbean literary tradition, a native literary patrimony, had come into existence. The movement on behalf of *créolité* therefore emerged against the background of a literary and political history in which a local struggle managed to achieve worldwide recognition. Ramuz, by contrast, could not look to a native literary history. Lacking any preexisting regional or national model and, therefore, any literary capital, he was forced to invent a tradition on the basis of nothing (or almost nothing): "Thus the sad state of affairs that awaited those of us who came back: no example; no certainty; no model among current writers; no model among ones before us. One could not fail to see that all those who until then had shown some vitality in this country had been elevated to true success and self-affirmation only *after having crossed the border, after having denied us, or more simply forgotten us.*"[104]

Yet despite these differences, the four writers underwent the same evolution. The two manifestos, published seventy-five years apart, were identical in their effect: instead of distancing their authors from the center, whose legitimacy they had initially rejected (and affirmed in the process of rejecting), and instead of breaking with it once and for all, these proclamations of independence had the paradoxical consequence of permitting them to be noticed and recognized by the authorities in Paris. Thus Ramuz was published ten years later by Bernard Grasset, who brought him recognition not only in France but internationally. His views on linguistic questions were the object of a lively critical debate: the famous *Pour ou contre C.-F. Ramuz* [For or against C.-F. Ramuz], in which he was accused of "writing badly," appeared in 1926.[105]

In similar fashion, critics in Paris transformed what the spokesmen of creoleness had conceived as a rupture with French linguistic and political norms into a simple stylistic and semantic innovation. Once again recognition was achieved at the cost of a reappropriation of peripheral concerns by the center, with the result that the Martinicans' desire to affirm a literary politics was neutralized by their acceptance into the class of writers of "French literature." The Parisian discovery of the Caribbean novel, which extended even to the most conservative precincts of fictional aesthetics in France—the Goncourt jury—was the occasion not of accepting the properly creole dimension of this writing, but of celebrating the greatness and genius of the national language and of rejoicing in the success and triumph of writers from the former colonies on the English model. Neither Confiant nor Chamoiseau any longer spoke, as they had done at the beginning of their careers, of writing in Creole and publishing in their countries; instead they abandoned West

Indian publishers for the most prestigious houses in Paris and adopted a creolized French that all Francophone readers could understand.

None of this, however, alters the fact that the desire to establish oneself through the assertion of a linguistic difference within a great literary language is one of the major ways to subvert the literary order, which is to say to challenge all at once the aesthetic, grammatical, political, and social legacies of a colonial past.

During the building of the wall and ever since to this very day I have occupied myself almost exclusively with the comparative history of races—there are certain questions which one can probe to the marrow, as it were, only by this method.
  —Franz Kafka, "The Great Wall of China"

The period 1900–1914 was that of the Dublin School—Yeats, Moore, Joyce, Synge, and Stephens. The sentiment of these writers was anti-English . . . For them England was the Philistine and since they could not use Gaelic, their aim was to discover what blend of Anglo-Irish and French would give them an explosive that would knock the pundits of London off their padded chairs.
  —Cyril Connolly, *Enemies of Promise*

IT CAN HARDLY be claimed that the general pattern of the great families of cases that we have just examined, a set of infinitely diversified strategies employed by writers from outlying countries in world literary space, captures reality in all its complexity. What I have hoped to do instead is to give a glimpse of the misfortunes, the contradictions, and the difficulties faced by writers on the periphery in relation to those in the center who, blinded by the obviousness of their centrality, cannot even imagine these things; but also to show the global structure of dependence in which they are caught up in relation to those who, as captives of the shadows of the periphery, have only a partial view of it.

Ideally it would have been possible to analyze carefully each of the examples sketched in the previous chapters, looking at them in relation to one another both at a given moment and over time. Since a precise and detailed description of every literary space is impossible in a work of this scope, however, and in order to avoid an overly abstract description—one whose very abstraction would reveal its arbitrariness—I propose instead to devote a separate chapter to the Irish case, which may serve here as a paradigm, in the Platonic sense, that will give some idea of what it would have been necessary to do to give a complete account of each of the cases already discussed.

An examination of the Irish Literary Revival, which took place over a period of about forty years, between roughly 1890 and 1930, makes it possible to lay out chronologically and spatially the entire set of solutions devised by writers to the problem of overturning the dominant order as well as the structural rivalries with which they are faced. The Irish Revival, in other words, furnishes a compact history of the revolt against the literary order. Reconstructing this case in detail will therefore also provide a paradigm for the generative model I have elaborated, containing the full range of political and linguistic solutions, the whole gamut of positions, from Shaw's assimilation to Joyce's exile: in short, a theoretical and practical framework making it possible to recreate and understand literary revolts in general (looking at both prior and later examples) and to give a comparative analysis of quite different historical situations and cultural contexts.[1]

The distinctive quality of the Irish case resides in the fact that over a fairly short period a literary space emerged and a literary heritage was created in an exemplary way. In the space of a few decades the Irish literary world traversed all the stages (and all the states) of rupture with the literature of the center, providing a model of the aesthetic, formal, linguistic, and political possibilities contained within outlying spaces. Here, within Europe itself, immobilized under colonial control for more than eight centuries, was a land that disposed of few literary resources of its own at the moment when the first calls for a national culture were issued; and yet it was there that some of the greatest literary revolutionaries of the twentieth century were to appear—reason enough, surely, for talking of an Irish "miracle." The Irish case therefore makes it possible to grasp the character of a literary space in both its synchronic and diachronic aspects at once; that is, its overall structure at a given moment and the genesis of this structure according to a process that, ignoring certain secondary historical differences, can be seen to be almost universal.

With Yeats's poetry and his work in theater, Shaw's London exile, O'Casey's realism, Joyce's continental exile, and the struggle of the members of the Gaelic League to de-Anglicize Ireland, one is confronted not merely with the unique experience of a particular history but with the general design of a nearly universal literary structure. Accordingly, it becomes possible to comprehend the full historical necessity of what Kafka called the "connection with politics" in small literatures; to comprehend the strange and complex link between aesthetics and politics, the collective labor of accumulating a literary heritage—the indispensable condition for entering international space—and the gradual development of literary inventions, which make it possible for new literatures over time to acquire an increasing measure of autonomy.[2] Irish literature stands as one of the first great subversions of the literary order.

YEATS: THE INVENTION OF TRADITION

The Irish Revival "invented" Ireland between 1890 and 1930.[3] Drawing inspiration from the Romantic movement, which had assigned writers the task of exhuming an ancient national and popular patrimony and establishing literature as the expression of the "popular soul," a group of intellectuals, Anglo-Irish for the most part—William Butler Yeats, Lady Augusta Gregory, Edward Martyn, and George Moore to begin with; then George Russell (known as Æ), Padraic Colum, John Millington Synge (whom Yeats was to meet in Paris), and James Stephens—undertook to manufacture a national literature out of oral practices, collecting, transcribing, translating, and rewriting Celtic tales and legends. In seeking to give popular narratives and legends literary stature, ennobled through poetry and drama, their collective enterprise was oriented in two principal directions: toward the revival and dramatic presentation of the great narrative cycles of the Gaelic tradition, now seen as incarnating the Irish people; and the evocation of an idyllic peasantry as the repository of the "national spirit" and instrument of a Gaelic mysticism. Thus Cuchulain and Deirdre were regarded as incarnating the grandeur of the Irish people and of the Irish nation. The work of earlier authors, particularly Standish O'Grady, who published a two-volume *History of Ireland: Heroic Period* (1878–1880) in London, supplied an initial repertoire of legends that revivalist writers adapted to a variety of theatrical and narrative purposes:[4] the version of the legend of Cuchulain was often reworked, thus making this character into a model of national heroism.

Yeats began by bringing together popular narratives that collectively restored a sort of Gaelic golden age. *Fairy and Folk Tales of the Irish Peasantry* (1888) did much to disseminate and lend distinction to the genre of the popular tale in Ireland. It was immediately followed by *The Wanderings of Oisin* (1889) and, several years later, still in the same vein, by *The Countess Cathleen and Various Legends and Lyrics* (1892) and the celebrated *Celtic Twilight* (1893), a collection of essays, narratives, and descriptive accounts. These volumes serve to verify the hypothesis advanced here that in spaces deprived of all literary resources the first impulse of writers influenced by Herder's ideas was to embrace a popular definition of literature and to collect specimens of the popular cultural practice of their countries in order to convert them into national capital. Literature was first defined, then, as an archive of popular legends, tales, and traditions.

Yeats, like all intellectuals determined to found a national literature and repertoire, very quickly turned his attention toward the theater: from 1899 to 1911 he worked to create a distinctively Irish theater, conceived both as the privileged instrument for communicating a national literature and as a pedagogical tool for educating the Irish people. Together with Lady Gregory and Edward Martyn, Yeats founded the Irish Literary Theatre in 1899. In 1902, now called the Irish National Theatre, it presented Yeats's famous *Cathleen ni Houlihan,*[5] and next his adaptation for the stage, with George Moore, of a story from the Ossianic cycle, *Diarmuid and Gráinne.* From 1904, having in the meantime found a permanent home at the Abbey Theatre, the company put on plays by Synge, Lady Gregory, and Padraic Colum, all of whom deliberately sought to elaborate a native idiom: thus Synge used the language of the Aran Islands, and Lady Gregory—with whom Yeats was to collaborate for a time—wrote plays in the Kiltartan dialect.[6] The explicit intention of this enterprise, at least at first, was to found a new Irish national literature that could speak to the people. "Our movement," Yeats wrote in 1902, "is a return to the people, like the Russian movement of the early seventies"; a decade earlier, in *The Celtic Twilight,* he had claimed: "Folk art is, indeed, the oldest of the aristocracies of thought . . . it is the soil where all great art is rooted."[7]

After this first, largely collective phase of elaborating a national literary corpus, Yeats—the promoter and the leader of the Irish Revival and the founder of the Abbey Theatre—came to be regarded in Dublin as in a sense embodying Irish poetry. The Abbey quickly established itself as a national institution: thanks to its initial accumulation of capital, Ireland was able at last to claim its own literary existence. Later, in 1923, as though his own newly official status in the world of letters had been confirmed through the recognition of Ireland's literary "difference," Yeats received the Nobel Prize for Literature.

At the same time his political moderation and growing hesitancy, at least after the 1916 uprising, made him an ambiguous figure, the founding father of a new Irish literature and at the same time a writer associated with London literary circles, where his work had long been admired. The performance in London, in 1903, by the infant Irish National Theatre of five plays it had just put on in Dublin won the unanimous approval of the critics. This, together with the aid of an English patron, enabled Yeats to acquire a fame that the Dublin critics alone could not have given him. But it was this very fame that signaled his dependence in relation to a center from which he nonetheless professed to keep his distance.

THE GAELIC LEAGUE: RECREATION OF A NATIONAL LANGUAGE
At the same time as the Protestant architects of the Irish renaissance were imparting literary value to the nation's literary "heritage" and supplying, in English, the foundations for a new national literature, an influential group of scholars and writers sought to promote a national language in order to put an end to the linguistic and cultural ascendancy of the English colonizer. The Gaelic League (Connradh na Gaeilge), founded in 1893 under the leadership of the Protestant linguist Douglas Hyde and the Catholic historian Eoin Mac Néill, had as its stated purpose the elimination of English in Ireland, once British soldiers had been expelled from the country, and the reintroduction of the Gaelic language, whose use had greatly declined since the late eighteenth century. Generally speaking, the proponents of Gaelic were Catholic intellectuals, men such as Patrick Pearse (later the leader of the 1916 rebellion) and Padraic O'Conaire, who were much more committed to political and nationalist action than their Protestant counterparts.

The revival of Gaelic was an entirely new idea. No nationalist political leader, neither O'Connell nor Parnell, had ever made it a political theme. And yet, although the literary movement had been born of political despair, the embrace of the native tongue represented a politicization of the larger movement of cultural emancipation. Even though Irish had ceased to be a language of intellectual creation and communication, at least since the early seventeenth century, it was still spoken by more than half of the population until 1840. With the great famine of 1847 Gaelic was further marginalized, so that by the second half of the nineteenth century its use was limited to some 250,000 rural speakers, among them the poorest in the land. Indeed, as Declan Kiberd has argued, the Irish language was now "the language of the poor and, in truth, a decisive mark of their poverty."[8] From then on the demands for linguistic and national independence amounted to a sort of reversal of values portending a genuine cultural upheaval—all the more as the country's political leaders had undertaken a campaign to promote the learning of English, the language of business and modernity, which was to encourage emigration to America.

The success of the Gaelic League was so immediate that Yeats had to make a diplomatic alliance with it. Very shortly thereafter, in October 1901, he put on the first play performed in Gaelic, Douglas Hyde's *Casadh an tSúgáin* (The Twisting of the Rope), taken from a Connacht folktale. Joyce himself, despite his reservations, acknowledged the League's success in a lecture titled "Ireland, Island of Saints and Sages," delivered in Trieste in 1907:

> Now the Gaelic League has revived [the] use [of this language]. Every Irish newspaper, with the exception of the Unionist organs, has at least one special headline printed in Irish. The correspondence of the principal cities is written in Irish, the Irish language is taught in most of the primary and secondary schools, and, in the universities, it has been set on a level with the other modern languages, such as French, German, Italian, and Spanish. In Dublin, the names of the streets are printed in both languages. The league organizes concerts, debates, and socials at which the speaker of *beurla* (that is, English) feels like a fish out of water, confused in the midst of a crowd that chatters in a harsh and guttural tongue.[9]

Despite the publication of a few works written during this period in Gaelic, among them the first novel in Irish, by Padraic O'Conaire, and the texts of Patrick Pearse, the literary status of the language was long to remain equivocal. The fact that it was not really used in daily life, together with the absence of both a genuine literary tradition (interrupted for almost three centuries) and a popular audience, meant that the proponents of Gaelic had first to carry out the technical task of establishing grammatical and orthographic norms, and then to lobby for the introduction of the language in the educational system. The marginality and artificiality of the literary use of Gaelic made translation necessary, with the result that writers who chose it found themselves in a paradoxical position from the first: either to write in the Irish language and remain unknown, without a real audience; or to be translated into English and so repudiate the linguistic and cultural rupture with the authority of London that writing in Gaelic represented. The situation in which Douglas Hyde found himself was more paradoxical still: although he campaigned on behalf of an Irish national literature in Gaelic, he was also "a founder of the Anglo-Irish literary revival," which is to say of Irish literature in English.[10] His works—including a *Literary History of Ireland* (1899), which described and analyzed the great epic cycles and reproduced long translated extracts from them; and a bilingual collection, *The Love Songs of Connacht* (1893)—were to serve as a catalogue of legends and folktales for writers of the renaissance who did not know Irish. The predicament faced by the partisans of Gaelic is common to all national writers who choose a language distinct from the colonial language, since the struggle to establish a small language is inevitably linked from the start with issues of national politics—a proposition that is borne out by the experience of Czechoslovakia, Hungary, Norway at the end of the nineteenth century, Kenya in the 1970s, Brazil in the 1930s, and Algeria in the 1960s, among other countries. Because the linguistic battle involves the creation of a literature that itself is subject to political criteria and the judgment of political authorities, it is at once an essential moment in the affirmation of a national difference and the starting point for the constitution of an independent heritage.

In Ireland, the desire to bring about the de-Anglicization of the country, explicitly advocated by the Gaelic League, and to restore the native language to its former position of preeminence also represented a challenge to the influence of Protestant intellectuals and their aesthetic preferences upon the nascent national literature. The defense and promotion of Gaelic by itself changed the nature of cultural and political debate, making it possible at last to inquire into the nature of the cultural bonds uniting Ireland and England, the definition of an independent national culture, and the relation between national culture and language. The break with the English language amounted to a declaration of cultural independence, a refusal to go on seeing the success of Irish books (and plays) depend on the verdict of London; or, more precisely, the independent existence claimed for a neglected language peculiar to Ireland, which was now championed in the name of a national culture and literature, permitted Catholic writers to reappropriate literary nationalism and to challenge the hegemony of Yeats and the revivalists of the first generation—Protestants for the most part—over Irish literary production and aesthetics. The linguistic gambit was a bold attempt, then, in the name of the nation and the people, to deny Protestant intellectuals a monopoly over national cultural property.

Debate over the comparative merits of the two cultural options continued for a very long time and profoundly marked the whole founding phase of modern Irish literature by perpetuating the division and rivalries between the proponents of Gaelic and the partisans of English.[11] The former were recognized only in Ireland for literary activity connected with politics; the latter very quickly achieved broad recognition in London literary circles and beyond.

SYNGE: THE WRITTEN ORAL LANGUAGE

Rejecting the cut-and-dried political (and politicized) alternative between Gaelic and English that presented Irish writers with an undecidable choice, John Millington Synge (1871–1909) introduced in his plays the spoken language of Irish peasants, beggars, and vagabonds—something without precedent in the history of European drama. This language, Anglo-Irish ("extracted from dialects forbidden to writing," as his French translator Françoise Morvan has put it), a sort of creole mixing the two tongues, was "neither good English nor good Irish but creation at the confluence of two languages."[12] Like all defenders of a true literary autonomy conceived in terms of a language within a language, as it were—a new, free, modern idiom, impertinent in its rejection of the usages of a written language that was fixed, dead, rigidified—Synge worked out the writing of Anglo-Irish for the theater. In so doing he refused to cut himself off completely from the formal possibilities offered by English, without, however, thereby submitting to the norms and canons of "English" literature. Yeats had emphasized how subversive and courageous the use of rural speech as the language of theater and poetry could be. But the question of the literary and national status of the popular language, recreated for the stage by Synge, was ambiguously posed. Indeed, the scandal caused by the first performance of *The Playboy of the Western World* at the Abbey Theatre in 1907 is partly explained by this ambiguity: the play was condemned on the ground either that it was "false," and therefore insufficiently realistic; or that it was too realistic, indeed prosaic, and therefore contrary to the aesthetic conventions of the theater.

Moreover, Synge clearly aligned himself with a moderate realism, rejecting both the aestheticism and abstraction associated with Mallarmé and the style of drama represented by Ibsen, understood in England as a form of social criticism:

> In the modern literature of towns, however, richness is found only in sonnets, or prose poems, or in one or two elaborate books that are far away from the profound and common interests of life. One has, on one side, Mallarmé and Huysmans producing this literature; and on the other Ibsen and Zola dealing with the reality of life in joyless and pallid words. On the stage one must have reality, and one must have joy . . . the rich joy found only in what is superb and wild in reality.[13]

O'CASEY: THE REALIST OPPOSITION

Yeats's aesthetic principles were not only criticized by the Gaelicizers. They were also challenged by a younger generation of English-language Catholic writers who upheld the claims of realism against those of poetic drama. From the moment the Irish Literary Theatre was founded in 1899 Yeats found himself opposed from this quarter by men such as George Moore and Edward Martyn, who had begun as an Ibsenite and whose departure hastened the birth of the Irish National Theatre in 1902. And despite the strong imprint and great influence of the Symbolism advocated by Yeats at the Abbey Theatre, aesthetic ambivalence remained the rule: at the same time as Yeats's works were being produced, Padraic Colum and Lady Gregory were staging farces, comedies of manners, and peasant dramas.

After 1912–13, but especially following the sudden rupture of 1916—when Yeats distanced himself from his colleagues and took refuge behind a hieratic, formalized drama, inspired by the Japanese Noh, and in his poetry celebrated solitude and the past—the realist aesthetic became established at the Abbey Theatre. The new generation of Catholic writers tried at first to contradict the legendary and rural world of Yeats and his friends by adopting the "peasant realism" later associated with the work of the Cork realists, notably T. C. Murray and Lennox Robinson, for many years the director of the Abbey Theatre. Then, chiefly under the influence of Sean O'Casey, they turned toward an urban, more political realism—this at a pivotal moment in the political transformation of the term "people," whose evolution can be monitored in an almost empirical way. In the 1920s the old Herderian sense of the word, tied to national and rural values, was still current, but its new proclaimed equivalence with the proletariat, a consequence of the Russian Revolution and the increasing power of Communist parties in Europe, now began to be established and to transform the aesthetic assumptions of popular drama inherited from Herder and his followers.

It was the work of Sean O'Casey (1880–1964) that established this new type of popular realism in Ireland. By birth a Protestant, but from a very poor family, O'Casey was closer, socially and aesthetically, to Irish Catholics than to the Protestant bourgeoisie.[14] Self-taught, and a union activist, he was briefly in 1914 a member of a socialist paramilitary group, the Irish Citizen Army, which he quit the same year and shortly thereafter began writing plays that celebrated nationalism while pointing out the ambiguity and danger of heroic national mythologies. He was also one of the first Irish writers openly to affirm his Communist loyalties.[15] His first plays, *The Shadow of a Gunman* and *Cathleen Listens In,* were produced in 1923; *Juno and the Paycock,* performed the following year, was an immense success. It was praised by Yeats, who believed that it "contained the promise of a new idea . . . [and] foreshadowed a new direction in Irish drama."[16] *The Plough and the Stars,* staged in 1926, scarcely three years after Ireland had won its independence, was a high-spirited and implacable attack on the false heroes of the resistance to English rule. Taking as his subject the famous Easter 1916 uprising, an event erected into a foundational myth of national legend during the years since, O'Casey lambasted the improvisational character of the revolutionary struggle and, above all, the influence wielded by the Catholic church in its eagerness to take over from the English oppressor. The play provoked riots, forcing its author to go into exile in England.

Despite the huge scandals that his work aroused, the urban and political realism of O'Casey and his followers was adopted in turn by the vast majority of Irish dramatists. The passage from neoromanticism—the idealization and aestheticization of the peasantry, seen as incarnating the essence of the popular "soul"—to realism—at first rural, then associated with urban life and literary and political modernity—summarizes the history and succession of popular aesthetics.

O'Casey's example, together with those of Yeats and Synge, illustrates precisely the importance of the theater in all emergent literatures. But here, as elsewhere, the aesthetics, language, form, and content involved in each of his works were the object of struggles and conflicts that helped unify the space by diversifying the range of positions within it. Just as Jorge Amado in Brazil during the 1930s chose to devote himself to the proletarian political novel and privileged the social notion of the "people," Sean O'Casey opted for a style of theater that was political, popular, and realistic.

SHAW: ASSIMILATION IN LONDON

Like all nascent literary worlds on the periphery, the Irish space spread beyond the nation's borders. Thus George Bernard Shaw, born in Dublin in 1856, became a great figure of the London theater. Awarded the Nobel Prize in Literature two years after Yeats, in 1925, he incarnated the canonical and obligatory career of Irish writers before the emergence of a peculiarly Irish space: exile to London—a move that by the end of the nineteenth century had come to be considered a betrayal of the Irish national cause.

Shaw belonged so completely to the same literary space as the revivalists that he felt it necessary to state his opposition plainly, in the name of reason, both to Yeats's folkloristic and spiritualist irrationalism and to Joyce's iconoclastic ambitions in fiction. Placing himself at an equal distance from his two countrymen, he, too, sought to subvert English norms, only by rejecting Irish national (and nationalist) values. Thus *John Bull's Other Island* (1904) was a deliberately anti-Yeatsian play. But Shaw was every bit as much opposed, and symmetrically so, to Joyce's literary purposes. In 1921 he delivered an ambiguous tribute (to say the least) to *Ulysses* in a letter addressed to Sylvia Beach, who had sent him serialized extracts of the text in the hope that he might agree to join in a subscription aimed at covering the costs of the book's publication: "Dear Madam, I have read several fragments of *Ulysses* in serial form. It is a revolting record of a disgusting phase of civilization; but it is a truthful one . . . To you, possibly, it may appeal as art . . . But to me it is all hideously real."[17] Not only did Shaw thus refuse to elevate to the rank of art a realistic portrait that seemed to him contrary to the requirements of literature, but moreover he challenged the assumption that, as an Irishman, he should have felt obliged to ascribe a special artistic interest to it.

Shaw nonetheless recognized the necessity and the legitimacy of Irish nationalist demands and constantly called attention to the poverty and backwardness of Ireland, which were as much economic as intellectual, in relation to Europe as a whole. He defended his dual rejection of English imperialism and Irish nationalism by imputing to England the evils of Ireland and, refusing to make a cause of Irish exceptionalism, converted it into a subversive socialist conviction instead. The social and political criticism at work in his drama reflected a determination to go beyond the opposition between imperialism and nationalism. Shaw had a horror of entrapment by and within national (or nationalist) issues, which he saw as provincializing literary production. Taken together, all the things that he regarded as contributing to the historical backwardness of Ireland, including the intellectual underdevelopment of a country singlemindedly bent upon winning its independence, trace the exact boundaries of what he considered the sole homeland of literature in English: London.

Integration with the center seemed to Shaw to assure the certainty of a degree of aesthetic freedom and critical tolerance that a small national capital such as Dublin, torn between the centrifugal pull of British literary space and internal self-affirmation, could not guarantee. Paradoxically, then, some writers are prepared to leave leave their country and take up residence abroad in a literary capital in the name of denationalizing literature, of rejecting the systematic appropriation of literature for national purposes—a characteristic strategy of small nations in the process of defining themselves or in danger of intellectual absorption by a larger nation. In response to the accusations of national betrayal that were brought against him, Shaw maintained that he had not "chosen" London over Dublin. London for him was a neutral place to which he had sworn no oaths of loyalty or attachment, a place that assured him of literary success and liberty while also granting him the leisure of fully exercising his critical faculty.

Shaw's career encapsulates the experience of all those writers whom I have called "assimilated"—those who, in the absence of any other alternative, or out of a refusal to yield to the aesthetic injunctions of small literatures, integrate themselves, as Michaux, Cioran, and Naipaul were to do in the twentieth century, with one of the literary centers.

JOYCE AND BECKETT: AUTONOMY

The rupture provoked by James Joyce was the final step in the constitution of Irish literary space. Exploiting all the literary projects, experiments, and debates of the late nineteenth century, which is to say the literary capital accumulated by all those who came before him, Joyce invented and proclaimed an almost absolute autonomy. In this highly politicized space, and in opposition to the movement of the Irish renaissance, which, as he said in *Ulysses,* threatened to become "all too Irish,"[18] he managed to establish an autonomous, purely literary pole, thus helping to obtain recognition for the whole of Irish literature by liberating it to some extent from political domination. As a young man, in 1903, he had mocked Lady Gregory's excursions into folklore: "In fine, her book, wherever it treats of the 'folk,' sets forth in the fullness of its senility a class of mind which Mr. Yeats has set forth with such delicate skepticism in his happiest book, 'The Celtic Twilight.'"[19] Two years earlier, in fact, he had already strongly criticized the theatrical undertaking of Yeats, Martyn, and Moore on the ground that it represented a loss of literary autonomy and signaled the submission of writers to what he considered the dictates of the public: "But an aesthete has a floating will, and Mr. Yeats's treacherous instinct of adaptability must be blamed for his recent association with a platform from which even self-respect should have urged him to refrain. Mr. Martyn and Mr. Moore are not writers of much originality."[20]

The question of literary autonomy in Ireland was played out through a subversive use of language and of the national and social codes connected with it. Joyce condensed and, in his own fashion, settled the debate—inseparably literary, linguistic, and political—that pitted the proponents of Gaelic against those of English. His whole literary work can be seen as a very subtle Irish reappropriation of the English language. Joyce dislocated English, the language of colonization, not only by incorporating in it elements of every European language but also by subverting the norms of English propriety and, in keeping with Irish practice, using obscene and scatalogical vernaculars to make a laughingstock of English literary tradition—to the point, in *Finnegans Wake,* of making this subverted language of domination a quasi-foreign tongue. A main part of his purpose, then, was to disrupt the hierarchical relation between London and Dublin so that Ireland would be able to assume its rightful place in the literary world. "The Irish," as Joyce was fond of saying already in Trieste, "condemned to express themselves in a language not their own, have stamped on it the mark of their own genius and compete for glory with the civilised nations."[21]

Although he belonged to the next generation, Joyce in a sense pursued the same end as the revivalists. First in *Dubliners*—the majority of whose stories were written in 1904–05, which is to say at the very time when the Abbey Theatre was founded—and then in *Ulysses,* he sought to confer literary status upon Dublin by transforming it into a literary place par excellence, ennobling it through literary description. But already in the early collection of stories the stylistic methods employed, and the aesthetic perspective they represented, were wholly at odds with the underlying assumptions of both Yeats's Symbolism and the rural realism that was opposed to it. From the very beginning, Joyce's exclusive concern with Dublin and urban life signaled his rejection of the peasant folklore tradition and his determination to bring Irish literature into European modernity. *Dubliners* proclaimed Joyce's refusal to take up the cause of the revivalists. Through the urban realism of these stories he sought to imbue Irish life with a certain mundaneness, to abandon the grandiloquence of the literature of legendary heroism in order to embrace the novel trivialities of modern Dublin. "I have written [the book] for the most part in a style of scrupulous meanness," Joyce said in a letter to his publisher.[22] He dismissed the project of the founders of the Revival as a piece of aesthetic archaism that reflected the "backward" character of the country,[23] emphasized earlier by Shaw, which was as much political as intellectual and artistic. It was this total rupture with the dominant literary aesthetic of the day in Ireland that explains the immense difficulties Joyce encountered in trying to get his first collection of stories published.

These difficulties were therefore the product of a double rejection, not only of English literary norms but also of the aesthetic tenets of the nationalist literature then being created. Determined to get past the oversimplified alternative presented by colonial dependence—literary emancipation or submission to the London authorities—Joyce attacked "the national temper" in an effort to defend "the region of literature . . . assailed so fiercely by the enthusiast and the doctrinaire,"[24] on the one hand, and, on the other, denounced those who "surrender to the trolls," allowing the Irish theater to become "the property of the rabblement of the most belated race in Europe."[25] In other words, he opposed both Catholic writers who transformed literature into an instrument of nationalist propaganda and Protestant intellectuals who reduced it to the transcription of popular myths.

Joyce's dual opposition was spatial as well as literary: refusing to obey either the law of London or that of Dublin, he chose exile on the continent in order to produce an Irish literature. Ultimately it was in Paris, a politically neutral ground and an international literary capital, that he was to try to achieve this apparently contradictory result—thus placing himself in a position that was eccentric in the fullest sense of the word. Joyce settled in Paris, not in order to draw upon any models he might have found there, but to subvert the language of oppression itself. His purpose was therefore both literary and political.[26] In the passage quoted as an epigraph to this chapter, the Irish Protestant Cyril Connolly, who left his native land and became a celebrated writer and critic in London, expressed the British view of the detour taken by Joyce. Arguing that the aim of Joyce and other Irish writers of his generation was to discover "a blend of Anglo-Irish and French" that would shock the London critics, Connolly noted that "all [of them] had lived in Paris, and all had absorbed French culture." He went on to indicate the place of Paris and Dublin in the literary war unleashed against London: "The second quarter was Paris which held in the attack on the new Mandarins the line taken by Dublin against their predecessors thirty years before. It was here that conspirators met in Sylvia Beach's little bookshop where *Ulysses* lay stacked up like dynamite in a revolutionary cellar and then scattered down the Rue de l'Odéon on the missions assigned to them."[27]

The history of Irish literature was not finished with James Joyce. Through his claim to literary extraterritoriality he not only gave Irish literary space its contemporary form; he opened up a connection to Paris, thus providing a solution for all those who rejected the colonial alternative of retreat to Dublin or treasonous emigration to London. With Joyce, Irish literature was constituted in terms of a triangle of capitals formed by London, Dublin, Paris—a triangle that was less geographic than aesthetic and that had been imagined and created in the space of some thirty or forty years: Yeats staked out the first national literary position in Dublin; in London, Shaw occupied the canonical position of the Irishman adapted to suit English requirements; Joyce, refusing to choose between these cities, succeeded in reconciling contraries by establishing Paris as a new stronghold for the Irish, ruling out both conformity to the standards of national poetry and submission to English literary norms.

The design of the literary structure constituted by these three cities distilled the entire history of Irish literature, insofar as it had been "invented" between 1890 and 1930, and held out to every aspiring Irish author a range of aesthetic possibilities, engagements, positions, and choices. This polycentric configuration became so much a part of the mental habits of Irish writers, and of their view of the world, that still today a writer such as Seamus Heaney, undoubtedly the greatest contemporary Irish poet—born in 1939 in County Derry, Northern Ireland, professor from 1966 to 1972 at Queen's University of Belfast, where he had been a student, and winner of the 1995 Nobel Prize for Literature, whose decision to settle in the Republic of Ireland a few years earlier caused a scandal in his own country—can describe the choices available to him in exactly the same terms. In an interview with the French press he remarked: "If, like Joyce and Beckett, I had gone to live in Paris, I would only have conformed to a cliché. If I had gone off to London, this would have been considered an ambitious but normal course of action. But to go to [County] Wicklow was an act charged with meaning . . . When I crossed the border, my private life fell into the public domain and the newspapers wrote editorials about my decision. A queer paradox!"[28] To this foundational and historic triangle must now be added New York, which, owing to the presence there of a sizable Irish-American community, represents at once an alternative to London within the English-speaking world and a powerful pole of consecration in its own right.

After Joyce, Samuel Beckett represented a sort of end point in the constitution of Irish literary space and its process of emancipation. The whole history of this national literary world is at once present and denied in his career; but it can be grasped only by recognizing exactly what he had to do to rescue himself from the danger of national, linguistic, political, and aesthetic rootedness. In other words, to understand the very "purity" of Beckett's work, his progressive detachment from all external definition, his almost absolute autonomy, it is necessary to retrace the route by which he achieved formal and stylistic freedom—a route that is indissociable from the apparently more contingent and external one that brought him from Dublin to Paris.

As a young writer in Dublin in the late 1920s, Beckett was heir to the tripolar configuration of Irish space I have just described. One cannot fail to be struck by the importance it conferred upon these three capital cities. Beckett's displacements between Dublin, London, and Paris were so many aesthetic attempts to find his place in a literary space that was at once national and international. Because he found himself in the same situation that Joyce had twenty years earlier,[29] Beckett took exactly the same path—relying on Joyce to guide and justify his tastes, admiring the writers Joyce admired and dismissing the ones he did not, following Joyce in his exaltation of Dante and his sarcastic suspicions of the Celtic prophets, and so on.

Paralyzed by his boundless admiration for an author who then represented for him the highest imaginable degree of freedom from the norms imposed by nationalism, and, more than this, dumbfounded by the power of the position Joyce had created in Paris, Beckett had great difficulties until the war years finding his own way. Joyce's manner of fictional invention was the only one he could conceive of. Seemingly condemned to imitation or, worse, blind conformity, and driven to despair at not being able to settle upon a literary project to which he could commit himself, or even to choose a city where he could live (hesitating between retreat to Dublin and exile—another form of imitation—in Paris), Beckett searched for more than a decade for a way out from the aesthetic and existential impasse in which he found himself.

Though he was determined to use the autonomy that Joyce had achieved to his own advantage, he sought to follow in the footsteps of the older writer by other means. This meant relying upon the entire Irish literary heritage, in addition to Joyce's own innovations, in order to create a new and still more independent position. He therefore first had to find a way around the literary alternative—realism or Symbolism—imposed by the internal struggles of the Irish field, then to overcome what he called, in a letter in German addressed to Axel Kaun in 1937, speaking of Joyce's enterprise, "the apotheosis of the word"—that is, the willful belief in the power of words;[30] and, finally, to take his place, beyond Joyce, in an artistic genealogy that would inaugurate a new formal modernity. Beckett's invention of the most absolute literary autonomy, the highest degree of literary subversion and emancipation ever achieved, was therefore the paradoxical product of Irish literary history. Accordingly, it can be perceived and understood only on the basis of the whole of the history of Irish literary space.

GENESIS AND STRUCTURE OF A LITERARY SPACE

As against the commonly held view that each national particularism, each literary event, each work of literature is reducible to nothing other than itself, and remains incomparable to any other event in the world, the Irish case furnishes a paradigm that covers virtually the entire range of literary solutions to the problem of domination—and these in almost perfectly distilled form.

I have wished to examine the case of Ireland in order to show that the model proposed here is not an a priori construction of abstract elements, but rather one that may be directly applied to the historical formation of individual literatures. It has several essential aspects. First, it demonstrates that no literary project, not even the most formalistic, can be explained in a monadic fashion: every project must be put in relation to the totality of rival projects within the same literary space. Second, the Irish example makes it possible to explain how and why at any given moment of its history a particular literary field can be described in its entirety with reference to the set of competing contemporary positions. Finally, the Irish case is a way of showing that each new path of invention that is opened up, along with all those that have been blazed before, helps to form and unify the literary space in which it appears and asserts itself.[31]

Contrary to what the individual case studies of the previous chapters, considered in isolation from one another, may seem to suggest, the solutions devised by deprived writers take on their full meaning only once they have been put back into the context of the specific history of their respective literary spaces, which itself is part of an almost universal chronology. Thus Beckett's relationship to Joyce, for example, conceived as something absolutely unique (a notion that itself derives from belief in a literature that produces "pure" ideas in a sort of Platonic heaven), is typically taken to demonstrate the artistic independence of the disciple.[32] But even if it is true that Joyce was absent from Beckett's mature work (from the 1950s on), he nonetheless remained central to Beckett's aesthetic position and choices: Beckett was a descendant—a paradoxical one, to be sure, unacknowledged but nonetheless real—of Joycean invention.

Some theorists, such as Edward Said, have tried to incorporate Ireland in a general model of the postcolonial world. For Said, taking issue with the fundamental assumptions of "pure" criticism, literature was one of the main instruments by which colonialism and cultural domination are justified. In order to break with these assumptions, which he saw as having been reinforced, first by the "New Criticism" of the 1940s and 1950s, and then by deconstructivist criticism, Said sought in works such as *Orientalism* (1978), and still more so in *Culture and Imperialism* (1993), to give a new definition of literature and of literary reality by describing the political unconscious that is at work in the French and English novels of the nineteenth and twentieth centuries. Once the insistent but always unnoticed presence of colonial empire and colonized peoples is recognized, through a method of interpretation that he calls "contrapuntal," since it inverts the ordinary position of the reader in the structure and purpose of these novels (whether by Flaubert, Austen, Dickens, Thackeray, or Camus), it is no longer possible to sustain the view of a radical disjunction between literature and the (political) events of the world. The presence in these works of a colonial conception of the world calls attention to the reality of relations of cultural domination and thereby reveals the political truth of literature, hitherto obscured. Said's work had the great merit of internationalizing literary debate, showing that what he called the historical experience of empire is common to everyone, colonizers and colonized alike, and of rejecting the exclusive claims of linguistic and national criteria in favor of a literary history whose groupings and classifications are informed by the historical experience of colonization and, later, imperialism.

Said therefore took an interest in the figure of W. B. Yeats, whom he described as "the indisputably great national poet who articulates the experiences, the aspirations, and the vision of a people suffering under the dominion of an offshore power."[33] Fredric Jameson, for his part, has tried to show that literary modernism—and notably Joyce's formal investigations in *Ulysses*—were directly associated with the historical phenomenon of imperialism, contending that the end of modernism "coincide[s] with the restructuration of the classical imperialist world system."[34] Said and Jameson were among the first critics, in other words, to make the connection between the political history of countries that have long suffered foreign domination and the emergence of new national literatures. In doing this they promoted a new type of comparativism, using imperialism as a model to relate to one another works that appeared in very different countries and historical contexts. Thus Said was able, for example, to link Yeats's early poems with those of the Chilean poet Pablo Neruda.[35] Similarly, both Said and Jameson have explicitly rejected what Said in *Culture and Imperialism* called "the comfortable autonomies"—the unquestioned assumptions of pure, dehistoricized interpretations of poetry and, more generally, literature. Each one in his own way has called for the rehistoricization—which is to say, the repoliticization—of literary practices, even the most formalistic, such as Joyce's *Ulysses*. In the same sense, and on the basis of the same critical assumptions, Enda Duffy has proposed a national reading of Joyce's novel, which she holds is a postcolonial work of literature that portrays a simple "national allegory" and gives a narrative form to the ideological and political conflicts of Ireland at the beginning of the twentieth century.[36]

The "connection between imperial politics and culture," Said maintained, "is astonishingly direct."[37] Although his readings of literary texts were extremely shrewd, he regarded the aesthetic nature of a given work, and its singularity, as matters for internal criticism to decide. As against this view, however, a plausible case can be made that the link between literary form and political history requires that texts be considered in relation to the national and international literary space that mediates political, ideological, national, and literary stakes. The analysis I have developed here tends to cast doubt upon the possibility and validity of a political reading of *Ulysses,* for example, on the basis of the factual chronology of Irish politics alone. With the emergence of a literary space that becomes progressively more autonomous, that acquires its own distinctive tempo and its own chronology, so that it is partially independent of the political world, it becomes difficult to insist upon a strict correspondence between the political events that unfolded in Ireland between 1914 and 1921—the period during which *Ulysses* was composed—and Joyce's text; to push the parallelism, as Enda Duffy does, to the point of seeing homologies, or structural similarities, between the narrative strategies of the novel and the political forces at work during the Irish conflict of these years is even harder to justify. Nor can one wholly endorse the claims of Declan Kiberd, though he does recognize that "it was less easy to decolonize the mind than the territory" and acknowledges that the effects of dependence in Irish literature extended far beyond the official dates of national independence. Kiberd's novel and passionate approach to postcolonialism in Ireland, which he tries to relate to the literatures of Africa and India, likewise interprets literary events in terms of political structures and events ("the Irish were the first modern people to decolonize in the twentieth century") without taking into account, in its full historical complexity, the structure of the world republic of letters as a whole and the position occupied in it by Irish literary space.[38]

11 | *The Revolutionaries*

The Irish, condemned to express themselves in a language not their own, have stamped on it the mark of their own genius and compete for glory with the civilised nations.
  —James Joyce, lectures, 1905–06

For centuries correct national languages did not yet exist . . . On the one hand there had been Latin, which is to say the learned tongue, and on the other national languages, which is to say vulgar tongues . . . The end was [finally] reached, evreetheeng, absolootleeevreetheeng wuz expresst in the formerly vulgur langwedge . . . and this is preesycelee where mattersstandtooday withlitrachoor . . . since there is not, in a global way, any separation or demarcation between the literary language and the correct national language . . . the goal is to create pleasure and not linguistic purity . . . As a result writers can employ any method, achieve everything that is achievable, evreetheeng, absolootlee evreetheenggoze! There is therefore no obligation to respect linguistic norms . . . You stop thinking that you must defend the correct national language.
  —Katalin Molnár, *On Language*

WHEN THE FIRST effects of revolt, which is to say of literary differentiation, make themselves felt, and the first literary resources are able to be claimed and appropriated for both political and literary purposes, the conditions for the formation and unification of a new national literary space are brought together: a national literary heritage, if only a minimal one, has now been accumulated. It is at this stage that second-generation writers such as James Joyce appear. Exploiting national literary resources

that for the first time are regarded as such, they break away from the national and nationalist model of literature and, in inventing the conditions of their autonomy, achieve freedom. In other words, whereas the
first national intellectuals refer to a political idea of literature in order to
create a particular national identity, the newcomers refer to autonomous
international literary laws in order to bring into existence, still on a national level, another type of literature and literary capital.

The case of Latin America is exemplary in this regard. The period
known as the "boom," when writers from Central and South America
achieved international recognition following the award of the Nobel
Prize to Asturias in 1967, represents the beginning of a proclamation of
autonomy. The consecration of these novelists and the recognition of a
distinctive aesthetic permitted them collectively to detach themselves
from what Alfonso Reyes (1889–1959) called the "ancillary" vocation of
Hispano-American literature and to reject pure political functionalism.
"The literature of Spanish America," Carlos Fuentes has written, "had
to overcome, in order to exist, the obstacles of flat realism, commemorative nationalism, and dogmatic commitment. With Borges, Asturias,
Carpentier, Rulfo, and Onetti, the Hispano-American novel developed
in violation of realism and its codes."[1] In the early years of the "boom," a
debate developed within this transnational literary space between the
upholders of literature in the service of national and political causes (at
the time usually associated with the Cuban regime) and advocates of literary autonomy. The very emergence of this debate is a significant indication that the process of autonomization was then under way. In 1967
the Argentinian writer Julio Cortázar (1914–1984), committed to the
cause of the Cuban and Nicaraguan revolutionaries, and a member of
the Russell tribunal on the Vietnam War, nonetheless defended a position of literary autonomy. In a letter written in the aftermath of two
trips to Cuba, he told the editor of the Havana review *Casa de las
Américas*:

> When I came back to France after these two trips, there were two
> things that I understood better. On the one hand, my personal and in-
> tellectual involvement in the struggle for socialism . . . On the other,
> my work as a writer followed the orientation that my way of being
> impressed upon it, and even if at a given moment my work reflected
> this involvement, I did it for the same reasons of aesthetic freedom that
> currently lead me to write a novel that takes place virtually outside of

time and historical space. At the risk of disappointing the catechists and partisans of art in the service of the masses, I continue to be this "cronopio" who writes for his own personal pleasure and suffering, without the least concession, without "Latin American" or "Socialist" obligations understood as pragmatic a priori assumptions.[2]

These second-generation writers—"eccentric" in the fullest sense of the word—become the architects of the great literary revolutions: each using his own weapons, they fight to change the established literary order. They are innovators who undermine the forms, styles, and codes accepted at the literary Greenwich meridian, thus thoroughly changing, renewing, sometimes even shattering the criteria of modernity and, as a result, the practices of world literature as a whole. Joyce and Faulkner, two of the greatest innovators of the twentieth century, each carried out a revolution so great that the measure of literary time itself was profoundly altered. They became—and to a large extent still are—measuring instruments, points of reference by which every work claiming a place in the literary world can be evaluated.

International creators gradually build up a set of aesthetic solutions that, once tested and modified in different historical and social contexts, produce a genuinely international patrimony, a pool of specific strategies reserved for the privileged use of writers on the periphery. Drawn upon more or less everywhere in the world, endlessly reused and reinvented, the capital constituted by all these new solutions to the problem of domination allows such authors to refine and deepen the complexity of their paths to revolt and liberation. As a consequence of this accumulation of a worldwide heritage, which enables writers in outlying spaces to borrow stylistic, linguistic, and political techniques (and later to be borrowed from in their turn), there exists today a range of possibilities that they can turn to in order to devise their own solutions—whether aesthetic, linguistic, formal, or other—in response to the needs of a particular cultural, linguistic, or national situation. Those who, like Darío, Paz, Kiš, and Benet, go to the center to seek—to understand, assimilate, conquer, rob . . .—literary wealth and possibilities that hitherto had been denied them help accelerate the process of building up literary assets in the small nations of the world.

It will be recalled that Octavio Paz, upon grasping the necessity of entering the game, which is to say of gaining access to central time—the literary present that could not be found in his own country—decided "to go and look for it and bring it back home." This, Paz remarked, was "why there was frequent talk of 'modernizing' our countries: the modern was outside and had to be imported."[3] The major resource such writers lack is time. Like national writers, but in different forms and ways, they therefore have either to devise shortcuts or to accelerate literary time. In the course of enlarging literary space, the great innovators from the margins of the world of letters gradually make use of the whole of the heretical transnational heritage that has been accumulated since the first successful revolutions. Thus, in the nineteenth and twentieth centuries, the naturalist revolution, Surrealism, the Joycean revolution, and the Faulknerian revolution—products of different political and historical spaces and contexts—furnished eccentric writers with tools for modifying the relation of dependence in which they found themselves.

Whereas national writers, fomenters of the first literary revolts, rely on the literary models of national tradition, international writers draw upon this transnational repertoire of literary techniques in order to escape being imprisoned in national tradition. Through recourse to the values that enjoy currency at the Greenwich meridian, they create an autonomous pole in a space that previously had been shut off from international revolutions and, in this way, help to unify it. By the same token, the most autonomous writers of the small literatures are also for the most part, as we have seen, translators: they import, directly by means of translation or indirectly through their own work, the innovations of literary modernity. In countries of great but devalued historical capital, international writers are at once introducers of central modernity and internal translators, which is to say promoters of a national capital. Thus Sadiq Hidayat was both the translator of Omar Khayyáam into modern Persian, as we have already noted, and the translator of Kafka.

Once consecrated, the great revolutionaries are themselves co-opted in turn by the most subversive writers in deprived spaces and their advances incorporated into the body of transnational resources constituted by the work of literary innovators everywhere. Joyce was thus at once the creator of the first autonomous position within Irish literary space and the inventor of a new aesthetic, political, and above all linguistic solution to literary dependence. There is an international genealogy, then, that includes all the great innovators honored as true liberators in the peripheral lands of literary space, a pantheon of great authors regarded as universal classics (such as Ibsen, Joyce, and Faulkner) that writers from outlying countries can oppose both to central literary histories and to the academic genealogies of national and colonial pantheons.

Combining the lucidity of the dominated with a knowledge of the current supply of autonomous aesthetic innovations, these writers are now able to draw upon a fund of international resources whose availability throughout the world of letters leads to a considerable increase in the range of technical possibilities and causes the frontier of the literarily unthinkable to begin to recede. Still more importantly, they are the only ones who are able to discover and reproduce the aims and trajectories of the great literary heretics, the great revolutionaries who, once they have been canonized by their respective centers and declared universal classics, lose a part of their historical context and, as a result, a part of their power of subversion. Only the great subversives know how to search for and recognize in history itself—that is, in the structure of domination in literary space—authors who were in the same situation in which they find themselves and who managed to discover the solutions that *made* universal literature. In this way they turn the central classics to their own advantage and put them to new and specific uses, as Beckett and Joyce did with Dante, as Henry Roth was later to do with Joyce, Juan Benet with Faulkner, and so on.

Revolutionaries such as Joyce and Faulkner provide the literarily destitute with a variety of new means for reducing the distance that separates them from their centers.[4] They are able to accelerate literary time because their formal and stylistic innovations make it possible to transform the signs of cultural, literary, and often economic destitution into literary resources and thus to gain access to the highest modernity. By radically transforming the definition and limits assigned to literature (with regard not only to wordplay but also to the sexual, the scatalogical, and the prosaic aspects of urban life in the case of Joyce; in the case of Faulkner, to the destitution of rural life), they enable writers on the periphery who previously were denied access to literary modernity to take part in international competition, using instruments that they themselves have forged.

DANTE AND THE IRISH

The paradigm of all these subversive reworkings is surely the use that the Irish (first Joyce, then Beckett and Heaney) made of Dante. They reappropriated the work of the Tuscan poet—noble before all others—as an instrument of struggle on behalf of cosmopolitan and antinationalist Irish poets. Through a sort of reactualization of the linguistic and literary project laid out in *De vulgari eloquentia* (On Vernacular Eloquence)—a project that only writers concretely and directly concerned with the status of a national language in relation to the literary language of their space could understand—Joyce and Beckett in turn recreated, recovered, and invoked Dante's subversive power.[5] Dante became at once a resource and a weapon in the struggle of the most international writers in the Irish space.

Joyce's fascination with Dante is well known. Nicknamed "the Dante of Dublin" at the age of eighteen, he identified himself with the great Tuscan exile throughout his life. But it was Beckett, whose admiration for Dante and knowledge of Dante's work was no less great, who was to insist explicitly upon the structural similarity of their positions. His first published text was an essay written in early 1929 at Joyce's request for *Our Exagmination round his Factification for Incamination of Work in Progress,* a volume conceived by Joyce in response to the sharp criticism in England and America directed against what was to become *Finnegans Wake,* fragments of which had appeared in various reviews. The essay, "Dante . . . Bruno. Vico . . . Joyce," made use of the sophisticated tools furnished by Dante's *On Vernacular Eloquence* to mount a defense of the linguistic—which is to say political—dimension of Joyce's enterprise. At bottom it was both an anti-English manifesto and an attack against the Gaelicizing Irish, challenging the stranglehold of the English language over literature in Ireland while at the same time rejecting the inward-looking impulse of the Irish Revival. Beckett drew upon Dante's arguments in favor of an "illustrious vulgar tongue" in order to show that Joyce's *Work in Progress* was ultimately a refusal to submit to the tyranny of English: just as Dante had proposed the creation of an ideal language that would have synthesized all the dialects of Italy, so Joyce, in creating a sort of synthesis of all the languages of Europe, had invented an utterly novel answer to English political and linguistic domination.

Beckett himself, whose early fictions featured a Dantesque character named Belacqua, was to remain faithful to Dante's work throughout his career as well. In rejecting in a specifically literary way the national norms then current in Ireland, he took the same approach as Dante; and Dante, revamped and made the contemporary of the most international of Irish writers, took on a new dimension in his turn. Having been rehistoricized and transformed into one of the founding fathers of modern Irish literature, Dante now assumed his place in the legitimate heritage of all heretics, of all autonomous authors, of all Irish writers who refused to yield to the narrow limits of national realism.

Above all, the Irish embrace of Dante reveals the extraordinary continuity of the formation and unification of world literary space. At a distance of almost six hundred years, Joyce and Beckett reactualized a founding text that constituted the first specific call for emancipation, the first revolt against a dominant order (then represented by Latin). Like du Bellay, who had also invoked him as the inventor of non-Latin poetical forms, Joyce and Beckett, finding themselves in a homologous position, made Dante an instrument of their own liberation. This use—at once literary and political—of a text essential to the constitution of world literary space, one that allowed it to come into existence, attests to the validity of the genetic model proposed in the present work. Although they sought a way out from a situation of domination that, despite its historical differences, was very similar structurally, Joyce and Beckett completed and crowned the genesis and emergence of a world republic of letters: in coming full circle and rediscovering the inventor of the weapons forged against Latin oppression, they restored to Dante's work its full subversive charge by raising it as the standard of their own revolutionary ambitions.

THE JOYCEAN FAMILY

It is commonly said that *Finnegans Wake* is a limiting case, calling into question the very idea of literature and of readability; and that after Joyce no one could either take this path or go beyond it. This central (and above all Parisian—which is to say exclusively formalistic) reading makes an abstraction of Joyce's historical situation in Ireland and ignores the fact that, far from being pure and purely formal enterprises, both *Finnegans Wake* and *Ulysses*, which relied on Dante's model as well as the antiuniversalist theories of Vico,[6] were manifestos and programs for escaping a state of literary and political dependence. As Beckett showed in his 1929 essay, Joyce's *Work in Progress* proposed a sophisticated solution to the structural dilemma of writers from dominated territories of international literary space. Writers occupying a homologous position who grasped the import of Joyce's experiment were later to take this path, using methods of their own, among them Henry Roth in New York in the 1920s, Arno Schmidt in postwar Germany, and, today, Njabulo Ndebele in South Africa and Salman Rushdie in England and India.

Joyce in the Moors of Lunebourg

Arno Schmidt (1914–1979) adopted exactly the same posture during the postwar years in Germany as Joyce had done during the 1920s in Ireland, both because of the structural similarity of their positions—Schmidt in a sense reinvented the same literary revolution—and because he found in Joyce's work and outlook, albeit belatedly and without acknowledging it, a sort of noble precedent authorizing him to push his own aesthetic breakthrough still further than Joyce had done.[7]

Just as Joyce had defined his literary purpose in opposition to Irish nationalist literature, Schmidt conceived himself first and foremost in opposition to Germany and the whole of its intellectual tradition. An autodidact who came late to literature, he had in common with his contemporaries who founded Gruppe 47 a provocative mistrust of his native land. The very things that led Heinrich Böll, Uwe Johnson, and Alfred Andersch to place politics at the center of their theoretical and fictional writing after the war, to inquire into the intellectual roots of Nazism and the false assumptions of the German Democatic Republic, led Schmidt by contrast to carry out this same national critique on the terrain of language, to reject straightforward political discourse and to propose instead a "literary politics." As against the "renovation" of literature advocated by Gruppe 47, which was to be achieved using the methods of realism and with the "political" aim of stripping down the language—on the model of Sartre, for the purpose of combating the Germanic tradition of aestheticism—Schmidt was practically alone in undertaking a systematic critique of language and fictional form.

Like Joyce, Schmidt broke with the conservatism and aestheticism that were characteristic of the national culture of the day, but he was also in disagreement with the political critique that Gruppe 47 directed against this culture: "I hereby solemnly protest," he exclaimed, "against the term 'German writer' by which this nation of stupid fools will seek one day to claim me as one of their own."[8] Like Joyce again, he was to cast this dual rejection in specifically literary terms—the only writer in Germany to do so for many years. Fascinated by the work of the Irish novelist, he proposed in 1960 to undertake an annotated translation of

Finnegans Wake, but no publisher would take on the project. Nonetheless his familiarity with literature in the English language gave him access to European modernity and avant-garde techniques, which in turn enabled him to avoid the stylistic and narrative constraints of postwar German realism.

As brothers in revolt against language and nationalist hierarchies, Joyce and Schmidt had much in common. Like Joyce, Schmidt chose to contradict the national aesthetic model: against seriousness, he praised lightness, humor, and farce; against poetry, prose and prosaism—the title of his collection of stories *Rosen und Porree* (Roses and Leeks, 1959) is by itself an extraordinary summary of his poetics, devoted to upending clichés and standing poetry on its head, and in this way, by making concrete the faintest and most abstract sensations, revitalizing the most trivial descriptions of literature; and against lyricism and metaphysics, sarcasm:

> Every writer should grab hold of the nettle of reality, and then show us all of it, the black filthy roots; the poison-green viper stalk; the gaudy flower(y pot). And as for the critics, those intellectual street-porters and volunteer firemen, they ought to stop tatting lace nets to snare poets and produce something "refined" themselves for once: that would make the world sit up and take roaring notice! Of course, as with every other grand and beautiful thing, poetry is hedged in by its complement of geldings; but: the genuine blackamoors are the ones who rejoice in the sun's black spots! (All of this for the reviewers' album.)[9]

Just as Joyce in *Finnegans Wake* had proclaimed an autonomous literary language, Schmidt fought for a revitalized punctuation and a simplified spelling in German, forcing his typographical innovations upon publishers and printers: "I have shown that it is neither a matter of sensationalism nor of ostentatious display, but of . . . the further improvement, the necessary refinement of the writer's tools."[10] He made the difference between "two" and "2" the pivot of his expressiveness, and the subtlety of pauses, according to their increasing order of duration, the very symbol of his freedom: "If we were not *given* such freedom, we'll simply take it! For it's necessary."[11] In short, he called for the perfecting of a literary language freed from conventions and official norms, an autonomous tool in the service of writing and the writer. Hence his decision to quit his publishers once and for all and to publish his last works—among them *Abend mit Goldrand* (Evening Edged in Gold, 1975)—in the form of typescripts, all of whose stages of production he could personally supervise.

Schmidt also shared Joyce's disdain for national tradition. In all his books he proclaimed his defiance of Goethe, regarded as the greatest of all German writers, and his rejection, not of Goethe's poetry, but of Goethe's prose ("Whereas Goethe daubed all over the joints with his amorphous prose pap . . ."; "With Goethe, prose is not an art form but a junk pile").[12] While denouncing Goethe's undisputed hegemony over German letters, he restored "minor" writers—Wieland, Fouqué, Tieck, Wezel—to the first rank. And above all he insisted upon his total artistic independence in the face of national hierarchies that submitted texts to the judgment of the "people": "Should you receive the applause of the people," he wrote in *Brand's Haide* (Brand's Heath, 1951), "ask yourself: what have I done wrong?! And if your second book is so received as well, then cast away your pen: you can never be great . . . Art for the people?!: leave that slogan to the Nazis and the Communists."[13] This position is identical in almost every respect with that of Joyce when he protested against what he considered the Abbey Theatre's mistaken emphasis on popular drama: "the artist, though he may employ the crowd, is very careful to isolate himself . . . your popular devil is more dangerous than your vulgar devil."[14]

James Joyce and Arno Schmidt did what no one before them had dared to do: disregarding national taboos and the restrictions these assert, they imposed their own language and grammar together with a new style of narrative discontinuity—"My life?! is not a continuum," Schmidt declared, "(not simply fractured into black and white pieces by day and night! . . .) man of a thousand thoughts; of fragmenting categories . . . a tray full of glistening snapshots . . . that's how my life runs, how my memories run (as if some spasm-shaken man were watching a thunderstorm in the night)"—and overturned the hierarchies of national pantheons.[15] The kinship between Schmidt and Joyce—like the one that, as we shall see, links Faulkner with Juan Benet, Rachid Boudjedra, and Mario Vargas Llosa—is not a matter merely of historical similarity; the similarity is also, and especially, structural. Occupying the same place in their respective national spaces, they were able to upset the same established literary values. Their common defiance of a national language allowed each of them to bring to bear his formidable irony, to revitalize literary language, and to carry out an immense literary revolution.

Ulysses in Harlem

Henry Roth (1906–1995), the son of Yiddish-speaking Jewish immigrants, discovered Joyce's *Ulysses* in New York during the 1920s. For a young man who had grown up in terrible poverty, deprived of almost all intellectual and literary resources, in East Harlem, the book was an utter revelation. He later described in detail in *From Bondage,* the third of four volumes of his autobiographical novel *Mercy of a Rude Stream* (1994–1998), how Joyce's book had come to him, almost by chance, through the intervention of a young woman, a professor of literature at the City College of New York, who had smuggled back into the country a copy of the edition published in Paris by Sylvia Beach ("a blue paper-bound book, an untitled copy of James Joyce's *Ulysses*"). Roth's experience provides further evidence in support of the account of the structure of literary space given here, as well as of the role of Paris in the manufacture and diffusion of literary modernity. Joyce's book was already famous in literary and student circles in New York: "The rare one who had read the book seemed invested with a veritable luster; he was like one inducted into an esoteric sodality, an ultramodern one. Even to demonstrate familiarity with the book warranted pretensions to the intellectual vanguard."[16]

Roth understood at once that Joyce's novel could provide him with a unique means for attaining literary modernity—for transforming his wretched everyday life into literary gold. His enthusiastic pages can only be read as so many testimonies to the "economic" reality—habitually denied—of literary creation:

> the *Ulysses* demonstrated to him not only that it was possible to commute the dross of the mundane and the sordid into literary treasure, but how it was done. It showed him how to address whole slag heaps of squalor, and make them available for exploitation in art . . . What was there in the stodgy variety of Dublin city through which Bloom and Dedalus went to and fro that was so very different from the stodgy variety of Harlem's environs, the environs Ira[17] knew so well—and the East Side environments that memory retained like a reserve of impressions? . . . Hell, of nastiness, of sordidness, perversity, and squalor—compared to anyone in the *Ulysses,* he had loads, he had droves, he had

troves. But it was language, language, that could magically transmogrify the baseness of his days and ways into precious literature—into the highly touted *Ulysses* itself . . . The forlorn backyards of tenements, the dreary Felsnaphthamopped hallways, enlivened sometimes by homely emanations of cabbage . . . Speak of the worn lip of the stoop stairs, the battered brass letter boxes in the foyer, the dilapidated flight of linoleum-covered steps past the window at the turn of the landing, and up to the "first floor" . . . Didn't it qualify for *alchemical transformation* . . .? If that was latent wealth in the domain of letters, why, he was rich beyond compare: his whole world was a junkyard. All those myriad, myriad squalid impressions he took for granted, all were convertible from base to precious, from pig iron to gold ingot.[18]

Roth stated all the literary possibilities that existed in America at the time, all the models that were available to him:

No, you didn't have to go cruisin o'er the billows to the South Sea Isles on a sailing vessel crowded with canvas, or fist a t'gallant, like a character in *The Sea Wolf,* or prospect for gold in the faraway Klondike, or float down the Mississippi in a raft with Huck Finn, or fight Indians in the young Wild West nickel magazines . . . You didn't need to go anywhere, anywhere at all. It was all here, right here, in Harlem, on Manhattan Island, anywhere from Harlem to the Jersey City Pier . . . Language was the conjuror, indeed the philosopher's stone, *language was a form of alchemy.* It was language that elevated meanness to the heights of art . . . What a discovery that was! He, Ira Stigman, was a *mehvin*[19] of misery, of the dismal, of the pathetic, the deprived. Everywhere he looked, whole treasuries were exposed, repositories of priceless potential ignored, and hence they were his . . . It was indecent, but it was literary, and Ira had paid his fee in full for the right to use it.[20]

Here Roth describes almost in its raw state the principle of literary "transmutation"—a word that, as we have seen, is not carelessly chosen. His economic vocabulary ("treasure," "latent wealth," "gold," "priceless potential") reveals the actual mechanisms of *littérarisation,* stripped of the usual literary euphemisms, and demonstrates the practical function of what I have called literary heritage, or capital. For it was only on the basis of his recognition of a structural similarity between his position and that of a writer from a wholly different linguistic, literary, political, and historical world, and by relying upon the model that this artist supplied him with, that Roth managed to create his own world for himself, to convert (Roth's own term) his economic and literary poverty into a fictional project and, equipped with this passport to modernity, to grapple directly with the most current issues of the literary world. Thus he wrote, with reference to his first astonished reading of Joyce's *Ulysses:*

> But as the days passed, and he read and wrestled . . . the strange conviction took firmer and firmer hold of him, that within himself was graven a crude analogue of the Joycean model, just as he felt within himself a humble affinity for the Joycean temperament, a diffident aptitude for the Joycean method. Opaque though many and many a passage might be, Ira sensed that he was a *mehvin* of that same kind of world of which Joyce was an incomparable connoisseur: of that same kind of pocked and pitted reality. There were keys that evoked that world, signatures by which they were recognized, and he was ever receptive to them—why, he couldn't say.[21]

The novel that Roth wrote after this Joycean revelation, *Call It Sleep* (1934), was to be a failure—perhaps because the gap between his position as an author on the far periphery of the world of letters, American literary space at the time, and the places where certificates of literary modernity were awarded was too great. Thirty years later Roth's book was rediscovered and consecrated, and went on to sell more than a million copies.

THE FAULKNERIAN REVOLUTION

William Faulkner, no less than Joyce, was responsible for one of the greatest revolutions in the world of letters, comparable in its extent, and in the depth of the changes it introduced in the novel, to the naturalist revolution of the late nineteenth century. But while in the centers, and especially in Paris, the technical innovations of the American novelist were understood and valued only as formalistic devices, in the outlying countries of the literary world they were welcomed as tools of liberation. Faulkner's work, more than that of any other writer, henceforth belonged to the explicit repertoire of international writers in dominated literary spaces who sought to escape the imposition of national rules, for he had found a solution to a commonly experienced political, aesthetic, and literary impasse.

Though he enjoys a great reputation in the highest circles of the literary world and ranks among the great literary revolutionaries, Faulkner is also a figure with whom all writers in countries on the periphery can identify—still more than Joyce, who has been annexed by critics in the centers and so thoroughly dehistoricized that deprived writers, bowing to the monopoly power of the capitals over literary consecration, tend to overlook the subversive dimension of his work. In putting an end to the curse of backwardness that lay over these regions, by offering the novelists of the poorest countries the possibility of giving acceptable literary form to the most repugnant realities of the margins of the world, Faulkner has been a formidable force for accelerating literary time.

If Faulkner's work has succeeded in linking very different literary enterprises, and if its power has been recognized for almost half a century by writers from very different backgrounds, this is surely because it reconciles properties that normally are thought to be incompatible. As a citizen of the most powerful nation in the world, and as a writer consecrated by Paris, Faulkner nonetheless evoked in all his books (at least all those of his early period) characters, landscapes, ways of thinking, and stories that exactly coincided with the reality of all those countries said to lie in the "South"—a rural and archaic world prey to magical styles of thought and trapped in the closed life of families and villages. In his famous preface to the French translation of *As I Lay Dying*, Valery Larbaud confirmed—in order immediately to insist upon the fallacy of this interpretation—that Faulkner's early works had been received in France as examples of the lowest of all fictional genres, the *roman paysan:* "Here is a novel of rural manners that comes to us, in a good translation, from the state of Mississippi . . . *As I Lay Dying* holds certainly more interest and possesses, in my opinion, much higher aesthetic value than the great majority of the books among which stores arrange it for the convenience of their customers, which is to say under the category of 'rural novels.'"[22]

Faulkner thus helped a primitive and rural world that until then had seemed to demand a codified and descriptive realism to achieve novelistic modernity: in his hands, a violent, tribal civilization, impressed with the mark of biblical mythologies, opposed in every respect to urban modernity (which was typically associated with the stylistic avant-garde), became the privileged object of one of the most daring exercises in style of the century. Faulkner singlehandedly resolved the contradictions in which writers from disadvantaged countries found themselves mired, lifting the curse of imposed literary hierarchies and bringing about a prodigious reversal of values. With a single stroke he wiped out the accumulated backwardness of literatures that hitherto had been excluded from the literary present, which is to say from stylistic modernity. The Spanish writer Juan Benet was indisputably one of the first to have understood this; but after him all writers from the South, in the broad sense of the term, from the West Indies to Portugal and from South America to Africa, recognized that Faulkner had revealed to them a way of attaining the Greenwich meridian without in the least denying their cultural heritage. The kinship that immediately disclosed itself to eccentric writers, despite differences of language, period, and civilization, allowed him to be claimed as a legitimate ancestor. Moreover, it is clear that the mechanism of identification was the same in the case both of Joyce and of Faulkner. Their work, so far as it resolved in an utterly new and masterly fashion the dilemma and difficulties of deprived writers, could be appreciated only by writers who were placed in a homologous position: whereas Joyce is typically, and unsurprisingly, honored by novelists from disadvantaged urban backgrounds, Faulkner is recognized by authors from rural countries with archaic cultural structures.

Faulkner in León

"William Faulkner was my reason for becoming a writer," Juan Benet once said. "He was the greatest influence of my entire life."[23] The debt to Faulkner acknowledged by Benet, the direct line of descent he recognized between his own work and that of the American novelist, the absolute admiration that he reserved for a writer whom he looked up to as a master before all others are an extraordinary illustration of the complexity of the circulatory network of literature. This elective affinity, ordinarily described using the language of "influence," was in no way the product of a preordained meeting in some heavenly realm of ideas.[24]

By the time they reached Benet in Spain in the 1950s, Faulkner's novels had traveled a very long way in time and space. They took twenty years to make the trip from Mississippi to Madrid, by a route that owed nothing to chance, for they had gone through Paris. Benet read Faulkner in French translation—not, he later confirmed, out of any special fascination with France or its language, but because at this time speaking and reading French assured access to the literature of the whole world. And he discovered literary modernity not because he had any particular interest in the American or English novel, but because Faulkner had long been regarded by the highest critical authorities in France as one of the founders of the modern novel. The eminent position occupied by Paris in the world of letters meant that Benet could not help but place his full confidence in the French endorsement of Faulkner, and he approached Faulkner as a great writer whose enduring reputation was secure. But the sense of revelation he felt on encountering Faulkner's work (rather than that of any other author) was plainly connected with the striking coincidence between two worlds that apparently had nothing in common, the South of the United States described by Faulkner and the Spanish province of León, where Benet was working at the time. Looking back upon his early career as an engineer and a writer, Benet recalled: "I was in a region that I knew very little: the northwest of Spain, south of the Cantabrian Mountains, in León. It was a very backward region at the time, with very few people—there was nothing, no roads, no electricity, everything had to be done. I traveled a great deal [at this time] in the poorest and most remote regions of Spain."[25] Valery Larbaud, in his preface to the French version of *As I Lay Dying,* had earlier described Faulkner's American landscape in almost the same terms: "The reader will not fail to be struck by the purely agricultural character of these vast areas, the absence of large cities, the underdeveloped system of roads and communications, and the sparse population of farmers who work their own land, whose life seems much more difficult than that of the majority of rural folk, freehold and tenant farmers alike, in central and eastern Europe."[26]

The worn notion of "influence" is plainly both too simple and too vague to be of any use in trying to account for the affinity Benet felt for Faulkner. Far from dissimulating, or remaining silent about what he owed to Faulkner—unlike the majority of "influenced" writers, who insist above all upon the originality of their inspiration—Benet openly acknowledged his filiation and constantly emphasized, by way of explicit homage, the many parallels between their work.[27] He proclaimed his indebtedness as though he wished to understand better the nature of his borrowings: to describe a homologous reality, he employed in a functional (and not only, for example, an aesthetic) way elements that by definition were similar. The recognition of a kinship between the two worlds implies in practice the reproduction of stylistic and structural elements, excluding any straightforward imitation of literary "procedures." Attention has, of course, been called to the fact that Benet situated all his novels in a region called "Región," just as Faulkner had circumscribed the action of his books within Yoknapatawpha County—both authors also provided precise topographical maps for their fictive regions, Faulkner for the *Portable Faulkner* (1946) edited by Malcolm Cowley and Benet in *Herrumbrosas Lanzas* (1983)—to say nothing of similarities with respect to narrative complexity, temporal nonlinearity, chronological disruptions, and so on. Maurice-Edgar Coindreau, rejecting the particularist interpretation that associated Faulkner's work solely with the American South, insisted in his preface to the French edition of *The Wild Palms* (1939) that "Faulkner's true domain is that of eternal myths, especially those that the Bible has popularized" and went on to describe Faulkner as a "great primitive, servant of the old myths."[28]

Benet likewise appealed to myth, but in order to evoke an altogether different cultural context. In all his novels he mixed myths with popular beliefs, superstitions, and ancestral customs, as though his intention was to conduct a sort of ethnological inquiry. In drawing upon ancient myths, if only in an imprecise and allusive way, he ennobled and universalized the structures of thought of isolated peasants in the Cantabrian Mountains: the menacing and labyrinthine peaks that loom over the opening of *Volverás a Región* (Return to Región, 1967), watched over by a ghostly and omnipresent guardian, subtly evoke all Hades and all labyrinthine hells, the strange birds of the region ("beautiful, black, hungry, and silent") that attack human beings by plunging a terrible and sudden barb into their back, calling to mind the guardians of some infernal circle.[29] In laying emphasis on the interaction of beliefs, fears, and legends, Benet developed a long and complex line of thought concerning the archaism and underdevelopment of his country, doomed to endure obscure combats for antiquated prizes: "and there, in a ditch . . . died the man who, by mobilizing an entire army, had attempted, with the pretext of an old affront, to violate the inaccessibility of that mountain and bring to light the secret that its backwardness holds."[30] Benet's recourse to magical thought was not at all a matter of idealizing the rural world as a repository of the purest traces of a national culture; to the contrary, through a curious reflectiveness, no doubt made possible by the action of a Faulknerian sort of recollection, it underlay his political and historical inquiry into Spanish backwardness and resistance to change.

The freedom Benet discovered from reading Faulkner permitted him to frame questions pertinent to Spanish experience. It is in this sense that all his analyses must be understood: despite their apparently enigmatic (and therefore strictly literary) quality, they are unquestionably historical and ethnographic, aimed at deciphering archaic national structures. Thus he evoked the "head of King Sidonio—as legend tells—leaping over the swirling waters of the Torce . . . and the madness of young Aviza, opening the insides of his father's corpse . . . [which will] shape forever the behavior of a dispossessed and degraded people driven toward decadence and backwardness in order to preserve its legitimate authority."[31] In the same way Benet adopted a resolutely provocative point of view with regard to the Spanish civil war. There is no trace in his writings of the heroic mythology that furnished the point of departure for so many works by Republican exiles. In his first book (and subsequently in almost all his novels in one form or another) Benet directly addressed the question of the war—the most taboo subject of all, the source of all political stances in the Spanish intellectual world of the 1950s and 1960s. The utterly new perspective that he brought to bear upon the war was that of a historian; his tone was clinical, descriptive, impartial, refusing to endorse the cause of either republicans or nationalists, all of whom seemed to him to display the same reckless bellicosity.

Benet's disillusionment (no doubt rooted in personal experience—his father, a republican, had been executed in Madrid by the republican army) could only lead to a total rupture with literary conventions. Thus he plainly announced his purpose in *Return to Región:* "The whole course of the civil war in the Región sector begins to be clearly seen when one understands that, in more than one aspect, it is a paradigm on a lesser scale and with a slower rhythm than peninsular-wide events." A few lines later, describing the republican campaign in Región, he writes: "It was republican by negligence or omission, revolutionary by sound, and bellicose not out of any spirit of revenge for an age-old oppressive order, but out of the anger and candor born of a natural ominous and tedious condition."[32] In describing the civil war as one of the innumerable avatars of Spanish underdevelopment,[33] as one of the most terrible consequences of an isolation that had deliberately been imposed upon a country subject to the most archaic practices and beliefs, Benet drew attention in this book, published while Franco was still in power, to the historical logic of the advent of a dictatorship. Thus he observed in connection with Numa, guardian of the accursed mountain of Región: "He gives up nothing, but, at least, he doesn't allow the slightest progress; he doesn't squeeze, he smothers. Don't look for a superstition in him; he's not a whim of nature or the result of a civil war; perhaps the whole organized process of a religion, joined to the growth of poverty, necessarily produces such a creature: a cowardly, selfish, and coarse people always prefers suppression to doubt; the latter, it might be said, is a privilege of the rich."[34]

Faulkner in Algeria

Rachid Boudjedra, who attempted to do the same sort of thing in Arabic as Juan Benet had done with respect to Spanish language and culture, also sought to make use of the Faulknerian heritage in order to recast the national questions facing the Algerian novel and to find an alternative to the unsatisfactory choice between writing in French or Arabic. He therefore looked to a fictional modernity that the educational tradition of his country, shaped by colonization, had not allowed to develop there:

> I want my country to be modern, and for the moment it isn't; and in my writing, actually, I am fascinated by the modernity of writing, by writers whom I consider to be making modernity in the world, whether they are contemporary or avant-garde writers: Faulkner, even if he has long been dead, because he invented fictional modernity; and Claude Simon. All of Claude Simon's novels take place in and around Perpignan. The whole world of his books unfolds in this small city and the small village [outside it]. And in the same way Faulkner also set all his stories in Jefferson, a tiny town in Mississippi. And so I find myself there, and I call this the Southern novel and I am part of this Southern novel, I want to be part of it. It's the South that makes me feel close to Claude Simon because he spoke of the women of the 1930s [in Perpignan] exactly as I speak of the women of the 1990s in Algeria today: the confinement, the heat . . . All that is the same world as my own, the world in which I was born. Faulkner is the same thing, the South, the mosquitoes, all that.[35]

Boudjedra's reference to Claude Simon, who also acknowledged his indebtedness to Faulkner, is further evidence of a wide-ranging appropriation of the American heritage. Moreover, the avowal of a fictional modernity that supplies the means for expressing the reality of a country without using the outmoded devices of naturalism implies the affirma-

tion of total literary and aesthetic autonomy: Boudjedra rejected the political co-optation of Algerian writers and instead sought to join battle
with politics on another terrain, that of literature. This effort, it should
be emphasized, did not amount to retreat into an apolitical aestheticism.
Undermining the literary norms of the Arabic language and the traditional respect for a language associated with religion and social life profoundly revitalized literary practices in Algeria. Boudjedra employed the
weapons of writers in the center in order to subvert social and religious
proprieties (surely no less difficult to do in Algeria today than it was in
Ireland in the 1920s) and to transform from within the practices of a literature that believed itself to be liberated from colonial constraints by
the general adoption of a narrative model that, in fact, only reproduced
the French academic tradition of *belle écriture:* "Ours is a literature of
teachers, a pedagogical literature . . . the Algerian writer sees things in an
objective, external, sociological, anthropological way. It must also be said
that colonization was a great help to him and even confined him within
[this perspective] and applauded his efforts . . . And in this literature
of teachers there is a desire to teach, a desire to instruct." To Boudjedra's
mind, the problem was "above all one of questioning sacredness, what is
considered by a people, rightly or wrongly, to be sacred . . . it is necessary
to talk in Arabic about things that haven't been talked about. Sexuality,
for instance." The appearance of the Arabic translation of *Sunstroke,* his
second novel published in France, was "an enormous scandal at the time
in Algeria," he recalled, "precisely because I'd challenged the sacred
text—I'd made puns on the Koranic text just as we did as children, as
every Algerian, Arab, Muslim child does in primary school. The whole
subversive side, the whole subversive thrust comes through better in
Arabic . . . I subvert the language; this is important for us, that we subvert the language, because it's so sacralized, so strictly channeled, it's
good to subvert it."[36]

Some fifteen years earlier Boudjedra's countryman Kateb Yacine had
expressed himself in rather similar terms while seeking to qualify the
tendency of critics to view Faulkner as his sole model and to explain
Faulkner's importance for him in terms of the similarities between the
American South and Algeria:

> Let's take the example of Camus. He was also a writer, undeniably, but
> his books on Algeria ring false and hollow . . . As for Faulkner, he rep-

resents the type of man I detest most of all. He was a colonist, a white Puritan, a product of the United States . . . Only Faulkner was brilliant. He was a slave to literature . . . He couldn't not have influenced me, especially since Algeria was a sort of Southern America, a South of the United States, at the moment when I was writing, with its sizable minority of whites and a host of very similar problems. And so there is a reason for the fascination with Faulkner. But the way in which Faulkner's influence has been described is misleading. Naturally publishers put that sort of thing on the book cover. Which is fine, because Faulkner is very well known. It's convenient—but it has to be explained, Faulkner's influence. If one explains it in a few words, as I have just done, things are put back in perspective.[37]

Faulkner in Latin America

The American novelist also became the standard-bearer of the literary liberation of the writers of the Latin American "boom." We know that his work was essential for Gabriel García Márquez, who has repeatedly testified to this. But it was also essential for Mario Vargas Llosa, who has insisted on the importance of Faulkner's writing for writers of his generation:

> I read the American novelists, especially those of the "lost generation"—Faulkner, Hemingway, Fitzgerald, Dos Passos—above all Faulkner. Of the authors I read in my youth, he is one of the few who still remains a living presence for me. I have never been disappointed rereading Faulkner, as I have sometimes been with Hemingway, for example . . . [Faulkner] was the first novelist whom I wanted to study closely, to reconstruct rationally, trying to see how time was organized in his novels, for example, how the planes of space and chronology intersected, [to see] its jumps, its ability to tell a story from various contrary perspectives so as to create an ambiguity, an enigma, a sense of mystery and depth. Faulkner's technique dazzled me, apart from the fact that he is one of the great novelists of the twentieth century. I believe that, for a Latin American writer, reading his books at the time I did was very useful, because they provided a valuable set of techniques for describing a reality that, in a certain sense, had a great deal in common with Faulkner's reality, that of the South of the United States.[38]

The "geopolitical" kinship emphasized by Vargas Llosa is the very same one detected by Benet and Boudjedra, proof of a structural affinity that does not make Faulkner the object of a vague admiration for one of the most eminent members of the pantheon of fictional modernity, but the precursor and inventor of a specific—narrative, technical, formal—solution that made it possible to reconcile the most modern aesthetics with the most archaic social structures and landscapes.[39]

TOWARD THE INVENTION OF LITERARY LANGUAGES

In the course of a long history that led writers from a condition of dependence to one of at least relative independence, a slow process of accumulating resources that led to the gradual invention of literary freedom and specificity, the most uncertain and most difficult struggle (and also the one most rarely encountered) has been over language. Because it is at once a political instrument, a national standard, and a writer's raw material, language is always liable—by virtue of this very ambiguity—to be used as a means for achieving national ends, whether nationalist or populist or both. The inescapable dependence upon political and national authorities explains why the only admission of membership and dependence that writers in the most autonomous territories of the world republic of letters can permit themselves almost invariably takes the form, regardless of their homeland, of the universally adopted watchword "My country is my language"—an explicit and economical way of repudiating political nationalism (banished from the most independent countries) while at the same time pledging allegiance to a tongue that is tied to the nation.

This is why the ultimate step in the liberation of writing and writers, their final proclamation of independence, consists in affirming the autonomous use of a purely literary language, one that submits to none of the laws of grammatical or even orthographic correctness (which, of course, are imposed by states) and that refuses to yield to the usual requirements of intelligibility associated with the most elementary forms of communication, remaining loyal only to the conditions dictated by literary creation itself.

Joyce was the first, in *Finnegans Wake,* to break with the imperatives of linear narrative, immediate readability, and grammaticality, and to herald with this multilingual work the advent and use of a specifically literary language. Arno Schmidt followed him along this path, changing the nature of narrative through typographical alterations, notably in *Abend mit Goldrand,* in which several narrations are found on the same page. Katalin Molnár, a Hungarian writer living and working in France, recently took yet another step with an attack on the French language that explicitly challenged the national—which is to say political—assumptions on which submission to a linguistic order rests.[40] In the passage that serves as an epigraph to this chapter, she uses a phonetic language—that is, one that is the same in both written and spoken form—both ironically and subversively to argue that literary language must enjoy complete autonomy.[41]

Surely no writer up until the present day has gone further in the invention of a literary language than Samuel Beckett, whose texts are among the most autonomous ever imagined. His position as an Irish writer exiled in Paris, together with the bilingual character of his work (self-translated in both directions), proved to be an unsurpassably efficient engine for challenging accepted linguistic and narrative practices. His increasingly rigorous and precise quest for a radical autonomy led him to break with all the forms of national dependence peculiar to writers: the nation in the political sense, of course, but to a still greater degree the debates concerning national literary history, the aesthetic choices dictated by national literary space, and finally language itself, conceived as a set of laws and rules imposed by political authorities that work to subject writers to the national norms of the national language.

It is in this sense that Beckett's passionate interest in the painting of Bram van Velde is to be understood: turning away from the figurative conventions of his own art, he looked to abstract painting. By transposing one of the great revolutions in painting to literature he succeeded in upsetting its usual assumptions. Little by little, but ever more radically in extending Joyce's effort to undermine the edifice of realism, Beckett challenged all the illusions of reality on which fictional narration rests. Rejecting first the assumption of spatial and temporal verisimilitude, then of characters and even first names, he labored to invent a pure and autonomous literature freed from the rules of traditional representation. This emancipation required a novel use of language, liberated from the ordinary constraints of plain readability.

To achieve this unprecedented degree of abstraction, Beckett had to invent an utterly new set of technical tools that made it possible to escape meaning—which is to say narration, representation, succession, description, setting, even character—without thereby resigning himself to inarticulateness. In short, he had to create an autonomous literary language, or at least the most autonomous language ever imagined by a writer. To silence meaning as far as possible, in order to attain literary autonomy—this was Beckett's wager, one of the maddest and most ambitious in the history of literature. The result of this magisterial attempt to create an absolutely self-sufficient writing was *Worstward Ho* (1983)— posthumously translated into French as *Cap au pire* (1991)—which generated its own syntax and vocabulary, decreed its own grammar, even created words answering solely to the logic of the pure space of a text whose very possibility was due to itself alone. It is perhaps in this respect that Beckett finally attained total literary abstraction, having managed to create a pure object of language, totally autonomous since it refers to nothing other than itself.

In order to rescue literature from its final form of dependence, then, Beckett broke with the very idea of a common language. Having set off in search of a literature of the "non-word,"[42] he created the most independent world conceivable—a literature delivered from verbal meaning itself. Beckett wrote in neither French nor English. He manufactured a unique aesthetic material solely on the basis of his own aesthetic principles, thus perhaps managing to bring about, in the most total incomprehension, the first truly autonomous literary revolution.

CONCLUSION | *The World and the Literary Trousers*

Customer: God made the world in six days and you, you couldn't be bothered to make me a
    pair of trousers in six months.
Tailor: But sir, look at the world, and look at your trousers.
    —Samuel Beckett, The World and the Trousers

BECKETT, ALTHOUGH HE sought to tear himself away from traditional conceptions of a literature that, like Kafka, he thought was literally impossible, worked very briefly at the end of the war as an art critic. Seeking to describe and make known the work of the van Velde brothers, he reviewed all the possibilities available to the critic: "Let us not speak of criticism proper. The best criticism—by men such as Fromentin, Grohmann, MacGreevy, Sauerlandt—is that of Amiel . . . Otherwise one does general aesthetics, like Lessing. This is a charming game. Or one deals in anecdotes, like Vasari and *Harper's Magazine*. Or one puts together catalogues raisonnés, like Smith. Or one frankly devotes oneself to a disagreeable and confused chatter."[1]

What, then, is left for the critic to do? Perhaps just this: to restore the lost relationship between the world and the trousers of literature, to patiently retie the threads that link these two universes, which otherwise are condemned to exist in parallel without ever meeting each other. Literary theory has long renounced history by pretending that it is necessary to choose between the two, which it holds to be mutually exclusive—indeed Roland Barthes wrote an essay on this question titled

"History or Literature"[2]—and that to do literary history amounts to renouncing the text, which is to say literature itself. The author as exception and the text as unattainable infinite have been declared consubstantial with the very definition of literary activity. This in turn has led to their exclusion or expulsion—to use the language of the church, their definitive excommunication—from history, which stands accused of being incapable of rising high enough in the heaven of the pure forms of literary art.

The two universes—the "world" and "literature"—were thus declared incommensurable. Barthes spoke of two continents: "On the one hand the world, with its profusion of facts, political, social, economic, ideological; and on the other the work, apparently solitary, always ambiguous, since it lends itself to several meanings *at the same time* . . . From one continent to the other a few signals are exchanged, a few connivances underscored. But for the most part the study of each of these two continents proceeds in an autonomous fashion: the two geographies seldom coincide."[3]

The obstacle, usually thought to be insurmountable, to establishing a link between these two universes is the one mentioned by Barthes, namely, geography. But it is above all time. Theorists and historians of literature maintain that literary forms do not change with the same rhythm; they are subject to "another temporality," as Marc Fumaroli calls it, that is irreducible to the chronology of the ordinary world.[4] But in fact it appears possible to stand the question of what Antoine Compagnon has called "differential chronology" on its head,[5] and to describe instead the ways in which literary time comes into existence, which is to say a world that is structured according to its own laws, its specific geography and chronology. This world is quite separate from the ordinary world, but it is only *relatively* autonomous, only relatively independent of it—which is to say, by the same token, relatively *dependent* upon it. In a sense, Barthes's dream has been realized: "The dream, obviously, is that these two continents have complementary forms; that, distant [though they are from each other] on the map, they can nonetheless, through an ideal translation, be brought together, be interlocked with each other, rather as Wegener rejoined Africa and America."[6]

But how are we to conceive a history of everything that, in Beckett's words, "moves, swims, flies away, comes back, unmakes and remakes itself . . . [of] these shifting planes, these shimmering contours, these equilibria that the least disturbance disrupts, that break apart and come back together again if one looks long enough? How are we to speak . . . of this world without weight, without force, without shadow? . . . This is what literature is." Moreover, he goes on to ask, how are we to represent change—not only specific changes in literary forms, genres, and styles but also literary ruptures and revolutions? Above all, how are we to understand the most distinctive works *in time,* without either denying or diminishing their singularity, when art "is waiting to be gotten out of there"—to be rescued from time?[7]

Making Barthes's dream come true assumes an inversion of the ordinary view of literature and, through a sort of Husserlian *epochē,* a momentary suspension of the belief that attaches to it. To go against common sense by making literature a temporal object is not to reduce it to a series of worldly events, causing individual works to depend on ordinary historical chronology; to the contrary, it causes them to enter into a dual temporality. Writing the history of literature is a paradoxical activity that consists in placing it in historical time and then showing how literature gradually tears itself away from this temporality, creating in turn its own temporality, one that has gone unperceived until the present day. It is true that there is a temporal imbalance between the world and literature, but it is literary time that allows literature to free itself from political time. In other words, the elaboration of a properly literary temporality is the condition of being able to create a literary history of literature (by contrast with—and by reference to—what Lucien Febvre called the "historical history of literature").[8] Hence the necessity of reestablishing the original historical bond between literature and the world—a bond that, as we have seen, is primarily political and national in nature—in order to show how literature subsequently managed, through a gradual acquisition of autonomy, to escape the ordinary laws of history. By the same token, literature may be defined—without contradiction—both as an object that is irreducible to history and as a historical object, albeit one that enjoys a strictly literary historicity. What I have called the genesis of literary space is this very process by which literary freedom is invented, slowly, painfully, and with great difficulty, through endless struggles and rivalries, and against all the extrinsic limitations—political, national, linguistic, commercial, diplomatic—that are imposed upon it.

To account fully for this invisible and secret measure of time, it is therefore necessary to show how the emergence of literary time led to the creation of a literary space endowed with its own laws. This space may be said to be "inter-national" in the sense that it has been constructed and unified by means of struggles and rivalries among national spaces—to the point that today it covers the entire world. The structure of world space, what Barthes called "geography," is itself a function of time: each national literary space (and therefore each writer) is situated not spatially but temporally. There is a time specific to literature, measured with reference to what I have called the literary Greenwich meridian, in terms of which it becomes possible to draw an aesthetic map of the world, the position of each national space being determined by its temporal distance from the center.

The simple pattern of inequality that structures this space has the immediate consequence of rendering obsolete the most common representations of the writer as a pure being, standing outside history and without ties to the world: everything that is divine, Barthes used to say, is light. If it is true that this literary world has been constituted as a sort of parallel reality, then every writer is ineluctably situated in this space: "And not only does everyone have this feeling that we occupy a place in Time," Proust wrote at the end of À la recherche du temps perdu (In Search of Lost Time, 1913–1927), "but this 'place' is something that the simplest among us habitually measures in an approximate fashion, as he might measure with his eye the place which we occupy in space."[9] Indeed, the writer is twice situated in literary space-time: once according to the position of the national literary space from which he comes, and once according to the place that he occupies within this national space.

In other words, in proposing to describe the world republic of letters, which is to say the genesis and structure of international literary space, I have tried not only to lay the foundations for a true literary history, but also to give the principles of a new method for interpreting literary texts. Whence the enormous difficulty of the enterprise: by its very nature it requires the critic to continually shift perspective, to change lenses, as it were—one moment looking to clarify a view of the whole by what might seem to be an insignificant detail, the next to explicating the most particular aspect of a work by taking a detour through what might appear to be observations of the most general sort. In this problem I thought I recognized the one evoked by Proust when he recalled in the final volume of À la Recherche the misunderstandings encountered during his first attempts to convey the purpose of his work as a whole:

Before long I was able to show a few sketches. No one understood anything of them. Even those who commended my perception of the truths which I wanted eventually to engrave within the temple, congratulated me on having discovered them "with a microscope," when on the contrary it was a telescope that I had used to observe things which were indeed very small to the naked eye, but only because they were situated at a great distance, and which were each one of them in itself a world. Those passages in which I was trying to arrive at general laws were described as so much pedantic investigation of detail.[10]

This constant passing back and forth between that which is nearest and that which is farthest away, between the microscopic and the macroscopic, between the individual writer and the vast literary world, demands a new hermeneutic logic, at once specific—since it seeks to account for a text in its very singularity and literariness—and historical. To read a text in a way that is inseparably literary and historical, then, is to restore it to its own distinctive time; to situate it in its own world, with reference only to the literary Greenwich meridian.

But time, the sole source of literary value (converted into antiquity, into credit, resources, and literariness), is also the source of the inequality of the literary world. A genuinely literary history of literature can be written only by taking into account the unequal status of the players in the literary game and the specific mechanisms of domination that are manifested in it. The oldest literary spaces are also the most endowed, which is to say that they exert an uncontested dominion over the whole of the literary world. The idea of a pure literature, freed from history, is a historical invention that, on account of the distance that separates the oldest spaces from the ones that have most recently entered the literary world, has been universally imposed throughout the world of letters.

The denial of history and, above all, the denial of the unequal structure of literary space prevent an understanding—and an acceptance—of national, political, and popular categories as constitutive of less endowed literary spaces, thereby making it impossible to grasp the purpose of many enterprises from the suburbs of literary space, even (as in the case of Kafka) to recognize them as such. "Pure" criticism, in the fullness of its ignorance, projects its own aesthetic categories upon texts whose history is much more complex than it is willing to acknowledge. At the pole of pure literature, national and political categories are not only ignored; they are excluded from the very definition of literature. In other words, in those lands where the most ancient resources have permitted literature to emancipate itself (or nearly so) from all forms of external dependence, a remorseless ethnocentrism causes the formidable hierarchical structure of the literary world—the de facto inequality of its participants—to be rejected. Political dependence, internal translations, national and linguistic concerns, the necessity of constituting a patrimony in order to enter into literary time—all these things that constrain the purpose and the form of literary works from the margins of the republic of letters are at once denied and disregarded by those who lay down its laws in the center. This is why eccentric works are either dismissed out of hand as nonliterary, which is to say inconsistent with the pure criteria of pure literature, or, less often, consecrated at the price of immense misunderstandings that are elevated to the status of principles of literary recognition. Thus the denial of hierarchical structure, of rivalry, of the inequality of literary spaces transforms the haughty regard of ethnocentric ignorance into either universalizing consecration or wholesale excommunication.

The example of Kafka shows that for the most part this ethnocentrism takes the form of anachronism. Since his fame was entirely posthumous, these anachronisms had to do with the distance that separated the literary (and political and intellectual) space in which he produced his texts from the corresponding space in which his work was received. With Kafka's entrance into the international literary world that anointed him after 1945 as one of the founders of literary modernity, the criteria that were then current at the literary Greenwich meridian—the criteria of the literary present, reactualized by each generation in appropriating texts for its own use: autonomy, formalism, polysemy, modernity, and so on—were applied to his work. Kafka thereby lost all of his national and cultural characteristics, now obscured by the process of universalization. By historicizing his position and purpose, however, it becomes possible to show that he was in fact a writer from a dominated country, that he believed himself to be one, and that he lived as though he was one. Given this much, it may reasonably be concluded on the basis of the model that has been developed in these pages that his writing was devoted to the ceaseless investigation of a problematic identity. He took part in the constitution of a national literature, seeking to contribute through his writing to the emancipation of his people and to hasten its accession to nationality. No matter that Kafka was a writer from a small country, he was completely opposed to literary formalism; and it was with full knowledge and awareness of his predicament that he embarked upon the collective and communitarian path. Yet the existence of literary hierarchies imposed by the critical ethnocentrism of the great literary nations prevented this type of literary enterprise from being recognized as worthy of the highest conception of literature.

Only the international and historical model that has been proposed here, and quite particularly an appreciation of the historical link established since the sixteenth century between literature and the nation, can give the literary projects of writers on the periphery their justification and their aesthetic and political coherence. By drawing up a map of the literary world and highlighting the gap between great and small literary nations, one may hope to be delivered at last from the prejudices inculcated by literary critics in the center. By accepting that Kafka, for example, possessed the traits proper and common to writers from emerging and dominated nations, it becomes possible to free oneself from the inherent blindnesses of the consecrating authorities. The same mechanism by which political and historical specificity is denied can be seen at work in authors as various as Ibsen, Yacine, Joyce, Beckett, and Benet: though they traveled very different paths, each of them owed his universal recognition to a huge misunderstanding of what he was trying to do. Each of their careers poses, in an exemplary way, the question of how literary universality is manufactured.[11]

I do not mean, of course, to contest Kafka's universal consecration. His extraordinary investigations, combined with his untenable position, no doubt obliged him to invent a literature that, through the subversion of the ordinary codes of literary representation and, above all, the questioning of Jewish identity as a social destiny, raised a universal kind of questioning to its point of highest intensity. But the deliberate dehistoricization practiced by critics in the center favored a univeralization that rests on an equally deliberate and obvious ignorance. This is why the application of a new method for interpreting literary texts, founded on a fresh conception of literary history, is an indispensable tool in the constitution of a new literary universality. For it is only on the condition of understanding the extreme particularism of a literary project that one can go on to state the true principle of its universal appeal.

My hope is that the present work may become a sort of critical weapon in the service of all deprived and dominated writers on the periphery of the literary world. I hope that my reading of the texts of du Bellay, Kafka, Joyce, and Faulkner may serve as an instrument for struggling against the presumptions, the arrogance, and the fiats of critics in the center, who ignore the basic fact of the inequality of access to literary existence. There is a kind of universality that escapes the centers: the universal domination of writers that, though historically it has taken different forms, has nonetheless managed to produce the same effects everywhere in the world over the last four hundred years. The incredible constancy—I myself was amazed to discover it—of the literary struggles, proclamations, and manifestos that lead from du Bellay to Kateb Yacine, via Yeats, Kiš and Beckett, ought in the future to encourage "latecomers" to the world of letters to claim as their ancestors some of the most prestigious writers in literary history and, above all, to find in the work of these writers the justification for their own work, with regard not only to the forms they adopt but also to the language they use and the political and national perspectives they express.

It would not be an exaggeration to say that ever since 1549, the date of the first printed edition of *The Defense and Illustration of the French Language,* the greatest revolutions have been fomented by eccentric writers. The revolutions brought about by authors such as Rubén Darío, Georg Brandes, Mário de Andrade, James Joyce, Franz Kafka, Samuel Beckett, and William Faulkner helped to profoundly alter current literary practices and to change the very measure of time and literary modernity. Because this book has been composed for—and even through—its readers, I hope I may be forgiven for quoting Proust once more in closing, using the same words that he used at the end of *In Search of Lost Time:*

> I thought [more modestly] of my book and it would be inaccurate even to say that I thought of those who would read it as "my" readers. For it seemed to me that they would not be "my" readers but the readers of their own selves, my book being merely a sort of magnifying glass like those that the optician at Combray used to offer his customers—it would be my book, but with its help I would furnish them with the means of reading what lay inside themselves. So that I should not ask them to praise me or to censure me, but simply to tell me whether "it is really like that," I should ask them whether the words that they read within themselves are the same as those which I have written.[12]

Notes

Introduction

1. Henry James, *The Figure in the Carpet and Other Stories,* ed. Frank Kermode (New York: Penguin, 1986), 368.
2. Ibid., 364, 368, 366–367, 368.
3. Ibid., 366, 374, 381, 367.
4. Ferdinand Braudel, *Civilization and Capitalism: 15th–18th Century,* vol. 3: *The Perspective of the World,* trans. Siân Reynolds (Berkeley: University of California Press, 1992), 19.
5. Ibid., 18–19, 17.
6. Valery Larbaud, "Paris de France," in *Jaune, bleu, blanc* (Paris: Gallimard, 1927), 15.
7. Valery Larbaud, "Vers l'Internationale," in *Sous l'invocation de saint Jérôme* (Paris: Gallimard, 1946), 147. This article is devoted to the *Précis d'histoire littéraire de l'Europe depuis la Renaissance* (1925), by Larbaud's friend the celebrated comparativist Paul Van Tieghem, who was one of the first in France to lay the basis for an international literary history.
8. Larbaud, *Sous l'invocation de saint Jérôme,* 151.
9. James, *The Figure in the Carpet,* 385.

1. Principles of a World History of Literature

1. Valery Larbaud, *Ce vice impuni, la lecture: Domaine anglais* (Paris: Gallimard, 1925), 33–34. A revised and substantially enlarged version of the book, edited by Béatrice Mousli, was published by Gallimard in 1988.
2. Ferdinand Braudel, *Civilization and Capitalism: 15th–18th Century,* vol. 3: *The*

Perspective of the World, trans. Siân Reynolds (Berkeley: University of California Press, 1992), 68.

3. The phrase *instances de consécration* is due originally to Pierre Bourdieu, whose many translators have tended to render the first term of the phrase either by the same word in English or, with somewhat greater justification, as "agencies." I have preferred "authorities," a more natural and surely no less precise translation. It should be plain in any case that the phrase refers to the class of critics, translators, publishers, academies, and other institutions that jointly are responsible for conferring literary prestige and reputation.—Trans.

4. See Braudel, *The Perspective of the World,* especially the chapter "Divisions of Space and Time in Europe," 21–88.

5. Paul Valéry, "La liberté de l'esprit," in *Regards sur le monde actuel,* in *Oeuvres,* ed. Jean Hytier, 2 vols. (Paris: Gallimard, 1957–1960), 2:1081; emphasis added.

6. Ibid., 1081, 1082, 1090.

7. Johann Wolfgang von Goethe, letter to Carlyle (1827), quoted in Antoine Berman, *L'épreuve de l'étranger: Culture et traduction dans l'Allemagne romantique* (Paris: Gallimard, 1984), 92–93.

8. Ibid., 90.

9. Fritz Strich, *Goethe und die Weltliteratur* (Bern: Franke Verlag, 1946), 17–18; Goethe quoted in ibid., 18.

10. Valéry, "La liberté de l'esprit," 1090.

11. It goes without saying that, in order to clarify the use made by Valéry of the notion of cultural (or literary) capital, I rely on the notion of "symbolic capital" developed by Pierre Bourdieu, notably in "Le marché des biens symboliques," *L'Année sociologique* 22 (1971): 49–126; and Randal Johnson, ed., *The Field of Cultural Production* (New York: Columbia University Press, 1993); and that of "literary capital" proposed by Bourdieu in *Les règles de l'art* (Paris: Seuil, 1992).

12. Valéry, "La liberté de l'esprit," 1090.

13. In 1973, for every 100,000 inhabitants, 52.2 titles were published in France as against 39.7 in the United States. Analysis of eighty-one countries reveals between 9 and 100 titles published per 100,000 inhabitants; more than half of this number (fifty-one countries) published fewer than 20 titles per 100,000 inhabitants. See Priscilla Parkhurst Clark, *Literary France: The Making of a Culture* (Berkeley: University of California Press, 1987), 217. Each of these indicators has been studied comparatively in several European countries and the United States. In each case France turns out to be by far the most "literary" country, which is to say the one having the largest volume of literary capital.

14. Paul Valéry, "Pensée et art français," in *Regards sur le monde actuel,* 1050.

15. Antonio Candido, *On Literature and Society,* trans. Howard S. Becker (Princeton: Princeton University Press, 1995).

16. Ezra Pound, *ABC of Reading* (New York: New Directions, 1960), 25.

17. The word "credit"—from the Latin *credere,* to believe—is synonymous with power, consideration, authority, importance.

18. Paul Valéry, "Fonction et mystère de l'Académie," in *Regards sur le monde actuel,* 1120.

19. It will, of course, be understood that writers from outlying spaces are impoverished *(démunis)* not in any material or psychological sense, though their standard of living may well be lower than that of writers nearer the center, but in the specific sense plainly defined in the preceding pages—namely, that they are deprived, or destitute, of literary capital.—Trans.

20. I use the term *littérarité* in a sense very close to that of Roman Jakobson, for whom literariness is that by virtue of which a language or a text is literary, or may be said to be literary: "The subject of literary science is not literature, but 'literariness' [*literaturnost*], i.e., that which makes a given work a literary work"; see *Noveishaia russkaia poeziia* (Prague: Tipografiia "Politika," 1921), 11, quoted by B. M. Eikhenbaum, "La Théorie de la 'méthode formelle,'" in *Théorie de la littérature: Textes des Formalistes russes,* ed. Tzvetan Todorov (Paris: Seuil, 1965), 37. Eikhenbaum adds: "We posited, and continue to posit, as a fundamental principle that the object of literary science must be the study of the specific particularities of literary objects that distinguish them from all other material . . . R. Jakobson gave this idea its definitive formulation."

21. See Abram de Swaan, "The Emergent World Language System," *International Political Science Review* 14 (July 1993).

22. Antoine de Rivarol was declared the winner of the competition sponsored three years later, in 1783, by the Academy of Berlin for his *Discours sur l'universalité de la langue française,* in recognition of which Frederick II awarded him a seat in the Academy.

23. Frederick II of Prussia, *De la littérature allemande* (Paris: Gallimard, 1994), 47.

24. Quoted in Max Daireaux, *Panorama de la littérature hispano-américaine* (Paris: Kra, 1930), 96.

25. Khlebnikov's aesthetic program was constructed both in conscious opposition to the "West" and its culture and as a means of affirming the existence of an inalienable Slavic spirit.

26. Velimir Khlebnikov, "Artists of the World!: A Written Language for Planet Earth; a Common System of Hieroglyphs for the People of our Planet," in *Collected Works of Velimir Khlebnikov,* ed. Charlotte Douglas, trans. Paul Schmidt, 3 vols. (Cambridge, Mass.: Harvard University Press, 1987–1997), 1:364.

27. Swaan, "The Emergent World Language System," 219.

28. Ibid., 222.

29. See Valérie Gannes and Marc Minon, "Géographie de la traduction," in *Traduire l'Europe,* ed. Françoise Barret-Ducrocq (Paris: Payot, 1992), 55–95. The authors distinguish "in-translation" *(intraduction),* the importation of foreign literary texts into a national language by means of translation, from "out-translation" *(extraduction),* the exportation of national literary texts.

30. Larbaud, *Ce vice impuni, la lecture,* 11.

31. Ibid., 22–23.

32. Valéry, "La liberté de l'esprit," 1091; emphasis added. "Judges" is also the term that Cocteau uses to refer—angrily—to theater critics.

33. Valery Larbaud, *Sous l'invocation de saint Jérôme* (Paris: Gallimard, 1946), 76–77.

34. Charles Ferdinand Ramuz, *Paris: Notes d'un Vaudois* (Lausanne: Éditions de l'Aire, 1978), 65.

35. See Paul Valéry, "Fonction de Paris," in *Regards sur le monde actuel,* 1007–10.

36. Louis Ulbach, ed., *Paris guide, par les principaux écrivains et artistes de la France* (Paris: A. Lacroix, 1867), xviii–xix. This work, which appeared shortly after the opening of the second Universal Exposition of Paris, was the result of collaboration by 125 men and women of letters.

37. Georg K. Glaser, *Secret et violence,* trans. Lucienne Foucrault (Paris: Correa, 1951), 157.

38. Walter Benjamin, "Ancient Paris, Catacombs, Demolitions, Decline of Paris," in *The Arcades Project,* trans. Howard Eiland and Kevin McLaughlin (Cambridge, Mass.: Belknap Press of Harvard University Press, 1999), 83. This work, unfinished at the time of Benjamin's death in 1940, first appeared in 1983 in a two-volume edition prepared by Rolf Tiedemann.

39. On this "accursed pair" see Benjamin's 6 January 1938 letter to Max Horkheimer in *The Correspondence of Walter Benjamin, 1910–1940,* ed. Gershom Scholem and Theodor Adorno, trans. Manfred R. Jacobson and Evelyn M. Jacobson (Chicago: University of Chicago Press, 1994), 549.

40. Roger Caillois, "Puissance du roman. Un example: Balzac," in *Approches de l'imaginaire* (Paris: Gallimard, 1974), 234.

41. Daniel Oster, "Paris-guide: D'Edmond Texier à Charles Virmaître," in *Écrire Paris* (Paris: Éditions Seesam-Fondation Singer-Polignac, 1990), 116. Thus Balzac styled it a "monstrous marvel," "head of the world," and "shimmering queen of cities." See Caillois, "Puissance du roman," 237.

42. See Daniel Oster and Jean-Marie Goulemot, *La vie parisienne: Anthologie des moeurs au XIXe siècle* (Paris: Sand-Conti, 1989), 19–21.

43. Quoted in Oster, "Paris-guide: D'Edmond Texier à Charles Virmaître," 108.

44. As Savinio put it, in both ironic and deferential terms: "No, the Greek gods have not degenerated . . . It is here [to Paris] . . . that sacred Delphi has

transported its mysteries, its soothing operations against the wrath of the mountain gods, and the famous *omphalos* thanks to which it had justly deserved the name navel of the world"; *Souvenirs,* trans. Jean-Marie Laclavetine (Paris: Fayard, 1986), 200–201.

45. Ernst Robert Curtius, *The Civilization of France,* trans. Olive Wyon (New York: Vintage, 1962), 184.

46. See Oster and Goulemot, *La vie parisienne,* 24.

47. Maxime Du Camp, *Paris, ses organes, ses fonctions et sa vie dans la seconde moitié du XIXe siècle* (1869), quoted in ibid., 25.

48. On this subject see also Giovanni Macchia, *Paris en ruines,* trans. Paul Bédarida (Paris: Flammarion, 1988), particularly the third part ("Les ruines de Paris"), 360–412: "Having become an ancient city like Rome, Athens, Memphis, and Babylon, Paris seemed obliged in turn to give evidence of its own grandeur through the spectacle of its destruction" (363).

49. Caillois, "La ville fabuleuse," in *Approches de l'imaginaire,* 234.

50. Endre Ady, Hungarian poet (1877–1919) and one of the leaders of the literary movement associated with the review *Nyugat,* spent several years in Paris, where he became acquainted with the work of the French symbolist poets. As the French correspondent for several Hungarian newspapers, he chronicled the Paris of the Belle Époque and went on to become one of the great modernizers of Hungarian thought and poetry. Kiš, having translated his poems, spent many years looking for a publisher.

51. Danilo Kiš, "Excursion à Paris," trans. Pascale Delpech, *Nouvelle revue française,* no. 525 (October 1996): 88–115.

52. Ibid.

53. Octavio Paz, *In Light of India,* trans. Eliot Weinberger (New York: Harcourt, Brace, 1995), 3.

54. Juan Benet, *Otoño en Madrid hacia 1950* (Madrid: Alianza Editorial, 1987), 81. [Here, as in the case of quotation from other foreign works cited in their original editions, usually because published English versions do not exist, I have made my own translations.—Trans.]

55. Henri Michaux, "Lieux lointains," *Mercure de France,* no. 1109 (1 January 1956) (special issue in memory of Adrienne Monnier): 52.

56. Quoted by Alexandra Parigoris, "Brancusi: En art il n'y a pas d'étrangers," in *Le Paris des étrangers: Depuis un siècle,* ed. André Kaspi and Antoine Marès (Paris: Imprimerie Nationale, 1989), 213.

57. Valery Larbaud, "Paris de France," in *Jaune, bleu, blanc* (Paris: Gallimard, 1927), 15.

58. On the foreign communities settled in Paris, see also Christophe Charle, *Les intellectuels en Europe au XIXe siècle: Essai d'histoire comparée* (Paris: Seuil, 1996), 110–113.

59. Arthur Koestler, *The Invisible Writing* (New York: Macmillan, 1954), 277.

60. See Christiane Séris, "Microcosme dans la capitale ou l'histoire de la colonie intellectuelle hispano-américaine à Paris entre 1890 et 1914," in Kaspi and Marès, *Le Paris des étrangers,* 299–312.

61. See Antoine Marès, "Tchèques et Slovaques à Paris: D'une résistance à l'autre," in ibid., 73–89.

62. Harold Rosenberg, *The Tradition of the New* (New York: Horizon, 1959), 212.

63. Quoted by Mario Carelli, "Les Brésiliens à Paris de la naissance du romanticisme aux avant-gardes," in Kaspi and Marès, *Le Paris des étrangers,* 290.

64. Quoted in Claude Cymerman and Claude Fell, *Histoire de la littérature hispano-américaine de 1940 à nos jours* (Paris: Nathan, 1997), 11.

65. Quoted by Anna Wessely, "The Status of Authors in Nineteenth-Century Hungary: The Influence of the French Model," in *Écrire en France au XIXe siècle,* ed. Graziella Pagliano and Antonio Gomez-Moriana (Longueuil, Quebec: La Préambule, 1989), 204. See also Béla Köpeczi and Istvan Söter, eds., *Eszmék és találkozások* (Budapest: Akedemiai Kiado, 1970), 162.

66. Letter to the Spanish painter Ignacio Zuloaga y Zabaleta (12 February 1923), quoted by Danièle Pistone, "Les musiciens étrangers à Paris au XXe siècle," in Kaspi and Marès, *Le Paris des étrangers,* 249.

67. See Philippe Dewitte, "Le Paris noir de l'entre-deux-guerres," in ibid., 157–181.

68. Rubén Darío, *Obras completas,* ed. M. Sanmiguel Raimundez, 5 vols. (Madrid: Aguado, 1950–1955), I:102.

69. Quoted in Haruhisa Kato, "L'image culturelle de la France au Japon," *Dialogues et cultures* 36 (1992): 39.

70. See Gabriela Mistral, *Poesías completas* (Madrid: Aguilar, 1958).

71. Walt Whitman, *Complete Poetry and Collected Prose,* ed. Justin Kaplan (New York: Viking, 1982), 519–520. The adjective "frivolous" captures the entire ambiguity of the image of Paris, capital of liberty but also of libertinism.

72. See Pierre Bourdieu, "Deux impérialismes de l'universel," in *L'Amérique des Français,* ed. Christine Fauré and Tom Bishop (Paris: François Bourin, 1992), 149–155.

73. The terms "nation" and "national" are used here for the sake of convenience, while taking care to guard against the risk of anachronism.

74. See particularly Daniel Baggioni, *Langues et nations en Europe* (Paris: Payot, 1997), 74–77. Baggioni distinguishes between "common" and "national" languages in order to avoid confusion and anachronism.

75. See Benedict Anderson, *Imagined Communities: Reflections on the Origin and Spread of Nationalism* (London: Verso, 1983).

76. Thus Jacques Revel has been able to show how languages were very gradually associated (through maps) with spaces delimited by "linguistic bound-

aries." See Daniel Nordman and Jacques Revel, "La formation de l'espace français," in *Histoire de la France,* ed. André Burguière and Jacques Revel, 4 vols. (Paris: Seuil, 1989–1993), 1:155–162.

77. The Italian poet Bembo, du Bellay and Ronsard in France, Thomas More in England, and Sebastian Brant in Germany all took part in the humanist movement, advocating a return to ancient literatures while defending their own "illustrious vulgar tongue" (in Dante's phrase).

78. See Charles Tilly, *European Revolutions, 1492–1992* (Oxford: Blackwell, 1993), 29–36.

79. See Michael Jeismann, *Das Vaterland der Feinde: Studien zum nationalen Feindbegriff und Selbstverständnis in Deutschland und Frankreich, 1792–1918* (Stuttgart: Klett-Cotta, 1992).

80. See Linda Colley, *Britons: Forging the Nation, 1707–1837* (New Haven: Yale University Press, 1992).

81. Danilo Kiš, *La leçon d'anatomie,* trans. Pascale Delpech (Paris: Fayard, 1993), 29–31. [Selected passages are available in English in Susan Sontag's edition of Kiš's *Homo Poeticus,* trans. Michael Heim et al. (New York: Farrar, Straus and Giroux, 1995).—Trans.]

82. In the Dreyfus Affair, Zola abruptly broke with everything that until than had linked the writer with the nation, national honor, and nationalist discourse, and, by betraying the nationalist right, proclaimed his own autonomy. He thereby put himself in a position, in the very name of his own autonomy and freedom, to proclaim Dreyfus' innocence. This amounted to inventing a totally new relation to politics: a sort of denationalized politicization of literature.

83. Isaiah Berlin, "The Bent Twig: On the Rise of Nationalism," in *The Crooked Timber of Humanity: Chapters in the History of Ideas,* ed. Henry Hardy (New York: Knopf, 1991), 246.

84. This neglect is due also to the primacy always accorded in literary criticism to the "psychology" of a writer.

85. Originally published in an edition of 500 copies, printed in Dijon in 1925 by Maurice Darantière for Contact Éditions of Paris.

86. Octavio Paz, *In Search of the Present: 1990 Nobel Lecture,* bilingual ed., trans. Anthony Stanton (San Diego: Harcourt Brace Jovanovich, 1990), 17.

2. The Invention of Literature

1. In France, from the second half of the seventeenth century onward, it was the state that ordered the exclusive use of the French language. See Michel de Certeau, Dominique Julia, and Jacques Revel, *Une politique de la langue: La Révolution française et les patois: L'enquête de Grégoire* (Paris: Gallimard, 1975).

2. See Samuel Beckett's article "Dante . . . Bruno. Vico . . . Joyce," in *Our Exagmination round His Factification for Incamination of Work in Progress* (Paris: Shakespeare & Co., 1929), a volume of essays conceived by Joyce in response to sharp criticism in Britain and the United States of *Finnegans Wake*, which was then appearing in fragments in various reviews under the generic title *Work in Progress*.

3. Benedict Anderson, *Imagined Communities: Reflections on the Origin and Spread of Nationalism* (London: Verso, 1983), 66. The sociolinguist Daniel Baggioni characterizes the same phenomenon as the first "ecolinguistic revolution in Western Europe"; see *Langues et nations en Europe* (Paris: Payot, 1997), 73–94.

4. Anderson, *Imagined Communities*, 80.

5. See Eric Hobsbawm and Terence Ranger, *The Invention of Tradition* (Cambridge: Cambridge University Press, 1983).

6. Marc Fumaroli, "The Genius of the French Language," in *Realms of Memory*, ed. Lawrence D. Kritzman, trans. Arthur Goldhammer, 3 vols. (New York: Columbia University Press, 1998), 3:558.

7. Humanism was also a return to two other languages of antiquity, Greek and Hebrew, on the basis of which one could correct "bad" medieval Latin and consider oneself closer to the ancients than the clerics were. Knowledge of Greek made it possible finally to read the Bible independently of the Vulgate.

8. The anachronism "intellectual" is used here to subsume under a single term the fields of literature and scholarship. See Fernand Braudel, *Le modèle italien* (Paris: Arthaud, 1989), 42–47.

9. Ibid., 45, 46.

10. See Françoise Waquet, *Le modèle français et l'Italie savante: Conscience de soi et perception de l'autre dans la République des Lettres, 1660–1750* (Rome: École Française de Rome, 1989).

11. Luther was not the first to translate the Bible. Others had translated it, wholly or in part, at the same time or a bit earlier in an attempt to reform the Church from within.

12. See Baggioni, *Langues et nations en Europe*, 109.

13. Fumaroli, "The Genius of the French Language," 560, 565.

14. See Robert-Henri Bautier, *Chartes, sceaux et chancelleries: Études de diplomatique et de sigillographie médiévales* (Geneva: Droz/Paris: Champion, 1990).

15. Joachim du Bellay, *The Defence and Illustration of the French Language*, trans. Gladys M. Turquet (London: J. M. Dent and Sons, 1939), 37. See Joseph Jurt, "Autonomie ou hétéronomie: Le champ littéraire en France et en Allemagne," *Regards Sociologiques*, no. 4 (1992): 12. The "second rhetoric" was a science of versification referred to by this name in fifteenth-century

treatises on the practice of poetry in the vulgar tongue. Accordingly, it stood in opposition to the Latin rhetoric taught in the schools and the conventional theory of discourse of the period.

16. See Reinhard Krüger, "Der Kampf der literarischen Moderne in Frankreich (1548–1554)," in *Nation und Literatur im Europa der frühen Neuzeit,* ed. Klaus Garber (Tübingen: Niemeyer, 1989), 344–381.

17. See Colette Beaune, *Naissance de la nation France* (Paris: Gallimard, 1985), 300 ff.

18. Fumaroli, "The Genius of the French Language," 563.

19. Du Bellay, *Defence and Illustration of French Language,* 54–56, 39, 40; emphasis added.

20. This metaphor was to be met with later in almost the same terms when the German romantics were putting their ideas about translation into effect; and also in the "cannibalistic" manifesto of the Brazilian modernists during the 1920s. See the essay by Pierre Rivas, "Modernisme et primitivisme dans *Macounaïma,*" in his critical edition of Mário de Andrade's *Macounaïma* (Paris: Stock-UNESCO, 1996). The ethnologist Roger Bastide has compared the Pléiade's enterprise with that of the Brazilian modernists in "*Macunaíma* visto por um francês," *Revista do Arquivo municipal* (São Paulo), no. 106 (January 1946).

21. Du Bellay, *Defence and Illustration of French Language,* 37; emphasis added.

22. Fumaroli, "The Genius of the French Language," 572.

23. François Lopez, "Le retard de l'Espagne: La fin du Siècle d'or," in *Histoire de la littérature espagnole,* ed. Jean Canavaggio, 2 vols. (Paris: Fayard, 1993–94), 2:14.

24. Fumaroli, "The Genius of the French Language," 568.

25. Baggioni distinguishes between "grammatization" and "grammaticalization," endorsing the definition of the former term given by Sylvain Auroux, namely, as a process that leads to describing and using a language on the basis of two techniques: a grammar and a dictionary; see *Langues et nations en Europe,* 93.

26. See ibid., 62–65.

27. See Jean-Pierre Chauveau, *Poésie française du XVIIe siècle* (Paris: Gallimard, 1987), 19; also Jacques Roubaud, *La vieillesse d'Alexandre: Essai sur quelques états du vers français* (Paris: Ramsay, 1988).

28. See Anthony Lodge, *French: From Dialect to Standard* (London: Routledge, 1993), 153–188.

29. Thomas Pavel, *L'art de l'éloignement: Essai sur l'imagination classique* (Paris: Gallimard, 1996), 152–155. See also Georges Snyders, *La pédagogie en France aux XVIIe et XVIIIe siècles* (Paris: Presses Universitaires de France, 1965), chap. 3 ("Le rôle de l'Antiquité: Le monde latin comme clôture"), 67–83.

30. Émile Durkheim, *L'évolution pédagogique en France* (Paris: Press Universitaires de France, 1990), 287, 306–307.

31. Quoted in Fumaroli, "The Genius of the French Language," 600.

32. The pejorative sense of the term *pédant* was beginning to develop in just this context in the mid-seventeenth century; until then the word retained its originally favorable sense (from the Italian *pedante,* meaning one who instructs children). See Gaston Cayrou, *Dictionnaire du français classique,* 2d ed. (1924; reprint, Paris: Klincksieck, 2000), 576.—Trans.

33. Quoted in Fumaroli, "The Genius of the French Language," 600.

34. Ibid., 583.

35. Honorat de Bueil, Marquis de Racan, *Vie de monsieur de Malherbe* (Paris: Gallimard, 1991), 42–43; quoted in Fumaroli, "The Genius of the French Language," 584.

36. "Crocheteurs du Port-au-Foin," or naive authorities on the actual spoken language of Île-de-France: "When [Malherbe] was asked his opinion about some French word, he usually referred to the hay-pitchers at Port-au-Foin, and said that these were his masters for language"; see Racan, *Vie de monsieur de Malherbe,* 41.

37. Lodge, *French,* 174.

38. Claude Favre de Vaugelas, *Remarques sur la langue françoise, utiles à ceux qui veulent bien parler et bien écrire,* ed. Jean-Claude Streicher (Geneva: Slatkine, 1970), 3.

39. Fumaroli, "The Genius of the French Language," 585.

40. Lodge, *French,* 172.

41. Walther von Wartburg, *Évolution et structure de la langue française* (Bern: Franke, 1962).

42. See Pierre Bourdieu, *Ce que parler veut dire* (Paris: Fayard, 1982), 47–49; also Alain Viala, *Naissance de l'écrivain* (Paris: Éditions de Minuit, 1985), 270 ff.

43. See René Bray, *La formation de la doctrine classique en France* (Paris: Nizet, 1951).

44. Ferdinand Brunot, *Histoire de la langue française,* 13 vols. (Paris: Colin, 1966), 3:4.

45. See Lodge, *French,* 159.

46. René Descartes, *Oeuvres de Descartes,* ed. Charles Adam and Paul Tannery, 2d ed., 11 vols. (Paris: Vrin, 1974–1989), 6:77. Descartes' decision to write in French is an overlooked aspect of his opposition to the scholastics.

47. Baggioni, *Langues et nations en Europe,* 187. Baggioni interprets "the process of standardization of common languages during the sixteenth, seventeenth, and eighteenth centuries" as the result of a combination of "epilinguistic resources," including guides to proper spelling, grammars, and dictionaries, with "an instrumentalization of the language through theory (manuals of

logic, rhetoric, poetics) and practice (reference works and a prestigious literary corpus)" and "institutions and instruments of linguistic dissemination and control (schools, academies, and so on)"; ibid., 125.

48. Lodge, *French,* 173; the reference is to Brunot, *Histoire de la langue française,* 3:17.

49. Vincent Voiture, *Oeuvres de Voiture: Lettres et poésies,* ed. A. Ubicini, 2 vols. (Geneva: Slatkine, 1967), 1:294–295.

50. Fumaroli, "The Genius of the French Language," 599. See Georges Doncieux, *Un jésuite homme de lettres au XVIIe siècle: Le père Bouhours* (Paris: Hachette, 1886).

51. Quoted in Fumaroli, "The Genius of the French Language," 595.

52. See Bernard Magné, *La crise de la littérature française sous Louis XIV: Humanisme et rationalisme,* 2 vols. (Lille: Atelier Reproduction des Thèses, Université Lille-III/Paris: H. Champion, 1976).

53. For a critical look at the traditional view of this quarrel, see Jean-Marie Goulemot, *Le règne de l'histoire: Discours historiques et révolutions, XVIIe–XVIIe siècles* (Paris: Albin Michel, 1996), 164–172.

54. See Joseph Jurt, "Sprache, Literatur, Nation, Kosmopolitismus, Internationalismus: Historische Bedingungen des deutsch-französischen Kulturaustauches," in *Le Français aujourd'hui: Une langue à comprendre,* ed. Gilles Dorion, Franz-Joseph Meissner, Janos Riesz, and Ulf Wielandt (Frankfurt: Diesterweg, 1992), 230–241.

55. Quoted in Fumaroli, "The Genius of the French Language," 602–603.

56. Ibid., 604. See also Norbert Elias, *The Civilizing Process,* trans. Edmund Jephcott (New York: Urizen, 1978).

57. Still today a whole part of the literary historiography of French classicism is the direct heir, or possibly the victim, of this partial and biased view; see, for example, Goulemot, *Le règne de l'histoire,* 164.

58. Voltaire, *Le siècle de Louis XIV,* 3 vols. (Frankfurt: Vve. Knoch and J. G. Eslinger, 1753), 3:81.

59. It is well known, of course, that Frederick the Great maintained a correspondence with Voltaire before ascending the throne and that Voltaire resided at his court in Berlin between 1750 and 1753. It was precisely during this period that the French writer composed and published *Le siècle de Louis XIV.*

60. Frederick II of Prussia, *De la littérature allemande* (Paris: Gallimard, 1994), 81–82.

61. Antoine de Rivarol, *De l'universalité de la langue française* (Paris: Obsidiane, 1991), 9.

62. Ibid., 34; quoted in Fumaroli, "The Genius of the French Language," 605–606.

63. Rivarol, *De l'universalité de la langue française,* 39.

64. Ibid., 20, 37.

65. Louis Réau, *L'Europe française au siècle des Lumières* (Paris: Albin Michel, 1971), 291.

66. Baggioni, *Langues et nations en Europe,* 153.

67. Ibid., 154.

68. See Stefan Collini, *Public Moralists: Political Thought and Intellectual Life in Britain, 1850–1930* (Oxford: Clarendon Press, 1991), 347.

69. See Linda Colley's treatment of this subject in *Britons: Forging the Nation, 1707–1837* (New Haven: Yale University Press, 1992).

70. Thus the argument of Collini in *Public Moralists.*

71. Ibid., 357.

72. Ibid., 351–358.

73. Hagen Schulze notes the immense cultural consequences of the national passion in nineteenth-century Germany for the Middle Ages, particularly the enthusiasm for the neo-Gothic style in architecture, which the Germans were convinced was "the only properly German style to which it was necessary to 'return'"; see *État et nation dans l'histoire de l'Europe,* trans. Denis-Armand Canal (Paris: Seuil, 1996), 198–199.

74. Jurt, "Autonomie ou hétéronomie," 12.

75. See Pierre Pénisson, *Johann Gottfried Herder: La raison dans les peuples* (Paris: Éditions du Cerf, 1992), 200, 201.

76. See George Bancroft, "The Life and Genius of Goethe," *North American Review* 19 (1824): 303–325. Note that the use of the expression "The literature of a nation is national" shows that it was not yet considered a tautology, but instead was quite a novel idea.

77. Quoted by Frank E. Manuel in his abridged edition of Herder's *Ideen: Reflections on the Philosophy of the History of Mankind* (Chicago: University of Chicago Press, 1968), 98. See also Kurt Mueller-Vollmer, "Herder and the Formation of an American National Consciousness during the Early Republic," in *Herder Today: Contributions from the International Herder Conference, November 5–8, 1987, Stanford, California,* ed. Mueller-Vollmer (Berlin: Walter de Gruyter, 1990), 415–430; and Pénisson, *Johann Gottfried Herder,* 204–205.

78. See Eric Hobsbawm, *Nations and Nationalism since 1780* (New York: Cambridge University Press, 1990), 54; also Anderson, *Imagined Communities,* 82–85; and William M. Johnston, *The Austrian Mind: An Intellectual and Social History, 1848–1938* (Berkeley: University of California Press, 1972), 265–273 and 344–356.

79. As Benedict Anderson notes, "vernacularizing lexicographers, grammarians, philologists, and litterateurs . . . were central to the shaping of nineteenth-century European nationalisms"; *Imagined Communities,* 69.

80. Baggioni, *Langues et nations en Europe,* 298.

3. World Literary Space

1. Ferdinand Braudel, *Civilization and Capitalism: 15th–18th Century,* vol. 3: *The Perspective of the World,* trans. Siân Reynolds (Berkeley: University of California Press, 1992), 3:47–50.
2. Benedict Anderson, *Imagined Communities: Reflections on the Origin and Spread of Nationalism* (London: Verso, 1983), 50.
3. See Marc Ferro, *Histoire des colonisations: Des conquêtes aux indépendances, XIIIe–XXe siècles* (Paris: Seuil, 1994), especially chap. 7.
4. See Anderson, *Imagined Communities,* 50–65.
5. Arturo Uslar Pietri, *Insurgés et visionnaires d'Amérique latine,* trans. Philippe Dessommes Florez (Paris: Criterion, 1995), 7–8.
6. Octavio Paz, *In Search of the Present: 1990 Nobel Lecture,* bilingual ed., trans. Anthony Stanton (San Diego: Harcourt Brace Jovanovich, 1990), 5 [translation slightly modified].
7. See the chapter titled "La conquête de l'autonomie," in Pierre Bourdieu, *Les règles de l'art* (Paris: Seuil, 1992), 75–164.
8. Evidence of this may be found particularly in the role played by writers in debates over spelling reforms. The defense of the national language by the most conservative authors, who regard it not only as the specific tool of their trade but also as an element of national property that it is their duty to protect, reveals their political dependence—this despite their claim to take part in these debates in the very name of literary specificity.
9. Valery Larbaud, *Sous l'invocation de saint Jérôme* (Paris: Gallimard, 1946), 150.
10. Pierre Bourdieu, *Homo academicus* (Paris: Éditions de Minuit, 1984), 226.
11. Gertrude Stein, *Paris, France* (New York: Charles Scribner's Sons, 1940), 11.
12. Louis Ulbach, ed., *Paris guide, par les principaux écrivains et artistes de la France* (Paris: A. Lacroix, 1867), xxix, xxx.
13. Stein, *Paris, France,* 8–12.
14. Frederick II of Prussia, *De la littérature allemande* (Paris: Gallimard, 1994), 28, 33, 49.
15. See Jean-Claude Marcadé, "Alexis Kroutchonykh et Vélimir Khlebnikov: Le mot comme tel," in *L'année 1913: Les formes esthétiques de l'oeuvre d'art à la veille de la Première Guerre,* ed. Liliane Brion-Guerry, 3 vols. (Paris: Klincksieck, 1971–1973), 3:359–361.
16. Octavio Paz, *The Labyrinth of Solitude,* trans. Lysander Kemp (New York: Grove, 1985), 194.
17. Danilo Kiš, "The Conscience of an Unknown Europe," in *Homo Poeticus,* ed. Susan Sontag, trans. Ralph Mannheim et al. (New York: Farrar, Straus and Giroux, 1995), 218.
18. Paul Valéry, "La liberté de l'esprit," in *Regards sur le monde actuel,* in *Oeuvres,* ed. Jean Hytier, 2 vols. (Paris: Gallimard, 1957–1960), 2:1083.
19. Paz, *The Labyrinth of Solitude,* 218.

20. Paz, *In Search of the Present,* 10, 14–16.

21. Ibid., 16.

22. Ibid., 16–17; emphasis added.

23. "It was precisely by contrast, by the vision of the old and the new, the two great worlds between which he shuttled, the American in Europe, the European in America, the polarities of the parochial and the cosmopolitan, that Henry [James] was to live"; Leon Edel, *Henry James,* 5 vols. (Philadelphia: J. P. Lippincott, 1953–1972), 2:193.

24. Mario Vargas Llosa, "The Mandarin," in *Making Waves,* ed. and trans. John King (London: Faber and Faber, 1996), 132.

25. Danilo Kiš, *Le résidu amer de l'expérience,* trans. Pascale Delpech (Paris: Fayard, 1995), 71.

26. Danilo Kiš, "Nous prêchons dans le désert," in *Homo poeticus,* trans. Pascale Delpech (Paris: Fayard, 1993), 11.

27. See Max Daireaux, *Panorama de la littérature hispano-américaine* (Paris: Kra, 1930), 95–106.

28. Rubén Darío, *Historia de mis libros,* in *Obras completas,* ed. Alberto Ghiraldo, 22 vols. (Madrid: Editorial Mundo Latino, 1917–1921), 17:170; emphasis added.

29. Quoted by Gérard de Cortanze in the introduction ("Rubén Darío ou le gallicisme mental") to his translation of Rubén Darío, *Azul* (Paris: La Différence, 1991), 15.

30. Jorge Luis Borges and Osvaldo Ferrari, "Diálogo sobre el Modernismo y Rubén Darío," in *Libro de diálogos* (Buenos Aires: Editorial Sudamericana, 1987), 118–119.

31. Quoted in Régis Boyer, *Histoire des littératures scandinaves* (Paris: Fayard, 1996), 152.

32. See ibid., esp. 135–195.

33. Brandes translated John Stuart Mill's *On the Subjection of Women* in 1869.

34. Thure Stenström, "Les relations culturelles franco-suédoises de 1870 à 1900," in *Une amitié millénaire: Les relations entre la France et la Suède à travers les âges,* ed. Marianne Battail and Jean-François Battail (Paris: Beauchesne, 1993), 295–296.

35. Hjalmar Söderberg (1869–1941), a novelist, playwright, and essayist, was no less famous in Scandinavian countries than his contemporary August Strindberg. He is remembered today chiefly for his play *Gertrud* (1906), which was adapted for the cinema by Carl Theodor Dreyer in 1964. His most important works are *Förvillelser* (Aberrations, 1895), *Martin Bircks ungdom* (The Youth of Martin Birck, 1901), and *Den allvarsamma leken* (The Serious Game, 1912).

36. Henrik Stangerup, interview with the author, September 1993.

37. Ibid.

38. Antonio Candido, *On Literature and Society,* trans. Howard S. Becker (Princeton: Princeton University Press, 1995), 126–127, 128–129.

39. Juan Benet, interview with the author, July 1991; Vargas Llosa, "The Mandarin," 132.

40. Vargas Llosa, interview with the author, July 1991.

41. See Joseph Jurt, "The Reception of Naturalism in Germany," in *Naturalism in the European Novel: New Critical Perspectives,* ed. Brian Nelson (New York: Berg, 1992), 99–119.

42. Joseph Jurt, "Sprache, Literatur, Nation, Kosmopolitismus, Internationalismus: Historische Bedingungen des deutsch-französischen Kulturaustauches," in *Le Français aujourd'hui: Une langue à comprendre,* ed. Gilles Dorion, Franz-Joseph Meissner, Janos Riesz, and Ulf Wielandt (Frankfurt: Diesterweg, 1992), 235.

43. See Michel Espagne and Michael Werner, eds., *Qu'est-ce qu'une littérature nationale? Approches pour une théorie interculturelle du champ littéraire: Philologues III* (Paris: Éditions de la Maison des Sciences de l'Homme, 1994).

44. Stefan Collini, *Public Moralists: Political Thought and Intellectual Life in Britain, 1850–1930* (Oxford: Clarendon Press, 1991), 357.

45. Ibid.

46. Pedro Salinas (1892–1951) was a member of the "generation of 1927." A cosmopolite and translator, influenced in the early part of his career by futurism, Salinas left Spain in 1939 and settled in the United States, where he died in Boston.

47. Benet, interview with the author, July 1991. I conducted two interviews with Juan Benet, one in October 1987 and the other in July 1991, hoping to understand the reasons for his sudden and improbable emergence on the Spanish literary scene and his place in it.

48. See Michel Espagne, *Le paradigme de l'étranger: Les chairs de littérature étrangère au XIXe siècle* (Paris: Cerf, 1993).

49. Christophe Charle has described the same dichotemy in nineteenth-century European intellectual life: "The different conceptions of the role of intellectuals in Europe can be reduced to an opposition between those intellectuals who crossed boundaries and those who guarded them"; see "Pour une histoire comparée des intellectuels en Europe," *Liber: Revue internationale des livres,* no. 26 (March 1996): 11.

50. Valery Larbaud, *Ce vice impuni, la lecture: Domaine anglais* (Paris: Gallimard, 1925), 407–408.

51. James Joyce, *A Portrait of the Artist as a Young Man* (New York: Viking, 1968), 247.

52. Benet, interview with the author, July 1991.

53. Thanks to his brother, who lived in Paris, Benet received French books by diplomatic pouch; see *Otoño en Madrid hacia 1950* (Madrid: Alianza Editorial, 1987), 18.

54. After the end of the civil war in 1939, despite its pro-German sympathies Spain stayed out of the world war that followed. France, in accordance with a resolution approved by the United Nations on 12 December 1946 condemning Franco's regime, sealed off its borders with Spain. Between 1945 and 1949 Spain had no ambassadorial representation abroad.

55. Benet, interview with the author, July 1991.

56. Ibid.

57. Ibid.

58. Danilo Kiš, "The Anatomy Lesson: Borges," in Sontag, ed., *Homo Poeticus*, 41.

59. Danilo Kiš, *La leçon d'anatomie,* trans. Pascale Delpech (Paris: Fayard, 1993), 115.

60. Ibid.

61. Ibid., 29.

62. Ibid., 53–54.

63. See Taha Hussein, *Le livre des jours,* with a preface by André Gide (Paris: Gallimard, 1947); Rabindranath Tagore, *L'offrande lyrique,* trans. André Gide (Paris: Gallimard, 1914); and Marguerite Yourcenar, *Mishima, ou la vision du vide* (Paris: Gallimard, 1981).

64. See especially Florence Harlow, *Resistance Literature* (New York: Methuen, 1987).

65. Salman Rushdie, "The New Empire within Britain," in *Imaginary Homelands: Essays and Criticism, 1981–1991* (London: Granta, 1991), 130.

66. Édouard Glissant, *Poetics of Relation,* trans. Betsy Wing (Ann Arbor: University of Michigan Press, 1997), 23, 19.

67. Salman Rushdie, *The Satanic Verses* (New York: Viking Penguin, 1989), 398–399.

68. See Valérie Gannes and Marc Minon, "Géographie de la traduction," in *Traduire l'Europe,* ed. Françoise Barret-Ducrocq (Paris: Payot, 1992).

69. Quoted in Pico Iyer, "L'empire contre-attaque, plume en main," *Gulliver, revue littérarire,* no. 11 (summer 1993): 41.

70. Salman Rushdie, "Commonwealth Literature Does Not Exist," in *Imaginary Homelands,* 66.

71. Margaret Atwood, interview with the author, November 1991.

72. On 18 June 1812 the United States declared war on England with a view to annexing Canada. The English moved to defend their North American territories against the threat of invasion and sought to recover lands lost in the west. The fighting ended in a restoration of the status quo ante, ratified by the Treaty of Ghent (1814).

73. Jane Urquhart, *The Whirlpool* (Boston: David R. Godine, 1990), 63, 72, 59.

74. See Mia Couto, *Terra sonâmbula* (Lisbon: Caminho, 1992).

75. Mia Couto, interview with the author, November 1994.

76. Raphaël Confiant, *Aimé Césaire: Une traversée paradoxale du siècle* (Paris: Stock, 1993), 88.

77. Tierno Monénembo, interview with the author, March 1993.

4. The Fabric of the Universal

1. Paul Valéry, "La liberté de l'esprit," in *Regards sur le monde actuel,* in *Oeuvres,* ed. Jean Hytier, 2 vols. (Paris: Gallimard, 1957–1960), 2: 1081. The full text of this quotation is given above, Chapter 1, near note 5.

2. Samuel Beckett, *Le monde et le pantalon* (Paris: Éditions de Minuit, 1989), 21. The essay originally appeared in *Cahiers d'art,* vols. 20–21 (1945–1946): 349–356.

3. Valery Larbaud, *Ce vice impuni, la lecture: Domaine anglais* (Paris: Gallimard, 1925), 215.

4. See Paul de Man, "A Modern Master: Jorge Luis Borges," in *Critical Writings, 1953–1978* (Minneapolis: University of Minnesota Press, 1989), 123.

5. Larbaud, *Ce vice impuni, la lecture,* 233.

6. Danilo Kiš, *Le résidu amer de l'expérience,* trans. Pascale Delpech (Paris: Fayard, 1995), 105.

7. Anna Boschetti has shown that in the person of Sartre were concentrated every available form of capital—philosophical, literary, critical, political—held by Paris; see *Sartre et Les Temps modernes: Une entreprise intellectuelle* (Paris: Éditions de Minuit, 1985).

8. Vargas Llosa, "The Mandarin," in *Making Waves,* ed. and trans. John King (London: Faber and Faber, 1996), 140–141.

9. Ibid., 131–132.

10. Maurice-Edgar Coindreau, "William Faulkner," *Nouvelle revue française,* no. 19 (June 1931): 926–930.

11. See Michel Gresset's preface to *Le bruit et la fureur* in the Pléiade edition of Faulkner's novels, *Oeuvres romanesques* (Paris: Gallimard, 1977), 1253.

12. Sartre's review appeared in the July 1939 edition of the *Nouvelle revue française* and was reprinted in *Situations I* (Paris: Gallimard, 1947), 65–75.

13. Christophe Charle argues that, at least in the first half of the nineteenth century, "London and Brussels were the two other alternative liberal capitals, places of refuge for exiles judged to be dangerous and expelled by the French government"; see *Les intellectuels en Europe au XIXe siècle: Essai d'histoire comparée* (Paris: Seuil, 1996), 112.

14. See Bertrand Marchal's edition of Stéphane Mallarmé, *Oeuvres complètes,* 2 vols. to date (Paris: Gallimard, 1998–), 1:32.

15. Here I intend to stress only a very particular function of translation that studies devoted to it seem to have passed over in silence, failing to take into account the difference between linguistic capital and the transfer of capital (including the specific ways in which it can be exchanged).

16. See Itamar Even-Zohar, "Laws of Literary Interference" and "Translation and Transfer," *Poetics Today: International Journal for Theory and Analysis of Literature and Communication* 11, no. 1 (spring 1990): 53–72 and 73–78.

17. Hence the term *intraduction* ("in-translation") used by Ganne and Minon to refer to the importation of foreign literary texts; see Valérie Gannes and Marc Minon, "Géographie de la traduction," in *Traduire l'Europe,* ed. Françoise Barret-Ducrocq (Paris: Payot, 1992), 58.

18. Though Schmidt never published a complete version of any of Joyce's work, brief selections from his unfinished translation of *Finnegans Wake* appeared posthumously under the title *Arno Schmidts Arbeitsexemplar von Finnegans Wake* (Zurich: Arno Schmidt Stiftung, 1984).

19. See de Man, "A Modern Master," 123.

20. Thus Ganne and Minon refer to the exportation of national texts into another language as *extraduction* ("out-translation"); see "Géographie de la traduction," 58.

21. Pius Ngandu Nkashama, *Littératures et écritures en langues africaines* (Paris: L'Harmattan, 1992), 24–30.

22. Salman Rushdie, *Imaginary Homelands: Essays and Criticism, 1981–1991* (London: Granta, 1991), 17.

23. See Carl Gustav Bjurström's essay, "Strindberg écrivain français," in his edition of Strindberg's *Oeuvre autobiographique,* 2 vols. (Paris: Mercure de France, 1990), 2:1199.

24. The Théâtre-Libre, founded in Paris by André Antoine in 1887 with Zola's patronage, sought to adapt the novelist's naturalist theories and innovations to the theater, staging a number of his plays and novels. The *succès de scandale* triggered by Antoine's first productions had tremendous repercussions throughout Europe. Strindberg, for his part, understood at once that with the appearance of this new theater he had a chance of being read—and perhaps recognized—by Zola, then one of the most famous and influential men of letters.

25. August Strindberg, letter to Carl Larsson (22 April 1884), in *Letters,* ed. and trans. Michael Robinson, 2 vols. (Chicago: University of Chicago Press, 1992), 1:136.

26. August Strindberg, *Brev,* ed. Torsten Hedlund and Bjørn Meidal, 22 vols. (Stockholm: Bonniers, 1948–2001), letter no. 1091, 5:124–126.

27. There are a good many indications that he also wanted to protect his private life and not reveal to Swedish readers the story of his marriage.

28. See Mark Raeff, "La culture russe et l'émigration," in *Histoire de la littérature russe: Le XXe siècle,* 3 vols. (Paris: Fayard, 1987–1990), 2:87–103.

29. At the beginning of the 1930s there were only 30,000 Russians left in Berlin, and half of these, partly German by birth, no longer belonged to the Russian colony. By contrast, the émigré press and publishing prospered in Paris, home to the majority of the 400,000 Russian refugees who now lived in France.

30. Fayard published the novel in 1934 under the title *La course du fou.* Thirty years later a new translation appeared with Gallimard as *La défense Loujine.*

31. See Brian Boyd, *Vladimir Nabokov: The Russian Years* (Princeton: Princeton University Press, 1990), 369.

32. The book was initially published in four consecutive issues of *Sovremennyia Zapiski* from May 1932 to May 1933 (nos. 49–52).

33. The book first appeared in English as *Camera Obscura;* it was throughly revised by the author and reissued in 1938 as *Laughter in the Dark.*

34. Boyd, *Vladimir Nabokov,* 419.

35. Letter to Zinaida Chakhovskaya (October 1935), quoted in ibid., 421.

36. Nabokov moved to Paris from Berlin in 1937 and lived there until 1940.

37. The original version of this novel was eventually published in Paris, by the Olympia Press in 1953, and then translated into French by the author in collaboration with Ludovic and Agnès Janvier.

38. The English version of *Molloy* (translated in collaboration with Paul Bowles) appeared in 1955. *Texts for Nothing* was not published until 1967.

39. Though Larbaud is mentioned in various dictionaries (invariably as a "writer" first), Coindreau's name does not even appear.

40. Quoted in Larbaud, *Ce vice impuni, la lecture,* 36–37. Thus Larbaud tried to defend the task of translators by giving them, at once seriously and ironically, a patron saint. He chose Saint Jerome, the author of the Vulgate (or Latin version of the Bible), insisting on the importance of the cultural change brought about by Jerome's translation. It was Jerome "who gave the Hebrew Bible to the Western world, and constructed the broad viaduct that linked Jerusalem to Rome and Rome to all the peoples of the Romance languages . . . What other translator carried out so colossal an enterprise with such success and with consequences so far-reaching in time and space? . . . Words issuing from his words praise the Lord to the sound of banjos in negro spirituals, and sob on guitars, in *tristes* and *modinhas,* in places where the speech of the peasants of Latium meets the speech of Guarani Indians"; *Sous l'invocation de saint Jérôme* (Paris: Gallimard, 1946), 54.

41. Larbaud, *Ce vice impuni, la lecture,* 31–32.

42. Maurice Nadeau, *Grâces leur soient rendues* (Paris: Albin Michel, 1990), 343.

43. Quoted in Rita Gombrowicz, *Gombrowicz en Europe: Témoignages et docu-*

ments, 1963–1969 (Paris: Denoël, 1988), 16. The Congrès pour la Liberté de la Culture was an international organization based in Paris (with covert funding from U.S. intelligence services) and devoted to combatting Communist influence among intellectuals; see Pierre Grémion, *Intelligence de l'anticommunisme: Le Congrès pour la Liberté de la Culture à Paris (1950–1975)* (Paris: Fayard, 1995).

44. Jelenski first translated extracts of *Ferdydurke* and *Trans-Atlantyk* and submitted the text to a number of publishers in Paris, all of whom turned it down. Through him François Bondy, editor of the review *Preuves,* discovered the Spanish edition of *Ferdydurke* and published the first review of it in France ("Note sur *Ferdydurke*," *Preuves,* no. 32 [October 1953]). This notice aroused the interest of the publisher Maurice Nadeau, who five years later brought out a French translation in Julliard's "Les Lettres Nouvelles" series. Jelenski also published a great many articles on Gombrowicz's work, including three pieces in *Preuves:* "Witold Gombrowicz," no. 34 (December 1953); "Witold Gombrowicz ou l'immaturité adulte," no. 95 (January 1959); and "Gombrowicz et Ionesco," (no. 188 [October 1966]). In addition to the preface he wrote for the first French edition of *Ferdydurke* and his own translation of *Trans-Atlantyk,* Jelenski collaborated with Geneviève Serreau on translations of four other works by Gombrowicz and, with Dominique de Roux, edited *Le cahier Gombrowicz* (Paris: Éditions de l'Herne, 1971).

45. Witold Gombrowicz, *Diary,* ed. Jan Kott, trans. Lillian Vallee, 3 vols. (Evanston: Northwestern University Press, 1988–1993), 3:84.

46. Witold Gombrowicz, *Journal,* trans. Allan Kosko et al., 3 vols. (Paris: Christian Bourgois, 1981), 3:62.

47. Ibid., 1:366.

48. The first French translation of *Ferdydurke* was by Gombrowicz himself (under the pseudonym of Brone) with the assistance of Roland Martin, a French journalist working in Argentina.

49. See "Ulysse: Note sur l'histoire du texte," in James Joyce, *Oeuvres complètes,* ed. Jacques Aubert et al., 2 vols. (Paris: Gallimard, 1995–1996), 2:1030–33.

50. Philippe Soupault implied in his preface that "the first attempt [at translation] made by Samuel Beckett, an Irishman and teaching assistant at the École Normale . . . assisted in this task by Alfred Péron, an *agrégé de l'université,*" had been largely revised and altered.

51. From time to time one encounters a few ritual criticisms regarding the appropriateness of this or that choice (which only serve to emphasize the lofty conception of the prize) but also the institution itself, such as George Steiner's diatribe, "The Scandal of the Nobel Prize," *New York Times Book Review,* 30 September 1984, whose infuriated tone demonstrates, if any further proof were needed, the undeniable importance of the prize.

52. There have been a few attempts at creating a rival prize, such as the Neu-

stadt Prize, established in 1969 and awarded by an international jury of writers, but none has met with unanimous approval.

53. *Korea Herald,* 17 October 1995; Nicole Zand, "Prodigieuse Corée," *Le Monde,* 24 November 1995.

54. See Patrick Maurus, ed. and trans., *La chanteuse de P'ansori: Prose coréenne contemporain* (Arles: Actes Sud, 1997), 53.

55. Tsu-Yü Hwang, quoted in *Göteborgs-Posten,* 24 June 1984.

56. Jorge Amado, interview with the author, September 1993. Torga has since died.

57. It is to be regretted, however, that in choosing between José Saramago and António Lobo Antunes the Swedish Academy should have priviledged the more "national" of the two and the upholder of a conservative aesthetic of the novel. Antunes, an innovator, the creator of new literary forms, is unquestionably the only true Portuguese "classic of the future."

58. For all historical details, descriptions of the internal functioning of the committee, and citations from the archives of the Swedish Academy I rely on the history of the prize recounted by Kjell Espmark—himself a member of the Academy—in *The Nobel Prize in Literature: A Study of the Criteria behind the Choices* (Boston: G. K. Hall, 1986). An internal, descriptive, and commemorative history that is too closely bound up with the institution it describes, Espmark's work is valuable more as an insider's account than as an attempt at analysis.

59. These phrases are found in the Nobel Committee's recommendations for the years 1901, 1903, and 1908, respectively; see ibid., 32–33.

60. Ibid., 32, 57, 41.

61. Ibid., 59.

62. Ibid., 136.

63. Ibid., 132. The second Nobel Prize awarded to an East Asian writer also went to a Japanese author, Kenzaburo Oe, though not until 1994.

64. The monopolistic nature of the system is sometimes unwittingly acknowledged. Thus, for example, Donald Keene was quoted (in the 8 December 1968 issue of the *New York Times Book Review*) as saying that the Nobel jury wished to incorporate the Japanese novel, through the prize given to Kawabata, into "the mainstream of world literature." A professor of Japanese literature and civilization at Columbia University, Keene was one of three experts appointed by the Nobel Committee to evaluate Kawabata's work.

65. Gao Xingjian, interview with the author, 28 December 2000.

66. Ibid.

67. See Gao Xingjian, *La montagne de l'âme,* trans. Noël and Liliane Dutrait (Paris: L'Aube, 1995), subsequently published in English as *Soul Mountain,* trans. Mabel Lee (New York: HarperCollins, 2000).

68. Epsmark, *The Nobel Prize in Literature,* 73, 76.

69. In this connection one recalls the French writer René Étiemble's attack on "Eurocentrism" and his plea on behalf of "exotic," "marginal," and "small" literatures in *Essais de littérature (vraiment) générale* (Paris: Gallimard, 1974). See also his earlier work *Comparaison n'est pas raison* (Paris: Gallimard, 1963).

70. Ernest Boyd, *Ireland's Literary Renaissance,* rev. ed. (New York: Alfred A. Knopf, 1922), 404, 406. Boyd attacked Larbaud on another occasion, in an article published in the 15 June 1924 issue of the *New York Herald Tribune.*

71. Larbaud, *Ce vice impuni, la lecture,* 234.

72. See Béatrice Mousli, *Valery Larbaud* (Paris: Flammarion, 1998), 369–370.

73. Valery Larbaud, "À propos de James Joyce et de 'Ulysse': Réponse à M. Ernest Boyd," *Nouvelle revue française,* no. 24 (January 1925): 1–17.

74. Marthe Robert, "Kafka en France," in *Le siècle de Kafka* (Paris: Centre Georges-Pompidou, 1984), 15–16.

75. Larson has published widely on African literature and, in particular, on Achebe's own work; see, for example, *The Emergence of African Fiction,* rev. ed. (London: Macmillan, 1978).

76. Chinua Achebe, "Colonialist Criticism," in *Hopes and Impediments* (London: Heinemann International, 1988), 51–52.

77. Charles Ferdinand Ramuz, "Lettre à Bernard Grasset," in *Oeuvres complètes,* 20 vols. (Lausanne: Rencontre, 1967–1968), 12:272.

78. Jean Cassou, *Nouvelle revue française,* no. 23 (July–December 1924): 144.

79. Octave Crémazie, "Lettre à l'abbé Casgrain du 29 janvier 1867," in *Oeuvres complètes* (Montreal: Beauchemin, 1896); quoted in Dominique Combe, *Poétiques francophones* (Paris: Hachette, 1995), 29.

80. From a letter written by Ibsen to the king, quoted by Régis Boyer in the introduction to his translation of Ibsen's *Peer Gynt* (Paris: Flammarion, 1994), 13.

81. In 1898 Shaw published *The Perfect Wagnerite,* in which he examined *The Ring* in the light of the anarchist and socialist ideas of the German revolutionary movement to which the composer had belonged in 1848–49.

82. Arthur Wing Pinero (1855–1934) was a popular author of light comedies who had recently turned to psychological drama.

83. George Bernard Shaw, "Wagner in Bayreuth," *English Illustrated Magazine,* October 1889; reprinted in Dan H. Laurence, ed., *Shaw's Music: The Complete Musical Criticism,* 3 vols. (New York: Dodd, Mead, 1981), 1:802.

84. George Bernard Shaw, "A Neglected Moral of the Wagner Centenary," *New Statesman,* 31 May 1913; reprinted in Laurence, *Shaw's Music,* 3:645.

85. George Bernard Shaw, "The Performance of Grieg's *Peer Gynt* in London," *Dagbladet* (Oslo), 18 March 1889; reprinted in Laurence, *Shaw's Music,* 1:582.

86. See Jacques Robichez, *Le symbolisme au théâtre: Lugné-Poë et les débuts de l'oeuvre* (Paris: L'Arche, 1957), 99.

87. Ibid., 155.

88. Henrik Ibsen, interview in *Le Figaro,* 4 January 1893, quoted in ibid., 157.

89. Ibid., 272.

90. Ibid., 276, 288.

91. G. B. Shaw, "L'oeuvre," *Saturday Review,* 30 March 1895; reprinted in Ayot St. Lawrence, ed., *Collected Works of G. B. Shaw,* 30 vols. (New York: William H. Wise, 1931), 23:76–77.

5. From Literary Internationalism to Commercial Globalization?

1. See Daniel Oster and Jean-Marie Goulemot, *La vie parisienne: Anthologie des moeurs au XIXe siècle* (Paris: Sand-Conti, 1989), 24–25.

2. Danilo Kiš, "Paris, la grande cuisine des idées," in *Homo poeticus,* trans. Pascale Delpech (Paris: Fayard, 1993), 52.

3. Valérie Gannes and Marc Minon, "Géographie de la traduction," in Françoise Barret-Ducrocq, ed., *Traduire l'Europe* (Paris: Payot, 1992), 64.

4. See Martin Chalmers, "La réception de la littérature allemande en Angleterre: Un splendide isolement," *Liber: Revue internationale des livres,* no. 18 (June 1994): 20–22.

5. Ibid., 22.

6. See Gannes and Minon, "Géographie de la traduction," 67.

7. See Bourdieu's chapter "Le point de vue de l'auteur: Quelques propriétés générales des champs de production culturelle," in *Les règles de l'art* (Paris: Seuil, 1992), 298–390.

8. Valery Larbaud, *Ce vice impuni, la lecture: Domaine anglais* (Paris: Gallimard, 1925), 407–408.

9. André Schiffrin, "La nouvelle structure de l'édition aux États-Unis," *Liber: Revue internationale des livres,* no. 29 (December 1996): 2–5. The argument of this article is developed more fully in Schiffrin, *The Business of Books: How International Conglomerates Took Over Publishing and Changed the Way We Read* (New York: Verso, 2000).

10. This figure includes purely commercial houses as well as ones that have sought to preserve a balance between profitability and traditional standards of editorial responsibility; see Schiffrin, "La nouvelle structure de l'édition," 2.

11. Ibid., 3.

12. Thus Jean-Marie Bouvaist quotes the American publisher Richard Snyder as saying, "It is better to publish anything than not to publish at all"; see *Crise et mutation dans l'édition française* (Paris: Éditions du Cercle de la Librairie, 1993), 7. See also Bourdieu, *Les règles de l'art,* 202–210.

13. See Bouvaist, *Crise et mutation dans l'édition française,* 400.

14. I use the term "neocolonial novel" to refer to the work of writers from formerly colonized countries who, while giving the impression of breaking

with tradition, reproduce the narrative techniques of the colonial novel in its most conservative form.

15. See, for example, Arturo Pérez-Reverte's novel *El Club Dumas* (Madrid: Alfaguara, 1993).

16. See Bouvaist, Crise et mutation dans l'édition française, 14.

6. The Small Literatures

1. André de Ridder, *La littérature flamande contemporaine* (Antwerp: L. Opde-beek/Paris: Champion, 1923), 15.

2. Édouard Glissant, *Poetics of Relation,* trans. Betsy Wing (Ann Arbor: University of Michigan Press, 1997), 103.

3. Octavio Paz, *In Search of the Present: 1990 Nobel Lecture,* bilingual ed., trans. Anthony Stanton (San Diego: Harcourt Brace Jovanovich, 1990), 6–7.

4. Glissant, *Poetics of Relation,* 107n.

5. Charles Ferdinand Ramuz, *Questions* (Lausanne: Éditions d'Aujourd'hui, 1935); reprinted in *La pensée remonte les fleuves* (Paris: Plon, 1979), 292.

6. István Bibó, *Misère des petits états d'Europe de l'Est,* trans. Gyorgy Kassai (Paris: Albin Michel, 1993), 176.

7. Interview with Nicole Zand in the November 1992 literary supplement of *Le Monde,* "Carrefour des littératures européennes."

8. Miroslav Krleža, "Choix de textes," trans. Janine Matillon, *Le messager européen,* no. 8 (1994): 357–358.

9. Milan Kundera, "The Unloved Child of the Family," in *Testments Betrayed,* trans. Linda Asher (New York: HarperCollins, 1995), 192.

10. Janine Matillon, "Hommes dans de sombres temps: Miroslav Krleža," *Le messager européen,* no. 8 (1994): 349.

11. Charles Ferdinand Ramuz, "Besoin de grandeur," in *La pensée remonte les fleuves,* 97.

12. Ramuz, *Questions,* in ibid., 320.

13. Samuel Beckett, "Home Olga," quoted in Lawrence E. Harvey, *Samuel Beckett: Poet and Critic* (Princeton: Princeton University Press, 1970), 296. The poem was composed in 1932 and published two years later in *Contempo III* (Chapel Hill, N.C.), 15 February 1934.

14. Samuel Beckett, *Dream of Fair and Middling Women,* ed. Eoin O'Brien and Edith Fournier (Dublin: Black Cat Press, 1992), 158; quoted in Harvey, *Samuel Beckett,* 338.

15. E. M. Cioran, "Entretien avec Fritz J. Raddatz," *Die Zeit,* 4 April 1986; quoted in Gabriel Liiceanu, *Itinéraires d'une vie: E. M. Cioran, suivi de "Les continents de l'insomnie": Entretien avec E. M. Cioran* (Paris: Michalon, 1995), 63.

16. "Concerning our people, I think more than ever that no illusion is permitted. I feel toward it a sort of despairing contempt"; letter to Aurel Cioran,

30 August 1979, quoted in ibid., 101; E. M. Cioran, *Schimbarea la față a Romaniei* (Bucharest: Editura Vremea, 1936); quoted in Liiceanu, *Itinéraires d'une vie,* 50.

17. E. M. Cioran, "Mon pays," *Le messager européen,* no. 9 (1995): 67.

18. Quoted in Liiceanu, *Itinéraires d'une vie,* 36.

19. See Max Daireaux, *Panorama de la littérature hispano-américaine* (Paris: Kra, 1930), 32.

20. This phrase occurs in the French translation of Farah's 1990 essay "Childhood of My Schizophrenia," which appeared as "L'enfance de ma schizophrénie," *Le serpent à plumes,* no. 21 (fall 1993): 6. The original text (which refers to "colonial contradiction") is quoted in Chapter 9, near note 9.

21. Witold Gombrowicz, *Diary,* ed. Jan Kott, trans. Lillian Vallee, 3 vols. (Evanston: Northwestern University Press, 1988–1993), 1:4–6.

22. Krleža, "Choix de textes," 355.

23. Samuel Beckett, "Recent Irish Poetry," in *Disjecta: Miscellaneous Writings and a Dramatic Fragment,* ed. Ruby Cohn (London: John Calder, 1983), 70.

24. Henri Michaux, "Lettre de Belgique," *Transatlantic Review* 2 (December 1924): 678–681; reprinted in Henri Michaux, *Oeuvres complètes,* ed. Raymond Bellour with Ysé Tran, 3 vols. (Paris: Gallimard, 1998–2004), 1:51–55.

25. Pierre Bourdieu, "Existe-t-il une littérature belge? Limites d'un champ et frontières politiques," *Études de lettres,* October–December 1985, 3–6.

26. Michaux, "Lettre de Belgique," in *Oeuvres complètes,* 1:51.

27. Ibid.

28. See Henri Michaux, "Quelques renseignements sur cinquante-neuf années d'existence," first published in Robert Bréchon, *Henri Michaux* (Paris: Gallimard, 1959); reprinted in Michaux, *Oeuvres complètes,* 1:cxxix–cxxxv.

29. Michaux, "Lettre de Belgique," in *Oeuvres complètes,* 1:52.

30. Ibid., 53.

31. Samuel Putnam, Maida Castelhun Darnton, George Reavey, and Jacob Bronowski, eds., *The European Caravan: An Anthology of the New Spirit in European Literature* (New York: Brewer, Warren and Putnam, 1931).

32. Quoted in Deirdre Bair, *Samuel Beckett: A Biography* (New York: Harcourt Brace Jovanovich, 1978), 129–130.

33. Michaux, "Lettre de Belgique," in *Oeuvres complètes,* 1:54.

34. See Declan Kiberd, *Inventing Ireland: The Literature of the Modern Nation* (Cambridge, Mass.: Harvard University Press, 1995), 23–25.

35. Quoted in Kiberd, *Inventing Ireland,* 197. Cuchulain was the mythical Irish hero of the "Ulster cycle" (ninth to thirteenth centuries), restored to honor by W. B. Yeats. Son of the god Lug, having seven fingers on each hand and seven toes on each foot, as well as seven pupils in each eye, Cuchulain was the incarnation of Irish national anger and independence.

36. Kim Yun-Sik, "Histoire de la littérature coréenne moderne," trans. A. Fabre, *Culture coréenne,* no. 40 (September 1995): 4.

37. Kundera, "The Unloved Child of the Family," 193.

38. Quoted in Kiberd, *Inventing Ireland,* 218.

39. James Joyce, "The Day of the Rabblement," in *The Critical Writings of James Joyce,* ed. Ellsworth Mason and Richard Ellmann (New York: Viking, 1959), 70–71; emphasis added.

40. "Prises de position" in the French text—another phrase familiar from the work of Pierre Bourdieu, which has standardly been translated as "position-takings." I have taken similar liberties in the case of a number of other "technical" terms, especially *spécifique,* which seldom needs to be translated by the same word in English, as is so often done. No reader, I believe, is likely to be confused or otherwise inconvenienced by these mild departures from customary practice. The scope and meaning of "prise de position" are discussed by Randal Johnson in his introduction to *The Field of Cultural Production* (New York: Columbia University Press, 1993), 16–17; see also Bourdieu's own elucidation of the term in *Les règles de l'art* (Paris: Seuil, 1992), 131–138.—Trans.

41. See Gisèle Sapiro, *La guerre des écrivains: 1940–1953* (Paris: Fayard, 1999), especially the first part, "Logiques littérarires de l'engagement," 21–247; also Anne Simonin, *Les Éditions de Minuit, 1942–1955: Le devoir d'insoumission* (Paris: IMEC Éditions, 1994), especially chap. 2, "Littérature oblige," 55–99.

42. Thus the title of Ramuz's 1914 manifesto, originally published as the first issue of *Cahiers vaudois* and subsequently in book form as *Raison d'être* (Lausanne: Éditions du Verseau, 1926).

43. James Ngugi, "Response to Wole Soyinka's 'The Writer in a Modern African State,'" in *The Writer in Modern Africa,* ed. Per Wästberg (New York: Africana Publishing, 1969), 56; quoted in Neil Lazarus, *Resistance in Postcolonial African Fiction* (New Haven: Yale University Press, 1990), 207.

44. Quoted in Denise Coussy, *Le roman nigérian anglophone* (Paris: Éditions Silex, 1988), 491.

45. Chinua Achebe, "The Novelist as Teacher," in *Hopes and Impediments* (London: Heinemann International, 1988), 30. This essay first appeared in the *New Statesman* (29 January 1965) and was subsequently reprinted in *Morning Yet on Creation Day* (London: Heinemann, 1975) and again in *Hopes and Impediments,* 27–31. "The Role of a Writer in a New Nation" was first published in *Africa Report* 15 (March 1970).

46. André Burguière and Jacques Revel have also stressed the role of historical narratives in the construction of France as a political entity; see Burguière and Revel, eds., *Histoire de la France,* 4 vols. (Paris: Seuil, 1989–1993), 1:10–13.

47. Roland Barthes, "L'effet de réel," in *Littérature et réalité*, ed. Gérard Genette and Tzvetan Todorov (Paris: Seuil, 1982), 81–90; Michael Riffaterre, "L'illusion référentielle," in ibid., 93.

48. See Jean-Pierre Morel, *Le roman insupportable: L'Internationale littérarire et la France, 1920–1932* (Paris: Gallimard, 1985).

49. Juan Benet, interview with the author, July 1991.

50. Danilo Kiš, "Nous préchons dans le désert," in *Homo poeticus,* trans. Pascale Delpech (Paris: Fayard, 1993), 13–14.

51. Danilo Kiš, "Homo Poeticus, Regardless," in *Homo Poeticus,* ed. Susan Sontag (New York: Farrar, Straus and Giroux, 1995), 78.

52. Danilo Kiš, "Variations on Central European Themes," in ibid., 106. The Serbs' avowed submission to Moscow encouraged the Croats to distinguish themselves by choosing Paris as their intellectual pole.

53. "In [South] Korea . . . nationalism is a generic, all-encompassing, primary term. All discourse is nationalist. One is nationalist—or, more exactly, nationalist-messianic—before being 'on the Left' or identifying oneself with the 'masses' or claiming to be a liberal or a Buddhist": see Patrick Maurus' introduction to his annotated edition of selected poems by Shin Kyong-Nim, *Le rêve d'un homme abattu: Choix de poèmes* (Paris: Gallimard, 1995), 10.

54. Ibid., 10–11.

55. Carlos Fuentes, *Geografía de la novela* (Mexico City: Fondo de Cultura Económica, 1993), 14.

56. And not "minor" literatures—a term found in a translation by Marthe Robert that another translator of Kafka, Bernard Lortholary, has called "inexact and tendentious"; see "Le testament de l'écrivain," in *Un jeûneur et autres nouvelles* (Paris: Flammarion, 1993), 35. Kafka used the German word *klein.*

57. Franz Kafka, *The Diaries of Franz Kafka,* ed. Max Brod, trans. Joseph Kresh (New York: Schocken, 1948), 191.

58. Max Brod, *Franz Kafka: A Biography,* trans. G. Humphreys-Roberts and Richard Winston, 2d ed. (New York: Schocken, 1960), 111.

59. Kafka, *Diaries,* 194, 191–192, 194.

60. From Kafka's entry for 8 October 1911, ibid., 87.

61. Ibid., 193, 194.

62. Ibid., 194.

63. See Gilles Deleuze and Félix Guattari, *Kafka: Pour une littérature mineure* (Paris: Éditions de Minuit, 1975).

64. Ibid., 75–77.

65. See Klaus Wagenbach, *Franz Kafka: Eine Biographie seiner Jugend, 1883–1912* (Bern: Franke, 1958), available in French as *Franz Kafka: Années de jeunesse (1883–1912),* trans. Élisabeth Gaspar (Paris: Mercure de France, 1967).

66. Deleuze and Guattari, *Kafka,* 35, 33.

67. Ibid., 75, 74, 32.

7. The Assimilated

1. See, for example, Kazimierz Brandys, *A Warsaw Diary: 1978–1981,* trans. Richard Lourie (New York: Random House, 1983).

2. Israel Zangwill, "Anglicization," in *Ghetto Comedies* (New York: Macmillan, 1907), 59.

3. James Joyce, "Oscar Wilde: The Poet of 'Salomé,'" in *The Critical Writings of James Joyce,* ed. Ellsworth Mason and Richard Ellmann (New York: Viking, 1959), 202.

4. James Joyce, *Ulysses* (New York: Modern Library, 1961), 6.

5. See V. S. Naipaul, *India: A Million Mutinies Now* (London: Heinemann, 1990), 6–7.

6. See V. S. Naipaul, *The Enigma of Arrival* (New York: Vintage, 1988), 97–179.

7. Salman Rushdie, "V. S. Naipaul," in *Imaginary Homelands: Essays and Criticism, 1981–1991* (London: Granta, 1991), 148,

8. Naipaul, *The Enigma of Arrival,* 130, 111.

9. Ibid., 30, 196, 20–21, 92.

10. V. S. Naipaul, "Our Universal Civilization," adapted from the Walter B. Wriston lecture delivered by Naipaul at the Manhattan Institute in New York and published in the *New York Review of Books,* 31 January 1991, 22–25.

11. Ibid., 22–23. See also V. S. Naipaul, *Among the Believers: An Islamic Journey* (London: Deutsch, 1981).

12. A perspective that has changed over the years, from his first trip in 1962, recounted in *An Area of Darkness* (1964), his next visit in 1975, which produced *India: A Wounded Civilization* (1977), and then the most recent one, in 1990, reported in *India: A Million Mutinies Now* (1990).

13. Naipaul, *India: A Million Mutinies Now,* 392, 398.

14. Salman Rushdie, "Naipaul among the Believers," in *Imaginary Homelands,* 375. See, for example, V. S. Naipaul, *Guerrillas* (London: Deutsch, 1975).

15. The Nobel awarded to Naipaul broke with the entire unspoken tradition of the prize's political progressivism.

16. See Jean-Pierre Martin, *Henri Michaux: Écritures de soi, expatriations* (Paris: José Corti, 1994), 288.

17. "It is my faults of elocution," Cioran wrote, "my stammerings, my jerky way of speaking, my art of mumbling; it is my voice, my 'r's from the other end of Europe that led me by way of reaction to take some care over what I write and to make myself more or less worthy of an idiom that I misuse every time I open my mouth"; *Écartèlement* (Paris: Gallimard, 1979), 76.

18. Foreigners in Michaux's writings are often suspect: "Foreigners are cor-
ralled in camps, on the edges of the territory. They are admitted inside the
country only gradually and after many ordeals." See the definitive version of
Voyage en Grande Garabagne published as part of *Ailleurs* (Paris: Gallimard,
1948), 50–51.

19. Henri Michaux, "Quelques renseignements sur cinquante-neuf années
d'existence," in Robert Bréchon, *Henri Michaux* (Paris: Gallimard, 1959).

20. Ibid., 12.

21. Henri Michaux, *Plume, précédée par Lointain intérieur* (Paris: Gallimard, 1938),
68. As an adolescent he was fascinated by problems associated with heredity
and genealogy, obsessed by a concern with personal freedom and by the
tormenting question of whether he could free himself from his origins.

22. Michaux, "Quelques renseignements," 17.

23. Quoted in Gabriel Liiceanu, *Itinéraires d'une vie: E. M. Cioran, suivi de "Les
continents de l'insomnie": Entretien avec E. M. Cioran* (Paris: Michalon, 1995),
d'une vie, 114.

24. See ibid., 124: "We were very close friends, he even asked me to be his literary executor, but I declined."

25. Charles Ferdinand Ramuz, *Raison d'être* (Paris: La Différence, 1991), 29.

26. Charles Ferdinand Ramuz, *Paris: Notes d'un Vaudois* (Lausanne: Éditions de
l'Aire, 1978), 66.

8. The Rebels

1. Within the general process of literary dissimilation, a founding phase (during which a literary heritage is constituted) must be distinguished from subsequent stages during which the literary emancipation of a national space
takes place.

2. Samuel Burdy, *The History of Ireland from the Earliest Ages to the Union* (Edinburgh: Doig and Stirling, 1817), 567.

3. Quoted in Patrick Rafroidi, *L'Irlande et le Romantisme* (Lille: Presses Universitaires de Lille, 1972), 11.

4. Joachim du Bellay, *The Defence and Illustration of the French Language,* trans.
Gladys M. Turquet (London: J. M. Dent and Sons, 1939), 26.

5. Ralph Waldo Emerson, "The American Scholar," in *Selections from Ralph
Waldo Emerson,* ed. Stephen E. Whicher (Cambridge, Mass.: Riverside Press,
1960), 68, 67, 79.

6. See the chapter "Realismo mágico," in Arturo Uslar Pietri, *Godos, insur-
gentes y visionarios* (Barcelona: Seix Barral, 1986), 135–140.

7. Ibid., 40.

8. Alejo Carpentier, "América ante la joven literatura europea," first published

in *Cartelas* (28 June 1931) and reprinted in *La novela latinoamericana en visperas de un nuevo siglo y otras ensayos* (Mexico City: Siglo XXI, 1981), 51–59; quotation on 55–56.

9. Charles Ferdinand Ramuz, *Paris: Notes d'un Vaudois* (Lausanne: Éditions de l'Aire, 1978), 65.

10. Thus Kim Yun-Sik observes that in the second half of the 1920s "Korean literature exhibited two poles: proletarian literature on the one hand and, on the other, the nationalist literature that was constituted in opposition to it"; see "Histoire de la littérature coréenne moderne," trans. A. Fabre, *Culture coréenne,* no. 40 (September 1995): 7.

11. Plays: Mouloud Mammeri, *La mort absurde des Aztèques, suivi de Le Banquet* (Paris: Perrin, 1973); *Le Foehn, ou, la Preuve par neuf* (Paris: Publisud, 1982); *La cité du soleil* (Algiers: Laphomic, 1987). Grammar: Mouloud Mammeri, *Grammaire berbère* (Paris: Maspero, 1976). Folktale collections: Mouloud Mammeri, ed., *Tellem Chaho! et Machaho!: Contes berbères de Kabylie* (Paris: Bordas, 1980). Poetry: Mouloud Mammeri, ed., *Poèmes kabyles anciens* (Paris: Maspero, 1980); see also Mammeri's earlier edition of *Les Isefra: Poèmes de Si-Mohand-ou-Mhand* (Paris: Maspero, 1969).

12. From an unpublished preface to the novel composed in 1926 and quoted by Michel Riaudel, "Toupi or not toupi: Une aporie de l'être national," in Pierre Rivas's critical edition of the French translation, *Macounaïma* (Paris: Stock, 1996), 300.

13. See Alain Ricard, *Livre et communication au Nigeria* (Paris: Présence Africaine, 1975), 40–46.

14. D. O. Fagunwa, *The Forest of a Thousand Daemons: A Hunter's Saga,* trans. Wole Soyinka (New York: Random House, 1982), 1.

15. The book was originally published in London by Faber. A French translation by Raymond Queneau appeared the following year with Gallimard under the title *L'ivrogne dans la brousse.*

16. Quoted in Denise Coussy, *Le roman nigérian anglophone* (Paris: Éditions Silex, 1988), 20.

17. The cinema can promote the same sort of subversion and opposition in countries where authoritarian regimes exercise strict censorship over artists.

18. Pius Ngandu Nkashama has pointed out the importance in the 1960s of theatrical associations and groups such as the Makerere Travelling Theater, which made it possible for great works of drama to be staged in African languages in both Uganda and Kenya; see *Littératures et écritures en langues africaines* (Paris: L'Harmattan, 1992), 326.

19. Franz Kafka, *The Diaries of Franz Kafka,* ed. Max Brod, trans. Joseph Kresh (New York: Schocken, 1948), 87; emphasis added.

20. From Gilles Carpentier's introduction to his edited volume of interviews with Kateb Yacine, *Le poète comme boxeur: Entretiens, 1958–1989* (Paris: Seuil, 1994), 9.

21. Kateb Yacine, interview with Jacques Alessandra, "Le théâtre n'est pas sorcier," in ibid., 77–78.

22. Ibid., 58, 67, 74.

23. Six years earlier he had published a series of essays under the title *Homecoming: Essays on African and Caribbean Literature* (London: Heinemann, 1972).

24. See Neil Lazarus, *Resistance in Postcolonial African Fiction* (New Haven: Yale University Press, 1990), 214.

25. See Jacqueline Bardolph, *Ngugi wa Thiong'o: L'homme et l'oeuvre* (Paris: Présence Africaine, 1991), 26; also 58–59.

26. The term refers to any of a number of regional forms of Canadian French thought to be substandard and associated with a lack of education.—Trans.

27. Haruhisa Kato has proposed the term "phagocytosis" to describe one of the constant features of Japanese civilization, noting that "capturing, ingesting, and digesting foreign bodies is the most efficient means of conserving one's own identity while deriving enrichment from this external contribution"; see his "L'image culturelle de la France au Japon," *Dialogues et cultures* 36 (1992): 36–41.

28. Carpentier developed his famous theory of "lo real maravilloso" in the preface to his novel *El reino de este mundo* (The Kingdom of this World, 1949).

29. As a result of the Great Depression, whose effects were felt in Europe no less than in America, the review's first issue (April 1931) was to be its last; see Claude Cymerman and Claude Fell, *Histoire de la littérature hispano-américaine de 1940 à nos jours* (Paris: Nathan, 1997), 47.

30. Mexican painter (1886–1957), renowned as one of his country's greatest muralists.

31. Carpentier, "América ante la joven literatura europea," 56–57.

32. Antonio Candido, *On Literature and Society,* trans. Howard S. Becker (Princeton: Princeton University Press, 1995), 131.

33. See Mohammed Dib, "Le voleur de feu," in *Jean Amrouche: L'éternel Jugurtha, 1906–1962,* ed. Marc Faigre (Marseilles: Archives de la Ville de Marseille, 1985).

34. It is in exactly this way that the translations of Shakespeare into Swahili by Julius Nyerere, the former president of Tanzania, are to be understood. Nyerere's versions of *Julius Caesar* (1963) and *The Merchant of Venice* (1969) gave rise to a great many commentaries; see Pius Ngandu Nkashama, *Littératures et écritures en langues africaines,* 339–350.

35. See Antoine Berman, *L'épreuve de l'étranger: Culture et traduction dans l'Allemagne romantique* (Paris: Gallimard, 1984), 29.

36. Quoted in Fritz Strich, *Goethe und die Weltliteratur* (Bern: Franke Verlag, 1946), 18; emphasis added.

37. Quoted in ibid., 57; emphasis added.

38. Quoted in Winfried Sdun, *Probleme und Theorien des Übersetzens in Deutschland vom 18. bis zum 20. Jahrhundert* (Munich: Max Hüber, 1967), 25.

39. Walter Benjamin, "The Concept of Criticism," in *Selected Writings,* ed. Marcus Bullock and Michael W. Jennings, 4 vols. to date (Cambridge, Mass.: Harvard University Press, 1996–), 1:158.

40. See Berman, *L'épreuve de l'étranger,* 33.

41. Quoted in ibid., 92, 93.

42. August Wilhelm von Schlegel, *Geschichte der klassischen Literatur,* ed. Edgar Lohner (Stuttgart: Kohlhammer, 1964), 17; quoted in Berman, *L'épreuve de l'étranger,* 62.

43. Quoted in Sdun, *Probleme und Theorien,* 27.

44. Sadegh Hedayat, ed., *Les Chants d'Omar Khayam, édition critique,* trans. M. F. Farzaneh and Jean Malaplate (Paris: José Corti, 1993).

45. See M. F. Farzaneh, ed. and trans. (with F. Farzaneh), *Rencontres avec Sadegh Hedayat: Le parcours d'une initiation* (Paris: José Corti, 1993), 8.

46. Sadegh Hedayet, *La chouette aveugle,* trans. Roger Lescot (Paris: José Corti, 1953). The book was written in India between 1935 and 1937 and privately printed for friends, in a small run in Bombay, on its completion; it was then serialized in the newspaper *Iran* and finally published in Tehran in 1941.

47. Youssef Ishaghpour, *Le tombeau de Sadegh Hedayat* (Paris: Fourbis, 1991), 14.

48. Ibid., 35.

49. There was a first German version of the *Rubáiyát* in 1818 by the Austrian philosopher Baron Josef von Hammer-Purgstall; then, in 1857, a French prose version by the interpreter to the French Embassy in Persia, Jean-Baptiste Nicolas, annotated by Théophile Gautier and Ernst Renan. Khayyám's glory in the West dates from the publication in 1859 of Edward Fitzgerald's English translation of seventy-five quatrains. Fitzgerald's version enjoyed a great success among the pre-Raphaelites and remains one of the classics of the English language. Many other translations were to follow, all of which took liberties with the original manuscripts and poetical forms; see Jean Malaplate's "Note sur l'adaptation des Quatrains," in Hidayet's critical edition of the *Rubáiyát,* 115–119.

50. Stefan Collini, *Public Moralists: Political Thought and Intellectual Life in Britain, 1850–1930* (Oxford: Clarendon Press, 1991), 359.

51. Quoted in ibid.

52. Octavio Paz, *In Search of the Present: 1990 Nobel Lecture,* bilingual ed., trans. Anthony Stanton (San Diego: Harcourt Brace Jovanovich, 1990), 8.

53. Carlos Fuentes, *The Buried Mirror: Reflections on Spain and the New World* (Boston: Houghton Mifflin, 1992), 9–10.

54. See Jacques Bouchard, "Une renaissance: La formation de la conscience nationale chez les Grecs modernes," *Études françaises* 10, no. 4 (1974): 397–410; also Mario Vitti, *Histoire de la littérature grecque moderne* (Paris: Hatier, 1989), 185 ff.

55. Gertrude Stein, *The Autobiography of Alice B. Toklas,* in *The Writings of Gertrude Stein, 1903–1932,* ed. Catherine Stimpson and Harriet Chessman (New York: Library of America, 1998), 739.

56. James Joyce, "Ireland, Island of Saints and Sages," in *The Critical Writings of James Joyce,* ed. Ellsworth Mason and Richard Ellmann (New York: Viking, 1959), 173.

57. Walt Whitman, "Mississippi Valley Literature," in *Specimen Days,* in *Complete Poetry and Collected Prose,* ed. Justin Kaplan (New York: Literary Classics of the United States/Viking, 1982), 866–867.

58. Walt Whitman, *Leaves of Grass,* in ibid., 165, 167.

59. Whitman, "The Prairies and Great Plains of Poetry," in *Specimen Days,* 863.

60. Ramuz, *Paris: Notes d'un Vaudois,* 91; emphasis added.

61. Rubén Darío, *España contemporánea* (Paris: Garnier Hermanos, 1901), quoted by Hilda Torres-Varela, "1910–1914 en Espagne," in *L'année 1913: Les formes esthétiques de l'oeuvre d'art à la veille de la Première Guerre mondiale,* ed. Liliane Brion-Guerry, 2 vols. (Paris: Klincksieck, 1971), 2:1054.

62. Manuel Vázquez Montalbán, interview with the author, March 1991.

63. See H. Gustav Klaus, "1984 Glasgow: Alasdair Gray, Tom Leonard, James Kelman," *Liber: Revue internationale des livres,* no. 24 (October 1995): 12.

64. See John Kelly, "*The Irish Review,*" in Brion-Guerry, *L'année 1913,* 2:1028.

65. See ibid.

66. Very probably in 1898, when he was sixteen, and for reasons very similar to those of Shaw.

67. See Richard Ellmann, *James Joyce* (New York: Oxford University Press, 1982), 73.

68. See Jean-Michel Rabaté, *James Joyce* (Paris: Hachette, 1993), 71–72.

69. The schedule announced in October 1901 included *Casadh an tSúgáin,* a drama by Douglas Hyde written in Gaelic, and a play by Yeats and Moore based on an Irish heroic legend, titled *Diarmuid and Gráinne;* see Ellmann, *James Joyce,* 88.

70. Joyce, "The Day of the Rabblement," in Mason and Ellmann, *Critical Writings,* 69–70.

71. James Joyce, "Ibsen's New Drama," ibid., 48.

72. Similarly, Catalonia and Quebec today serve as models and points of reference for each other.

73. Quoted in Françoise Lalande, *Christian Dotremont, l'inventeur de Cobra: Une biographie* (Paris: Stock, 1998), 112.

74. Quoted in Richard Miller, *Cobra* (Paris: Nouvelles Éditions Françaises, 1994), 28.

75. Quoted in ibid., 49.

76. Quoted in ibid., 21.

77. Quoted in ibid., 190.

9. The Tragedy of Translated Men

1. See Louis-Jean Calvet, *La guerre des langues et les politiques linguistiques* (Paris: Payot, 1987).

2. On the complexity of the linguistic situation in Francophone Africa and its literary consequences, see Bernard Mouralis, *Littérature et développement: Essai sur le statut, la fonction et la représentation de la littérature négro-africaine d'expression française* (Paris: Honoré Champion, 1981), 131–147.

3. The term "translated men," it will be recalled, comes from Salman Rushdie, "Imaginary Homelands," in *Imaginary Homelands: Essays and Criticism, 1981–1991* (London: Granta, 1991), 17.

4. Interview with Abdellâtif Laâbi, *La quinzaine littéraire,* no. 436 (16–31 March 1985): 51.

5. Albert Memmi, *Portrait du colonisé, précédé de Portrait du colonisateur,* with a preface by Jean-Paul Sartre (Paris: Corréa, 1957), 126.

6. Quoted in Alain Ricard, *Littératures d'Afrique noire: Des langues aux livres* (Paris: CNRS Éditions-Kartala, 1995), 156. Couchoro became a citizen of the neighboring country of Togo in 1940.

7. Kateb Yacine, "Toujours la ruée vers l'or," in *Le poète comme boxeur: Entretiens, 1958–1989,* ed. Gilles Carpentier (Paris: Seuil, 1994), 132.

8. Nuruddin Farah, *Maps* (London: Picador, 1986), 171.

9. Nuruddin Farah, "Childhood of My Schizophrenia," *Times Literary Supplement,* 23–29 November 1990, 1264.

10. Anatole Riovallan, *Littérature irlandaise contemporaine* (Paris: Librarie Hachette, 1939), vii–viii.

11. See Njabulo Ndebele, *Rediscovery of the Ordinary and Other Essays* (Johannesburg: Ravan, 1989).

12. See, for example, Njabulo Ndebele, *Fools and Other Stories* (Johannesburg: Ravan, 1983).

13. Jean Amrouche, "Colonisation et langage," in *Un Algérien s'adresse aux*

Français ou l'histoire de l'Algérie par les textes, ed. Tassadit Yacine (Paris: Awal-L'Harmattan, 1994), 332.

14. Quoted by Mohammed Dib, "Le voleur de feu," in *Jean Amrouche: L'éternel Jugurtha, 1906–1962,* ed. Marc Faigre (Marseilles: Archives de la Ville de Marseille, 1985), 15; emphasis added.

15. Amrouche, "Colonisation et langage," 329.

16. Ibid., 15–17. Analysts of African literatures note, however, that in countries that were subject to British colonial rule the relation of writers to the colonial language generally seems less tense than in countries colonized by France, and that the need to choose a literary language has been experienced in a less dramatic way. In leaving greater freedom to native peoples in educational matters, insisting that local communities take responsibility for their own education, British practice allowed an Islamic literature in Hausa to develop in West Africa, for example, and in East Africa it encouraged new work to be produced in Swahili. Even so, the situation cannot be characterized in any simple way, and one finds many writers from former British colonies who face difficult choices with regard to language. See Ricard, *Littératures d'Afrique noire,* 152–162.

17. See Rushdie, "Imaginary Homelands," 15.

18. But also in France: see, for example, Janheinz Jahn, *Manuel de littérature négro-africaine* (Paris: Resma, 1969), 229–230.

19. William Shakespeare, *The Tempest,* ed. Robert Langbaum (New York: Signet Classic, 1964), act 1, scene ii, 55.

20. Rachid Boudjedra, in an interview with the author (November 1991), characterized Algerian literature as a whole—notwithstanding certain great exceptions such as Kateb Yacine—as a "literature of schoolteachers." This interview was subsequently published as "Entretien avec Rachid Boudjedra," *Liber,* no. 17 (March 1994): 11–14.

21. Salman Rushdie, "'Commonwealth Literature' Does Not Exist," in *Imaginary Homelands,* 69–70. Rushdie also emphasizes that the hegemony of English, now the "international language," is no longer only—and perhaps not even primarily—a consequence of the British heritage. It is also the language of the United States, now the most powerful country in the world. This ambiguity makes it possible for former colonies to escape exclusive British domination and sustains the ambivalent relation between the English language as the language used by the English and as the language used by much of the world—between a new literature produced by "translated men" and a denationalized international culture.

22. Ibid., 70.

23. Rushdie, "Imaginary Homelands," 17.

24. Rushdie, "'Commonwealth Literature' Does not Exist," 64.

25. See Ricard, *Littératures d'Afrique noire,* especially 151–172.

26. See Bernard Magnier, "Entretien avec Ahmadou Kourouma," *Notre librairie,* April–June 1987.

27. In the literary magazine *Cahiers de Barbarie,* edited by Jean Amrouche and Armand Guibert.

28. Hova is the written language of the Merina, a people of ancient Indonesian ancestry who occupied the high plateau of the island's interior and were the dominant kingdom of Madagascar in the nineteenth century.

29. See Jean Paulhan, *Les Hain-teny mérinas: Poésies populaires malgaches* (Paris: P. Geuthner, 1913). [Originally a means of resolving lawsuits, the oral genre of *hain teny* ("science of words") was marked by improvised dialogue between two opponents or, by metaphorical extension, quarreling lovers.—Trans.]

30. Boudjedra, "Entretien," 14.

31. The General Union (Bund) of Jewish Workers in Lithuania, Poland, and Russia was an organization of revolutionary Jewish workers founded in 1897 in Vilna; independent of the Mencheviks and Bolsheviks, and opposed to the Zionist movement, which it saw as a "romantic" form of bourgeois nationalism, it played an important role before and during the Russian Revolution of 1917, after which it was repressed.—Trans.

32. An informal group of German Jewish writers and artists led by Max Broad whose inner circle included Felix Weltsch, Oskar Baum, and (after Kafka's death) Ludwig Winter. Among the peripheral members were Ernst Weiss, Rudolf Fuchs, Willy Hass, and Hermann Ungar.—Trans.

33. The term "anti-Zionist" is used here exclusively in connection with the internal debates of Jewish nationalist movements at the beginning of the twentieth century—debates that opposed Zionists and Bundists—and the historical context surrounding them.

34. Thus the French title of this work: see Claude David, "'Notice' de *L'Amérique [L'oublié],*" in his edition of Franz Kafka, *Oeuvres complètes,* trans. Alexandre Vialatte, 3 vols. (Gallimard: 1976–84), 1:811. A more literal rendering of the German would be "The Missing Person," which is to say, as David notes, someone of whom all trace has been lost.—Trans.

35. Franz Kafka, *Letters to Friends, Family and Editors,* trans. Richard and Clara Winston (New York: Schocken, 1977), 288–289. In the German text Kafka distinguishes three ways of appropriating the German language: the appropriation may be openly admitted *(laut),* or tacit *(stillschweigend),* or else achieved only at the cost of an internal struggle amounting to mental torture for the writer *(selbstquälerisch).*

36. Franx Kafka, *Diaries,* ed. Max Brod, trans. Joseph Kresh and Martin Green-berg, 2 vols. (New York: Schocken, 1948–49), 1:111.

37. Eric Hobsbawm, *Nations and Nationalism since 1780* (New York: Cambridge University Press, 1990), 54.

38. Note the distinction made by Daniel Baggioni between "normalization," defined as "establishment of a norm . . . concerning the symbolic cap-italization necessary for creating a consensus that will allow its diffusion and adoption," and "standardization," which has to do with "the work of lan-guage professionals, grammarians, philologists, writers, and so on"; *Langues et nations en Europe* (Paris: Payot, 1997), 91.

39. Ricard, *Littératures d'Afrique noire,* 118.

40. Kikuyu is not the national language of Kenya, which in 1971 declared Swa-hili the sole official language, a distinction that until then had been shared with English.

41. From an edited version of a talk originally given by Ngugi wa Thiong'o at the Kenya Press Club, Nairobi, on 17 July 1979 and reprinted as "Return to the Roots: Language, Culture and Politics in Kenya," in *Writers in Politics: A Reengagement with Issues of Literature and Society,* ed. James Currey, rev. ed. (Portsmouth: Heinemann, 1997), 58.

42. Rushdie, "'Commonwealth Literature' Does Not Exist," 62–63.

43. Ricard, *Littératures d'Afrique noire,* 148.

44. Or a "diglossia" in the sense given this term by sociolinguists; see Baggioni, *Langues et nations en Europe,* 55.

45. Henrik Stangerup, *The Seducer: It Is Hard to Die in Dieppe,* trans. Sean Martin (New York: Marion Boyars, 1990), 199.

46. Antonio Candido, *On Literature and Society,* trans. Howard S. Becker (Prince-ton: Princeton University Press, 1995), 105–106.

47. Howard S. Becker, introduction to ibid., xxi.

48. E. M. Cioran, "Lettre à Bacur Tincu, 29 décembre 1973," quoted in Gabriel Liiceanu, *Itinéraires d'une vie: E. M. Cioran, suivi de "Les continents de l'in-somnie": Entretien avec E. M. Cioran* (Paris: Michalon, 1995), 30.

49. I have already noted that a relatively autonomous "national" space may be formed and unified in the absence of a state in the strict political sense of the term. In certain politically dependent regions that have a strong indige-nous cultural tradition and within which forces of cultural and political na-tionalism (or movements aimed at achieving political independence) have grown up, as in Ireland at the end of the nineteenth century, and in Cata-lonia and Martinique today, one may speak of the emergence of a relatively autonomous literary space.

50. Juan Benet, *Otoño en Madrid hacia 1950* (Madrid: Alianza Editorial, 1987), 38–40.

51. Milan Kundera, "La parole de Kundera," *Le Monde,* 24 September 1993, 44.

52. They are exceptions because there political independence was proclaimed not by the colonized but by the colonists, as a consequence of which the relation of the present-day residents of these areas to the languages they speak is not one of subjection or imposition but of "legitimate" inheritance.

53. The partly national struggle of Egyptian writers during this period to introduce literary and linguistic realism—so-called dialectal and popular Arabic, until then restricted to the production of a second-class literature—as against the overrefinement of the classical language among aesthetes, can be described in exactly the same terms and according to the same logic.

54. Jean Bernabé, Patrick Chamoiseau, and Raphaël Confiant, *Éloge de la créolité/In Praise of Creoleness,* bilingual ed. (Paris: Gallimard; Baltimore: Johns Hopkins University Press, 1990), 80.

55. Quoted in Mario Carelli and Walnice Nogueira Galvão, *Le roman brésilien: Une littérature anthropophage au XXe siècle* (Paris: Presses Universitaires de France, 1995), 60.

56. Mário de Andrade, *Macunaima,* trans. E. A. Goodland (New York: Random House, 1984), 108.

57. Notable among those who came before is José de Alencar (1829–1877), to whom Andrade dedicated *Macunaíma* and who had sought to promote a Brazilian language; see Carelli and Galvão, *Le roman brésilien,* 10–11.

58. Already in the 1940s the ethnologist Roger Bastide had suggested a parallel between *Macunaíma* and the enterprise of the Pléiade: see his article "*Macunaíma* visto por um francês," *Revista do Arquivo municipal* (São Paulo), no. 106 (January 1946).

59. Oswald de Andrade, "Manifesto da poesia Pau-Brasil," in *Do Pau-Brasil a Antropafagia e as Utopias,* vol. 6 of *Obras completas* (Rio de Janeiro: Civilização Brasileira, 1972), 7.

60. Quoted by Gilles Lapouge in his preface to Mário de Andrade, *L'apprenti touriste,* trans. Monique Le Moing and Marie-Pierre Mazéas (Paris: La Quinzaine Littérarie–Louis Vuitton, 1996), 13.

61. See Mario Carelli, "Les Brésiliens à Paris de la naissance du romantisme aux avant-gardes," in *Le Paris des étrangers: Depuis un siècle,* ed. André Kaspi and Antoine Marès (Paris: Imprimerie Nationale, 1989), 287–298.

62. From Andrade's third letter to Alberto de Oliveira, quoted in Carelli and Galvão, *Le roman brésilien,* 53.

63. From Andrade's letter to Manuel Bandeira, quoted in ibid.

64. Andrade, *Macunaima,* 80.

65. Ibid., 78.

66. Samuel Beckett, "Dante . . . Bruno. Vico . . . Joyce," in *Our Exagmination*

Round His Factification for Incamination of Work in Progress (Paris: Shakespeare & Co., 1929), 30.

67. Mário de Andrade, *O turista aprendeiz* (São Paulo: Libraria Duas Cidades/ Secretária de Cultura, Ciência e Technologia, 1976), 207.

68. Theodor Koch-Grünberg, *Vom Roroima zum Orinoco: Mythen und Legenden der Taulipang und Arekuná Indianern* (Stuttgart: Strecker und Schroeder, 1924). See Telê Porto Ancona Lopez, "*Macounaïma* et Mário de Andrade," in *Macounaïma,* ed. Pierre Rivas (Paris: Stock, 1996), 242–243.

69. Mário de Andrade, letter to Souza de Oliveira (26 April 1935), quoted by Michel Riaudel, "Toupi or not toupi: Une aporie de l'être national," in ibid., 300. Andrade thus opposed regionalist literature, which had been very important in Brazil since the end of the nineteenth century.

70. Quoted in ibid., 301.

71. A bit later João Guimarães Rosa (1908–1967) was to proceed in a very similar fashion, in his stories and especially in his great novel, *Grande sertão: Veredas* (The Devil to Pay in the Backlands, 1956), decisively enriching the national Brazilian vocabulary through his inexhaustible enumeration of terms referring to the flora and fauna of the *sertão.*

72. Andrade, *Macunaima,* 28.

73. Joachim du Bellay, *The Defence and Illustration of the French Language,* trans. Gladys M. Turquet (London: J. M. Dent and Sons, 1939), 95.

74. See Riaudel, "Toupi or not toupi," 290.

75. Quoted by Pierre Rivas, "Réception critique de *Macounaïma* en France," in Rivas, *Macounaïma,* 315.

76. Conversely, Andrade's fellow countryman Oswald de Andrade, who made many trips to Paris, sought to make himself known and to arrange for translation of his work. He managed to meet Larbaud—despite the warnings of Mathilde Pomès, who regarded Latin Americans as "people thirsting for European fame"—and, in addition to his own work (which, however, remained untranslated), acquainted Larbaud with modern Brazilian writing. It is known that he gave Larbaud a volume of the works of the great nineteenth-century Brazilian novelist Machado de Assis. See Béatrice Mousli, *Valery Larbaud* (Paris: Flammarion, 1998), 378.

77. Quoted in Riaudel, "Toupi or not toupi," 304.

78. Andrade, *Macunaima,* 13.

79. Pierre Rivas, "Modernisme et primitivisme dans *Macounaïma,*" in Rivas, *Macounaïma,* 11.

80. Quoted in ibid.

81. See Angela McRobbie, "Wet, wet, wet," *Liber: Revue internationale des livres,* no. 24 (October 1995): 8–11.

82. Ernest Hemingway, *The Green Hills of Africa* (New York: Scribner, 1935), 22.

83. Quoted in Duncan McLean, "James Kelman Interviewed," *Edinburgh Review* 71 (1985): 77.

84. See Alfredo Almeida, *Jorge Amado: Politica e literatura* (Rio de Janeiro: Campus, 1979).

85. Jorge Amado, *Conversations avec Alice Raillard* (Paris: Gallimard, 1990), 38, 20; emphasis added.

86. Ibid., 42–43.

87. Bernabé, Chamoiseau, and Confiant, *Éloge de la créolité/In Praise of Creoleness,* 102.

88. Charles Ferdinand Ramuz, *Raison d'être* (Paris: La Différence, 1991), 56.

89. The difference in status between creole French, claimed to be a "language" by its defenders, and the Vaudois dialect (or "patois") can be one only of degree of independence in relation to the norms of French.

90. Ramuz, *Raison d'être,* 55.

91. Bernabé, Chamoiseau, and Confiant, *Éloge de la créolité/In Praise of Creoleness,* 105 [translation slightly modified].

92. Ibid., 76.

93. Ibid., 95–98; emphasis added.

94. Charles Ferdinand Ramuz, letter to Paul Claudel (22 April 1925), quoted in Jérôme Meizoz, "Le droit de mal écrire," *Actes de la recherche en sciences sociales,* nos. 111–112 (March 1996): 106.

95. In much the same way the Danish novelist Henrik Stangerup, in *The Seducer,* made his literary and historical hero Møller a literary critic who set out for Paris in search of the "Danish tone" in order to found a new Danish literature, freed from the yoke of German domination.

96. Ramuz, *Raison d'être,* 64.

97. Bernabé, Chamoiseau, and Confiant, *Éloge de la créolité/In Praise of Creoleness,* 102.

98. Ibid., 100.

99. Ibid., 96 [translation slightly modified].

100. Ramuz, *Raison d'être,* 66.

101. Ibid., 67. This last sentence may be read as a vow to make the *pays vaudois* a simple detour on the road to Paris, which is to say to universality.

102. Ibid., 68–69; emphasis added.

103. Bernabé, Chamoiseau, and Confiant, *Éloge de la créolité/In Praise of Creoleness,* 102, 111–115 [translation slightly modified].

104. Ramuz, *Raison d'être,* 43; emphasis added.

105. *Pour ou contre C.-F. Ramuz: Cahier des témoignages* (Paris: Éditions du Siècle, 1926).

10. The Irish Paradigm

1. Irish literary space has the additional and rare distinction of combining every form of domination. Like all European literatures it was from the beginning relatively well endowed with resources, while at the same time exhibiting all the characteristics of economic and cultural colonization.

2. Bourdieu's notion of "progressive autonomization" (as the term is ritually translated in English) is developed in several essays; see particularly *The Field of Cultural Production* (New York: Columbia University Press, 1993), 52–55 and 112–114.—Trans.

3. See Declan Kiberd, *Inventing Ireland: The Literature of the Modern Nation* (Cambridge, Mass.: Harvard University Press, 1995), 1–8.

4. Lady Gregory was to publish her *Cuchulain of Muirthemne* in 1902. The legend of Deirdre was adapted for the stage by Yeats, Æ, and Synge; James Stephens gave a narrative version of it.

5. This play associated the legendary figure of Cathleen, the symbol of Ireland, and the memory of the French landing at Killala in 1798.

6. Kiltartan, a dialect of English that preserves Elizabethan and Jacobean archaicisms as well as underlying Gaelic turns of phrase, is the speech of the peasants of County Galway, the home of Lady Gregory. See Robert Welch, ed., *The Oxford Companion to Irish Literature* (Oxford: Clarendon Press, 1996), 226.

7. W. B. Yeats, "The Irish Dramatic Movement, Samhain 1902," in *The Collected Works of William Butler Yeats* (Stratford-on-Avon: A. H. Bullen/Shakespeare Head Press, 1908), 102–103; idem, *The Celtic Twilight* (London: A. H. Bullen, 1902), 232–233.

8. Kiberd, *Inventing Ireland,* 133.

9. James Joyce, "Ireland, Island of Saints and Sages," in *The Critical Writings of James Joyce,* ed. Ellsworth Mason and Richard Ellmann (New York: Viking, 1959), 155–156.

10. Kiberd, *Inventing Ireland,* 155.

11. See John Kelly, "*The Irish Review,*" in *L'année 1913: Les formes esthétiques de l'oeuvre d'art à la veille de la Première Guerre mondiale,* ed. Liliane Brion-Guerry, 2 vols. (Paris: Klincksieck, 1971), 2:1024. See also Luke Gibbons, "Constructing the Canon: Versions of National Identity," in Seamus Deane, Andrew Carpenter, and Jonathan Williams, eds., *The Field Day Anthology of Irish Writing,* 3 vols. (Lawrence Hill, Derry, Northern Ireland: Field Day, 1991), 3:950–955.

12. From Françoise Morvan's introduction to her edition of J. M. Synge, *Théâtre* (Paris: Babel, 1996), 16–17.

13. J. M. Synge, "1907 Preface to *The Playboy of the Western World,*" in Robin

Skelton, ed., *J. M. Synge: Collected Works*, 4 vols. (London: Oxford University Press, 1962–1968), 2:53–54.

14. Born John Casey, he Gaelicized his first name (Sean) and his patronymic (O'Casey) in order to identify and integrate himself more completely with the nationalist struggle.

15. See in particular the section "A Terrible Beauty is Borneo," in *Inishfallen, Fare Thee Well* (New York: Macmillan, 1949), 219–222.

16. Quoted in Sean O'Casey, *Rose and Crown* (London: Macmillan, 1952), 41–42.

17. G. B. Shaw, letter to Sylvia Beach (11 June 1921), quoted in Richard Ellmann, *James Joyce* (New York: Oxford University Press, 1982), 506–507.

18. See Richard Ellmann's preface to "An Irish Poet," in Mason and Ellmann, *Critical Writings*, 84.

19. James Joyce, "The Soul of Ireland,' in ibid., 104.

20. James Joyce, "The Day of the Rabblement," in ibid., 71.

21. See Alessandro Francini-Bruni, *Joyce intimo spogliatto in paizza* (Trieste: Editoriale Libraria, 1922); quoted in Ellmann, *James Joyce*, 226.

22. James Joyce, letter to Grant Richards (5 May 1906), quoted in "An Irish Poet," 85, n. 5.

23. See Joyce, "Ireland, Island of Saints and Sages," 172–174.

24. Joyce, "An Irish Poet," 85.

25. Joyce, "The Day of the Rabblement," 70–71.

26. Among the reasons for Joyce's prolonged exile (and that of many other Irish artists), one must not neglect the Catholic censorship established in Ireland after 1921, which imposed very strict aesthetic norms and moral prohibitions upon artists.

27. Cyril Connolly, *Enemies of Promise* (New York: Macmillan, 1948), 30, 58.

28. Interview with Seamus Heaney in *Libération*, 24 November 1988.

29. In Bourdieu's terms, used by the author here and elsewhere, Beckett occupied the same "positions" and exhibited the same "dispositions" that Joyce had; see the discussion of these concepts in *The Field of Cultural Production*, 61–73.—Trans.

30. Samuel Beckett, "German Letter of 1937," in *Disjecta: Miscellaneous Writings and a Dramatic Fragment,* ed. Ruby Cohn (London: John Calder, 1983), 52–53.

31. Among recent studies in this direction, see in particular János Riesz, "La notion de champ littérarire appliquée à la littérature togoloise," in *Le champ littéraire togolais,* ed. János Riesz and Alain Ricard (Bayreuth: E. Breitinger/ Universität Bayreuth, 1991), 11–20.

32. Of the many studies that rely solely on the uncertain notion of "influence"

in seeking to relate writers in Irish literary space to one another, see, for example, Martha Fodaski Black, *Shaw and Joyce: The Last Word in Stolentelling* (Gainesville: University Press of Florida, 1995).

33. Edward Said, "Yeats and Decolonization," in *Nationalism, Colonialism, and Literature,* ed. Terry Eagleton, Fredric Jameson, and Edward Said (Minneapolis: University of Minnesota Press, 1990), 69.

34. Fredric Jameson, "Modernism and Imperialism," in ibid., 45.

35. See Said, "Yeats and Decolonization," 73.

36. See Enda Duffy, *The Subaltern Ulysses* (Minneapolis: University of Minnesota Press, 1994).

37. Edward Said, *Culture and Imperialism* (New York: Knopf, 1994), 8.

38. Kiberd, Inventing Ireland, 6, 5.

11. The Revolutionaries

1. Carlos Fuentes, "Ha Muerto la novela?" in *Geografía de la novela* (Mexico City: Fondo de Cultura Económica, 1993), 27.

2. Quoted in Claude Cymerman and Claude Fell, *Histoire de la littérature hispano-américaine de 1940 à nos jours* (Paris: Nathan, 1997), 13–14. On the term "cronopio," see Cortázar's novel *Historias de cronopios y de famas* (1962).

3. Octavio Paz, *In Search of the Present: 1990 Nobel Lecture,* bilingual ed., trans. Anthony Stanton (San Diego: Harcourt Brace Jovanovich, 1990), 16, 19.

4. Here I propose only a very partial study of a few heretical genealogies. To this list would have to be added in particular the name of Jorge Luis Borges, recognized as a master by a great many novelists both in the center and on the periphery (among them Danilo Kiš).

5. See the chapter "Usages politiques et littéraires de Dante" in Pascale Casanova, *Beckett l'abstracteur: Anatomie d'une révolution littéraire* (Paris: Seuil, 1997), 64–80.

6. Giambattista Vico (1668–1744), Neapolitan historian, jurist, and philosopher who used a comparative method to study the formation, development, and decline of nations, served as a sort of substitute for Herder for writers and intellectuals distant from the Germanic cultural area.

7. The notion that there is an affinity between the two writers, or even that Joyce exerted any influence upon Schmidt, is continually denied by critics. Relying on statements made by the German writer, who rightly refused to be regarded—as commentators on his work insisted—as a mere imitator, they thus succeed only in obeying one of the tacit laws of the literary world, namely, that an author cannot be declared great unless he demonstrates total originality, which is to say unless he qualifies for a certificate of historical virginity.

8. Arno Schmidt, excerpt from letter to Ernst Krawehl, 3 March 1963, quoted in Schmidt, *Der Briefwechsel mit Alfred Andersch,* vol. 1 of *Arno-Schmidt-Briefedition* (Zurich: Haffmans Verlag, 1986), 224 (note to letter 235).

9. Arno Schmidt, *Scenes from the Life of a Faun,* in *Collected Early Fiction, 1949–1964,* 4 vols., trans. John E. Woods (Normal, Ill.: Dalkey Archive, 1994–1997), 2:19.

10. Arno Schmidt, *Calculations III,* trans. Freidrich Peter Ott, in *Review of Contemporary Fiction* 8 (spring 1988): 88.

11. Ibid., 72.

12. Arno Schmidt, *Calculations I,* in ibid., 55; idem, *Scenes from the Life of a Faun,* trans. John E. Woods (London: Marion Boyars, 1983), 93.

13. Arno Schmidt, *Brand's Heath,* in *Collected Early Fiction,* 2:115.

14. James Joyce, "The Day of the Rabblement," in *The Critical Writings of James Joyce,* ed. Ellsworth Mason and Richard Ellmann (New York: Viking, 1959), 69–70.

15. Schmidt, *Scenes from the Life of a Faun,* trans. Woods (Boyars edition), 9–10.

16. Henry Roth, *From Bondage* (New York: St. Martin's, 1996), 62, 64.

17. Roth himself figures as a character in *From Bondage,* under the name of Ira Stigman.

18. Ibid., 73–75; emphasis added.

19. The Yiddish expression for someone who is an expert, a connoisseur, which has given English the word "maven."—Trans.

20. Roth, *From Bondage,* 76–77; emphasis added.

21. Ibid., 74.

22. From Larbaud's preface to William Faulkner, *Tandis que j'agonise,* trans. Maurice-Edgar Coindreau (Paris: Gallimard, 1934), i.

23. Juan Benet, interview with the author, October 1987.

24. The assertion of stylistic kinship and similarity between Benet's work and that of Claude Simon, for example, which no French reader could fail to note and which was emphasized by the jacket copy of Éditions de Minuit, their common publisher, are in fact the result of an error of perspective and Francocentric interpretation. Benet insisted on his unfamiliarity with the *nouveau roman,* and his lack of interest in it, when he was starting out as a writer: "No, the *nouveau roman* wasn't that important for me. It was reading William Faulkner that really awakened me to all the possibilities of writing. After him, of course, I read the French novelists of the *nouveau roman,* and the German, English, South American writers, but [by then] I was already too mature and too far along in writing my books to feel the influence of these authors" (interview with the author, October 1987). Rather, a certain state of the novel, combined with the existence of an international literary culture, was capable of producing quite similar projects in different

places and contexts. Claude Simon, for his part, was a self-proclaimed descendant of Faulkner as well.

25. Juan Benet, interview with the author, July 1991.
26. Valery Larbaud, preface to Faulkner, *Tandis que j'agonise,* ii.
27. Benet even went so far as to embed phrases from Faulkner in his own fictional texts. Thus he refers, for example, to "the barking 'unreal, sonorous, and regular, stamped by that sad and resigned desolation' with which the dogs were calling to each other"; *Return to Región,* trans. Gregory Rabassa (New York: Columbia University Press, 1985), 265.
28. Preface to William Faulkner, *Les palmiers sauvages,* trans. Maurice-Edgar Coindreau (Paris: Gallimard, 1952), 4, 5.
29. Benet, *Return to Región,* 3–4.
30. Ibid., 76.
31. Ibid., 202.
32. Ibid., 63, 64.
33. In "Tres Fechas: Sobre la estrategia en la Guerra Civil española," in *La construcción de la torre de Babel* (Madrid: Siruela, 1990), 85–116, Benet speaks of the "theoretical backwardness" of Spanish military leaders.
34. Benet, *Return to Región,* 201 [translation slightly modified].
35. Rachid Boudjedra, interview with the author, November 1991, published as "Entretien avec Rachid Boudjedra," *Liber,* no. 17 (March 1994): 13.
36. Ibid., 13, 11, 12, 14.
37. Kateb Yacine, interview with Mireille Djaider and K. Nekkouri-Khelladi, 4 April 1975, published as "Le génie est collectif," in *Kateb Yacine: Éclats de mémoire,* ed. Olivier Corpet and Albert Dichy (Paris: IMEC Éditions, 1994), 61–62.
38. Mario Vargas Llosa, *Sobre la vida y la política: Diálogo con Vargas Llosa,* ed. Ricardo A. Setti (Buenos Aires: Editorial Intermundo, 1989), 17–18.
39. Along with the majority of Latin American novelists today, mention must be made of Patrick Chamoiseau and Raphaël Confiant, as well as Édouard Glissant, all of whom claim kinship with Faulkner and membership in the community of the "American creole novel," as Chamoiseau described it in my September 1992 interview with him.
40. Katalin Molnár, "Dlalang," *Revue de littérature générale,* February 1996.
41. The phonetic portion of Molnár's original text reads: "Le but a été atteint, tou, absolumantou sèksprim danlélang jadis vulguèr . . . écéla justeman ouçafoir ôjourd'hui avèklalitératur . . . Par conséquent, ils peuvent utiliser n'importe quel procédé, réaliser tout ce qui est réalisable, tou, absoluman toutépermi!"—Trans.
42. Samuel Beckett, "German Letter of 1937," in *Disjecta: Miscellaneous Writings and a Dramatic Fragment,* ed. Ruby Cohn (London: John Calder, 1983), 53.

Conclusion

1. Samuel Beckett, *Le monde et le pantalon* (Paris: Éditions de Minuit, 1989), 8–9.
2. Roland Barthes, "Histoire ou littérature," in *Sur Racine* (Paris: Seuil, 1963), 145–167.
3. Ibid., 148.
4. Marc Fumaroli, *Trois institutions littéraires* (Paris: Gallimard, 1994), xii.
5. Antoine Compagnon, *Le démon de la théorie: Littérature et sens commun* (Paris: Seuil, 1998), 239.
6. Barthes, "Histoire ou littérature," 148.
7. Beckett, *Le monde et le pantalon,* 33, 10–11.
8. See Lucien Febvre, "Littérature et vie sociale. De Lanson à Daniel Mornet: Un renoncement?" *Annales d'histoire économique et sociale* 13, no. 3 (1941).
9. Marcel Proust, *Remembrance of Things Past,* trans. C. K. Scott-Moncrieff, Terence Kilmartin, and Andreas Mayor, 3 vols. (New York: Random House, 1981), 3:1104.
10. Ibid., 1098–99.
11. Throughout the text, where I have spoken of a writer's "career" in preference to literal renderings of *itinéraire* or *trajectoire,* terms often found in the French text, it will of course be understood that the reference is not to his or her occupation, or to a reputation determined by critics or other literary authorities, but, in keeping with the root sense of the English word and with the author's own conceptions, the path and passage of a writer through literary space and literary time.—Trans.
12. Proust, *Remembrance of Things Past,* 1089.

Index

Croats, 78, 182, 187
Cuba, 206, 222, 232–234, 325
Cuchulain (Irish legendary figure), 190, 305, 306, 381n35
Cummings, E. E., 134
Curtius, Ernst, 27. WORKS: *French Culture (Die französische Kultur)*, 27
Czech language, 201, 274, 281–282
Czech nationalism, 269
Czechoslovakia, 196, 200, 309
Czechs, 78, 84, 191

Dadaism, 279
Dahomey, 260
Daireaux, Max, 184
Daive, Jean, 281
Danish language, 256, 277
Dante Alighieri, 14, 46, 49, 52, 55, 56, 57, 249, 319, 328–330. WORKS: *The Banquet (Il Convivio)*, 55; *On Vernacular Eloquence (De vulgari eloquentia)*, 46, 55, 329
Danton, Georges-Jacques, 25
Darantière, Maurice, 363n85
Darío, Rubén, 91, 95, 96–97, 99, 223, 246, 326, 355; on attraction of Paris, 32–33; "mental Gallicism" of, 19, 138, 258, 266. WORKS: *Azul*, 96; *Prosas profanas*, 96
Defauconpret, A. J. B., 146
Deirdre, Irish legend of, 305, 397n4
Deleuze, Gilles, 165, 166, 203–204
Delibes, Miguel, 110, 280
DeLillo, Don, 169
Delphi, 27
Demolder, Eugène, 188
Demosthenes, 70
Denmark, 99, 159, 162, 168
Derrida, Jacques, 165, 166
Descartes, René, 64, 366n46. WORKS: *Discourse on Method (Discours de la méthode)*, 64; *General and Analytical Grammar (Grammaire générale et raisonnée)*, 64
Desfontaine, Pierre-François Guyot, Abbé, 68
Desnos, Robert, 232
Desportes, Philippe, 60
Diaghilev, Sergei Pavlovich, 126
Dib, Mohammed, 220, 235. WORKS: "Thief of Fire," 220
Dickens, Charles, 121, 321
Disque Vert, Le (review), 189
Djibouti, 260
Dongala, Emmanuel, 259–260

Dorat (Jean Dinemandi), 51
Dos Passos, John, 130, 169, 344
Dostoevsky, Fyodor, 199, 260
Dotremont, Christian, 251, 252
Dowell, Coleman, 169
Drachmann, Holger, 98
Dreyfus Affair, 150, 363n82
Dryden, John, 73
Dublin, 109, 128, 140, 146, 160, 188, 191, 295, 319; literary description of, 247; relation to London, 314, 316; theater in, 307; Trinity College, 189
Dublin School, 303
Dubuffet, Jean, 253
Du Camp, Maxime, 27
Duffy, Enda, 322
Dumas, Alexandre, 32, 159
Dun Cow, Book of the, 243
Duriaud, Jean, 290
Durkheim, Émile, 59
Dutch language, 248, 256

Easter 1916 uprising (Ireland), 190, 312
Eckermann, Johann Peter, 236
Eckhoud, Georges, 188
Eco, Umberto, 101, 171
École Normale Supérieure, 189
Ecuador, 222
Edinburgh, 247
Éditions Bordas, 141
Éditions Parti Pris, 284
Egypt, 238, 283, 394n53
Eliot, T. S., 153
Elizabethan literature, 106
Ellison, Ralph, 173. WORKS: *Invisible Man*, 173
Éloge de la créolité (In Praise of Creoleness) (manifesto), 296
Emerson, Ralph Waldo, 222. WORKS: "The American Scholar," 222
England, 11, 36, 37, 55, 71, 73, 85, 105–106, 312. *See also* British Empire; Great Britain; London
English language, 32, 73–75, 139, 167, 258; global dominance of, 119, 391n21; in Ireland, 307, 310, 315; London as literary center, 117; Old and Middle English, 240; postcolonial literature and, 275–276; in United States, 62
"English Men of Letters" anthology, 106
Enlightenment, French, 84–85
Ernst, Max, 126

Monénembo, Tierno, 125
Monnier, Adrienne, 29, 145
Montale, Eugenio, 153
Montreal, 232, 283
Monzó, Quim, 247, 278
Moore, George, 154, 226, 303, 305, 306, 311, 315. WORKS: *Diarmuid and Gráinne* (with Yeats), 389n69
Moore, Thomas, 146
Morand, Paul, 134
More, Sir Thomas, 363n77
Morel, Auguste, 145
Morley, John, 106
Moro, César, 32
Morocco, 257
Morvan, Françoise, 310
Moscow, 95
Möser, Justus, 76, 77
Mozambique, 123–124
Mukherjee, Bharati, 120
Munich, 177
Murray, T. C., 312
Mutis, Álvaro, 206

Nabokov, Vladimir, 129, 134, 138, 164, 281. WORKS: *Camera Obscura / Laughter in the Dark* (*Kamera Obskura*), 139, 375n33; *Despair* (*Otchaianie*), 139; *King, Queen, Knave* (*Korol, dama, valet*), 138; *Lolita*, 129, 140, 169; *The Luzhin Defense* (*Zashchita Luzhina*), 138–139, 375n30; "Mademoiselle O," 140; *Mary* (*Mashen'ka*), 138; *Nikolai Gogol*, 164; "Pouchkine ou le vrai et le vraisemblable," 140; *The Real Life of Sebastian Knight*, 140
Nabuco, Joaquim, 32. WORKS: *The Choice* (*L'Option*), 32
Nadeau, Maurice, 144, 169, 376n44
Nagai, Kafu, 32
Naipaul, V. S., 4, 110, 120, 178, 205, 209–212, 215, 217, 315. WORKS: *An Area of Darkness*, 384n12; *The Enigma of Arrival*, 210; *India: A Million Mutinies Now*, 384n12; *India: A Wounded Civilization*, 384n12; "Our Universal Civilization," 205
Nairobi, University of (Kenya), 231
Naples, 24
Narayan, R. K., 118, 264
Nation Tchèque, La (journal), 31
Na Zdar (journal), 31
Nazism, 19, 30, 252, 331, 333
Ndebele, Njabulo, 261–262

Negritude, 297, 300
Neocolonial novel, 379n14
Neo-Gothic (architectural style), 368n73
Neoimpressionism, 132
Neruda, Pablo, 153, 234, 322
Neustadt Prize, 376n52
New Criticism, 321
New Directions (publishing house), 140
New York City, 92, 93, 109, 117, 164, 206; as city of Jewish immigration, 270, 334; Irish-Americans in, 318; rivalry with London, 119, 122, 123; rivalry with Paris, 165. *See also* United States
New York Society for the Suppression of Vice, 145
New Zealand, 117, 120
Ngugi wa Thiong'o, 195, 229, 231, 258, 275–276. WORKS: *The Black Hermit*, 231; *Devil on the Cross* (*Caitaani mutharaba-ini*), 231, 275; *A Grain of Wheat*, 231; *I Will Marry When I Want* (*Ngaahika ndeenda*), 231; *Petals of Blood*, 231; *The River Between*, 231; *Weep Not, Child*, 231
Nicaragua, 325
Nicolas, Jean-Baptiste, 388n49
Nietzsche, Friedrich, 129, 191
Nieuwenhuys, Constant, 251
Nigeria, 110, 120, 195, 227–228
Nineveh, 27
Nkashama, Pius Ngandu, 135–136, 386n18
Nobel, Alfred, 147, 149
Nobel Prize, 168, 212, 376n51, 384n15; African writers, 120, 227; East Asian (Chinese, Korean) writers, 147–148, 280; Hispano-American writers, 92, 94, 180, 206, 233, 234, 241, 325; Irish writers, 187, 307, 313, 318; North American writers, 131; Portuguese-speaking writers, 148; South Asian (Indian) writers, 135, 149
Noh theater, 311
Noiret, Joseph, 251, 252
Norman Conquest, 73
North America, 11
Norway, 50, 79, 98, 129, 158, 162, 248, 250, 309
Norwegian language, 78, 256, 274
Nouvelle Revue Française (journal), 131, 146, 157
Nouvelles Littéraires, Les (journal), 138–139
Novalis, Friedrich, 77, 236
Nyerere, Julius, 387n34. TRANSLATIONS: *Julius Caesar*, 387n34; *The Merchant of Venice*, 387n34

Nynorsk (new Norwegian), 158, 256, 274
Nyugat (journal), 361n50

O'Casey, Sean, 192, 193, 225, 305, 311–313,
    398n14. WORKS: *Cathleen Listens In*, 312;
    Juno and the Paycock, 312; *The Plough and the
    Stars*, 312; *The Shadow of a Gunman*, 192,
    312
O'Conaire, Padraic, 307, 308
O'Connell, Daniel, 308
Oe, Kenzaburo, 377n63
Oehlenschläger, Adam, 277
O'Grady, Standish James, 190, 196, 305.
    WORKS: *History of Ireland: Heroic Period*, 305
Okri, Ben, 120, 228. WORKS: *The Famished
    Road*, 228
Old English, 240
Old World, 243
Oliveira, Alberto de, 45, 286
Oliveira, Manuel de, 167
Olympia Press, 140
Ondaatje, Michael, 120, 122
O'Neill, Eugene, 151
Onetti, Juan Carlos, 325
Opéra Français, 132
Ordinance of Villers-Cotterêts, 51
Ors, Eugenio d', 246
Orthodox Christianity, 198
Ossian, 76, 306
Oster, Daniel, 26
Ottawa, 283
Oxford English Dictionary, 106

Pakistan, 121
Pak Kyong-Ni, 147, 280. WORKS: *Land (T'oji)*,
    147
Palestine, 270
Pámies, Sergi, 278
Paparrigopoulos, Konstantinos, 242. WORKS:
    *History of the Greek Nation (Historia tou
    hellenikou ethnous)*, 242
Pardo Bazán, Emilia, 102. WORKS: *The Burning
    Question (La cuestión palpitante)*, 102
Paris, 11, 23–24, 25–34, 87, 93, 109; artistic cen-
    trality challenged, 251–253; consecration in,
    127–131, 230; "decline" of, 164–165; émigrés
    in, 138–140, 143, 206, 232, 317, 375n29; mo-
    dernity and, 96, 126, 334; postcolonial writ-
    ers and, 122, 124–125; prestige of, 96; rivalry
    with Brussels, 131–133; rivalry with London,
    153, 165; rivalry with New York, 165; the-

ater in, 160; as universal capital, 108. *See also*
    France
Paris Guide (1867), 24, 88
Parnassism, 223, 265
Parnell, Charles Stewart, 190, 249, 308
Parti Pris (review), 284
Pascal, Blaise, 67
Paulhan, Jean, 266
Pavel, Thomas, 59
Pavić, Milorad, 101
Paz, Octavio, 28, 43, 82, 85, 92–94, 125, 244;
    Mexican national identity and, 241; mod-
    ernization and, 326–327; Nobel Prize and,
    234, 241; on tension in American literatures,
    180. WORKS: *In Light of India (Vislumbres de
    la India)*, 28; "In Search of the Present" ("La
    búsqueda del presente") (Nobel Prize ac-
    ceptance speech), 92–93; *The Labyrinth of
    Solitude*, 82, 92, 241
Pearse, Patrick, 190, 307, 309
Pellisson, Paul, 59
Pérez Galdós, Benito, 149
Pérez-Reverte, Arturo, 101
Péron, Alfred, 141, 146, 376n50
Perrault, Charles, 66–67. WORKS: *The Century
    of Louis the Great (Le siècle de Louis le Grand)*,
    66; *Parallels between the Ancients and the Mod-
    erns (Parallèles des anciens et des modernes)*, 66
Persian language, 239, 256, 327
Peru, 32
Peter the Great, 198
Pétillon, Pierre-Yves, 169
Petites Écoles des Messieurs de Port-Royal, 59
Petöfi, Sándor, 134
Petrarch, Francesco, 49, 56, 236
Picasso, Pablo, 126, 233
Pichot, Amédée, 146
Pietri, Arturo Uslar, 85, 222, 232
Pinero, Arthur Wing, 378n82
Pirandello, Luigi, 110
Plato, 70
Pléiade, 47, 51, 54, 55, 220, 255; France as liter-
    ary power and, 11; status of French language
    and, 57, 58, 60, 61
Poe, Edgar Allen, 97, 134
Poles and Poland, 78, 80, 144, 166, 186, 229,
    270
Polish language, 143, 274
Pomès, Mathilde, 395n76
Ponge, Francis, 152
Pope, Alexander, 73

Trinidad, 205, 209, 210, 211, 212
Trinity College (Dublin), 146, 189
Tsvetaeva, Marina, 134
Tupi Indians, 292
Turenne, Henri de La Tour d'Auvergne,
    vicomte de, 69
Tuscan dialect, 10–11, 49, 52, 55. *See also* Italian
    language
Tutea, Petre, 278
Tutuola, Amos, 227–228. WORKS: *The Palm-
    Wine Drinkard*, 227, 386n15
Twain, Mark, 62, 293. WORKS: *Huckleberry Finn*,
    293
Tzara, Tristan, 29

Uganda, 231, 386n18
Ujević, Tin, 28
Ukrainian language, 78, 274
Unamuno y Jugo, Miguel, 222
Ungar, Hermann, 392n32
United States, 11, 31, 42, 62, 78, 85, 121, 165,
    166; birth of American novel, 293; Canadian
    literature and, 122–123; émigré writers in,
    140; English as world language and, 391n21;
    Irish community in, 123; literary tutelage of
    London, 243–244; Nobel Prize winners
    from, 151; publishing industry in, 168–171,
    358n13; Yiddish-speaking Jews in, 229, 334.
    See also New York City
Updike, John, 156
Urquhart, Jane, 122–123. WORKS: *The Whirl-
    pool*, 122–123
Uruguay, 213

Valéry, Paul, 9, 10, 12–15, 16–17, 22, 24, 27, 266;
    Nobel Prize and, 150; on taste, 92; on trans-
    lators, 135; on value, 127. WORKS: "Spiritual
    Freedom" ("La Liberté de l'esprit"), 9, 13
Vallejo, César, 32
Vallès, Jules, 26. WORKS: *The Insurrectionist*
    (*L'Insurgé*), 26
Van Gogh, Vincent, 132
Van Velde, Abraham, 127–128, 346, 348
Van Velde, Gerardus, 127–128, 348
Vargas Llosa, Mario, 94, 100, 130, 166, 333,
    344
Vasari, Giorgio, 348
Vaud (Swiss canton), 157, 244, 282, 296
Vázquez Montalbán, Manuel, 246, 247, 264,
    278
Venice, 10, 24

Verhaeren, Émile, 188, 248
Verlaine, Paul, 134, 223, 266
Vico, Giambattista, 330, 399n6
Victoria, queen of United Kingdom, 240
Victorian literature, 106
Vieira, José Luandino, 123
Vietnam War, 325
Vigny, Alfred de, 143
Vingtistes, 132
Virgil, 53, 61, 287
Voiture, Vincent, 65
Voltaire (François-Marie Arouet), 67, 69–70,
    76, 130, 143, 367n59
Voss, Johann Heinrich, 236
Vraz, Stanko, 79

Waberi, Abdourahman, 260
Wagenbach, Klaus, 203
Wagner, Richard, 132, 160–161
Walloons, 213, 214
Walser, Robert, 177
Warburg, Walther von, 63
War of 1812, 122–123, 372n72
Warren, Robert Penn, 134
Warsaw, 143, 202, 247
Wegener, Alfred Lothar, 349
Weiss, Ernst, 392n32
Weiss, Peter, 167
Weltsch, Felix, 392n32
West Indies, 32, 125, 176, 180, 209, 283, 296,
    338
Wezel, Johann Carl, 333
Whitman, Walt, 33, 128, 243, 266, 293. WORKS:
    Leaves of Grass, 33, 244, 293; "Mississippi Val-
    ley Literature," 244; *Specimen Days*, 244
Wideman, John Edgar, 169
Wieland, Christoph Martin, 19, 333
Wilde, Oscar, 134, 163, 208. WORKS: *Lady
    Windermere's Fan*, 208
Williams, William Carlos, 32
Winter, Ludwig, 392n32
Wittgenstein, Ludwig, 82. WORKS: *Philosophical
    Investigations*, 82
Wolf, Christa, 167–168
Wordsworth, William, 123

Yacine, Kateb, 41, 176, 229, 230–231, 260, 272,
    343–344, 354, 391n20. WORKS: *Mohamed
    prend ta valise*, 231; *Nedjma*, 230
Yale University, 165
Yeats, William Butler, 41, 118, 153, 187, 190,

Yeats, William Butler *(continued)*
225, 226, 355; Abbey Theatre and, 249, 311–312; Belgian literature and, 248; invention of Irish tradition and, 305–307; London critics and, 264. WORKS: *Cathleen ni Houlihan*, 306; *Celtic Twilight*, 306, 315; *The Countess Cathleen and Various Legends and Lyrics*, 306; *Deirdre,* 397n4; *Diarmuid and Gráinne* (with George Moore), 306, 389n69; *Fairy and Folk Tales of the Irish Peasantry*, 306; *The Wanderings of Oisin*, 306
Yellow Book of Lecan, 243
Yesenin, Sergey Aleksandrovich, 134
Yiddish language, 200–203, 229, 259, 334. *See also* Jews
Yoruba language and people, 227, 259, 291

Yourcenar, Marguerite, 115, 206
Yugoslavia, 27, 80, 111, 113–115, 198

Zangwill, Israel, 208. WORKS: *Ghetto Comedies,* 208
Zionism, 269, 270, 392n31
Zola, Émile, 19, 25, 26, 37, 98, 101–102, 137; Dreyfus Affair and, 363n82; realism and, 311; theater and, 161, 162, 374n24. WORKS: *L'Assommoir,* 102; *The Belly of Paris (Le ventre de Paris)*, 26; "J'accuse," 37, 98; *Le Roman expérimental,* 102; *Les Rougon-Macquart,* 101; *The Spoils (La Curée)*, 26
Zulu language, 239, 268
Zurich, 30–31
Zweig, Stefan, 98